Foundations of Artificial Intelligence

Special Issues of Artificial Intelligence: An International Journal

The titles in this series are paperback, readily accessible editions of the Special Volumes of *Artificial Intelligence: An International Journal*, edited by Daniel G. Bobrow and produced by special agreement with Elsevier Science Publishers B.V.

Qualitative Reasoning about Physical Systems, edited by Daniel G. Bobrow, 1985.

Geometric Reasoning, edited by Deekpak Kapur and Joseph L. Mundy, 1989.

Machine Learning: Paradigms and Methods, edited by Jaime Carbonell, 1990.

Artificial Intelligence and Learning Environments, edited by William J. Clancey and Elliot Soloway, 1990.

Connectionist Symbol Processing, edited by G. E. Hinton, 1991.

Foundations of Artificial Intelligence, edited by David Kirsh, 1992.

Foundations of Artificial Intelligence

edited by

David Kirsh

purchased by
David Coore

A Bradford Book
The MIT Press
Cambridge, Massachusetts
London, England

First MIT Press edition, 1992

Reprinted from *Artificial Intelligence: An International Journal*, Volume 47, Numbers 1–3, 1991. The MIT Press has exclusive license to sell this English-language book edition throughout the world.

Printed and bound in the Netherlands. This book is printed on acid-free paper.

Library of Congress Cataloging-in-Publication Data

Foundations of artificial intelligence / edited by David Kirsh. — 1st MIT Press ed.
p. cm. — (Special issues of Artificial intelligence, an international journal)
"A Bradford Book."
"Reprinted from Artificial intelligence, an international journal, volume 47, numbers 1–3, 1991"—T.p. verso.
Includes bibliographical information and index.
ISBN 0-262-61075-2
1. Artificial intelligence. I. Kirsh, David. II. Series.
Q335.5.F68 1992
006.3—dc20

91-18104
CIP

Contents

Artificial Intelligence 47 (1991) 1
Elsevier

Foreword

The intent of this special issue on the Foundations of AI is to critically evaluate the fundamental assumptions underpinning the dominant approaches to AI. Theorists historically associated with each position were originally invited to a workshop at Endicott House, MIT, in 1987. They were asked to write a paper identifying the basic tenets of their position, to discuss the principles underpinning the method or approach, to describe the natural type of problems and tasks in which the approach succeeds, to explain where the power resides in the method or approach, and then to discuss its scope and limits. Theorists generally skeptical of the position were similarly asked to evaluate the source of power of the method or approach and to state why they thought the method/approach works and why it fails. Discussions and presentations there formed the basis for the papers published here. We gratefully acknowledge the support for the workshop provided for by the MIT Artificial Intelligence Laboratory, National Science Foundation, and AAAI.

David Kirsh
Department of Cognitive Science
University of California, San Diego
La Jolla, CA, USA

Artificial Intelligence 47 (1991) 3–30.
Elsevier

Foundations of AI: the big issues*

David Kirsh

Department of Cognitive Science C-015, University of California, San Diego, La Jolla, CA 92093, USA

Received December 1989
Revised October 1990

Abstract

Kirsh, D., Foundations of AI: the big issues, Artificial Intelligence 47 (1991) 3–30.

The objective of research in the foundations of AI is to explore such basic questions as: What is a theory in AI? What are the most abstract assumptions underlying the competing visions of intelligence? What are the basic arguments for and against each assumption? In this essay I discuss five foundational issues: (1) Core AI is the study of conceptualization and should begin with knowledge level theories. (2) Cognition can be studied as a disembodied process without solving the symbol grounding problem. (3) Cognition is nicely described in propositional terms. (4) We can study cognition separately from learning. (5) There is a single architecture underlying virtually all cognition. I explain what each of these implies and present arguments from both outside and inside AI why each has been seen as right or wrong.

1. Introduction

In AI, to date, there has been little discussion, and even less agreement, on methodology: What is a theory in AI? An architecture? An account of knowledge? Can a theory be tested by studying performance in abstract, simulated environments, or is it necessary to hook up implementations to actual visual input and actual motor output? Is there one level of analysis or a small set of problems which ought to be pursued first? For instance, should we try to identify the knowledge necessary for a skill before we concern ourselves with issues of representation and control? Is complexity theory relevant to the central problems of the field? Indeed, what are the central problems?

The objective of research in the foundations of AI is to address some of

* Support for this work has been provided in part by the Army Institute for Research in Management, Information and Communication Systems contract number DAKF11-88-C-0045.

these basic questions of method, theory and orientation. It is to self-consciously reappraise what AI is all about.

The pursuit of AI does not occur in isolation. Fields such as philosophy, linguistics, psychophysics and theoretical computer science have exercised a historical influence over the field and today there is as much dialogue as ever, particularly with the new field of cognitive science. One consequence of dialogue is that criticisms of positions held in one discipline frequently apply to positions held in other disciplines.

In this first essay, my objective is to bring together a variety of these arguments both for and against the dominant research programs of AI.

It is impossible, of course, to explore carefully all of these arguments in a single paper. The majority, in any event, are discussed in the papers in this volume, and it is not my intent to repeat them here. It may be of use, though, to stand back and consider several of the most abstract assumptions underlying the competing visions of intelligence. These assumptions—whether explicitly named by theorists or not—identify issues which have become focal points of debate and serve as dividing lines of positions.

Of these, five stand out as particularly fundamental:

- *Pre-eminence of knowledge and conceptualization*: Intelligence that transcends insect-level intelligence requires declarative knowledge and some form of reasoning-like computation—call this *cognition*.[1] Core AI is the study of the conceptualizations of the world presupposed and used by intelligent systems during cognition.
- *Disembodiment*: Cognition and the knowledge it presupposes can be studied largely in abstraction from the details of perception and motor control.
- *Kinematics of cognition are language-like*: It is possible to describe the trajectory of knowledge states or informational states created during cognition using a vocabulary very much like English or some regimented logico-mathematical version of English.
- *Learning can be added later*: The kinematics of cognition and the domain knowledge needed for cognition can be studied separately from the study of concept learning, psychological development, and evolutionary change.
- *Uniform architecture*: There is a single architecture underlying virtually all cognition.

Different research programs are based, more or less, on an admixture of these assumptions plus corollaries.

[1] By cognition I do not mean to take a stand on what the proper subject matter of cognitive science is. The term is meant to refer to computational processes that resemble both reasoning in a classical sense and computational processes that are more "peripheral" than reasoning, such as language recognition and object identification, where the representations are not about the entities and relations we have common sense terms for, but which may still usefully be construed as rules operating on representations.

Logicism [15, 32] as typified by formal theorists of the commonsense world, formal theorists of language and formal theorists of belief [17, 24], presupposes almost all of these assumptions. Logicism, as we know it today, is predicated on the pre-eminence of reasoning-like processes and conceptualization, the legitimacy of disembodied analysis, on interpreting rational kinematics as propositional, and the possibility of separating thought and learning. It remains neutral on the uniformity of the underlying architecture.

Other research progams make a virtue of denying one or more of these assumptions. Soar, [30, 35] for instance, differs from logicism in according learning a vital role in the basic theory and in assuming that all of cognition can be explained as processes occurring in a single uniform architecture. Rational kinematics in Soar are virtually propositional but differ slightly in containing control markers—preferences—to bias transitions. In other respects, Soar shares with logicism the assumption that reasoning-like processes and conceptualization are central, and that it is methodologically acceptable to treat central processes in abstraction from perceptual and motor processes.

Connectionists, [27, 38] by contrast, deny that reasoning-like processes are pre-eminent in cognition, that core AI is the study of the concepts underpinning domain understanding, and that rational kinematics is language-like. Yet like Soar, connectionists emphasize the centrality of learning in the study of cognition, and like logicists they remain agnostic about the uniformity of the underlying architecture. They are divided on the assumption of disembodiment.

Moboticists [3] take the most extreme stance and deny reasoning, conceptualization, rational kinematics, disembodiment, uniformity of architecture and the separability of knowledge and learning (more precisely evolution). Part of what is attractive in the mobotics approach is precisely its radicalness.

Similar profiles can be offered for Lenat and Feigenbaum's position [23], Minsky's society of mind theory [28], Schank's anti-formalist approach [40, 41] and Hewitt and Gasser's account [12, 14] of much of distributed AI research.

These five issues by no means exhaust the foundational issues posed by the various approaches. But each does, in my opinion, lie at the center of a cluster of deep questions.

In what follows I will explore arguments for and against each of these assumptions. I will explain what each of them implies and why they have been seen as right or wrong.

2. Are knowledge and conceptualization at the heart of AI?

Here is one answer to the question: what is a theory in AI?

> A theory in AI is a specification of the knowledge underpinning a cognitive skill.

A cognitive skill is the information-based control mechanism regulating performance in some domain. It is meant to cover the gamut of information-sensitive activities such as problem solving, language use, decision making, routine activity, perception and some elements of motor control.

In accepting the priority of knowledge level theories, one is not committed to supposing that knowledge is explicitly encoded declaratively and deployed in explicitly inferential processes, although frequently knowledge will be. One's commitment is that knowledge and conceptualization lie at the heart of AI: that a major goal of the field is to discover the basic knowledge units of cognition (of intelligent skills).

What are these knowledge units? In the case of qualitative theories of the commonsense world, and in the case of Lenat's CYC project [21, 23], these basic knowledge units are the conceptual units of *consensus reality*—the core concepts underpinning "the millions of things that we all know and that we assume everyone else knows" [21, p. 4]. Not surprisingly, these concepts are often familiar ideas with familiar names—though sometimes they will be theoretical ideas, having a technical meaning internal to the theory. For instance, in CYC, in addition to terms for tables, salt, Africa, and numbers—obvious elements of consensual reality—there are technical terms such as temporal subabstraction, temporal projectability, partition, change predicate which have no simple correlate in English, and which are included as abstract elements of consensual reality because of the difficulty of constructing an adequate account without them.

In the case of linguistics and higher vision these basic knowledge units tend more generally to be about theoretical entities. Only occasionally will there be pre-existing terms in English for them. Thus, noun phrase, sphere, pyramid and other shapes are commonsense concepts having familiar English names, but governing domain, animate movements, causal launchings[2] and most shape representations are, for most people, novel ideas that are not part of common parlance. The basic knowledge units of cognition—the conceptualizations underpinning cognitive skills—may range, then, from the familiar to the exotic and theoretical.

The basic idea that knowledge and conceptualization lie at the heart of AI stems from the seductive view that cognition is inference. Intelligent skills, an old truism of AI runs, are composed of two parts: a declarative knowledge base and an inference engine.

The inference engine is relatively uncomplicated; it is a domain-independent program that takes as input a set of statements about the current situation plus a fragment of the declarative knowledge base, it produces as output a stream of

[2] It is widely argued in the developmental literature that one of the earliest and visually most robust cues for distinguishing animate creatures like dogs and snakes from non-animate objects like toy dogs, and cars, which may also move, are cues about body part trajectories, and original causation [25].

inferred declaratives culminating in the case of decision making and routine activity, in directives for appropriate action.

In contrast to the inference engine, the knowledge base is domain-specific and is as complicated as a cognitive skill requires. Domain knowledge is what distinguishes the ability to troubleshoot a circuit from the ability to understand the meaning of a sentence. Both require knowledge but of different domains. It follows that the heart of the AI problem is to discover what an agent knows about the world which permits success. This idea, *in one form or another*, has been endorsed by logicists, by Lenat and Feigenbaum [23], Chomsky [6], Montague [29], and with variations by Schank [41], and Newell and Simon [32].

The qualification *in one form or another* is significant. As mentioned, a commitment to theorizing about knowledge and knowledge units is not in itself a commitment to large amounts of on-line logical reasoning or explicit representation of domain knowledge. It is well known that not all skills that require intelligent control require an *explicit* knowledge base. So it is a further thesis that declarative knowledge and logical inference are actually deployed in most cognitive skills. In such cases we still may say that cognition is inference, but we no longer expect to find explicit inference rules or even complete trajectories of inferential steps. In the source code of cognition we would find instructions for inferential processes throughout. But knowledge can be compiled into procedures or designed into control systems which have no distinct inference engines. So often our account of cognition is more of the form "The system is acting *as if* it were inferring . . .".

Knowledge compilation One question of considerable interest among theorists who accept the centrality of knowledge and the virtue of knowledge level theories, is "How far can this knowledge compilation go?"

According to Nilsson there are severe limits on this compilation. Overt declaratives have special virtues.

> The most versatile intelligent machines will represent much of their knowledge about their environment declaratively . . . [A declarative can] be used by the machine even for purposes unforeseen by the machine's designer, it [can] more easily be modified than could knowledge embodied in programs, and it facilitate[s] communication between machine and other machines and humans. [33]

For Nilsson, the theory of what is known is a good approximation of what is actually represented declaratively. He suggests that some reactions to situations and some useful inferences may be compiled. But storage and indexing costs militate against compiling knowledge overmuch. Real flexibility requires explicit declarative representation of knowledge. No doubt, it is an empirical question just how much of a cognitive skill can be compiled. But as long as a system uses some explicit declaratives, the apparatus of declarative representation must be in place, making it possible, when time permits, to control action through run time inference.

Rosenschein et al. [37] see the inflexibility of knowledge compilation as far less constraining. On their view, a significant range of tasks connected with adaptive response to the environment can be compiled. To determine the appropriate set of reactions to build into a machine, a designer performs the relevant knowledge level logical reasoning at compile time so that the results will be available at run time. Again, it is an empirical matter how many cognitive skills can be completely automatized in this fashion. But the research program of situated automata is to push the envelope as far as possible.

A similar line of thought applies to the work of Chomsky and Montague. When they claim to be offering a theory about the knowledge deployed in parsing and speech production it does not follow they require on-line inference. By offering their theories in the format of "here's the knowledge base use the obvious inference engine" they establish the effectiveness of their knowledge specification: it is a condition on their theory that when conjoined with the obvious inference engine it should generate all and only syntactic strings (or some specified fragment of that set). That is why their theories are called *generative*. But to date no one has offered a satisfactory account of how the theory is to be efficiently implemented. Parsing *may* involve considerable inference, but equally it may consist of highly automated retrieval processes where structures or fragments of structures previously found acceptable are recognized. To be sure, some theorists say that recognition is itself a type of inference: that recognizing a string of words *as* an NP involves inference. Hence even parsing construed as constraint satisfaction or as schema retrieval (instantiation) and so forth, is itself inferential at bottom. But this is not the dominant view. Whatever the answer, though, there are no *a priori* grounds for assuming that statements of linguistic principle are encoded explicitly in declaratives and operated on by explicit inference rules.

Whether knowledge be explicit or compiled, the view that cognition is inference and that theorizing at the *knowledge level* is at least the starting place of scientific AI is endorsed by a large fragment of the community.

Opposition In stark contrast is the position held by Rod Brooks. According to Brooks [3] a theory in AI is not an account of the knowledge units of cognition. Most tasks that seem to involve considerable world knowledge may yet be achievable without appeal to declaratives, to concepts, or to basic knowledge units, even at compile time. Knowledge level theories, he argues, too often chase fictions. If AI's overarching goal is to understand intelligent control of action, then if it turns out to be true, as Brooks believes it will, that most intelligent behaviour can be produced by a system of carefully tuned control systems interconnected in a simple but often ad hoc manner, then why study knowledge? A methodology more like experimental engineering is what is required.

If Brooks is right, intelligent control systems can be designed before a designer has an articulated conceptualization of the task environment. Moreover, the system itself can succeed without operating on a conceptualization in any interesting sense. New behaviours can be grown onto older behaviours in an evolutionary fashion that makes otiose the task of conceptualizing the world. The result is a system that, for a large class of tasks, might match the versatility of action achievable with declaratives, yet it never calls on the type of capacities we associate with having knowledge of a conceptualization and symbolic representation of basic world elements.

Whatever our belief about the viability of Brooks' position he has succeeded in exposing an important foundational question: *Why assume intelligence requires concepts*? If the AI community has largely ignored this problem it is not simply because it is a presupposition of the view that cognition is inference. It is also because the problem of designing intelligent systems has never been consciously formulated as one of discovering concepts in a *psychological* sense. In AI there is no marked difference between assuming a system to have a symbol in a declarative and assuming it to have a concept. The worry about what it is to have a concept is seldom articulated. Hence skepticism about concepts and conceptualization has been kept down.

2.1. Are concepts really necessary for most intelligence?

Evidence that the notion of concept is understudied in AI is easy to find. When Nilsson, for instance, unambiguously states that "The most important part of the 'AI problem' involves inventing an appropriate conceptualization" [33, p. 10], it would be natural to expect him to provide an account of what it is for a system to have a concept. But in fact by conceptualization he does not mean the concepts a system has about the world. Rather he means the *designer* of a machine's best guess about a "mathematical structure consisting of objects, functions, and relations" close enough to the real world for the machine to achieve its purposes. Admittedly, for Nilsson, the designer *builds his conceptualization into* a system by creating "linguistic terms to denote his invented objects, functions and relations", putting these terms in sentences in the predicate calculus, and giving "the machine declarative knowledge about the world by storing these sentences in the machine's memory". So in certain cases talk of conceptualization is short hand for talk of the concepts a machine has. But it is important to mark the logical distinction between:

(1) the conceptualization of a task the designer has;
(2) the conceptual system the machine embodying the skill has;
(3) the way the conceptual system is encoded.

The difference lies in the deeply philosophical question of what it is to *grasp* a concept. We cannot just assume that a machine which has a structure in memory that corresponds in name to a structure in the designer's conceptualization is sufficient for grasping the concept. The structure must play a role in a network of abilities; it must confer on the agent certain causal powers [1]. Some of these powers involve reasoning: being able to use the structure *appropriately* in deduction, induction and perhaps abduction. But other powers involve perception and action—hooking up the structure via causal mechanisms to the outside world.

Logicists are not unmindful of the need to explain what it is for a system to understand a proposition, or to grasp the concepts which constitute propositions. But the party line is that this job can be pursued independently from the designer's main task of inventing conceptualizations. The two activities—inventing conceptualizations and grounding concepts—are modular. Hence the grounding issue has not historically been treated as posing a challenge that might overturn the logicist program.

A similar belief in modularizing the theorist's job is shared by Lenat and Feigenbaum. They see the paramount task of AI to be to discover the conceptual knowledge underpinning cognitive skills and consensus reality. This leaves open the question of what exactly grasping a basic conceptual or knowledge unit of consensus reality amounts to. There certainly is a story of grounding to be told, but creatures with different perceptual-motor endowments will each require its own story. So why not regard the problem of conceptualization to be independent from the problem of grounding concepts?

This assumption of modularization—of disembodiment—is the core concern of Brian Smith [42] in his reply to Lenat and Feigenbaum. It pertains, as well, to worries Birnbaum expresses about model theoretic semantics [1]. Both Birnbaum and Smith emphasize that if knowing a concept, or if having knowledge about a particular conceptualization requires a machine to have a large background of behavioural, perceptual and even reasoning skills, then the greater part of the AI task may reside in understanding how concepts can refer, or how they can be used in reasoning, perceiving, acting, rather than in just identifying those concepts or stating their axiomatic relations.

Accordingly, it is time to explore what the logicist's conception of a concept amounts to. Only then can we intelligently consider whether it is fair to say that logicists and Lenat and Feigenbaum—by assuming they can provide a machine with symbols that are not *grounded* and so not truly grasped—are omitting an absolutely major part of the AI problem.

2.1.1. The logicist concept of concept

A concept, on anyone's view, is a modular component of knowledge. If we say John knows *the pen is on the desk*, and we mean this to imply that John grasps the fact of there being a particular pen on a particular desk, we assume that he has distinct concepts for *pen*, *desk* and *on*. We assume this because we believe that John must know what it is for something to be a pen, a desk, and something to be on something else. That is, we assume he has the referential apparatus to think about pens, desks, and being on. At a minimum, this implies having the capacity to substitute other appropriate concepts for x and y in (*On pen y*), (*On x desk*), and R in (*R pen desk*). If John could not just as easily understand what it is for a pen to be on something other than a desk, or a desk to have something other than a pen on it, he would not have enough understanding of *pen*, *desk*, and *on* to be able to display the minimal knowledge that pens and desks are distinct entities with enough causal individuality to appear separately, and in different combinations.

Now the basic premiss driving the logicist program, as well as Lenat and Feigenbaum's search for the underpinnings of consensus reality, is that to understand an agent's knowledge we must discover the structured system of concepts underpinning its skills. This structure can be discovered without explaining all that is involved in having the *referential apparatus* presupposed by concepts because it shows up in a number of purely disembodied, rational processes. If concepts and conceptual schemes seem to play enough of an explanatory role at the disembodied level to be seen as robust entities, then we can study their structure without concern for their grounding.

What then are these disembodied processes which can be explained so nicely by disembodied concepts? In the end we may decide that these do not sufficiently ground concepts. But it is important to note their variety. For too often arguments about grounding do not adequately attend to the range of phenomena explained by assuming modular concepts.

Inferential abilities First, and most obviously, is the capacity of an agent to draw inferences. For instance, given the premises that the pen is on the desk, that the pen is matte black, then a knowledgeable agent ought to be able to infer that the matte black pen is on the desk. It often happens that actual agents will not bother to draw this inference. But it is hard for us to imagine that they might have a grasp of what pens are etc, and not be *able* to draw it. Inferences are permissive not obligatory. Thus, as long as it makes sense to view agents to be *sometimes* drawing inferences about a domain, or performing reason-like operations, it makes sense to suppose they have a network of concepts which structures their knowledge.[3]

[3] The much discussed attribute of systematicity which Fodor and Pylyshyn cite in [11] as essential to symbolic reasoning and antithetical to the spirit of much connectionist work to date, is a version of this *generality constraint* on concepts. A few years earlier, Gareth Evans put the matter like this:

> If the subject can be credited with the thought that a is F, then he must have conceptual resources for entertaining the thought that a is G, for every property of being G of which he has a conception. We thus see the thought that a is F as lying at the intersection of two series of thoughts: on the one hand, the series of thoughts that a is F, b is F, c is F, . . ., and, on the other hand, the series of thoughts that a is F, a is G, a is H, ... [8, p. 104, footnote 22].

It must be appreciated, however, that when we say that John has the concepts of pen and desk we do not mean that John is able to draw inferences about pens and desks in only a few contexts. He must display his grasp of the terms extensively, otherwise we cannot be sure that he means *desk* by "desk" rather than *wooden object*, for instance. For this reason, if we attribute to a machine a grasp of a single concept we are obliged to attribute it a grasp of a whole system of concepts to structure its understanding. Otherwise its inferential abilities would be too spotty, displaying too many gaps to justify our attribution of genuine understanding. Experience shows that to prevent ridiculous displays of irrationality it is necessary to postulate an elaborate tissue of underlying conceptualizations and factual knowledge. The broader this knowledge base the more robust the understanding, and more reasonable the action. This is one very compelling reason for supposing that intelligence can be studied from a disembodied perspective.

Inferential breadth is only one of the rational capacities that is explained by assuming intelligent agents have concepts. Further capacities include identification and visual attention, learning, knowledge decay and portability of knowledge.

Knowledge and perception Kant once said, sensation without conception is blind. What he meant is that I do not know *what* I am seeing, if I have no concept to categorize my experience. Much of our experience is of a world populated with particular objects, events and processes. Our idea of these things may be abstractions—constructions from something more primitive, or fictional systematizers of experience. But if so, they are certainly robust abstractions, for they let us predict, retrodict, explain and plan events in the world.

It is hard to imagine how we could identify entities if we did not have concepts. The reason this is hard, I suspect, is because object identification is such an active process. Perception, it is now widely accepted, is not a passive system. It is a method for *systematically* gathering evidence about the environment. We can think of it as an oracle offering answers to questions about the external world. Not direct answers, but partial answers, perceptual answers, that serve as evidence for or against certain perceptual *conjectures*. One job of the perceptual system is to ask the right questions. Our eyes jump about an image looking for clues of identity; then shortly thereafter they search for confirmation of conjectures. The same holds for different modalities. Our eyes often confirm or disconfirm what our ears first detect. The notions of evidence, confirmation and falsification, however, are defined as relations between statements or propositions. Concepts are essential to perception then because perception provides evidence for conjectures about the world. It follows that the output of perception must be sufficiently evidence-like—that is, propositional—to be assigned a conceptual structure. How else could we see physical facts, such as the pen being on the desk *as* the structured facts—|*the pen*|⌒|*is on*|⌒|*the desk*|?

Growth of knowledge A third feature of rational intelligence—learning—can also be partly explained if we attribute to a system a set of disembodied concepts. From the logicist perspective, domain knowledge is much like a theory, it is a system of axioms relating basic concepts. Some axioms are empirical, others are definitional. Learning, on this account, is construed as movement along a trajectory of theories. It is conceptual advance. This approach brings us no closer to understanding the principles of learning, but we have at least defined what these principles are: principles of conceptual advance. A theory of intelligence which did not mention concepts would have to explain learning as a change in capacities behaviourally or functionally classified. Since two creatures with slightly different physical attributes would not have identical capacities, behaviourally defined, the two could not be said to learn identically. Yet from a more abstract perspective, what we are interested in is their knowledge of the domain, the two might indeed seem to learn the same way. Without concepts and conceptual knowledge it is not clear this similarity could be discovered, let alone be explained. But again the relevant notion of concept is not one that requires our knowing how it is grounded. Disembodied concepts serve well enough.

Decay of knowledge In a similar fashion, if a system has a network of disembodied concepts we can often notice and then later explain regularities in how its rational performance degrades. It is an empirical fact that knowledge and skill sometimes decay in existing reasoning systems, such as humans or animals, in a regular manner. Often it does not. Alzheimer's disease may bring about a loss of functionality that is sporadic or at times random. But often, when a system decays, deficits which at first seem to be unsystematic, can eventually be seen to follow a pattern, once we know the structure of the larger system from which they emerge. This is obviously desirable if we are cognitive scientists and wish to explain deficits and predict their etiology; but it is equally desirable if we are designers trying to determine why a design is faulty. If we interpret a system as having a network of concepts we are in a better position to locate where its bugs are. But the fact that we *can* track and *can* explain decay at the conceptual level without explaining grounding offers us further evidence of the robustness of disembodied concepts.

Portability of knowledge There is yet a fifth phenomenon of rationality which the postulation of disembodied concepts can help explain. If knowledge consists in compositions of concepts—that is, propositions—we have an explanation of why, in principle, any piece of knowledge in one microtheory can be combined with knowledge drawn from another microtheory. They can combine because they are structured in a similar fashion out of similar types of elements. At the object level, this explains how it is possible for a cognizer to receive generally useful information in one context, say astronomy, and end up using it in another, say calendar making. At the metalevel, it explains how, as designers, we can build on knowledge in different domains, thereby simplifying our overall account of the knowledge a system requires. Many of the decisions we make rely on information drawn from disparate domains. Knowledge which accrues in one domain can be useful in making decisions in another. This is a fact which Nilsson rightly emphasizes in his condition on portability as a hallmark of commonsense knowledge. Compositionality would explain portability.[4]

Given the virtues of concepts it is hard to imagine anyone seriously doubting that concepts—whose grounding we have yet to explain—lie at the heart of intelligence. Explanations of a system's conceptual system are clearly not the whole story of AI, but can it be reasonably denied that they are a cleanly modular major chapter?

I now turn to these reasonable doubts.

3. Are cognitive skills disembodied?

I have been presenting a justification for the view that, in the main, intelligence can be fruitfully studied on the assumption that the problems and tasks facing intelligent agents can be formally specified, and so pursued abstractly at the knowledge or conceptual level. For analytic purposes we can ask questions about cognitive skills using symbolic characterizations of the environment as input and symbolic characterizations of motor activity as output. Concerns about how conceptual knowledge is *grounded* in perceptual-motor skills can be addressed separately. These questions can be bracketed because what differentiates cognitive skills is not so much the perceptual-motor parameters of a task but the knowledge of the task domain which directs action in that domain. This is the methodological assumption of disembodiment. What are the arguments against it?

In his attack on core AI, Brooks identifies three assumptions related to disembodiment which, in his opinion, dangerously bias the way cognitive skills are studied:

[4] To be sure, this common language of concepts does not apply to *every* domain of knowledge. Microtheories about syntax and early vision, arguably are about domain elements not found in other microtheories. To the degree that the conceptual elements we attribute to syntax and early vision are inaccessible to other inferential processes we are justified in being skeptical of their robustness as concepts in the full blooded sense we mean when we talk of publicly shared concepts like chairs and tables. This concern that we should reserve the term concept for post-peripheral processes is discussed by Cussins [7].

- The output of vision is conceptualized and so the interface between perception and "central cognition" is clean and neatly characterizable in the language of predicate calculus, or some other language with terms denoting objects and terms denoting properties.
- Whenever we exercise our intelligence we call on a central representation of the world state where some substantial fraction of the world state is represented and regularly updated perceptually or by inference.
- When we seem to be pursuing our tasks in an organzied fashion our actions have been planned in advance by envisioning outcomes and choosing a sequence that best achieves the agent's goals.

The error in each of these assumptions, Brooks contends, is to suppose that the real world is somehow simple enough, sufficiently decomposable into concept-sized bites, that we can represent it, in real time, in all the detailed respects that might matter to achieving our goals. It is not. Even if we had enough concepts to cover its relevant aspects we would never be able to compute an updated world model in real time. Moreover, we don't need to. Real success in a causally dense world is achieved by tuning the perceptual system to *action-relevant* changes.

To take an example from J.J. Gibson, an earlier theorist who held similar views, if a creature's goals are to avoid obstacles on its path to a target, it is not necessary for it to constantly judge its distance from obstacles, update a world model with itself at the origin, and recalculate a trajectory given velocity projections. It can instead exploit the invariant relation between its current velocity and instantaneous time to contact obstacles in order to determine a new trajectory directly. It adapts its actions to changes in time to contact. If the environment is perceived in terms of actions that are *afforded* rather than in terms of objects and relations, the otherwise computationally intensive task is drastically simplified.

Now this is nothing short of a Ptolemaic revolution. If the world is always sensed from a perspective which views the environment as *a space of possibilities for action*, then every time an agent performs an action which changes the action potentials which the world affords it, it changes the world as it perceives it. In the last example, this occurs because as the agent changes its instantaneous speed and direction it may perceive significant changes in environmental affordances despite being in almost the same spatial relations to objects in the environment. Even slight actions can change the way a creature perceives the world. If these changes in perception regularly simplify the problem of attaining goals, then traditional accounts of the environment as a static structure composed of objects, relations and functions, may completely misstate the actual computational problems faced by creatures acting in the world. The real problem must be defined relative to the world-for-the-agent. The world-for-the-agent changes despite the world-in-itself remaining constant.

To take another example of how action and perception are intertwined, and so must be considered when stating the computational problems facing agents, consider the problem of grasp planning. Traditionally the problem is defined as follows: Given a target object, an initial configuration of hand joints and free space between hand and target, find a trajectory of joint changes that results in a stable grasp. At one time it was thought that to solve this problem it was necessary to compute the 3D shape of the target, the final configuration of joints, and the trajectory of joint changes between initial and final configurations—a substantial amount of computation by anyone's measure. Yet this is not the problem if we allow compliance. Instead we simply need locate a rough center of mass of the target, send the palm of the hand to that point with the instruction to close on contact, and rely on the hand to *comply* with the object. The problem is elegantly simplified. No longer must we know the shape of the object, the mapping relation between 3D shape and joint configuration, or the constraints on joint closure. The original definition of the grasp planning problem was a mis-statement. It led us to believe that certain subproblems and certain elements of knowledge would be required, when in fact they are not. Compliance changes everything. It alters the way the world should be interpreted.

The point is that the possibility of complying with shapes restructures the world. A creature with a compliant hand confronts a different world than a creature without. Accordingly, a knowledge level account of grasping which did not accommodate the simplifications due to compliance would be false. It would be working with an incorrect set of assumptions about the manipulator.

By analogy, one cardinal idea of the embodied approach to cognition, is that the hardware of the body—in particular, the details of the sensori-motor system—when taken in conjuction with an environment and goals shape the kinds of problems facing an agent. These problems in turn shape the cognitive skills agents have. Consequently, to specify these skills correctly it is necessary to pay close attention to the agent's interactions with its environment—to the actions it does and can do at any point. Disembodied approaches do not interpret the environment of action in this dynamic manner, and so inevitably give rise to false problems and false solutions. They tend to define problems in terms of task environments specified in the abstract perspective independent language of objects and relations.[5]

Now this argument, it seems to me, is sound. But how far does it go? It serves as a reminder to knowledge level theorists that they may easily misspecify a cognitive skill, and that to reliably theorize at the knowledge level one should often have a model of the agent's sensori-motor capacities. But it is

[5] Newell and Simon in their characterization of task environment emphasize that a given physical environment becomes a task environment only relative to a goal or task, and a set of actions. But one assumption they retain is that actions are basically STRIPS-like: they add or delete facts but do not engender wholesale revision of perspective.

an empirical question just how often hardware biases the definition of a cognitive problem. *A priori* one would expect a continuum of problems from the most situated—where the cognitive task cannot be correctly defined without a careful analysis of the possible compliances and possible agent environment invariants—to highly abstract problems, such as word problems, number problems, puzzles and so forth, where the task is essentially abstract, and its implementation in the world is largely irrelevant to performance.[6]

Ultimately, Brooks' rejection of disembodied AI is an empirical challenge: for a large class of problems facing an acting creature the only reliable method of discovering how they can succeed, and hence what their true cognitive skills are, is to study them *in situ*.

Frequently this is the way of foundational questions. One theorist argues that many of the assumptions underpinning the prevailing methodology are false. He then proposes a new methodology and looks for empirical support. But occasionally it is possible to offer, in addition to empirical support, a set of purely philosophical arguments against a methodology.

3.1. Philosophical objections to disembodied AI

At the top level we may distinguish two philosophical objections: first, that knowledge level accounts which leave out a theory of the body are too incomplete to serve the purpose for which they were proposed. Second, that axiomatic knowledge accounts fail to capture all the knowledge an agent has about a domain. Let us consider each in turn.

3.1.1. Why we need a theory of the body

The adequacy of a theory, whether in physics or AI, depends on the purpose it is meant to serve. It is possible to identify three rather different purposes AI theorists have in mind when they postulate a formal theory of the commonsense world. An axiomatic theory T of domain D is:

(1) adequate for *robotics* if it can be used by an acting perceiving machine to achieve its goals when operating in D;

(2) adequate for a *disembodied rational planner* if it entails all and only the intuitive truths of D as expressed in the language of the user of the planner;

(3) adequate for *cognitive science* if it effectively captures the knowledge of D which actual agents have.

[6] Clearly there are limits to how deviantly an abstract task may be implemented without effecting performance. Isomorphs of tic-tac-toe and the Tower of Hanoi are notoriously more difficult to solve than the standard problems. But the success in solving a problem often depends on finding its abstract structure—on understanding the constraints and options. Particular implementations or encodings of problems may make discovering this structure especially hard. But whenever success crucially depends on being mindful of that structure, knowledge level accounts of the problem are particularly appropriate.

The philosophical arguments I will now present are meant to show that a formal theory of D, unless accompanied by a theory about the sensori-motor capacities of the creature using the theory, will fail no matter which purpose a theorist has in mind. Theories of conceptualizations alone are inadequate, they require theories of embodiment.

Inadequacy for robotics According to Nilsson, the touchstone of adequacy of a logicist theory is that it marks the necessary domain distinctions and makes the necessary domain predictions for an acting perceiving machine to achieve its goals. Theoretical adequacy is a function of four variables: D: the actual subject-independent properties of a domain; P: the creature's perceptual capacities; A: the creature's action repertoire; and G: the creature's goals. In principle a change in any one of these can affect the theoretical adequacy of an axiomatization. For changes in perceptual abilities, no less than changes in action abilities or goals may render domain distinctions worthless, invisible to a creature.

If axioms are adequate only relative to $(D\ P\ A\ G)$ then formal theories are strictly speaking untestable without an account of $(D\ P\ A\ G)$. We can never know whether a given axiom set captures the distinctions and relations which a particular robot will need for coping with D. We cannot just assume that T is adequate if it satisfies our own intuitions of the useful distinctions inherent in a domain. The intuitions we ourselves have about the domain will be relative to our own action repertoire, perceptual capacities, and goals. Nor will appeal to model theory help. Model theoretic interpretations only establish consistency. They say nothing about the appropriateness, truth or utility of axiom sets for a given creature.

Moreover, this need to explicitly state A, P, and G is not restricted to robots or creatures having substantially different perceptual-motor capacities to our own. There is always the danger that between any two humans there are substantive differences about the intuitively useful distinctions inherent in a domain. The chemist, for instance, who wishes to axiomatize the knowledge a robot needs to cope with the many liquids it may encounter, has by dint of study refined his observational capacities to the point where he or she can notice theoretical properties of the liquid which remain invisible to the rest of us. She will use in her axiomatizations primitive terms that she believes are observational. For most of us they are not. We require axiomatic connections to tie those terms to more directly observational ones. As a result, there is in all probability a continuum of formal theories of the commonsense world ranging from ones understandable by novices to those understandable only by experts. Without an account of the observational capacities presupposed by a theory, however, it is an open question just which level of expertise a given T represents.

It may be objected that an account of the observational capacities presupposed by a theory is not actually part of the theory but of the metatheory of use—the theory that explains how to *apply* the theory. But this difference is in name alone. The domain knowledge that is required to tie a predicate to the observational conditions that are relevant to it is itself substantial. If a novice is to use the expert's theory he will have to know how to make all things considered judgements about whether a given phenomenon is an A-type event or B-type event. Similarly if the expert is to use the novice's theory he must likewise consult the novice's theory to decide the best way to collapse observational distinctions he notices. In either case, it is arbitrary where we say these world linking axioms are to be found. They are part and partial of domain knowledge. But they form the basis for a theory of embodiment.

Inadequacy for disembodied rational planners Despite the generality of the argument above it is hard to reject the seductive image of an omniscient angel—a disembodied intellect who by definition is unable to see or act—who nonetheless is fully knowledgeable of the properties of a domain and is able to draw inferences, make predictions and offer explanations in response to questions put to it.

The flaw in this image of a disembodied rational planner, once again, is to be found in the assumption that we can make sense of the angel's theoretical language without knowing how it would be hooked up to a body with sensors and effectors. Without some idea of what a creature would perceive the best we can do to identify the meaning it assigns to terms in its theory is to adopt a model theoretic stance and assume the creature operates with a consistent theory. In that case, the semantic content of a theory will be exhausted by the set of models satisfying it. Naturally, we would like to be able to single out one model, or one model family, as the *intended* models—the interpretation the angel has in mind when thinking about that theory. But there is no principle within model theory which justifies singling out one model as the intended model. Without some further ground for supposing the angel has one particular interpretation in mind we must acknowledge that the reference of the expressions in its theories are inscrutable.

It is not a weakness of model theory that it fails to state what a user of a language thinks his expressions are *about*. Model theory is a theory of validity, a theory of logical consequence. It states conditions under which an axiom set is consistent. It doesn't purport to be a theory of intentionality or a theory of meaning. This becomes important because unless all models are isomorphic to the intended model there will be possible interpretations that are so ridiculous given what we know that the axiom set is obviously empirically false. We know it doesn't correctly describe the entities and relations of the domain in question.

The way out of the model-theoretic straightjacket is once again by means of translation axioms linking terms in the axiom set to terms in our ordinary language. Thus if the angel uses a term such as "supports" as in "if you move a block supporting another block, the supported block moves" we assume that the meaning the angel has in mind for *support* is the same as that which we would have in the comparable English sentence. But now a problem arises. For unless we specify the meaning of these terms in English we cannot be confident the angel's theory is empirically adequate. The reason we must go this extra yard is that there are still too many possible interpretations of the terms in the axiom set. For instance, does the axiom "if you move a block supporting another, the supported block moves" seem correct? Perhaps. But consider cases where the upper block is resting on several lower blocks each supporting a corner of the upper block. Any single lower block can now be removed without disturbing the upper. Hence the axiom fails.

Were these cases intended? Exactly what range of cases did the angel have in mind? Without an account of intentionality, an account which explains what the angel would be disposed to recognize as a natural case and what as a deviant case, we know too little about the meaning of the angel's axioms to put them to use. Translation into English only shifts the burden because we still need to know what an English speaker would be disposed to recognize as a natural case and what as a deviant case. Without a theory of embodiment these questions are not meaningful.

Inadequacy for cognitive science I have been arguing that axiomatic accounts of common sense domains are incomplete for both robots and angels unless they include axioms specifying sensori-motor capacities, dispositions, and possibly goals. For the purposes of cognitive science, however, we may add yet another requirement to this list: that the predicates appearing in the axioms be extendable to new contexts in roughly the way the agents being modelled extend their predicates. We cannot say we have successfully captured the knowledge a given agent has about a domain unless we understand the concepts (or recognitional dispositions) it uses.

For instance, suppose an axiomatization of our knowledge of the blocks world fails to accommodate our judgements about novel blocks world cases. This will occur, for example, if we try to use our axioms of cubic blocks worlds to apply to blocks worlds containing pyramids. When our cubic blocks world axiomatization generates false predictions of this broader domain, shall we say the axiomatization fails to capture the single conceptualization of both worlds we operate with? Or shall we rather say that we must operate with more than one set of blocks world conceptions—one apt for cubic blocks, another for pyramidal, and so forth? One major school of thought maintains that it is the nature of human concepts that they be extendable to new domains without wholesale overhauling [19, 20]. Indeed that virtually all concepts, it is suggested, have this extensibility property.

Yet if extensibility is a feature of our conceptualizations then no axiomatization of our knowledge will be psychologically correct unless it also includes a set of axioms or principles for determining how we will extend our concepts to new domains. Axiomatizations without these principles will be too static, regularly giving rise to false predictions. On the other hand, extensibility dispositions cannot be stated without making reference to our sensori-motor dispositions and goals. Since these cannot be given without a theory of the agent's sense organs etc, axiomatizations in cognitive science must include a theory of embodiment.

3.1.2. Essential indexicality

The second set of arguments to show that an axiomatic theory of commonsense domains fail to capture all the knowledge the agents have about those domains turns on the rather severe assumptions implicit in model-theoretic interpretations of axioms that it be possible to state the intended interpretation of an axiom set in the language of sets and properties of objective spatial temporal regions. If it can be shown that systems often think about the world indexically, in an *egocentric* fashion, which cannot be adequately interpreted in terms of properties of objective space time regions, then there is some knowledge that an axiomatic theory fails to capture.

For example, my knowledge that my eyeglasses are *over there*, on my right, is not properly captured by describing my relation to a set of objective spatio-temporal models or geometric structures, because *over there* is not a standard function from words to worlds. If I am working with a data glove and manipulating objects on a display screen, *over there* means somewhere in data glove space. Similarly, if I am looking through a telescope, or I am wearing vision distorting glasses, what I mean when I say *over there* is not something context-independent; it very much matters on my action and perception space. What my knowledge of *over there* consists in is a set of dispositions to orient myself, to take certain actions which presuppose the location of the object relative to the type of actions I might perform. These dispositions cannot be described in terms of the public world of space and time, however, because they may have nothing to do with that shared world.[7]

Now if microtheories are meant to explain what we know about a domain that permits us to perform rational actions in that domain—for instance, if the microtheory of liquids is to partly explain why I open the tops of bottles, and upend them to extract their liquid contents—then that microtheory presupposes that we have the concept of *upending*. Yet if *upending* is a term that is meaningful egocentrically—and it must be for I may upend a bottle in data glove space—then our liquid microtheory does not capture our conceptual knowledge correctly. Many of the concepts we have are grounded in our egocentric understanding of our world of action and perception. Logicists tend

[7] The position I am cursorily describing derives from Gareth Evans in lecture and in [8].

to treat all concepts as designating entities in the public domain.[8] It is possible to introduce new constructs, such as perspectives, or situations to capture the agent's point of view on a space time region. But this still leaves unexplained the agent's perspective on virtual spaces which can be explained only by describing the agent's dispositions to behave in certain ways. Hence there are some things that an agent can know about a domain—such as where it is in a domain—which cannot be captured by standard axiomatic accounts.[9]

4. Is cognition rational kinematics?

I have been arguing that there are grave problems with the methodological assumption that cognitive skills can be studied in abstraction from the sensing and motor apparatus of the bodies that incorporate them. Both empirical and philosophical arguments can be presented to show that the body shows through. This does not vitiate the program of knowledge level theorists, but it does raise doubts about the probability of correctly modelling all cognitive skills on the knowledge-base/inference-engine model.

A further assumption related to disembodied AI is that we can use logic or English to track the trajectory of informational states a system creates as it processes a cognitive task. That is, either the predicate calculus or English can serve as a useful semantics for tracking the type of computation that goes on in cognition. They are helpful metalanguages.

From the logicist's point of view, when an agent computes its next behaviour it creates a trajectory of informational states that are *about* the objects, functions and relations designated in the designer's conceptualization of the environment. This language is, of course, a logical language. Hence the transitions between these informational states can be described as *rational transitions* or inferences in that logical language. If English is the semantic metalanguage, then rational transitions between sentences will be less well-defined, but ought nonetheless to make sense as *reasonable*.

There are two defects with this approach. First, that it is parochial: that in fact there are many types of computation which are not amenable to characterization in a logical metalanguage, but which still count as cognition. Second, because it is easy for a designer to mistake his own conceptualization for a machine's conceptualization there is a tendency to misinterpret the machine's informational trajectory, often attributing to the machine a deeper grasp of the world than is proper.

[8] For a brief account of the advantages of conceiving of the world as a public space, see my commentary on Rod Brooks [16].

[9] A third argument against model theoretic interpretations of knowledge is *inconsistency*. If there is an inconsistency in what I know about liquids, then there can be no models of this knowledge set. So I must know nothing at all. But of course I do know much about liquids, I just happen to be mistaken in one of my beliefs. Efforts to deal with such inconsistency exist in the literature [2].

Argument 1. Consider the second objection first. As mentioned earlier, it is necessary to distinguish those cases where:

(1) the designer uses concepts to describe the environment which the machine does not understand and perhaps could not;
(2) the designer uses only those concepts which the machine grasps, but the two represent those concepts differently;
(3) both designer and machine use the same concepts and encode them in the same way.

The first two cases concern the appropriate metalanguage of design, the last the object language of processing. Our goal as scientists is to represent a creature's cognition as accurately as possible, both so we can verify what it is doing, hence debug it better, and so we can design it better from the outset.

The trouble that regularly arises, though, is that the designer has a conceptualization of the task environment that is quite distinct from that of the system. There is always more than one way of *specifying* an ability, and more than one way of specifying an environment of action. Choice of a metalanguage should be made on pragmatic grounds: which formalism most simplifies the designer's task? But lurking in the background is the worry that if the designer uses a metalanguage that invokes concepts the system simply does not or could not have, then he may propose mistaken designs which he later verifies as correct using the same incorrect metalanguage.

For example, suppose we wish to design a procedure controlling a manipulator able to draw a circle using a pair of compasses. In our conceptualization we talk of a locus of points equidistant from a third point. Does the system itself operate with that conceptualization? Does it have *implicit* concepts of *locus*, *equidistance* and *points*?

Why does it matter? Well, suppose we now have the manipulator attempt to draw a circle on a crumpled piece of paper. The naive procedure will not produce a curve whose distance on the crumpled surface is equidistant. Its design works for flat surfaces, not for arbitrary surfaces. Yet if a system did have concepts for equidistance, locus and points it ought to be *adaptive* enough to accommodate deformations in surface topology. To be sure such a machine would have to have some way of sensing topology. That by itself is not enough, though. It is its dispositions to behave in possible worlds that matters. This is shown by the old comment that whether I have the concept *chordate* (creature having a heart) or *renate* (creature having kidneys) cannot be determined by studying my normal behaviour alone [34]. In normal worlds, all chordates are renates. Only in counterfactual worlds—where it is possible to come across viable creatures with hearts but no kidneys—could we display our individuating dispositions. The upshot is that a designer cannot assume that his characterization of the informational trajectory of a creature is correct, unless he confirms certain claims about the creature's dispositions to behave in a range of further

ceptualization are sufficiently distinct that the two can be studied separately. Indeed, learning is often understood as the mechanism for generating a trajectory of conceptualizations. This is clearly the belief of logic theorists and developmental psychologists who maintain that what an agent knows at a given stage of development is a theory, not fundamentally different in spirit than a scientific theory, about the domain [4].

There are several problems with this view. First, it assumes we can characterize the instantaneous conceptualization of a system without having to study its various earlier conceptualizations. But what if we cannot *elicit* the system's conceptualization using the standard techniques? To determine what a competent PDP system, for example, would know about its environment of action, it is necessary to train it until it satisfies some adequacy metric. We cannot say in advance what the system will know if it is perfectly competent because there are very many paths to competence, each of which potentially culminates in a different solution. Moreover if the account of PDP offered above is correct it may be impossible to characterize the system's conceptualization in a logical language or in English. It is necessary to analyze its dispositions. But to do that one needs an actual implementation displaying the competence. Hence the only way to know what a PDP system will know if it is competent is to build one and study it. A purely top-down stance, which asssumes that learning is irrelevant, is bound to fail in the case of PDP.

A second argument against detaching knowledge and learning also focusses on the *in practice* unpredictable nature of the learning trajectory. In Soar it is frequently said that chunking is more than mere speedup [35]. The results of repeatedly chunking solutions to impasses has a nonlinear effect on performance. Once we have nonlinear effects, however, we cannot predict the evolution of a system short of running it. Thus in order to determine the steady state knowledge underpinning a skill we need to run Soar with its chunking module on.[11]

A final reason we cannot study what a system knows without studying how it acquires that knowledge is that a system may have been special design features that let it acquire knowledge. It is organized to self-modify. Hence we cannot predict what knowledge it may contain unless we know how it integrates new information with old. There are many ways to self-modify.

For instance, according to Roger Schank, much of the knowledge a system contains is lodged in its indexing scheme [41]. As systems grow in size they generally have to revise their indexing scheme. The results of this process of revision cannot be anticipated *a priori* unless we have a good idea of the earlier indexing schemes. The reason is that much of its knowledge is stored in cases. Case knowledge may be sensitive to the order the cases were encountered.

[11] We can, of course, hand-simulate running the system and so predict its final states. But I take it this is not a significant difference from running Soar itself.

Consequently, we can never determine the knowledge a competent system has unless we know something of the cases it was exposed to and the order they were met. History counts.

This emphasis on cases goes along with a view that much of reasoning involves noticing analogies to past experiences. A common corrolary to this position is that concepts are not context-free intensions; they have a certain open texture, making it possible to flexibly extend their use and to apply them to new situations in creative ways. An agent which understands a concept should be able to recognize and generate analogical extensions of its concepts to new contexts.

Once we view concepts to be open textured, however, it becomes plausible to suppose that a concept's meaning is a function of history. It is easier to see an analogical extension of a word if it has already been extended in that direction before. But then, we can't say what an agent's concept of "container" is unless we know the variety of contexts it has seen the word in. If that is so, it is impossible to understand a creature's conceptualization in abstraction from its learning history. Much of cognition cannot be studied independently of learning.

6. Is the architecture of cognition homogeneous?

The final issue I will discuss is the claim made by Newell et al. that cognition is basically the product of running programs in a single architecture. According to Newell, too much of the research in AI and cognitive science aims at creating independent representational and control mechanisms for solving particular cognitive tasks. Each investigator has his or her preferred computational models which, clever as they may be, rarely meet a further constraint that they be integratable into a unified account of cognition. For Newell

> Psychology has arrived at the possibility of unified theories of cognition—theories that gain their power by positing a single system of mechanisms that operate together to produce the full range of human cognition [30].

The idea that there might be a general theory of intelligence is not new. At an abstract level anyone who believes that domain knowledge plus inferential abilities are responsible for intelligent performance, at least in one sense, operates with a general theory of cognition. For, on that view, it is knowledge, ultimately, that is the critical element in cognition.

But Newell's claim is more concrete: not only is knowledge the basis for intelligence; knowledge, he argues further, will be encoded in a Soar-like mechanism. This claim goes well beyond what most logicists would maintain. It is perfectly consistent with logicism that knowledge may be encoded, implemented or embedded in any of dozens of ways. A bare commitment to specification of cognitive skills at the knowledge level is hardly grounds for expecting a small set of "underlying mechanisms, whose interactions and compositions provide the answers to all the questions we have—predictions, explanations, designs, controls" [30, p. 14] pertaining to the full range of cognitive performances. The Soar project, however, is predicated on this very possibility. The goal of the group is to test the very strong claim that underpinning problem solving, decision making, routine action, memory, learning, skill, even perception and motor behaviour, there is a single architecture "a single system [that] produces all aspects of behaviour . . . Even if the mind has parts, modules, components, or whatever, they mesh together . . ." and work in accordance with a small set of principles.

It is not my intent to provide serious arguments for or against this position. I mention it largely because it is such a deep committment of the Soar research program and therefore an assumption that separates research orientations. The strongest support for it must surely be empirical, and it will become convincing only as the body of evidence builds up. There can be little doubt, though, that it is an assumption not universally shared.

Minsky, for instance, in *Society of Mind* [28], has argued that intelligence is the product of hundreds, probably thousands of specialized computational mechanisms he terms agents. There is no homogenous underlying architecture. In the society of mind theory, mental activity is the product of many agents of varying complexity interacting in hundreds of ways. The very purpose of the theory is to display the variety of mechanisms that are likely to be useful in a mind-like system, and to advocate the need for diversity. Evolution, Minsky, emphasizes is an opportunistic tinkerer likely to co-opt existing mechanisms in an *ad hoc* manner to create new functions meeting new needs. With such diversity and ad hoccery it would be surprising if most cognitive performances were the result of a few mechanisms comprising a principled architecture.

Brooks in a similar manner sets out to recreate intelligent capacities by building layer upon layer of mechanism, each with hooks into lower layers to suppress or bias input and output. Again, no non-empirical arguments may be offered to convince skeptics of the correctness of this view. The best that has been offered is that the brain seems to have diverse mechanisms of behaviour control, so it is plausible that systems with comparable functionality will too.

Again there is no quick way to justify the assumption of architecture homogeneity. More than any other foundational issue this is one for which non-empirical or philosophical arguments are misplaced.

7. Conclusion

I have presented five dimensions—five big issues—which theorists in AI, either tacitly or explicitly, take a stand on. Any selection of issues is bound to have a personal element to them. In my case I have focussed most deeply on the challenges of embodiment. How reliable can theories of cognition be if they assume that systems can be studied abstractly, without serious concern for the mechanisms that ground a system's conceptualization in perception and action? But other more traditional issues are of equal interest. How central is the role which knowledge plays in cognitive skills? Can most of cognition be seen as inference? What part does learning or psychological development play in the study of reasoning and performance? Will a few mechanisms of control and representation suffice for general intelligence? None of the arguments presented here even begin to be decisive. Nor were they meant to be. Their function is to encourage informed debate of the paramount issues informing our field.

Acknowledgement

I thank Farrel Ackerman, John Batali, Danny Bobrow, Pat Hayes, Paul Kube, Brian Smith and Patrick Winston for helpful and fun conversations on the topics of this paper.

References

[1] L. Birnbaum, Rigor mortis: a response to Nilsson's "Logic and artificial intelligence", *Artif. Intell.* **47** (1991) 57–77, this volume.
[2] M. Brandon and N. Rescher, *The Logic of Inconsistency* (Basil Blackwell, Oxford, 1978).
[3] R.A. Brooks, Intelligence without representation, *Artif. Intell.* **47** (1991) 139–159, this volume.
[4] S. Carey, *Conceptual Change in Childhood* (MIT Press/Bradford Books, Cambridge, MA, 1985).
[5] N. Chomsky, *Aspects of the Theory of Syntax* (MIT Press, Cambridge, MA, 1965).
[6] N. Chomsky, *Knowledge of Language: Its Nature Origin and Use* (Preager, New York, 1986).
[7] A. Cussins, Connectionist construction of concepts, in: M. Boden, ed., *Philosophy of Artificial Intelligence* (Oxford University Press, Oxford, 1986).
[8] G. Evans, *Varieties of Reference* (Oxford University Press, Oxford, 1983).
[9] J.A. Fodor, *Language of Thought* (Harvard University Press, Cambridge, MA, 1975).
[10] J.A. Fodor, *Psychosemantics* (MIT Press, Cambridge, MA, 1987).
[11] J.A. Fodor and Z.W. Pylyshyn, Connectionism and cognitive architecture: a critical analysis, *Cognition* **28** (1988) 3–71.
[12] L. Gasser, Social conceptions of knowledge and action: DAI foundations and open systems semantics, *Artif. Intell.* **47** (1991) 107–138, this volume.
[13] P.J. Hayes, A critique of pure treason, *Comput. Intell.* **3** (3) (1987).
[14] C. Hewitt, Open Information Systems Semantics for Distributed Artificial Intelligence, *Artif. Intell.* **47** (1991) 79–106, this volume.
[15] J.R. Hobbs and R. Moore, eds., *Formal Theories of the Commonsense World* (Ablex, Norwood, NJ, 1985).
[16] D. Kirsh, Today the earwig, tomorrow man?, *Artif. Intell.* **47** (1991) 161–184, this volume.
[17] K. Konolige, Belief and incompleteness, in: J.R. Hobbs and R. Moore, eds., *Formal Theories of the Commonsense World* (Ablex, Norwood, NJ, 1985).

[18] T. Kuhn, *The Structure of Scientific Revolutions* (University of Chicago Press, Chicago, IL, 1962).
[19] G. Lakoff, *Women, Fire, Dangerous Things: What Categories Reveal about the Mind* (University of Chicago Press, Chicago, IL, 1987).
[20] R. Langacker, *Foundations of Cognitive Grammar* (Stanford University Press, Stanford, CA, 1987).
[21] D.B. Lenat and R.V. Guha, *Building Large Knowledge-Based Systems, Representation and Inference in the Cyc Project* (Addison-Wesley, Reading, MA, 1989).
[22] D.B. Lenat and J.S. Brown, Why AM and EURISKO appear to work, *Artif. Intell.* **23** (1984) 269–294.
[23] D.B. Lenat and E.A. Feigenbaum, On the thresholds of knowledge, *Artif. Intell.* **47** (1991) 185–250, this volume.
[24] H.J. Levesque, Knowledge representation and reasoning, in: *Annual Review of Computer Science* **1** (Annual Reviews Inc., Palo Alto, CA, 1986) 255–287.
[25] J. Mandler, How to build a baby 2, unpublished manuscript.
[26] D. Marr, *Vision* (Freeman, San Francisco, CA, 1982).
[27] J.L. McClelland, D.E. Rumelhart and the PDP Research Group, eds., *Parallel Distributed Processing: Explorations in the Microstructure of Cognition* **2**: *Psychological and Biological Models* (MIT Press/Bradford Books, Cambridge, MA, 1986).
[28] M.L. Minsky, *The Society of Mind* (Simon and Schuster, New York, 1986).
[29] R. Montague, *Formal Philosophy: Selected Papers of Richard Montague*, edited by R.H. Thomason (Yale University Press, New Haven, CT, 1974).
[30] A. Newell, Unified theories of cognition: the William James lectures, manuscript.
[31] A. Newell, P.S. Rosenbloom and J.E. Laird, Symbolic architectures for cognition, in: M. Posner, ed., *Foundations of Cognitive Science* (MIT Press, Cambridge, MA, 1989).
[32] A. Newell and H.A. Simon, *Human Problem Solving* (Prentice-Hall, Englewood Cliffs, NJ, 1972).
[33] N.J. Nilsson, Logic and artificial intelligence, *Artif. Intell.* **47** (1991) 31–56, this volume.
[34] W.V.O. Quine, *Word and Object* (MIT Press, Cambridge, MA, 1960).
[35] P.S. Rosenbloom, J.E. Laird, A. Newell and R. McCarl, A preliminary analysis of the Soar architecture as a basis for general intelligence, *Artif. Intell.* **47** (1991) 289–325, this volume.
[36] S.J. Rosenschein, The logicist conception of knowledge is too narrow—but so is McDermott's, *Comput. Intell.* **3** (3) (1987).
[37] S.J. Rosenschein and L.P. Kaebling, The synthesis of machines with provably epistemic properties, in: J.Y. Halpern, ed., *Proceedings of the 1986 Conference on Theoretical Aspects of Reasoning about Knowledge* (Morgan Kaufmann, Los Altos, CA, 1986) 83–98.
[38] D.E. Rumelhart, J.L. McClelland and the PDP Research Group, eds., *Parallel Distributed Processing: Explorations in the Microstructure of Cognition* **1**: *Foundations* (MIT Press/Bradford Books, Cambridge, MA, 1986).
[39] D.E. Rumelhart et al., Schemata and sequential thought processes in PDP models, in: J.L. McClelland, D.E. Rumelhart and the PDP Research Group, eds., *Parallel Distributed Processing: Explorations in the Microstructure of Cognition* **2**: *Psychological and Biological Models* (MIT Press/Bradford Books, Cambridge, MA, 1986).
[40] R.C. Schank, *Dynamic Memory* (Erlbaum, Hillsdale, NJ, 1985).
[41] R.C. Schank and C. Riesbeck, *Inside Computer Understanding* (Erlbaum, Hillsdale, NJ, 1981).
[42] B.C. Smith, The owl and the electric encyclopedia, *Artif. Intell.* **47** (1991) 251–288, this volume.
[43] P. Smolensky, On the proper treatment of connectionism, *Behav. Brain Sci.* **11** (1988) 1–23.

Artificial Intelligence 47 (1991) 31–56
Elsevier

Logic and artificial intelligence

Nils J. Nilsson

Computer Science Department, Stanford University, Stanford, CA 94305, USA

Received February 1989

Abstract

Nilsson, N.J., Logic and artificial intelligence, Artificial Intelligence 47 (1990) 31–56.

The theoretical foundations of the logical approach to artificial intelligence are presented. Logical languages are widely used for expressing the declarative knowledge needed in artificial intelligence systems. Symbolic logic also provides a clear semantics for knowledge representation languages and a methodology for analyzing and comparing deductive inference techniques. Several observations gained from experience with the approach are discussed. Finally, we confront some challenging problems for artificial intelligence and describe what is being done in an attempt to solve them.

1. Introduction

Until a technological endeavor achieves a substantial number of its goals, several competing approaches are likely to be pursued. So it is with artificial intelligence (AI). AI researchers have programmed a number of demonstration systems that exhibit a fair degree of intelligence in limited domains (and some systems that even have commercial value). However, we are still far from achieving the versatile cognitive skills of humans. And so research continues along a number of paths—each with its ardent proponents. Although successful AI systems of the future will probably draw upon a combination of techniques, it is useful to study the different approaches in their pure forms in order to highlight strengths and weaknesses. Here, I present my view of what constitutes the "logical approach" to AI.

Some of the criticisms of the use of logic in AI stem from confusion about what it is that "logicists" claim for their approach. As we shall see, logicism provides a point of view and principles for constructing languages and procedures used by intelligent machines. It certainly does not promise a ready-made apparatus whose handle needs only to be turned to emit intelligence. Indeed, some researchers who might not count themselves among those following a logical approach can arguably be identified with the logicist position. (See, for example, Smith's review of a paper by Lenat and Feigenbaum [28, 54].) Other,

understand English well enough, it is too ambiguous a representational medium for present-day computers—the meanings of English sentences depend too much on the contexts in which they are uttered and understood.

AI researchers have experimented with a wide variety of languages in which to represent sentences. Some of these languages have limited expressive power. They might not have a means for saying that one or another of two facts is true without saying which fact is true. Some cannot say that a fact is not true without saying what is true instead. They might not be able to say that *all* the members of a class have a certain property without explicitly listing each of them. Finally, some are not able to state that at least one member of a class has a certain property without stating which member does. First-order predicate calculus, through its ability to formulate disjunctions, negations, and universally and existentially quantified sentences, does not suffer from these limitations and thus meets our minimal representational requirements.

3. Foundations of the logical approach

In addition to the three theses just stated, the logical approach to AI also embraces a point of view about what knowledge is, what the world is, how a machine interacts with the world, and the role and extent of special procedures in the design of intelligent machines.

Those designers who would claim that their machines possess declarative knowledge about the world are obliged to say something about what that claim means. The fact that a machine's knowledge base has an expression in it like $(\forall x)\mathrm{Box}(x) \supset \mathrm{Green}(x)$, for example, doesn't by itself justify the claim that the machine *believes* all boxes are green. (The mnemonic relation constants that we use in our design aren't mnemonic for the machine! We could just as well have written $(\forall x)\mathrm{GO11}(x) \supset \mathrm{GO23}(x)$.)

There are different views of what it means for a machine possessing a database of sentences to believe the facts intended by those sentences. The view that I favor involves making some (perhaps unusual) metaphysical

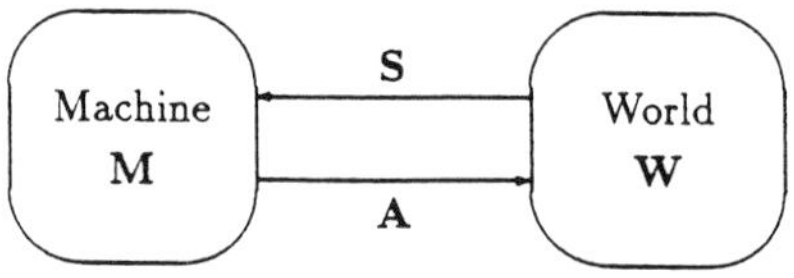

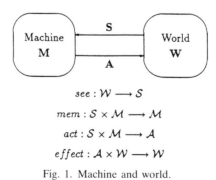

$$see : \mathcal{W} \longrightarrow \mathcal{S}$$

$$mem : \mathcal{S} \times \mathcal{M} \longrightarrow \mathcal{M}$$

$$act : \mathcal{S} \times \mathcal{M} \longrightarrow \mathcal{A}$$

$$effect : \mathcal{A} \times \mathcal{W} \longrightarrow \mathcal{W}$$

Fig. 1. Machine and world.

assumptions about what we take the "real world" to be and about how our machines interact with that world. I will give a simplified account of this view here. It is based, in part, on a discussion of intelligent agent architecture in [12, Chapter 13].

Figure 1 shows a machine interacting with the world. Both machine and world are regarded as finite-state machines. We denote the machine state by M; it is one of a set $\mathcal{M}$ of states. We denote the world state by W; it is one of a set $\mathcal{W}$ of states. The input to the machine is denoted by S—one of a set $\mathcal{S}$ of inputs; the output of the machine is denoted by A—one of a set $\mathcal{A}$ of outputs. States, inputs, and outputs are related as follows: the function *see* maps $\mathcal{W}$ into $\mathcal{S}$; the function *mem* maps $\mathcal{S} \times \mathcal{M}$ into $\mathcal{M}$; the function *act* maps $\mathcal{S} \times \mathcal{M}$ into $\mathcal{A}$; lastly, the function *effect* maps $\mathcal{A} \times \mathcal{W}$ into $\mathcal{W}$. The function *see* models the fact that the machine is not sensitive to every aspect of the world; it partitions the world into classes whose members, as far as the machine is concerned, are equivalent. The function *mem* models the machine's memory behavior; the machine's state at any instant is a function of the machine's input and its previous state. The function *act* describes how the machine acts on the world; its action is a function of its state and its input. We model the effects of these actions on the world (as well as the world's own internal dynamics) by *effect*.

This model of a machine and its world is sufficiently general to capture a number of approaches to intelligent machine design. To particularize it to the logical approach, we stipulate that the state of the machine is given by a set of sentences, which for concreteness we hereinafter take to be sentences in the first-order predicate calculus. The function *mem* transforms such a set of sentences (together with the input to the machine) into another set of sentences (and thus changes the machine's state). The function *act* is a function of such a set of sentences (and the machine's input) and produces as output a machine action.

Describing how the designer specifies *act*, *mem*, and an initial set of sentences requires some discussion about the relationship between these sentences and what the designer imagines the world of the machine to be like. We suppose that the designer thinks of the world literally as a finite-state machine which he describes as a mathematical structure consisting of *objects*, *functions*, and *relations*. Some of the objects in this mathematical structure might be states, others might be other entities that the designer thinks exist in the world—some of which are dependent on state. This structure must also account for the finite-state machine function *effect*, which produces a new world state depending on the action of the intelligent machine and the old world state, and the function *see*, which maps world states into the input to the intelligent machine. AI researchers have explored a variety of ways to conceive of the world in terms of objects, functions, and relations; while we will not describe any particular conceptualization here, they can all be accommodated by the account we are giving. (It may seem strange to think of the *real* world as a mathematical structure, but since our picture provides for the world to be affected by and affect itself and the intelligent machine, one shouldn't worry that our view of the world is impractically ethereal.)

Now, the designer of a machine that is to interact with the world never knows what the world objects, functions, and relations actually are. He must guess. Guessing involves *invention* on the designer's part. (Our machine designer is in the same predicament as is the scientist; scientists invent descriptions of the world and gradually refine them until they are more useful.) We use the term *conceptualization* to describe the designer's guess about the world objects, functions, and relations. The designer may not even be able to specify a single conceptualization; for example he may choose not to commit himself regarding whether an object he invents, say a block, has the color property green or blue. Thus, in general, the designer attempts to specify a set of conceptualizations such that, whatever the world actually is, he guesses it is a member of the set.

The designer realizes, of course, that his conceptualization might not accurately capture the world—even as he himself believes it to be. For example, his conceptualization may not discriminate between objects that he himself recognizes to be different but which can be considered to be the same considering his purposes for the machine. The designer need only invent a conceptualization that is *good enough*, and when and if it becomes apparent that it is deficient (and that this deficiency is the cause of inadequate machine performance), he can modify his conceptualization.

We stress that the objects guessed to exist in the world by the designer are *invented*. He is perfectly free to invent anything that makes the machine perform appropriately, and he doesn't ask whether or not some object *really* does or does not exist (whatever that might mean) apart from these invented structures. For many ordinary, concrete objects such as chairs, houses, people, and so on, we can be reasonably confident that our inventions mirror reality. But some of the things that we might want to include as world objects, such as *precambrian unconformities*, English sentences, *the Peloponnesian War*, π, and *truth*, have a somewhat more arbitrary ontological status. In fact, much of the designer's guess about the world may be quite arbitrary in the sense that other guesses would have suited his purposes equally well. (Even those researchers following other declarative, but putatively non-logical, approaches must invent the equivalent of objects, relations, and functions when they attempt to give their machines declarative knowledge.)

A logicist expresses his conceptualization of the world (for the machine) by a set of sentences. The sentences are made part of the machine's memory (comprising its state) and embody the machine's declarative knowledge. We assume that the sentences are in the first-order predicate calculus; this language and the sentences in it are constructed as follows: For every world object in the conceptualization we create an *object constant*; for every world relation, we create a *relation constant*; and for every world function, we create a *function constant*. Using these constructs, and the syntax of predicate calculus, we (the designer) then compose a set of sentences to express the declarative knowledge that we want the machine to have about the world.

When a designer cannot (or does not choose to) specify which of two relations holds, he uses a disjunction, such as: $\text{Box(Ob1)} \wedge [\text{Blue(Ob1)} \vee \text{Green(Ob1)}]$. Or he may use an existentially quantified statement; $(\exists x)\text{Box}(x) \wedge \text{Green}(x)$. Or, he might know that all boxes are green: $(\forall x)\text{Box}(x) \supset \text{Green}(x)$.

In what sense can we say that a collection of predicate calculus sentences represents *knowledge* about the world? Our answer to this question involves the notions of *interpretations* and *models* of sentences in the predicate calculus. Briefly, an interpretation consists of:

(1) an assignment of a relation to each relation constant;
(2) an assignment of an object to each object constant;
(3) an assignment of a function to each function constant;
(4) a procedure for assigning the values T (true) or F (false) to each closed formula. (This procedure involves *evaluating* ground atomic formulas using the relation/object/function assignments and then using the standard logical truth tables for non-atomic ground sentences. The description of how quantified sentences are evaluated is slightly more complex but respects the intuitive meanings of the quantifiers.)

Any interpretation for which all of the sentences in a set of sentences evaluates to T is called a *model* of the set of sentences.

In terms of these definitions, the designer's task can be re-stated as follows:

> Invent world objects, relations, and functions; a first-order predicate calculus language; an interpretation of the expressions of this language in terms of the objects, relations, and functions; and then compose a set of sentences in the language such that the interpretation of those sentences is a model of the set of sentences.

We will call the world objects, relations, and functions invented by the designer, the *intended model* of the sentences the designer uses to describe the world. Although this interpretation itself may never actually be represented explicitly as mathematical structure, it is important that it be firmly fixed in the mind of the designer. With this interpretation in mind, the designer invents linguistic terms to denote his invented objects, functions, and relations and writes down predicate calculus sentences for which the intended interpretation is a model.

The designer gives the machine declarative knowledge about the world by storing these sentences in the machine's memory. We call the set of sentences the *knowledge base* of the machine and denote the set by Δ. We assume that the designer fixes the initial state of the machine by specifying some Δ_0; when the machine is attached to the world, as in Fig. 1, *mem* produces a sequence of states $\Delta_0, \Delta_1, \ldots, \Delta_i, \ldots$.

Even when the designer has a single intended interpretation in mind, Δ, in general, will be satisfied by a set of interpretations—the intended one among them. The designer must provide sufficient sentences in the knowledge base such that its models are limited—limited so that even though the set has more than one model, it doesn't matter given the purposes for the machine. (To the extent that it *does* matter, the designer must then provide more sentences.) In designing knowledge bases, it frequently happens that the designer's idea of the intended interpretation is changed and articulated by the very act of writing down (and reasoning with) the sentences.

So, a machine possessing a set of sentences *knows* about the world in the sense that these sentences admit of a set of models, and this set is the designer's best approximation to what the world actually is, given the purposes for the machine. The *actual* world might not even be in the set (the designer's guess might be wrong), so we really should be talking about the machine's *beliefs* rather than the machine's *knowledge*. But, following the tradition established by the phrase "knowledge-based systems," we will continue to speak of the machine's knowledge.

The machine's procedural knowledge is represented in the functions *mem* and *act*. The function *mem* changes the sentences and thereby changes the machine's state. Perhaps new sentences are added or existing ones are modified or deleted in response to new sensory information. The function *mem* may also produce a change in the machine's state in the absence of sensory information; changes to Δ may occur through processes of deduction or other types of inference as will be described below.

The machine's declarative knowledge affects its actions through the function *act*. We take *act* to be a function (over sets of sentences) that produces actions. Note that *act* can thus only respond to sentences *qua sentences*, that is, as strings of symbols. It is not a function of the models of these sentences!

Given this picture, we can identify a spectrum of design choices. At one end, *act* and *mem* are highly specialized to the tasks the machine is expected to perform and to the environment in which it operates. We might say, in this case, that the machine's knowledge is mainly *procedurally* represented. At the other extreme, *act* and *mem* are general purpose and largely independent of the application. All application-specific knowledge is represented in Δ. The machine's knowledge in this case can be said to be mainly *declaratively* represented. The logical approach usually involves a commitment to represent most of the machine's knowledge declaratively. For a proposal at the extreme declarative end, see [12, Chapter 13]. It is not yet known to what extent this goal can be achieved while maintaining reasonable efficiency.

Because the actions emitted by *act* depend on the syntactic form of the sentences in Δ, it is necessary for *mem* to be able to rewrite these sentences in the form appropriate to the task at hand. This aspect of *mem* we call *reasoning*. Imagine, for example, a robot designed to paint boxes green. Its sentence-to-action process, *act*, may include a *production rule* like "If Δ includes the sentence Box(η) for some value of η, paint the object denoted by η green." But suppose Δ includes the sentences $(\forall x)\mathrm{Blue}(x) \supset \mathrm{Box}(x)$ and Blue(G17) but not Box(G17) explicitly. We might expect that correct behavior for this robot would be to paint the object denoted by G17 green, but there is no sentence-to-action rule to accomplish that unless Box(G17) occurs explicitly in Δ. Constructing the sentence Box(G17) from the sentences $(\forall x)\mathrm{Blue}(x) \supset \mathrm{Box}(x)$ and Blue(G17) is an example of one kind of sentence manipulation, or *inference*, that we want *mem* to do.

Often, as in the box-painting example, the new sentence constructed from ones already in memory does not tell us anything new about the world. (All of the models of $(\forall x)\mathrm{Blue}(x) \supset \mathrm{Box}(x)$ and Blue(G17) are also models of Box(G17). Thus, adding Box(G17) to Δ does not reduce the set of models.) What the new sentence tells us was already implicitly said by the sentences from which it was constructed.

If all of the models of Δ are also models of a sentence ϕ, we say that Δ *logically entails* ϕ and write $\Delta \models \phi$. Among the computations that we might want *mem* to perform are those which add sentences to Δ that are logically entailed by Δ. One apparent problem in devising such computations is the prospect of having to check *all* the models of Δ to see if they are also models of ϕ. But, fortunately, there exist strictly syntactic operations on Δ that are able to compute logically entailed formulas.

We use the phrase *rule of inference* to refer to any computation on a set of sentences that produces new sentences. If ψ can be derived from Δ by a sequence of applications of rules of inference, we say that ψ can be *deduced* from Δ and write $\Delta \vdash \psi$. An example is the rule of inference called *modus ponens*. From any sentences of the form $\rho \supset \sigma$ and ρ, we can deduce the sentence σ by modus ponens. The process of logical deduction involves using a set of rules of inference to deduce additional sentences from a set of sentences. Interestingly, it happens that there are rules of inference, modus ponens is an example, that have the property that if $\Delta \vdash \phi$, then $\Delta \models \phi$. Such rules of inference are called *sound*.

Sound rules of inference are extremely important because they allow us to compute sentences that are logically entailed by a set of sentences using computations on the sentences themselves (and not on their models).

We can also find sets of inference rules that have the property that if $\Delta \models \phi$ then the rules (successively applied) will eventually produce such a ϕ. Such a set of inference rules is called *complete*.

Although all logicists typically incorporate sound inference rules as part of the calculations performed by *mem*, there is no necessary reason to limit *mem* to performing sound inferences. Other computations are often desirable. We will describe some of these later in the paper.

In summary, intelligent machines designed according to the logical approach are state-machines whose states are sets of sentences. Machine state transitions are governed by a function, *mem*, acting on the sentence sets and the inputs to the machine. An important, but not the only, component of *mem* is sound logical inference. Machine actions are governed by a function, *act*, of the machine's state and inputs. The intended interpretation of the sentences in a machine's state involves objects, functions, and relations that are the designer's guesses about the world.

> Through naming comes knowing; we grasp an object, mentally, by giving it a name—hension, prehension, apprehension. And thus through language create a whole world, corresponding to the other world out there. Or we trust that it corresponds. Or perhaps, like a German poet, we cease to care, becoming more concerned with the naming than with the things named; the former becomes more real than the latter. And so in the end the world is lost again. No, the world remains—those unique, particular, incorrigibly individual junipers and sandstone monoliths—and it is we who are lost. Again. Round and round, through the endless labyrinth of thought—the maze. (Edward Abbey [1, pp. 288–289].)

4. Comments on the logical approach

The basic idea underlying the logical approach to AI is simple, but attempts to use it have resulted in several additional important insights.

4.1. The importance of conceptualization

The most important part of "the AI problem" involves inventing an appropriate conceptualization (intended model). It is not easy for a designer to squeeze his intuitive and commonsense ideas about the world into a coherent conceptualization involving objects, functions, and relations. Although this exercise has been carried out for several limited problem domains (most notably those to which expert systems have been successfully applied), there are some particularly difficult subjects to conceptualize. Among these are liquids and other "mass substances," processes, events, actions, beliefs, time, goals, intentions, and plans. Some researchers feel that the *frame problem*, for example, arises as it does as an artifact of an inappropriate (state-based) conceptualization of change [17]. Others feel that change must involve the notion of time (instead of the notion of state) [52]. Conceptualizing the "cognitive state" of intelligent agents has been the subject of recent intense study. (See, for example, [8] for a treatment of the intentions of agents and [24, 40] for treatments of the knowledge and beliefs of agents.) Interestingly, many of the most difficult conceptualization problems arise when attempting to express knowledge about the everyday, "commonsense" world (see [20, 21]). AI researchers join company with philosophers who have also been attempting to formalize some of these ideas.

Choosing to use first-order predicate calculus as a representation language does not relieve us of the chore of deciding *what* to say in that language. Deciding what to say is harder than designing the language in which to say it! The logical approach to AI carries with it no special insights into what conceptualizations to use. (Logic is often criticized for providing *form* but not *content*. Of course!)

It is important to stress that these conceptualization problems do not arise simply as an undesirable side effect of the use of logic. They must be confronted and resolved by any approach that attempts to represent knowledge of the world by sentence-like, declarative structures. The fact that these problems are exposed quite clearly in the coherent framework provided by the logical approach should be counted as an advantage.

4.2. Sound and unsound inferences

Another important observation concerns the subject of sound inference. Logicists are sometimes criticized for their alleged dependence on deduction. Much human thought, the critics rightly claim, involves leaps of intuition, inductive inference, and other guessing strategies that lie outside the realm of sound inference. There are two things that can be said about such criticism.

First, logicists regard sound inference as an important, but not the only, component of reasoning. We must be careful to note the circumstances under which both sound and unsound inferences might appropriately be used. Recall that the set of sentences Δ (with which a designer endows a machine) implicitly defines a set of models. Either the designer actually has some subset of these models in mind (as his guess about what the world is) or he is completely unbiased about which of the models might represent the world. If he really is unbiased, nothing other than sound inference would be desired by the designer. Any deduced sentence ϕ had better be logically entailed by Δ; if there are some models of Δ, for example, that are not models of ϕ, and if the designer wanted the machine to conclude ϕ, then he wouldn't have been completely unbiased about which of the models of Δ represented the world.

If the designer has some subset of the models of Δ in mind, and if (for one reason or another) he could not specify this subset by enlarging Δ, then there are circumstances under which unsound inference might be appropriate. For example, the designer may have some preference order over the models of Δ. He may want to focus, for example, on the minimal models (according to the preference order). These minimal models may be better guesses, in the designer's mind, about the real world than would be the other models of Δ. In that case, the inference ϕ would be appropriate if all the minimal models of Δ were models of ϕ. (We will see an example of the use of minimal models later.)

McCarthy [34] and Lifschitz [29] have studied a variety of such preference orders over models and have investigated an (unsound) inference computation, called *circumscription*, that is based on them. (We describe circumscription later in this paper.) Several aspects of commonsense reasoning, including inductive inference and default inference, appear to be mechanizable using circumscription or something very much like it.

Although inductive inference is a complex and well studied subject, we can use a simple version of it as an example of unsound inference. Consider the premises

$$\text{Emerald(Ob1)} \wedge \text{Color(Ob1, Green)},$$
$$\text{Emerald(Ob2)} \wedge \text{Color(Ob2, Green)},$$
$$\ldots,$$
$$\text{Emerald(Obn)} \wedge \text{Color(Obn, Green)}.$$

For some adequately large value of n, we may want to inductively infer (unsoundly but reasonably) $(\forall x)\text{Emerald}(x) \supset \text{Color}(x, \text{Green})$ if there is no η mentioned in Δ such that Δ entails $\text{Emerald}(\eta) \wedge \neg\text{Color}(\eta, \text{Green})$.

The second thing that can be said in defense of sound inference is that, in the context of sufficient additional information, sound conclusions can be drawn that might have seemed to have required unsound inference without the additional information. For example, suppose Δ contains the following statements:

$$(\exists y)(\forall x)\text{Emerald}(x) \supset \text{Color}(x, y)$$

(intended meaning: there is a color such that all emeralds have that color),

$$(\forall x, y, z)[\text{Color}(x, y) \wedge \text{Color}(x, z)] \supset (y = z)$$

(intended meaning: a thing can have only one color).

From these statements, we can deduce that if a thing is an emerald, it has a unique color. Now, if we subsequently learn

$$\text{Color(Ob1, Green)} \wedge \text{Emerald(Ob1)},$$

we can deduce (soundly) $(\forall x)\text{Emerald}(x) \supset \text{Color}(x, \text{Green})$. Δ already told us that all emeralds have the same unique color, but did not specify what that color was. Later information added to Δ allowed us to deduce a more specific general rule.

Although the logical approach might sanction unsound inferences, logicists would certainly want such inferences to have a well motivated model-theoretic justification. For example, circumscription is motivated by minimal-model entailment and thus might be called a "principled" inference even though not a sound one.

4.3. Efficiency and semantic attachment to partial models

Earlier, we mentioned that it was fortunate that sound inference techniques existed because it is impossible in most situations to check that all the models of Δ were also models of some formula ϕ. This "good fortune" is somewhat illusory however, because finding deductions is in general intractable and for many practical applications unworkably inefficient. Some people think that the inefficiency of the logical approach disqualifies it from serious consideration as a design strategy for intelligent machines.

There are several things to be said about logic and efficiency. First, it seems incontestable that knowledge can be brought to bear on a problem more efficiently when its use is tailored to the special features of that problem. When knowledge is encoded in a fashion that permits many different uses, several possible ways in which to use it may have to be tried in any given situation, and the resulting search process takes time. A price does have to be paid for generality, and the logical approach, it seems, pays a runtime cost to save accumulated design costs.

But even so, much progress has been made in making inference processes more efficient and practical for large problems. Stickel has developed one of the most powerful first-order-logic theorem provers [56, 57]. Several resolution refutation systems have been written that are able to solve large, nontrivial reasoning problems, including some open problems in mathematics [59, 61]. Many large-scale AI systems depend heavily on predicate calculus representations and reasoning methods. Among the more substantial of these are TEAM, a natural language interface to databases [14]; DART, a program for equipment design and repair [11]; and KAMP, a program that generates English sentences [3].

A very important technique for achieving efficiency in the context of the logical approach involves augmenting theorem-proving methods with calculations on model-like structures. Often, calculations on models are much more efficient than are inference processes, and we would be well advised to include them as part of a machine's reasoning apparatus.

We mentioned that seldom does a designer make explicit his guess about the world, the intended model. The set of models is implicitly defined by the set of sentences in Δ. Sometimes, however, it is possible to be explicit about at least part of the intended model. That is, we might be able to construct a part of the model as list structure and programs in, say, LISP. For example, we can represent objects as LISP atoms, functions as LISP functions, and relations as LISP predicates. In such cases we can perform reasoning by computations with these LISP constructs that we might otherwise have performed by logical inference on the predicate calculus sentences. This point has previously been made by a number of researchers[1]—most notably by Weyhrauch [58]. Typically, the LISP constructs will constitute only a *partial* model; that is, there might not be LISP referents for the expressions in all of the predicate calculus sentences, and/or the LISP functions and predicates themselves may be defined over just a subset of the intended domain. (In the following we will not always be careful about saying *partial* models and interpretations even though those are what we really mean.)

As an example, consider the predicate calculus sentences:

$$\mathsf{P(A)}, \qquad (\forall \mathsf{x})\mathsf{P(x)} \supset \mathsf{Q(x)} .$$

Presumably, these sentences stem from a certain conceptualization of the world. Suppose we can capture this conceptualization in LISP. Our intended interpretation for P is (represented by) a certain LISP predicate ***P***; our intended interpretation for Q is a certain LISP predicate ***Q***; and our intended interpretation for A is a certain LISP atom ***A***. If these intended interpretations are to be parts of models for Δ, then we know that (***P A***) and (**or** (**not** (***P A***)) (***Q A***)) will both evaluate to *T*. Thus, we must make sure that (***Q A***) evaluates to *T*.

So, this gives us two ways to compute the truth value of Q(A) with respect to the intended model. Given the initial sentences, we could deduce Q(A) using sound inference rules. That is, if a reasoning program needed to know whether or not Q(A) was true, it could find that it is true using logical inference. The fact that Q(A) can be (soundly) deduced from the other sentences means that Q(A) is logically entailed by them. And that means that *all* of the models of the initial sentences are also models of Q(A). That means, *a fortiori*, that the *intended* model of the initial sentence (whatever it is) is a model of Q(A).

The other way to compute the truth value of Q(A) is to associate Q(A) with (***Q A***) and evaluate (***Q A***) in LISP. We call this association *semantic attachment*. Semantic attachment to appropriate computational structures, when such are available, is sometimes more efficient than inference. It provides a means for determining the truth of an expression directly in the intended model rather than by establishing its truth in all models indirectly by sound inference.

It is my guess that practical AI systems will use a combination of logical inference and semantic attachment with the latter perhaps predominating in some applications and the former used as a "fall-back" method of great generality. Several standard structures and programs already commonly used in AI systems can be employed in semantic attachments. For example, tree structures are useful for representing taxonomic hierarchies (in fact, some knowledge representation languages use such tree-structure representations

[1] For a comprehensive recent treatment of attachment see: K.L. Myers, Automatically generating universal attachments through compilation, in: *Proceedings AAAI-90*, Boston, MA (1990) 252–257.

explicitly as part of the language [5]). Various LISP ordering predicates combined with appropriate directed-graph data structures are useful for representing transitive binary relations.

4.4. Reification of theories

Sometimes we will want our machines to reason about (rather than with) the sentences in its knowledge base. We may, for example, want them to reason about the lengths of sentences or about their complexity. Our conceptualizations will thus have to acknowledge that things called sentences exist in the world. Conferring *existence* on abstract concepts (such as sentences) is often called *reification*.

We might reify whole theories. This will allow us to say, for example, that some Δ_1 is more appropriate than is some Δ_2 when confronted with problems of diagnosing bacterial infections. Scientists are used to having different—even contradictory—theories to explain reality: quantum physics, Newtonian mechanics, relativity, wave theories of light, particle theories of light, and so on. Each is useful in certain circumstances. Although scientists search for a uniform, all-embracing, and consistent picture of reality, historically they have had to settle for a collection of somewhat different theories. There is nothing in the logicist approach that forces us, as machine designers, to use just *one* conceptualization of the world. There is no reason to think AI would be any more successful at that goal than scientists have been!

When theories are reified, *metatheory* (that is, a theory about theories) can be used to make decisions about which local theory should be used in which circumstances. For example, the metatheory might contain a predicate calculus statement having an intended meaning something like: "When planning a highway route, use the theory that treats roads as edges in a graph (rather than, for example, as solid objects made of asphalt or concrete)". Metatheory can also provide information to guide the inference procedures operating over local theories. For example, we might want to say that when two inferences are possible in some Δ_1, the inference that results in the most general conclusion should be preferred. Using metatheory to express knowledge about how to control inference is consistent with the logicists' desire to put as much knowledge as possible in declarative form (as opposed to "building it in" to the functions *mem* and *act*).

Weyhrauch [58] has pointed out that the process of semantic attachment in a metatheory can be particularly powerful. Commonly, even when no semantic attachments are possible to speed reasoning in a theory, the problem at hand can be dispatched efficiently by appropriate semantic attachment in the metatheory.

Some critics of the logical approach have claimed that since *anything* can be said in the metatheory, its use would seem to be a retreat to the same ad hoc tricks used by less disciplined AI researchers. But we think there are generally useful things to say in the metatheory that are not themselves problem dependent. That is, we think that knowledge about how to use knowledge can itself be expressed as context-free, declarative sentences. (Lenat's work has uncovered the best examples of generally useful statements about how to use knowledge [25–27].)

4.5. Other observations

Even though they frequently call the sentences in their knowledge bases *axioms*, logicists are not necessarily committed to represent knowledge by a minimal set of sentences. Indeed, some (or even most) of the sentences in Δ may be derivable from others. Since the "intelligence" of an agent depends on how much usable declarative knowledge it has, we agree completely with those who say "In the knowledge lies the power." We do not advocate systems that rely on search-based derivations of knowledge when it is possible to include the needed knowledge explicitly in the knowledge base. The use of very large knowledge bases, of course, presupposes efficient retrieval and indexing techniques.

The occasional criticism that logicists depend too heavily on their inference methods and not on the knowledge base must simply result from a misunderstanding of the goals of the logical approach. As has already been pointed out, logicists strive to make the inference process as uniform and domain independent as possible and to represent all knowledge (even the knowledge about how to use knowledge) declaratively.

5. Challenging problems

5.1. Language and the world

Few would deny that intelligent machines must have some kind of characterization or model of the world they inhabit. We have stressed that the main feature of machines designed using the logical approach is that they describe their worlds by *language*. Is language (any language) adequate to the task? As the writer Edward Abbey observed [1, p. x]:

> Language makes a mighty loose net with which to go fishing for simple facts, when facts are infinite.

A designer's intuitive ideas about the world are often difficult to capture in a conceptualization that can be described by a finite set of sentences. Usually these intuitive ideas are never complete at the time of design anyway, and the conceptualization expands making it difficult for the sentences to catch up.

John McCarthy humorously illustrates this difficulty by imagining how one might formulate a sentence that says that under certain conditions a car will start. In English we might say, for example: "If the fuel tank is not empty and if you turn the ignition key, the car will start." But this simple sentence is not true of a world in which the carburetor is broken, or in which the fuel tank (while not empty) is full of water, or in which the exhaust pipe has a potato stuck in it, or . . . . Indeed, it seems there might be an infinite number of *qualifications* that would need to be stated in order to make such a sentence true (in the world the designer has in mind—or comes to have in mind). Of course, just what it means for a designer to have a world in mind is problematical; he probably didn't even think of the possibility of the potato in the tailpipe until it was mentioned by someone else who happened to conceive of such a world.

There seem to be two related problems here. One is that we would like to have and use approximate, simple conceptualizations even when our view of the world would permit more accurate and detailed ones. The approximate ones are often sufficient for our purposes. Thus, even though we know full well that the carburetor must be working in order for a car to start, in many situations for which we want to reason about the car starting we don't need to know about the carburetor and can thus leave it out of our conceptualization. Using theories (Δ's) corresponding to approximate conceptualizations and successive refinements of them would seem to require the ability to have several such at hand and a metatheory to decide when to use which.

Another problem is that even the most detailed and accurate conceptualization may need to be revised as new information becomes available. Theories must be revisable to accomodate the designer's changing view of the world. As the machine interacts with its world, it too will learn new information which will in some cases add to its theory and in other cases require it to be modified.

Science has similar problems. Scientists and engineers knowingly and usefully employ approximate theories—such as frictionless models. Furthermore, all of our theories of the physical world are falsifiable, and, indeed, we expect scientific progress to falsify the theories we have and to replace them by others. When we conclude something based on a current physical theory, we admit the dependence of the conclusion on the theory and modify the theory if the conclusion is contradicted by subsequent facts. Those who would argue that logical languages are inappropriate for representing synthetic or contingent knowledge about the world [39] would also seem to have to doubt the utility of any of the languages that science uses to describe and predict reality. Merely because our conceptualization of the world at any stage of our progress toward understanding it may (inevitably will!) prove to be inaccurate does not mean that this conceptualization is not in the meantime useful.

Some AI researchers have suggested techniques for making useful inferences from an approximate, but not inaccurate, theory. We say that a theory is not inaccurate if its models include the world as conceived by the designer. If a theory is to be not inaccurate, it is typically impossible or overly cumbersome to include the universal statements needed to derive useful sound conclusions.

We illustrate the difficulty by an example. Suppose that we want our machine to decide whether or not an apple is edible. If Δ is to be not inaccurate, we cannot include in it the statement $(\forall x)\mathrm{Apple}(x) \wedge \mathrm{Ripe}(x) \supset \mathrm{Edible}(x)$ in the face of known exceptions such as $\mathrm{Wormy}(x)$ or $\mathrm{Rotten}(x)$. (We trust that the reader understands that the mnemonics we use in our examples must be backed up by sufficient additional statements in Δ to insure that these mnemonics are constrained to have roughly their intended meanings.) Suppose we cannot conclude from Δ that a given apple, say the apple denoted by apple1 is wormy or rotten; then we may want to conclude (even non-soundly) Edible(Apple1). If later, it is learned (say through sensory inputs) that Rotten(Apple1), then we must withdraw the earlier conclusion Edible(Apple1). The original inference is called *defeasible* because it can be defeated by additional information. Making such inferences involves what is usually called *nonmonotonic reasoning*. (Ordinary logical reasoning is monotonic in the sense that the set of conclusions that can be drawn from a set of sentences is not diminished if new sentences are added.)

Several researchers have proposed frameworks and techniques for nonmonotonic reasoning. McDermott and Doyle [37, 38] have developed a *nonmonotonic logic*. Reiter [46] has proposed inference rules (called *default rules*) whose applicability to a set of sentences Δ depends on what is *not* in Δ as well as what is. McCarthy [34] advocates the use of *circumscription* based on minimal models. Ginsberg [13] uses multiple (more than two) truth values to represent various degrees of knowledge. We will briefly describe one of these approaches, that based on minimal models, in order to illustrate what can be done. (See [47] for a thorough survey.)

Consider the general rule $(\forall x)Q(x) \supset P(x)$. We may know that this rule is not strictly correct without additional qualifications, and thus it cannot be included in a machine's knowledge base without making the knowledge base inaccurate. But we may want to use something like this rule to express the fact that "typically" all objects satisfying property Q also satisfy property P. Or we may want to use the rule in a system that can tolerate qualifications to be added later.

One way to hedge the rule (to avoid inaccuracy) is to introduce the concept of *abnormality*, denoted by the relation constant Ab [35]. Then we can say that all objects that are not abnormal and that satisfy property Q also satisfy property P:

$$(\forall x)Q(x) \wedge \neg \mathrm{Ab}(x) \supset P(x) .$$

Which objects are abnormal and which are not (if we know these facts) can be specified by other sentences in Δ. For example we may know that the objects denoted by A and B are abnormal: $\mathrm{Ab}(A) \wedge \mathrm{Ab}(B)$.

If we do not know whether or not something, say the object denoted by C, is abnormal, we might be prepared to assume that it is not. Later, if we learn that it is, we can add Ab(C) to Δ.

How do we say that something is not abnormal unless it is required to be by what we have already said in Δ? One way to do this is to specify that the intended model lies within a special subset of the models of Δ. The subset is characterized by those models having the smallest possible sets of abnormal objects consistent with what we know must be abnormal. These models are called minimal with respect to Ab. McCarthy [34] has shown how to compute a sentence ϕ such that the models of $\Delta \wedge \phi$ are just the models in this subset. The formula ϕ is called the *circumscription formula* of Ab in Δ.

In the case in which the only objects that can be proved abnormal are those denoted by A and B, McCarthy's method (with an elaboration that allows the predicate P to "vary") calculates ϕ to be:

$$(\forall x)\mathrm{Ab}(x) \equiv [(x = A) \vee (x = B)] .$$

If we additionally knew that $C \neq B$ and $C \neq A$, we could prove $\neg$Ab(C). Then, if Q(C), we could prove P(C).

Although the process of computing circumscription for general Δ is complex (ϕ might even be a second-order predicate calculus formula), there are some interesting special cases. Many of these have been investigated by Lifschitz [29] and are also described in [12].

5.2. Change

An intelligent machine must know something about how it perceives the world and about how its actions change the world. That is, it must know something about *see* and *effect*. The function *effect* characterizes how the world changes. If an agent is to perform appropriately in the world, it must be able to anticipate and influence these changes. Although it sounds unnecessarily tedious, an agent must know that after it moves from A to B, for example, it will be at B. It must also know that, all other things being equal, other objects will remain where they were before it moved to B. In summary, an agent must have as part of its knowledge some idea of how *effect* changes the world.

Several approaches have been pursued. Most work has been done using a conceptualization that includes objects called *states*. States are imagined as instantaneous snapshots of the world. Change is characterized as a transition from one state to another. Changes may occur as a result of actions on the part of the intelligent machine; we want our machines to be able to compute what actions they ought to perform in order that certain desirable states, called *goal states*, result. A key problem in characterizing the effects of a given machine action on the world involves how to specify which aspects of the world do not change. This has been called *the frame problem*.

The frame problem has been thoroughly treated in the literature. (See [7] and [44] for collections of articles. The latter collection includes several that discuss the problem from the standpoints of philosophy and cognitive psychology.) In attempting to deal with the frame problem in their system called STRIPS, Fikes and Nilsson [10] described the effects of a machine's actions by listing those relations that were changed by the action. They assumed that those relations not mentioned were not changed. Hayes [17, 18] introduced the notion of *histories* in an attempt to define a conceptualization in which the frame problem was less severe. McCarthy [35] and Reiter [46] proposed nonmonotonic reasoning methods for dealing with the frame problem. In the language of circumscription, their approaches assumed minimal changes consistent with the relations that were known to change. However, Hanks and McDermott [15] showed that a straightforward application of circumscription does not produce results strong enough to solve the frame problem. In response, Lifschitz [30] introduced a variant called *pointwise circumscription*. He also proposed reconceptualization of actions and their effects that permits the use of ordinary circumscription in solving the frame problem and the qualification problem [31]. Shoham [51] proposed an alternative minimization method related to circumscription, called *chronological ignorance*.

Although the frame problem has been extensively studied, it remains a formidable conceptual obstacle to the development of systems that must act in a changing world. This obstacle is faced by all such systems—even those whose knowledge about the world is represented in procedures. The designer of any intelligent machine must make assumptions (at least implicit ones) about how the world changes in response to the actions of the machine if the machine is to function effectively.

5.3. Uncertain knowledge

When one is uncertain about the world, one cannot specify precisely which relations hold in the world. Nevertheless, one might be able to say that at least one of a set of relations holds. Logical disjunctions permit us to express that kind of uncertain knowledge.

Logical representations (with their binary truth values) would seem to be inadequate for representing other types of uncertain knowledge. How do we say, for example, "It is likely that it will be sunny in Pasadena on New Year's day"? We could, of course embed probability information itself in the sentence, and this approach and others have been followed. Attempts to fuzz the crisp true/false semantics of logical languages have led to an active AI research subspecialty [23, 43, 53].

The approach followed by [41], for example, is to imagine that a probability value is associated with each of a set of possible conceptualizations (interpretations). The machine designer makes this assignment implicitly by composing a set of first-order predicate calculus sentences each having a probability value. Each of these values is the sum of the probabilities of those interpretations that are models of the associated sentence. In this way the set of sentences with their probabilities induce constraints on what the probabilities of the interpretations can be. These constraints can then be used to calculate bounds on the probabilities of other sentences about the world. This approach can be computationally intractable, however, and many approximate methods for dealing with uncertain knowledge are being explored and used.

Just as the logical approach to AI provides a coherent framework in which many of the problems of designing intelligent machines can be clearly posed and understood, we expect that some appropriate combination of logic and probability theory will similarly aid our understanding of the problem of reasoning with uncertain information.

5.4. Embedded systems

> Those who will not reason
> Perish in the act:
> Those who will not act
> Perish for that reason. (W.H. Auden [4, p. 42].)

To be effective in their environments, machines must both *react* appropriately to sensory inputs in bounded time and *reason*, less hurriedly, about what to do. Since logical reasoning may, in general, require unbounded time, these two requirements place conflicting demands on the architecture of intelligent machines. Combining the two abilities in a seamless and elegant architecture is proving to be a difficult problem.

One might approach this problem either from the point of view of control theory, in which case one needs to add symbolic reasoning abilities to the inherent real-time characteristics of control systems; or from the point of view of AI, in which case one needs to find a way to achieve real-time performance in systems that are able to plan and reason. Very little research has been done on the connection between reasoning mechanisms and their environments. Instead, the need for real-time response and the supposed inefficiencies of logical reasoning have inspired a number of AI researchers to explore action-computation mechanisms that seem more related to control theory than to AI.

Rosenschein and Kaelbling [48] have proposed *situated automata*—finite state machines that do not reason with explicit sentences but, rather, react within a bounded time interval to sensory stimuli. These machines are compiled from declarative sentences specified by the designer. From the designer's point of view, the machines can be said to know the propositions represented by these sentences, but the sentences themselves are not explicitly represented or reasoned with in the machine. In this approach, logical reasoning is done at compile time, and the results of this reasoning are available at run time. (Even though situated automata do not themselves perform explicit logical reasoning, some include them within the logical approach to AI because logic plays such an important role in their specification.)

Schoppers and Nilsson have each observed that in constructing a plan of actions the search process finds not only a path from the starting situation to a goal but finds several other paths as well. Ordinarily, these extraneous paths are discarded. Schoppers [50] suggests that with modest extra effort the paths from all possible starting states to a goal can be found during the plan-generation process. These paths can be stored as a *universal plan* that can be used to select appropriate actions in bounded time no matter how the unpredictable environment might throw the system off its current path. Nilsson [42] proposes that, in effect, multiple paths can be stored in a highly conditional plan structure called an *action network* consisting of a combinational circuit somewhat like those occuring in situated automata. Both universal plans and action networks share the virtue that actions appropriate to a wide range of environmental conditions can be selected in bounded time. Like situated automata, they pay for their improved runtime performance by investing extra time at compile or design time and by using extra space (to store the plan).

Other examples of architectures that do not rely (at run time at least) on the lumbering reasoning apparatus associated with explicit declarative representations can be found in the adaptive networks of the *connectionists* [49], in the finite-state machines of Brooks [6], in the PENGI system of Agre and Chapman [2], and in the *plan nets* of Drummond [9].

Good as they are for computing actions quickly however, systems that do no logical reasoning at run time may sometimes perish in the act. Imagine a Martian robot, for example, receiving a message from its Martian base that the base will not be able to refuel robots for five hours beginning in two hours. It would seem to be a reasonable strategy for robots to handle messages of this sort by receiving them as declarative sentences that are to be combined with other explicitly represented declarative knowledge and reasoned with to produce appropriate action. Anticipating what the appropriate responses should be for all possible such messages would seem to present untractable compilation and storage problems.

Connecting perception to reasoning and reasoning to action remains an important problem. For action nets and situated automata, for example, this problem becomes one of modifying the runtime system incrementally as new declarative knowledge is added to the system. Drummond [9] proposes the use of *situated control rules* generated by a planner to constrain the actions of a plan net. Kaelbling [22] has proposed hierarchical systems in which the lower levels are able to compute actions more quickly (if less intelligently) than the higher ones. Under time pressure, if the higher levels have not finished their more elaborate computations, the lower ones dominate.

I suspect that there are several other conceptual problems in connecting the world to systems that reason with explicitly represented sentences. As a columnist recently wrote [45] "... I sometimes worry about the men I know who live alone. I picture some of them thinking out loud about a ham and Swiss on rye, and then just sitting there, slowly starving to death. There's some synapse missing, the one that links desire and action." Transforming the highly indexical, situation-dependent information gleaned from sensors into context-free representations, and then converting information in those representations back into context-sensitive action, likely will involve "synapses" that have not yet been adequately considered by the logicists.

6. Conclusions

Logic provides the vocabulary and many of the techniques needed both for analyzing the processes of representation and reasoning and for synthesizing machines that represent and reason. The fact that we discover elements of reasoning and intelligent behavior that challenge the techniques of ordinary logic is no reason to abandon the solid base that we have already built. On the contrary, it appears that imaginative extensions to ordinary first-order logic are successfully dealing with many of its purported inadequacies.

Logic itself (originally invented to help formalize and explain human reasoning) has evolved dramatically in the last 2000 years. Anyone who attempts to develop theoretical apparatus relevant to systems that use and manipulate declaratively represented knowledge, and does so without taking into account the prior theoretical results of logicians on these topics, risks (at best) having to repeat some of the work done by the brightest minds of the last two millenia and (at worst) getting it wrong!

Of course, it may ultimately turn out that we cannot adequately and usefully represent knowledge needed by intelligent machines in declarative sentences. If we cannot, each application would seem to require a machine most of whose knowledge has to be designed in to procedures specialized to the application. Many of these specialized systems would have similar or identical bodies of knowledge, but even if largely identical, each body would have to be separately and specially (and thus expensively) crafted and re-crafted for each niche system. There is good reason to recoil from that prospect. There are too many niches! Considering the high payoff, the impressive results obtained so far, and the lack of promising alternatives, the grand vision of the logicists appears to me to be the approach of choice.

Acknowledgement

The author thanks the Palo Alto Laboratory of the Rockwell Scientific Center for support. Several people provided helpful suggestions, including Jon

Doyle, Michael Genesereth, Carl Hewitt, David Kirsh, Jean-Claude Latombe, John McCarthy, Devika Subramanian, Yoav Shoham, and many Stanford graduate students.

References

[1] E. Abbey, *Desert Solitaire* (Ballantine, New York, 1971).

[2] P. Agre and D. Chapman, Pengi: An implementation of a theory of activity, in: *Proceedings AAAI-87*, Seattle, WA (1987) 268–272.

[3] D.E. Appelt, *Planning English Sentences* (Cambridge University Press, Cambridge, 1985).

[4] W.H. Auden, *Collected Shorter Poems: 1927–1957* (Random House, New York, 1966).

[5] R. Brachman, V. Gilbert and H. Levesque, An essential hybrid reasoning system: knowledge and symbol level accounts of KRYPTON, in: *Proceedings IJCAI-85*, Los Angeles, CA (1985).

[6] R.A. Brooks, Intelligence without representation, *Artif. Intell.* **47** (1991) 139–159, this volume.

[7] F. Brown, ed., *The Frame Problem in Artificial Intelligence* (Morgan Kaufmann, San Mateo, CA, 1987).

[8] P.R. Cohen and H.J. Levesque, Intention is choice with commitment, *Artif. Intell.* **42** (1990) 213–261.

[9] M. Drummond, Situated control rules, in: J. Weber, J. Tenenberg and J. Allen, eds., *Proceedings of the Rochester Planning Workshop: From Formal Systems to Practical Systems*, Rochester, NY (1988).

[10] R.E. Fikes and N.J. Nilsson, STRIPS: A new approach to the application of theorem proving to problem solving, *Artif. Intell.* **2** (1971) 189–208.

[11] M.R. Genesereth, The use of design descriptions in automated diagnosis, *Artif. Intell.* **24** (1984) 411–436.

[12] M.R. Genesereth and N.J. Nilsson, *Logical Foundations of Artificial Intelligence* (Morgan Kaufmann, San Mateo, CA, 1987).

[13] M. Ginsberg, Multivalued logics: a uniform approach to inference in artificial intelligence, *Comput. Intell.* **4** (1988).

[14] B.J. Grosz, D.E. Appelt, P.A. Martin and F.C.N. Pereira, TEAM: An experiment in the design of transportable natural-language interfaces, *Artif. Intell.* **32** (1987) 173–243.

[15] S. Hanks and D. McDermott, Default reasoning, nonmonotonic logics, and the frame problem, in: *Proceedings AAAI-86*, Philadelphia, PA (1986).

[16] P.J. Hayes, In defence of logic, in: *Proceedings IJCAI-77*, Cambridge, MA (1977) 559–565.

[17] P.J. Hayes, The naive physics manifesto, in: D. Michie, ed., *Expert Systems in the Micro-Electronic Age* (Edinburgh University Press, Edinburgh, 1979) 242–270.

[18] P.J. Hayes, The second naive physics manifesto, in: J.R. Hobbs and R.C. Moore, eds., *Formal Theories of the Commonsense World* (Ablex, Norwood, NJ, 1985) 1–36; also in: R. Brachman and H. Levesque, eds., *Readings in Knowledge Representation* (Morgan Kaufmann, San Mateo, CA, 1985).

[19] B. Hayes-Roth, A blackboard architecture for control, *Artif. Intell.* **26** (1985) 251–321.

[20] J.R. Hobbs, ed., Commonsense Summer: final report, Rept. CSLI-85-35, Center for the Study of Language and Information, Stanford University, Stanford, CA (1985).

[21] J.R. Hobbs and R.C. Moore, eds., *Formal Theories of the Commonsense World* (Ablex, Norwood, NJ, 1985).

[22] L.P. Kaelbling, An architecture for intelligent reactive systems, in: M. Georgeff and A. Lansky, eds., *Reasoning about Actions and Plans* (Morgan Kaufmann, San Mateo, CA, 1987) 395–410.

[23] L.N. Kanal and J.F. Lemmer, eds., *Uncertainty in Artificial Intelligence* (North-Holland, Amsterdam, 1986).

[24] K. Konolige, Belief and incompleteness, in: J.R. Hobbs and R.C. Moore, eds., *Formal Theories of the Commonsense World* (Ablex, Norwood, NJ, 1985) 359–404.
[25] D.B. Lenat, The nature of heuristics, *Artif. Intell.* **19** (1982) 189–249.
[26] D.B. Lenat, Theory formation by heuristic search. The nature of heuristics II: Background and examples, *Artif. Intell.* **21** (1983) 31–59.
[27] D.B. Lenat, EURISKO: A program that learns new heuristics and domain concepts. The nature of heuristics III: Program design and results, *Artif. Intell.* **21** (1983) 61–98.
[28] D.B. Lenat and E.A. Feigenbaum, On the thresholds of knowledge, *Artif. Intell.* **47** (1991) 185–250, this volume.
[29] V. Lifschitz, Computing circumscription, in: *Proceedings IJCAI-85*, Los Angeles, CA (1985) 121–127.
[30] V. Lifschitz, Pointwise circumscription: preliminary report, in: *Proceedings AAAI-86*, Philadelphia, PA (1986) 406–410.
[31] V. Lifschitz, Formal theories of action, in: F. Brown, ed., *The Frame Problem in Artificial Intelligence* (Morgan Kaufmann, San Mateo, CA, 1987) 35–57.
[32] J. McCarthy, Programs with common sense, in: *Mechanisation of Thought Processes, Proc. Symp. Nat. Phys. Lab.* **1** (Her Majesty's Stationary Office, London, 1958) 77–84; also in: M. Minsky, ed., *Semantic Information Processing* (MIT Press, Cambridge, MA, 1968) 403–410; and in: R. Brachman and H. Levesque, eds., *Readings in Knowledge Representation* (Morgan Kaufmann, San Mateo, CA, 1985).
[33] J. McCarthy, Ascribing mental qualities to machines, Tech. Rept. STAN-CS-79-725, AIM-326, Department of Computer Science, Stanford University, Stanford, CA (1979).
[34] J. McCarthy, Circumscription—a form of non-monotonic reasoning, *Artif. Intell.* **13** (1980) 27–39; also in: B.L. Webber and N.J. Nilsson, eds., *Readings in Artificial Intelligence* (Morgan Kaufmann, San Mateo, CA, 1982).
[35] J. McCarthy, Applications of circumscription to formalizing commonsense knowledge, *Artif. Intell.* **28** (1986) 89–116.
[36] J. McCarthy, Mathematical logic in artificial intelligence, *Daedalus: J. Am. Acad. Arts Sci.* (1988) 297–311.
[37] D. McDermott and J. Doyle, Non-monotonic logic I, *Artif. Intell.* **13** (1980) 41–72.
[38] D. McDermott, Non-monotonic logic II: Non-monotonic modal theories, *J. ACM* **29** (1982) 33–57.
[39] D. McDermott, A critique of pure reason (with peer commentaries), *Comput. Intell.* **3** (1987) 151–237.
[40] R.C. Moore, A formal theory of knowledge and action, in: J.R. Hobbs and R.C. Moore, eds., *Formal Theories of the Commonsense World* (Ablex, Norwood, NJ, 1985).
[41] N.J. Nilsson, Probabilistic logic, *Artif. Intell.* **28** (1986) 71–87.
[42] N.J. Nilsson, Action networks, Unpublished working paper, Stanford University, Stanford, CA (1988); also in: J. Weber, J. Tenenberg and J. Allen, *Proceedings of the Rochester Planning Workshop: From Formal Systems to Practical Systems*, Rochester, NY (1988).
[43] J. Pearl, *Probabilistic Reasoning in Intelligent Systems: Networks of Plausible Inference* (Morgan Kaufmann, San Mateo, CA, 1988).
[44] Z. Pylyshyn, *The Robot's Dilemma: The Frame Problem in Artificial Intelligence* (Ablex, Norwood, NJ, 1987).
[45] A. Quindlen, Life in the 30's, *The New York Times* (May 5, 1988).
[46] R. Reiter, A logic for default reasoning, *Artif. Intell.* **13** (1980) 81–132.
[47] R. Reiter, Nonmonotonic reasoning, in: *Annual Reviews of Computer Science* **2** (Annual Reviews, Palo Alto, CA, 1987) 147–186.
[48] S.J. Rosenschein and L.P. Kaelbling, The synthesis of machines with provable epistemic properties, in: J.Y. Halpern, ed., *Proceedings of the 1986 Conference on Theoretical Aspects of Reasoning about Knowledge* (Morgan Kaufmann, San Mateo, CA, 1986) 83–98.
[49] D.E. Rumelhart, J.L. McClelland and the PDP Research Group, eds., *Parallel Distributed Processing: Explorations in the Microstructure of Cognition* **1**: *Foundations*; **2**: *Psychological and Biological Models* (MIT Press, Cambridge, MA, 1986).
[50] M.J. Schoppers, Universal plans for reactive robots in unpredictable domains, in: *Proceedings IJCAI-87*, Milan, Italy (1987).

[51] Y. Shoham, *Reasoning about Change: Time and Causation from the Standpoint of Artificial Intelligence* (MIT Press, Cambridge, MA, 1988) Chapter 4.
[52] Y. Shoham and N. Goyal, Temporal reasoning in artificial intelligence, in: H. Shrobe, ed., *Exploring Artificial Intelligence* (Morgan Kaufmann, San Mateo, CA, 1988) 419–438.
[53] E.H. Shortliffe, *Computer-Based Medical Consultations: MYCIN* (Elsevier, New York, 1976).
[54] B.C. Smith, The owl and the electric encyclopedia, *Artif. Intell.* **47** (1991) 251–288, this volume.
[55] P. Smolensky, On the proper treatment of connectionism, *Behav. Brain Sci.* (with peer commentary) **11** (1988) 1–74.
[56] M.E. Stickel, A nonclausal connection-graph resolution theorem-proving program, in: *Proceedings AAAI-82*, Pittsburgh, PA (1982) 229–233; also in: M. Stickel, A nonclausal connection-graph resolution theorem-proving program, SRI AI Center Tech. Note 268, SRI, Menlo Park, CA (1982).
[57] M.E. Stickel, A PROLOG technology theorem prover, in: *Proceedings IEEE Symposium on Logic Programming*, Atlanta City, NJ (1984) 211–217.
[58] R. Weyhrauch, Prolegomena to a theory of mechanized formal reasoning, *Artif. Intell.* **13** (1980) 133–170; also in: B.L. Webber and N.J. Nilsson, eds., *Readings in Artificial Intelligence* (Morgan Kaufmann, San Mateo, CA, 1982).
[59] S. Winker, Generation and verification of finite models and counterexamples using an automated theorem prover answering two open questions, *J. ACM* **29** (1982) 273–284.
[60] T. Winograd, Frame representations and the declarative/procedural controversy, in: D. Bobrow and A. Collins, eds., *Representation and Understanding: Studies in Cognitive Science* (Academic Press, New York, 1975) 185–210; also in: R. Brachman and H. Levesque, eds., *Readings in Knowledge Representation* (Morgan Kaufmann, San Mateo, CA, 1985).
[61] L. Wos, S. Winker, B. Smith, R. Veroff and L. Henschen, A new use of an automated reasoning assistant: open questions in equivalential calculus and the study of infinite domains, *Artif. Intell.* **22** (1984) 303–356.

Artificial Intelligence 47 (1991) 57–77
Elsevier

Rigor mortis: a response to Nilsson's "Logic and artificial intelligence"

Lawrence Birnbaum
The Institute for the Learning Sciences and Department of Electrical Engineering and Computer Science, Northwestern University, Evanston, IL 60201, USA

Received June 1988
Revised December 1989

Abstract

Birnbaum, L., Rigor mortis: a response to Nilsson's "Logic and artificial intelligence", Artificial Intelligence 47 (1991) 57–77.

Logicism has contributed greatly to progress in AI by emphasizing the central role of mental content and representational vocabulary in intelligent systems. Unfortunately, the logicists' dream of a completely use-independent characterization of knowledge has drawn their attention away from these fundamental AI problems, leading instead to a concentration on purely formalistic issues in deductive inference and model-theoretic "semantics". In addition, their failure to resist the lure of formalistic modes of expression has unnecessarily curtailed the prospects for intellectual interaction with other AI researchers.

1. Introduction

A good friend recently told me about a discussion he had with one of his colleagues about what to teach in a one-semester introductory artificial intelligence course for graduate students, given the rather limited time available in such a course. He proposed what he assumed were generally agreed to be central issues and techniques in AI—credit assignment in learning, means-ends analysis in problem-solving, the representation and use of abstract planning knowledge in the form of critics, and so on. Somewhat to his surprise, in his colleague's view one of the most important things for budding AI scientists to learn was . . . *Herbrand's theorem*.

I recount this anecdote here for two reasons. First, I suspect that most of us would have been surprised, as my friend was, by this response, and by the rather puzzling set of scientific and educational priorities that it reveals. It would, of course, be unfair to conclude that the scientific world-view displayed in this anecdote is representative of the logicist position in AI, at least as that

0004-3702/91/$03.50

position is portrayed by Nils Nilsson. Nevertheless, it is worth bearing in mind that, as the anecdote makes clear, this debate is not only—perhaps not even primarily—a technical one, but rather a question of scientific priorities.

The second reason I recount this anecdote here is to illustrate that when it comes to making a point, a good story is almost always more useful than a lot of abstract argumentation. We often lean more heavily on personal experience and specific stories than on "book learning" or other abstract knowledge, and we often draw general conclusions from a single experience, even when we know we shouldn't. Human reasoning is powerfully affected by concrete images, by illustrative anecdotes, and by memorable experiences. Of course, artificial intelligence is not psychology: Our goal is not to mimic human thought and behavior in minute detail. Nevertheless, such a pervasive characteristic of human thought cannot simply be ignored as if it were *prima facie* irrelevant to our own work. Although I can't imagine that anyone in AI seriously disagrees with the proposition that there are probably sound functional reasons why human thinking is the way it is, the point nevertheless often seems to need repeating. The role of concrete cases in reasoning is something that many of us think is an important piece of the puzzle of both artificial and human intelligence; it is also a good example of the kind of question that logicists never seem to address.

Of course, it is not necessarily fatal to the logicist enterprise that it addresses only a portion of the problems involved in artificial intelligence: Who would have expected otherwise? The answer, I'm afraid, is the logicists themselves. Despite Nilsson's rather sensible observation that "successful AI systems of the future will probably draw on a combination of techniques . . . ," logicists do not seem to view logicism as just one approach among many: They see it as the universal framework in terms of which everything else in AI must ultimately be expressed. For example, in his response to McDermott's [19] "A critique of pure reason", Nilsson [22] asserts that "While all AI researchers would acknowledge the general importance of procedures and procedural knowledge (as distinguished from declarative knowledge), they would seem to have no grounds for a special claim on those topics as a *subset* of computer science." In other words, in Nilsson's view AI is to be distinguished as a sub-area of computer science in general not by the *problems* it investigates—language understanding, learning, vision, planning, and so on—but by the *methods* it uses, and in fact by one and only one aspect of those methods, the use of declarative representations. Since Nilsson further makes it clear that in his view the use of declarative representations must, ultimately, entail embracing all of the apparatus of logic, the implication of this assertion is fairly obvious: Anything that doesn't fit the logicist paradigm—visual perception, goals, memory and indexing, attention, emotions, the control of physical movement, and so on—may be very nice computer science, thank you, but it isn't AI. This is not, it should be clear, a scientific proposition, but rather a political one, and as such its role in our field deserves careful scrutiny.

In addition to these sorts of political concerns, however, there are also good technical reasons for doubting the utility—or at the very least, the *special* utility—of logic, strictly speaking, as a framework for knowledge representation. I say "strictly speaking" because, in a broad sense, any computational scheme for knowledge representation and reasoning could be considered some form of logic, even connectionism. Moreover, most work in AI shares the logicist commitment to the centrality of explicit symbolic representations in mental processes.

How then does logicism differ from other approaches to AI? In my view, it is distinguished by two additional commitments. The first is its emphasis on sound, deductive inference, in the belief—for the most part implicit—that such inference plays a privileged role in mental life (see [19]). As a result of this emphasis, logicists tend to ignore other sorts of reasoning that seem quite central to intelligent behavior—probabilistic reasoning, reasoning from examples or by analogy, and reasoning based on the formation of faulty but useful conjectures and their subsequent elaboration and debugging, to name a few—or else, attempt (unsuccessfully, in my view) to re-cast plausible inference of the simplest sort as some species of sound inference.

The second distinguishing feature of logicism is the presumption that model-theoretic "semantics" is somehow central to knowledge representation in AI.[1] The primary justification for this presumption is its putative explanatory role, namely, that it is necessary in order to correctly characterize what it means for an agent to know or believe something, and thus to specify precisely what a given agent knows or believes. This, I take it, is Nilsson's argument.

Towards this claim, non-logicists seem to be of two minds: Some disagree with it—and I will explain why later in this paper—while others just don't see what difference it makes. In the face of the latter reaction—indifference—logicists often take another tack, and attempt to justify their preoccupation with model-theoretic "semantics" on methodological, rather than explanatory, grounds. In this vein, they stress its utility as a heuristic aid in solving knowledge representation problems, or to enable the AI researcher to prove things about his program, and so on. Whether the things that can be so proven are of any particular interest is debatable (see [4] for some arguments as to why proving that programs meet certain formal specifications is unlikely to be either possible or useful in software engineering; it seems doubtful that AI systems will prove more tractable in this regard). Whether such a "semantics" is in fact heuristically useful in solving representation problems is more difficult to debate, since that is a matter of personal taste. People should, obviously, work in the manner that they find most congenial and productive.

[1] I place scare quotes around "semantics" in this sense to emphasize that in logic this is a technical term, and that the theory to which it refers may or may not turn out to be a correct account of the meaning of mental representations.

2. The good news

The above criticisms notwithstanding—and I will take them up in greater detail shortly—it cannot be denied that logic and logicists have contributed a great deal to AI. Perhaps the logicists' most important contribution has been to focus attention on the fact that it is the *content* of our knowledge, and the concepts in terms of which that knowledge is expressed—what logicists refer to as "ontological" issues—that lie at the heart of our ability to think. Their arguments have played a key role in legitimizing the study of representations from the perspective of how well they capture certain contents, independently of the details of the particular processes that might employ them. Hayes's [11] "Naive physics manifesto", in particular, is a persuasive and historically important defense of this idea. As Nilsson puts it, "The most important part of "the AI problem" involves inventing an appropriate conceptualization . . . . " In fairness, however, the credit for this insight cannot be assigned solely to the logicists: Very much the same point can and has been made without any special commitment to logic, for example by Feigenbaum [6], Schank and Abelson [27], and Newell [21], among others. Moreover, as Nilsson acknowledges, "the [logicist] approach to AI carries with it no special insights into what conceptualizations to use."

The technical apparatus of logic itself—a clear and unambiguous syntax, the "ability to formulate disjunctions, negations, and universally and existentially quantified" expressions—indisputably plays an important role in AI, as does the technology of mechanical theorem proving. Although I am sympathetic with the view that it is a mistake to attempt to embed "scruffy" thinking in "neat" systems[2]—and that the real question is how "neat" thinking can emerge from a "scruffy" system—expressive apparatus of the sort provided by logic seems indispensable, especially when it comes to representing abstract concepts.[3] On the other hand, Nilsson's implicit criticism of knowledge representation schemes that lack this technical apparatus probably misses the point. Much research that might be criticized on these grounds has simply been directed towards other issues, primarily issues of content and conceptual vocabulary, or of memory organization and efficient access for a particular set of tasks.

Finally, there can be no question that logicists have led the battle for declarative representation in AI, a battle that they have largely won—though again, not entirely single-handedly. A particularly compelling argument, attributed by Nilsson to McCarthy, is that declaratively represented knowledge "[can] be used by the machine even for purposes unforeseen by the machine's designer . . . ." Putting this in somewhat different terms, there can be no question that cross-domain and -purpose application of knowledge is an

[2] See [1] for an enlightening discussion of these terms.

[3] Which aren't necessarily very technical or abstruse: Try representing the concept of "helping" in propositional logic.

important functional constraint on representations, and that declarative representations seem to meet this requirement better than anything else we know of. However, putting it this way makes it clear that what is at stake here is a type of *learning*—the ability to apply knowledge acquired in one situation, for one purpose, to other, different situations and purposes.

Yet, rather oddly, Nilsson, and logicists generally, pay no attention to this issue. There are several reasons for this, but the main one seems to be their attachment to sound inference and model-theoretic "semantics". For example, in his discussion of inference, Nilsson argues that

> Often, . . . the new sentence constructed from ones already in memory does not tell us anything new about the world. All of the models of [the sentences already in memory] are also models of [the new sentence]. Thus, adding [the new sentence] to [memory] does not reduce the set of models. What the new sentence tells us was already implicitly said by the sentences from which it was constructed.

Indeed, logicists sometimes go so far as to assert that sound inference cannot, in principle, generate any new knowledge. On this account of what knowledge is, or of what makes it "new", the problem of applying lessons learned in one domain for one purpose to other domains and other purposes doesn't exist, because it is already solved. Unfortunately, if this isn't true—and it strikes me as a rather dubious proposition on which to bet a research program—then we must conclude that the problem cannot even be properly *characterized* within the logicist framework. However, if the problem of cross-domain and -purpose application of knowledge cannot even be *characterized* within the logicist framework, then we have good reason to doubt that logic, as construed within that framework, in fact appropriately addresses the functional issues raised by the problem. Since, as Nilsson himself argues, this problem provides the fundamental justification for declarative representations in the first place, the logicists have some explaining to do.

3. The bad news

What drives logicists to adopt the obviously unrealistic position that inference does not change what an agent knows? It is their devotion to model-theoretic "semantics". And what motivates this devotion? Nilsson puts it as follows:

> Those designers who would claim that their machines possess declarative knowledge about the world are obliged to say something about what that claim means. The fact that a machine's knowledge

> base has an expression in it like $(\forall x)\mathrm{Box}(x) \supset \mathrm{Green}(x)$, for example, doesn't by itself justify the claim that the machine *believes* all boxes are green.

This is uncontroversial, as far as it goes. The leap of faith in the logicist program is the presumption that, in saying something about what it means for a machine to have beliefs, AI is obliged to reiterate a theory of how logical symbols are to be interpreted, developed over the last century in logic and mathematics for fundamentally different purposes—in particular, for proving the soundness and completeness of inference methods. Nilsson offers no argument why this should be so. But McDermott [19] is a bit more open about how the logicists arrived at this position: "The notation we use . . . must have a semantics; so it must have a Tarskian semantics, because there is no other candidate"—or to put his another way: "*You have a better theory*?"

I must admit that I do not have a better theory—at least, not one that would satisfy the logicists. But the absence of an alternative theory does not make a bad theory good. I find it difficult to understand the zeal with which logicists embrace and defend a theory that has so many problematic implications. Trying to define "knowledge" and "belief" at our current stage in theorizing about the mind is like biologists trying to define "life" a hundred years ago. Rather than seeing this as a complicated puzzle to be resolved by artificial intelligence and other cognitive sciences as they progress, logicists assume that the question has a simple, definitive answer, that logic has provided this definitive answer, and that all AI has to do is work out the details.

The obvious alternative to a model-theoretic "semantics" is a *functional* semantics, based on the idea that representations get their meaning by virtue of their causal role in the mental processes of the organism, and ultimately, in perception and action. On such a view the meaning of a term is not tied to the inferences that it could *in principle* license, but to those that it actually licenses *in practice*. The concept "prime number" does not mean the same thing to me as it does to a number theorist; and its meaning for me would change if I studied some number theory.

The problem with such an approach, from a logicist perspective, is that a theory of meaning based on functional role doesn't allow for a specification of what an organism knows independently of what it does. This is exactly right. Moreover, such a situation does not preclude applying the same knowledge in different domains, and for different purposes. Indeed, it seems clear that Nilsson's chief argument for the logicist position is based on a false dichotomy: Just because knowledge cannot be specified in *complete* independence of use doesn't mean that it can't be specified in a way that enables its application to many *different* uses. But for logicists, it isn't sufficient that the ability to apply the same knowledge in different domains, and for different purposes, be a functional constraint on mental representations—something that is, all other things being equal, to be desired. Such a formulation implies that generality of this sort might be involved in "grubby" engineering trade-offs (to use McDermott's colorful description), and this is exactly what logicism is trying to escape in the first place. As Dennett [5] cannily observes, logicism is the chief representative, within AI, of a belief in the "dignity and purity of the Crystalline Mind," and of the concomitant notion that psychology must be more like physics than like engineering or biology.

The upshot is that logicists believe there is no alternative to embracing model-theoretic "semantics" for mental representations. The major stumbling block in any straightforward application of this approach is, as has often been noted, consistency—or more precisely the lack of it (see, e.g., [12, 20]).[4] If the beliefs of an organism are inconsistent, then there is no model of those beliefs. This is problematic for a number of reasons. First, it means that the content of the organism's knowledge, which Nilsson asserts should be characterized as the "intended" model of the sentences representing that knowledge, cannot in fact be so characterized: In the technical sense, there are no such models. It follows that whatever the relationship between the organism's representations and the content they express, that relationship cannot be described by a model-theoretic "semantics". The second problem, of course, is that if the inference processes of the organism are to be construed as some form of logical deduction, then if its beliefs are inconsistent, anything at all can be deduced. Because its beliefs have no model, all models of its beliefs are also models of any other belief it might entertain.

Inconsistency poses such a severe problem for model-theoretic "semantics" because of its extremely "holistic" nature, in that the meaning of an individual symbol in a logical theory is determined by the set of models consistent with the entire theory in which it appears. As Hayes [11] puts it, "a token [in a formal theory] means a concept if, in every possible model of *the formalisation taken as a whole*, that token denotes an entity which one would agree was a satisfactory instantiation of the concept in the possible state of affairs represented by the model." There is a certain intuitive appeal to this holism; indeed, in any functional approach to semantics, the meaning of a symbol similarly depends upon the entire system in which it is embedded. The problem is that model-theoretic "semantics" takes the holism of meaning to its extreme: Either a theory is completely consistent, or it has no models, and hence no way to determine meaning at all. A knowledge base with a single bug that makes it inconsistent is as meaningless and incoherent as gibberish. There is no graded notion of coherence in this conception of semantics, and it seems clear that one is needed.

A contributing factor here is the logicist assumption, generally implicit, that a successful organism's beliefs about the world are such that the real world is in fact a model of those beliefs. As Nilsson puts it "the designer attempts to specify a set of conceptualizations such that, whatever the world actually is, he

[4] See [14, 28] for discussions of some other difficulties.

guesses it is a member of the set." In the talk upon which his paper is based, he went somewhat further and asserted that "the conceptualization *is* the world! (To the extent that it isn't and matters that it isn't—change the conceptualization.)" This assumption insulates logicists from one of the two potential sources of inconsistency, namely, the possibility that the set of beliefs about the world that an organism brings to any particular problem situation, whether innate or acquired, are themselves inherently inconsistent.[5] The ploy succeeds because we all assume that the real world is consistent; so if the real world is a model of the organism's beliefs, they must be consistent too. In his paper, Nilsson backs off to a certain extent from the claim that an organism's beliefs will have the real world as a model. Nevertheless, he asserts, without argument, that this is what we should aspire to. The fact of the matter is, however, that we have no reason to believe this is so. Naive physics is not physics, it is *psychology*: An organism's conceptualization of the world differs from the world in fundamental ways, and for very good functional reasons. If fidelity to the real world really were the paramount constraint on conceptualizations, then AI would seem best served simply by axiomatizing the latest theories of the physicists. If logicists don't believe this, then they must accept the fact that the primary constraints on conceptualizations are *pragmatic*, derived from the need to perform effectively in real-world tasks—in other words, that the content of our beliefs is determined in great measure by the uses which they must serve.

Now, is it reasonable to expect organisms to have perfectly consistent beliefs? Or is it more reasonable to expect that they will have some conflicting beliefs? Even the most committed logicists seem to acknowledge that the latter is more likely. Since an organism's beliefs arise, ultimately, from perception and learning, any mistakes in perception or learning would give rise to erroneous beliefs, and these would be likely to conflict with true beliefs of the organism, if not immediately then eventually—indeed, they had better, if the organism is ever to discover such errors.

One place to uncover concrete examples of contradictory beliefs is to consider questions about which we feel ambivalent or uncertain, such as tough moral questions. For example, I believe, on balance, that abortions ought to be freely available. On the other hand, I believe that killing a human being is unacceptable except in self-defense. So in order to reconcile these two beliefs, I have decided that fetuses are not human beings. Nevertheless, I also believe that abortions are somehow a bad thing, and should be avoided if possible. Moreover, I recently learned that there are reasons to believe that fetal tissue will be particularly effective in transplants, e.g., to cure Parkinson's disease. Should this prove to be the case, fetal tissue may come to be in high demand. This raises the following question: Would it be moral for a woman to conceive for the sole purpose of having an abortion to provide such tissue? I have

[5] The other possible source of inconsistency is unsound inference.

qualms about this. Now the problem is, given my ostensible belief that fetuses are not human beings, I'm not quite sure why I have any of these reservations. The best explanation I can give for my ambivalence about this issue is that, in fact, several conflicting beliefs bear on it.

But just as the person who is led down the garden path in an argument will squirm and wiggle and look for an implicit assumption that will let him off the hook, so the logicist argues that there are only *apparent* contradictions in an organism's beliefs: In fact, there are always additional qualifications attached to one or the other of two apparently inconsistent beliefs, and the organism has simply assumed, mistakenly, that all of these additional conditions on its beliefs hold true. Moreover, given any putative example of conflicting beliefs, this trick can always be pulled, and the argument can be made that the beliefs in question are in fact so qualified as to eliminate the apparent contradiction. This leads us, then, to the logicist characterization of plausible inference as deduction, given some extra assumption that may or may not turn out to be true—in other words, nonmonotonic logic.

In many ways, this is an attractive vision. The problem with this vision is that it seems difficult to characterize ahead of time all of the extra assumptions that one is in fact committed to in drawing a given conclusion, if one wants to view the drawing of that conclusion as a form of deduction. Nilsson makes this point using McCarthy's example of what might turn out to be involved in trying to determine the conditions under which we can infer that a car will start. The upshot is a kind of stand-off: Given any particular example of conflicting beliefs, logicists can plausibly argue that the beliefs in question are implicitly qualified so as not to conflict. But we are left with the suspicion that given more examples, such qualifications would have to be extended indefinitely, to the point of the ridiculous.

In any case, Nilsson concedes that organisms will have inconsistent beliefs in his discussion of the "reification" of theories. He accepts the view (espoused by Hewitt [12], among others) that problem-solving depends on the manipulation of relatively fragmented and mutually inconsistent *microtheories*—each perhaps internally consistent, and each constituting a valid way of looking at a problem:

> We might reify whole theories. This will allow us to say, for example, that some [set of beliefs] is more appropriate than some [other set of beliefs] when confronted with problems of diagnosing bacterial infections. Scientists are used to having different—even contradictory—theories to explain reality .... Each is useful in certain circumstances.

I agree that it is useful to have contradictory microtheories. But I find it difficult to understand how Nilsson reconciles this belief with the logicist program. What the phrase "each [theory] is useful in different circumstances" *really* means is that each is useful for different *purposes*. Such a proposal seems utterly inconsistent with the logicist dream of specifying knowledge in complete independence of use. Moreover, what status does Nilsson assign to the elements of the inconsistent theories that scientists "have": Are they beliefs, or not?[6] If so, then what is their model? For if model-theoretic "semantics" actually provides a correct account of what it means for an agent to know or believe something, as Nilsson asserts, then the elements of these inconsistent theories must have a model. But by virtue of their inconsistency, this is impossible. Alternatively, I suppose, Nilsson could argue that the elements of such inconsistent theories are not in fact beliefs. In that case, we may freely admit that logicism has provided a satisfactory account of what it means for organisms to have beliefs; it just turns out that beliefs, so construed, play little or no role in their reasoning processes.

The hard-core logicist response to this dilemma was enunciated, if I understood him correctly, by McCarthy at the workshop. Seemingly inconsistent microtheories, taken together, *do* have models: We must simply qualify *every* belief in *every* microtheory, if necessary, with the condition that the objects it concerns are not abnormal, conjoin all of the resulting microtheories, and then use *circumscription* [17] to limit the models of the resulting qualified and unified theory to those in which the number of abnormal objects is as small as possible.

Despite all its technical bravado, however, this proposal strikes me as a desperate strategem. *For there is no guarantee that the resulting models will bear any resemblance to the intended models underlying the initial (unqualified) microtheories.* It follows that the inferences we will be entitled to draw after following this procedure will, almost surely, be different from those we had in mind when the microtheories were originally constructed. Indeed, on the view that the meaning of a term is tied to the inferences it helps to license, the meanings of the concepts involved in a given microtheory are likely to be considerably different from what we originally intended.

What is most fatal to this proposal, however, is that we will almost surely be unable to tell whether or not these sorts of divergences from our original intentions have actually arisen in any given case. For although McCarthy's strategem guarantees that the resulting unified theory has models, not only does it fail to guarantee that those models have the properties we need, *it doesn't even guarantee that we know what those models are.* I take one of the larger lessons of Hanks and McDermott's [10] "shooting problem" to be that even given a small, simple set of initial beliefs, it is quite difficult to determine the models of those beliefs permitted by circumscription.[7] Since the task of

[6] I am indebted to Drew McDermott for pointing this problem out to me.

[7] To review briefly, the Hanks–McDermott problem is this: Given the event sequence (1) Fred is born, (2) a gun is loaded, and (3) Fred is shot with the gun, plus the belief that if someone is shot with a loaded gun they will die, infer that Fred is dead. Hanks and McDermott have shown that circumscription, along with other forms of nonmonotonic reasoning, permit unintended models in which the gun becomes unloaded after (2) but before (3), and Fred remains alive.

determining the models permitted by circumscription has proven so difficult for a small set of three or four beliefs, it seems unimaginable that it will be possible to determine those permitted a large knowledge base of conjoined, qualified microtheories. In short, although McCarthy's strategem does make it possible to ensure the consistency of a set of beliefs, and the existence of models for that set, the cost it exacts is that we no longer know what in fact those beliefs say, or whether the inferences we need actually follow from them. His proposal destroys semantics, in any meaningful sense, in order to save "semantics" in a technical sense.

Of course, the deeper question here is whether our conceptualizations of the world are or can be consistent and independent of use: The technical difficulties that surround model-theoretic "semantics" are, for the most part, a consequence of attempting to pursue the logicist dream of a completely context-free characterization of knowledge too far. And as I have already pointed out, Nilsson himself asserts, in his discussion of "reification", that the answer to this deeper question is no: Conceptualizations are not independent of use. However, this is true in a way that is even stronger than he implies. Nilsson's point is that different problem situations and different goals will require different—and incompatible—conceptualizations of the world. The fact is, however, that even if they *are* compatible, all conceptualizations of a situation are not the same.

This point was first made by Cordell Green in his discussion of QA3 [9], one of the earliest serious attempts to apply logical methods to problem solving. QA3 brought together the situation calculus [16] and resolution theorem proving [25] for the first time, and applied them to planning and automatic programming. In his experiments with it, Green discovered something interesting: When applied to relatively complicated problems such as the Tower of Hanoi, or writing a program for merge sort, whether or not QA3 could find a solution depended critically on how the axioms were formulated. The point he made then is still true now: One cannot in fact just "write down the axioms" in blissful ignorance of their intended uses. Logically equivalent ways of conceptualizing the world are not functionally equivalent. Nilsson seems to acknowledge this point when he writes that "Because the actions emitted by [the function that maps from an organism's beliefs to its actions] depend on the syntactic form of the sentences [representing those beliefs in the organism's memory], it is necessary . . . to be able to rewrite these sentences in the form appropriate to the task at hand." But I think it is fair to say that this acknowledgement, by focussing on the trivial and obvious dependence of an organism's effectors on the form of the signals that control them, draws attention away from the larger question of how the differences between logically equivalent conceptualizations might affect the task of reasoning itself, and thus seems to imply that such differences are far less important to the invention of appropriate conceptualizations than they actually are.

There is yet a further lesson about the interdependence of ontology and function to be drawn from Green's work. In his analysis of QA3's weaknesses, he made the following point:

> Let us divide information [needed for automatic programming problems] into three types: (1) Information concerning the problem description and semantics . . . (2) Information concerning the target programming language . . . (3) Information concerning the interrelation of the problem and the target language . . . . In the axiom systems presented, no distinction is made between such classes of information. Consequently, during the search for a proof the theorem prover might attempt to use axioms of type 1 for purposes where it needs information of type 2. Such attempts lead nowhere and generate useless clauses. However, . . . we can place in the proof strategy our knowledge of when such information is to be used, thus leading to more efficient proofs. [9, p. 235]

In other words, concepts about the world must be categorized in useful ways—in terms of abstractions whose definition is motivated not solely by the world itself, but by the need to organize knowledge about the world for effective problem solving. This is by now a widely accepted proposition. Still, I think it is fair to wonder about the status of such abstract categories within the logicist framework. As far as logic is concerned, an abstract category of this sort is really just a shorthand notation for the disjunction of all the concepts which it categorizes. If one were simply to eliminate all such abstractions from a set of axioms, and replace them with the equivalent disjunctions, the resulting set of axioms would be logically equivalent to the original set. Indeed, any set of such abstractions is as good as the next, logically speaking, since none makes the slightest difference to the conclusions that one can draw about the world. Thus, abstract concepts defined in order to usefully categorize knowledge are ontologically—and semantically—vacuous from a logicist perspective. In sum, if the "conceptualization" represented by a given knowledge base *is* (or should be) the world, as Nilsson asserts, then any additional concepts, categories, or relations defined in order to make reasoning more effective are not included by this term—it covers only a subset of the concepts, categories, and relations in terms of which we understand the world. It is, however, with conceptualizations in this larger sense that AI must be concerned, as Minsky [20] has forcefully argued.

It is worth pointing out that a similar argument forms a portion of Imre Lakatos' brilliant and entertaining critique of the logicist approach to mathematics, *Proofs and Refutations* [13]. Among other things, Lakatos shows how utterly inadequate the logicist conceptions of definitions as "theoretically dispensable but typographically convenient abbreviatory devices"—and ultimately, of proofs as formal deductions—actually are to explain what our mathematical concepts are and how they develop. It need hardly be added that the doubts Lakatos raises about whether logic can adequately account for how we think about mathematics should dampen anyone's enthusiasm about its ability to adequately account for how we think about everything else.

Given all of these difficulties, both theoretical and empirical, why do logicists continue to adhere to the position that conceptualizations are independent of use, and to the concomitant notion of model-theoretic "semantics"? I think the reasons have more to do with methodological hopes (and fears) than anything else. Process models of intelligence depend on knowledge; if the knowledge can't be formulated independently of the process models, where do we begin? How can we write down what a program needs to know before we know what the program looks like? And how can we write the program if we don't have some theory of what it needs to know? The logicists see the claim that knowledge can be formulated entirely independently of use as the only way to avoid this vicious circle.

It seems to me that this apparent circularity is based on an overly simplistic view of science (and for that matter, programming). We might, instead, view the process of constructing AI theories as proceeding by successive approximations, starting with an approximate theory of the necessary knowledge, constructing a preliminary algorithm, and then refining them both in concert. In reality, of course, this is exactly what everybody does. Moreover, viewed within the context of this more realistic characterization of AI methodology, our preliminary and descriptive theories of the contents of mental structures *sans* process models are merely that: preliminary and descriptive. There is no need to become obsessed with the formal properties of the notations we use in constructing such theories, because there is no reason to believe that these will play any explanatory role in the final theory.

To put this another way, any attempt to specify the contents of mental representations in complete independence of use is probably doomed to failure. Nevertheless, it is worth *pretending* that this is not so, since important and useful investigations of the knowledge necessary in order to behave intelligently are likely to result, and indeed *have* resulted, from such attempts. The question is how seriously we need to worry about the notations in which such investigations are carried out. As Hayes [11] points out, "Initially, the formalisations need be little more than carefully-worded English sentences. One can make considerable progress on ontological issues, for example, without actually *formalising* anything." He then goes on to argue that, in short order, it will be necessary to express such intuitions formally. I agree with him, but it seems to me that such formalizations must take place within the context of a set of actual tasks, so that we have some idea of the purposes to which the knowledge must actually be put. I don't mean to deny that the ability to apply the same knowledge to many different tasks should play a role in determining the appropriate formalization. But the only compelling reason to argue that such formalization must be in terms of logic, in the narrow sense, is if you assume that the knowledge will be applied by a deductive engine—i.e., a theorem prover. Without this assumption, the methodological imperative for formalization in terms of logic just isn't there. It is, after all, insights into "ontological issues" that are the point of the investigation in the first place. Painstaking attention to the formal properties of the notation in which such insights are expressed is misplaced. In those cases where content theories of what we know about some domain are expressed in English, for example, it seems difficult to imagine that Hayes or anybody else would advocate spending a lot of time worrying about linguistics.

This brings us, finally, to the logicists' preoccupation with deduction. The most straightforward argument for formalizing knowledge in logic, narrowly construed, is simply that if we do not do so, then we cannot rely on deduction, narrowly construed, as our model of reasoning. In my view, however, this has resulted in a reversal of priorities: The logicists have been led to embrace deduction as the process by which knowledge is applied in order to motivate the use of logic, rather than the other way around (McDermott [19] makes a similar point). Indeed, one can find clear evidence for this underlying motivation in the literature. Consider, for example, the following quote from Patel-Schneider [24]:

> [The undecidability of first-order logic] has led to many attempts to create [knowledge representation] systems based on [first-order logic] that always produce answers. Most of these systems retain the syntax of [first-order logic] while modifying its inferences in some way. The crudest of them simply take a theorem prover for [first-order logic] and place some *ad hoc* restrictions on it, such as terminating the search for a proof after a pre-set amount of time or a certain number of proof steps. Such modifications produce systems that cannot be given an adequate semantics and have no means of completely characterizing answers except by referring to the actions of the modified theorem prover. This destroys most of the advantages of using logic in the first place.

I agree with much of Patel-Schneider's discussion here: The sort of functionally motivated deviations from deductive inference which he stigmatizes as "ad hoc"[8] do, it seems to me, call into question the applicability and relevance of model-theoretic "semantics". But whereas this suggests to me that it is model-theoretic "semantics" that should be dispensed with, Patel-Schneider goes on to make it clear that in his view it is any deviation from pure deduction

[8] See [26] for an explanation of the political role that this term plays in the cognitive sciences. What "ad hoc" really means, of course, is "for a special case". Attempts to deal with fundamental constraints such as undecidability hardly strike me as being for a special case.

which must be abjured.[9] In this, the purest and most extreme form of the logicist world-view, the primary constraint on an inference process is not whether or how well it performs in some realistic task, but whether it can be given an "adequate" logical characterization. Needless to say, what we can expect from this approach are "logically characterized" systems that don't do anything particularly interesting. The literature is full of this sort of "result".

4. Residual problems

In this section, I would like to address some residual questions, having more to do with Nilsson's paper than logicism *per se*.

4.1. Addlists–deletelists and the frame problem

In his discussion of the frame problem [18]—the problem of determining what doesn't change in the world when an action is performed—Nilsson refers briefly to a number of approaches that have been suggested. Most of these fall squarely in the logicist camp, but at the head of the list he includes his and Fikes' use of addlists and deletelists in the STRIPS problem-solving system [7]. Leaving aside any perfectly understandable personal fondness that Nilsson might have for this approach, its inclusion of such a list, in a paper touting the virtues of logicism, seems completely incomprehensible. For whatever its other merits or deficiencies, this approach represents the antithesis of logicism. It may allow problem-solving systems to infer what changes and what doesn't change when actions are performed in certain simple domains—domains in which, e.g., the results of actions are not conditional on the state in which they are executed—but those inferences are by no means "logical" in the strict sense demanded by logicism. For better or for worse, the approach simply employs a procedure that updates the database by adding the assertions on the addlist, removing those on the deletelist, and leaving everything else alone. This may or may not be the right thing to do in certain circumstances, but surely it isn't the *logicist* thing to do—or if it is, then the label loses all significance.

4.2. Reasoning with models

Nilsson argues that in many cases it is possible to construct an analog of the "intended model" of a logical theory, or at least of a portion of it, and to

[9] Nor is he alone in this view: Levesque [15] dismisses such efforts as "pseudo-solutions" on the grounds that we cannot guarantee that the resulting reasoning systems will always get the right answer. I cannot imagine why anyone believes that we will be able to guarantee that intelligent systems will always get the right answer. Does Levesque believe that *people* always get the right answer?

reason about what is true in the model by directly examining it—a process that might turn out to be considerably cheaper than theorem proving. As he puts it, "because [sound logical deduction] guarantees that a derived sentence is satisfied by a whole set of interpretations (including the intended one), it may be too strong for most purposes—and thus too expensive. All that we really need is to know whether the *intended* interpretation is a model of the sentence in question." The question this raises is, why would we ever care about anything else? I also wonder what the logicist position on the semantics (in the informal sense) of such a model might be. I imagine that logicists would be tempted to argue that this is provided by the "semantics" of the logical theory of which it is the "intended model"—but that is of course circular. Indeed, it turns the relationship on its head. The only coherent option, then, is simply to examine the representation of the model and provide rigorous, informal arguments that it has the right properties. This, however, calls into question the methodological utility of model-theoretic "semantics" in general: Once again, the question is, if such arguments are good enough in this case, why would we ever want to do anything else?

4.3. The practicality of deduction

Nilsson acknowledges that logical deduction is computationally expensive (that's a bit of an understatement), but argues that it is nevertheless practical in many cases. As evidence, he claims that "many large-scale AI systems depend heavily on predicate calculus representations and reasoning methods." He then goes on to list a three such systems, among which is included Appelt's [2] natural language generator. I admire Appelt's work a great deal. However, the program to which Nilsson refers cannot by any stretch of the imagination be called a "large-scale AI system". It is an experimental AI program that handles a few interesting examples. Moreover, Appelt has been reputed to assert, in a mock boastful fashion, that his program is the slowest generator in existence. What he means by this, of course, is that his program implements the most detailed and faithful model of generation. The point remains, however, that this sort of work is hardly an argument for the large-scale practicability of logical methods.

5. A plea for plain speaking

Having reviewed what I see as the strong and weak points of the logicist enterprise, I would like to return to a theme I touched at the very beginning of this paper. It seems to me that the primary distinction between logicism and AI in general is not, as the logicists themselves seem to believe, a matter of technical issues, but rather a question of scientific world-view, of priorities and ways of looking at problems. Logicism represents, in my view, an understandable longing for a technical basis upon which to ground AI research. In this, it seems similar to certain forms of connectionism, a point to which Charniak [7] alludes when he identifies logicism with a larger trend that he terms "mathism". Although the assumptions, research programs, and even the personalities of the adherents differ radically, nonetheless from a sociological perspective, connectionism and logicism share a great deal. Connectionism has its neural nets, its energy function equations, its convergence theorems; logicism has its axiom schemata, its model-theoretic "semantics", its completeness theorems. Both appeal outside of AI for their foundations, logicism to analytic philosophy and mathematical logic, and connectionism to neurobiology and physics. Both represent something of a backlash against the dominance of expert systems in AI over the past ten to fifteen years.

The chief problem in both cases is that the appeal outside of the common heritage of AI inevitably makes communication more difficult, inhibiting the intellectual give and take that is so important to making progress on difficult issues. It takes a great deal of effort to read logicist papers, and unfortunately, the actual ideas and results being reported, once understood, rarely prove to be worth the cost in man hours required to put them in more straightforward terms. Nor am I alone in feeling this way. Forbus [8] indicates a similar annoyance with the opacity of logicist formulations:

> Anyone can write axioms. The problem is figuring out what should be said, and saying it precisely. . . . One can have ad hoc axiomatic theories just as easily as ad hoc theories stated in natural language. Everyone has their favorite examples. (I won't mention mine here, since it will only raise heat without shedding light.) The major difference is that, because more detail is involved, it usually takes more work to uncover bugs in axiomatic theories than in theories stated in English.

However, I disagree profoundly with Forbus' attribution of the problem to the allegedly greater detail to be found in logicist theories. I suspect, in fact, that he was merely being polite. Certainly, the work that he and others have done in qualitative physical reasoning is far more detailed than anything that has been produced by the logicists.

The inevitable result of the logicists' private language is that they end up talking primarily among themselves, and the larger dialectic into which they might enter is short-circuited. This is a loss both to the logicists—who are missing out on useful ideas, comments, and criticisms that non-logicists might offer—and to the rest of us. The fact of the matter is that one does not need a detailed understanding of circumscription, for example, to have useful and right-headed ideas about plausible reasoning. Unfortunately, the social utility of pretending otherwise has proven too great a temptation to logicists. Consider, for example, Nilsson's discussion outlining the motivations underlying the logicist approach to this problem:

> If the designer had some subset of the models of [a knowledge base] in mind, and if (for some reason) he could not specify this subset by enlarging [the knowledge base], then there are circumstances in which unsound inference might be appropriate. For example, the designer might have some preference function over models of [the knowledge base]. He may want to focus, for example, on the minimal models (according to the preference function). These minimal models may be better guesses, in the designer's mind, about the real world than would be the other models of [the knowledge base]. In that case, [an] inference . . . would be appropriate if all minimal models of [the knowledge base] were models of [the inference].

By using such terms as "minimal models" and "preference functions", there can be no question that in this paragraph Nilsson intends to convey the sense that logicism has progressed beyond the stage of naive, intuitive formulations of the issues involved in plausible inference. But has it really? There is, to my mind, something bizarrely syntactic about the way the problem is framed here. *What sort of* "better guesses . . . about the real world" would the designer of an AI program have which could not be specified by adding additional axioms? *When* and *why* would such a situation arise? *In what way* are preferred models "better" guesses about the world? *Why* would the designer of the program think so? *These* are the real questions that need to be addressed in developing a theory of plausible inference, but Nilsson's formulation of the problem makes no reference to these fundamental issues: What he describes are the shadows that the problem casts on the wall of the logicist cave.

I don't think this is an accident: Logicism *encourages* thinking about problems in this syntactic fashion, divorced from the functional concerns that, ultimately, constitute AI's unique contribution to the study of the mind. The proper formulation of plausible reasoning heuristics will ultimately depend on a good understanding of their utility, and utility can only be assessed in the context of the need to perform a set of tasks. In the absence of such functional constraints, one is free to postulate whatever heuristics "work" on the example at hand. Nowhere is this better illustrated than in the flood of putative solutions to Hanks and McDermott's "shooting problem". In fact, every one of these proposals suffers from severe defects, and moreover, defects which have nothing whatsoever to do with logic. However, only the fact that new ones keep being proposed would lead anyone outside of the logicist community to think anything was wrong.

To take just one example, several of the proposed solutions to the Hanks–

McDermott problem, stripped of their technical phraseology, come down to something like the following argument:

> (1) The problem here is that states should persist until something makes them go away—that's why our intuition is that Fred is dead, rather than that the gun became unloaded (since nothing made the gun become unloaded). (2) So that means, they should persist as long as possible. (3) So we'll formulate the following heuristic for plausible reasoning: Prefer scenarios in which things happen as late as possible (alternatively, in which our knowledge of things happening is as late as possible).

Put in plain English like this, of course, certain questions immediately come to mind: Is the first step really correct? Do the second and third steps really follow from it? In any event, once formulated in simple and clear language, it isn't hard to generate a lot of counterexamples—many of which, it turns out, have circulated privately within the logicist community for some time. For instance, if one modifies the Hanks–McDermott example so that it is asserted that Fred does not die, these heuristics lead to the inference that the gun becomes unloaded in the very split second before it is fired. This is, to say the least, a highly counter-intuitive result.

What such counterexamples reveal is that, although these heuristics indirectly *reflect* some of the factors involved in plausible inference, they neither exhaust the list of factors involved in this example, nor do they take the factors they do reflect into account in the appropriate way. What we have here are logical "theories" with all of the defects of the hacked-up programs we know so well—they are designed to work on a handful of examples, and fail on even minor permutations of these examples. Our intuition that Fred is dead is *not* due to our preference for scenarios in which our knowledge is delayed as long as possible: It is due to our preference for scenarios in which events have known causes.[10] Whether we are willing to conclude that Fred is dead, then, depends on our assessment of how complete our knowledge of the causes involved is likely to be. If we think that it is reasonably complete, then we are likely to infer that Fred is dead; if not, then we won't. Thus, for example, if a great deal of time passes—say, 100 years—we are less sure. Or if we leave the room for 20 minutes, again we are less sure. If we leave the room, come back, and the gun is then fired but Fred does not die, we are likely to conclude that the gun became unloaded while we were out of the room. The reason this conclusion seems sensible is that if anything happened to the gun that we didn't know about, it is most likely to have happened then. And this example, finally, reveals the grain of truth in the logicist heuristics described above: The earlier

[10] Why we seem to have this preference is exactly the sort of functional question that logicists never get around to addressing.

something happens, the more likely we are to see its effects. So, if something happened that we didn't know about, then it is more likely to have happened later rather than earlier—all other things being equal.

You don't have to be a logicist to understand this. On the contrary, the question that we must consider here is, how could they have missed it? A little more plain speaking would probably do the logicists at least as much good as the rest of us.

Acknowledgement

This paper is based on a talk given at the MIT Workshop on the Foundations of Artificial Intelligence, Dedham, Massachussetts, in June 1987. For many helpful discussions, and for invaluable comments on an earlier draft, I thank Gregg Collins, Jim Firby, Andrew Gelsey, Kris Hammond, Steve Hanks, Pat Hayes, Eric Jones, Alex Kass, David Kirsh, Paul Kube, Stan Letovsky, Nils Nilsson, Jordan Pollack, Chris Riesbeck, and Roger Schank. I owe a special debt to Drew McDermott for his many valiant attempts to set me straight, and for putting up with *my* attempts to set *him* straight. This work was supported in part by the Defense Advanced Research Projects Agency, monitored by the Office of Naval Research under contract N00014-85-K-0108 and by the Air Force Office of Scientific Research under contract F49620-88-C-0058. The Institute for the Learning Sciences was established in 1989 with the support of Andersen Consulting, part of The Arthur Andersen Worldwide Organization.

References

[1] R. Abelson, Constraint, construal, and cognitive science, in: *Proceedings Third Annual Conference of the Cognitive Science Society*, Berkeley, CA (1981) 1–9.

[2] D.E. Appelt, *Planning English Sentences* (Cambridge University Press, Cambridge, 1985).

[3] E. Charniak, Logic and explanation, *Comput. Intell.* **3** (1987) 172–174.

[4] R. DeMillo, R. Lipton, and A. Perlis, Social processes and proofs of theorems and programs, *Commun. ACM* **22** (1979) 271–280.

[5] D.C. Dennett, When philosophers encounter artificial intelligence, *Daedalus* **117** (1988) 283–295.

[6] E.A. Feigenbaum, The art of artificial intelligence: themes and case studies in knowledge engineering, in: *Proceedings IJCAI-77*, Cambridge, MA (1977) 1014–1029.

[7] R.E. Fikes and N.J. Nilsson, STRIPS: A new approach to the application of theorem proving to problem solving, *Artif. Intell.* **2** (1971) 189–208.

[8] K.D. Forbus, Logic versus logicism: A reply to McDermott, *Comput. Intell.* **3** (1987) 176–178.

[9] C. Green, Application of theorem proving to problem solving, in: *Proceedings IJCAI-69*, Washington, DC (1969) 219–239.

[10] S. Hanks and D.V. McDermott, Nonmonotonic logic and temporal projection, *Artif. Intell.* **33** (1987) 379–412.

[11] P.J. Hayes, The naive physics manifesto, in: D. Michie, ed., *Expert Systems in the Micro-Electronic Age* (Edinburgh University Press, Edinburgh, 1979).

[12] C. Hewitt, Metacritique of McDermott and the logicist approach, *Comput. Intell.* **3** (1987) 185–189.

[13] I. Lakatos, *Proofs and Refutations: The Logic of Mathematical Discovery* (Cambridge University Press, Cambridge, 1976).

[14] G. Lakoff, *Women, Fire, and Dangerous Things* (University of Chicago Press, Chicago, IL, 1987).

[15] H.J. Levesque, Knowledge representation and reasoning, in: J. Traub, B. Grosz, B. Lampson, and N. Nilsson, eds., *Annual Review of Computer Science* **1** (Annual Reviews Inc., Palo Alto, CA, 1986) 255–287.

[16] J. McCarthy, Programs with common sense, in: M. Minsky, ed., *Semantic Information Processing* (MIT Press, Cambridge, MA, 1968) 403–418.

[17] J. McCarthy, Circumscription—a form of non-monotonic reasoning, *Artif. Intell.* **13** (1980) 27–39.

[18] J. McCarthy and P.J. Hayes, Some philosophical problems from the standpoint of artificial intelligence, in: B. Meltzer and D. Michie, eds., *Machine Intelligence* **4** (1987) (American Elsevier, New York, 1969) 463–502.

[19] D.V. McDermott, A critique of pure reason, *Comput. Intell.* **3** 151–160.

[20] M. Minsky, A framework for representing knowledge, AI Memo No. 306, Artificial Intelligence Laboratory, MIT, Cambridge, MA (1974).

[21] A. Newell, The knowledge level, *Artif. Intell.* **18** (1982) 87–127.

[22] N.J. Nilsson, Commentary on McDermott, *Comput. Intell.* **3** (1987) 202–203.

[23] N. Nilsson, Logic and artificial intelligence, *Artif. Intell.* **47** (1991) 31–56, this volume.

[24] P.F. Patel-Schneider, A decidable first-order logic for knowledge representation, in: *Proceedings IJCAI-85*, Los Angeles, CA (1985) 455–458.

[25] J. Robinson, A machine-oriented logic based on the resolution principle, *J. ACM* **12** (1965) 23–41.

[26] R.C. Schank, What makes something "ad hoc", in: *Proceedings Second Workshop on Theoretical Issues in Natural Language Processing*, Urbana, IL (1978) 8–13.

[27] R.C. Schank, and R. Abelson, *Scripts, Plans, Goals, and Understanding* (Erlbaum, Hillsdale, NJ, 1977).

[28] W.A. Woods, Don't blame the tool, *Comput. Intell.* **3** (1987) 228–237.

Artificial Intelligence 47 (1991) 79–106
Elsevier

Open Information Systems Semantics for Distributed Artificial Intelligence

Carl Hewitt
AI Laboratory, 545 Technology Square, Cambridge, MA 02139, USA

Received June 1989
Revised January 1990

Abstract

Hewitt, C., Open Information Systems Semantics for Distributed Artificial Intelligence, Artificial Intelligence 47 (1991) 79–106.

Distributed Artificial Intelligence (henceforth called DAI) deals with issues of large-scale *Open Systems* (i.e. systems which are always subject to unanticipated outcomes in their operation and which can receive new information from outside themselves at any time). *Open Information Systems* (henceforth called OIS) are Open Systems that are implemented using digital storage, operations, and communications technology. OIS Semantics aims to provide a scientific foundation for understanding such large-scale OIS projects and for developing new technology.

The literature of DAI speaks of many important concepts such as *commitment*, *conflict*, *negotiation*, *cooperation*, *distributed problem solving*, *representation*, etc. However there is currently no framework for comparing the usage of such concepts in one publication with usage in other publications. *Open Information System Semantics* (henceforth called OIS Semantics) is a step toward remedying this problem by providing a framework which integrates methods from Sociology with methods from Concurrent Systems Science into a foundation that provides a framework for analyzing previous work in DAI and a powerful foundation for its further development.

Deduction, one of the most powerful and well-understood methods for information systems, has recently been applied to foundational issues in DAI thereby raising important new issues and problems above and beyond those of applying deduction to the problems of classical AI. OIS Semantics provides answers to many important questions about the uses of deduction in OIS. It provides a characterization of Deduction that encompasses *N*th-Order Logics, Meta-theories, Modal Logics, Circumscription, Default Logic, Autoepistemic Logic, Restricted Scope Nonmonotonic Logics, etc. OIS Semantics develops the concept of *Deductive Indecision* as a fundamental aspect of Deductive systems, thereby characterizing the scope and limits of Deduction for operational and representational activities in OIS.

Negotiations play a fundamental role in OIS Semantics. They are creative processes that go beyond the capabilities of Deduction. OIS Semantics characterizes the role of Negotiation as a powerful method for increasing understanding of large-scale OIS projects.

The ambitious goal of OIS Semantics for DAI is to provide an integrated foundation for Sociology and Concurrent Systems Science. This paper provides a snapshot of where we currently stand in the process of developing these foundations

1. Introduction

Distributed Artificial Intelligence (henceforth called DAI) *Open Information Systems* (henceforth called OIS) are large-scale information systems that are always subject to unanticipated outcomes in their operations and new information from their environment). This paper is concerned with Information Systems that are implemented using digital storage, operations, and communications technology. Information must be digitized in order to become part of an Information System. If information is not processed digitally, then it falls outside the scope of Information Systems as used in this paper.

This paper deals with *large-scale* projects. A good example is an enterprise-wide information system of the future for managing flexible semiconductor manufacturing including the connected information systems of the Sales, Marketing, and Research and Development departments. Large-scale OIS projects cover a large geography over a long period of time with many mutual dependencies with overlapping subprojects.

For excellent collections of readings on DAI and related topics see [9, 16, 28]. DAI OIS include projects such as designing a permanent space station and the software engineering of an international electronic funds transfer system. The literature of DAI speaks of many important concepts such as *commitment* [6], *conflict* [1], *negotiation* [13, 34, 46, 53], *cooperation* [11], *distributed problem solving* [21], *representation* [17], etc.

However, there is currently no framework for comparing the usage of such concepts in one publication with usage in other publications. OIS Semantics is a step toward remedying this problem by providing a framework which integrates methods from Sociology [18, 19, 35, 50] with methods from Concurrent Systems Science [25] into a foundation that provides a context for previous work in DAI and a powerful conceptual and operational foundation for the further development of DAI for OIS.

The development of this paper proceeds as follows. Section 2 presents issues and problems that arise in consideration of developing an adequate semantics for DAI OIS. Section 3 analyzes the role of deduction. Section 4 presents new foundations for dealing with the issues and problems covered in Sections 2 and 3. Section 5 outlines how we are attempting to *use* the new foundations.

2. Issues and problems in OIS Semantics for DAI

OIS Semantics provides a framework for analyzing the scope and goals of DAI OIS. It provides a characterization of the role of Deduction. In addition it provides a framework for analyzing the issues and problems that must be addressed by new foundations for DAI OIS.

2.1. Self-reliance and interdependence

OIS proposes *self-reliance* and *interdependence* as fundamental issues for DAI. It takes *Self-reliance*[1] to be the capability to act using the resources available locally and *Interdependence* to be the requirement to obtain resources elsewhere in order to act. In this regard *permission* is taken to be a resource that may be needed in order to act. Analysis in terms of *Self-reliance* and *Interdependence* provides a useful perspective towards analysis of terms such as "global coherence with local control" which mix together several issues besides the fact that no Open System is ever truly "global" since it is always subject to unanticipated interactions. As we shall see below, having both Self-reliance and Interdependence often leads to conflict.

- *Asynchrony* enables each participant to operate as quickly as possible, given local circumstances. Otherwise, the pace of the activity of each participant could only proceed at the pace of a distant scheduler. Asynchrony makes the component of a system more impervious to communications failures and consequently allows them to be more self-reliant. However, this often produces conflict because new information can generate new commitments that conflict with pre-existing local commitments.
- *Local authority* enables participants to react immediately to changing circumstances. Otherwise, they would have to consult a distant decision maker for each decision. When conflicts arise they can immediately take action, thereby creating new commitments. However, these new commitments will often conflict with those of other participants who are not yet aware of the new commitments.
- *Late-arriving information* enables participants to increase the effectiveness of their decision making by taking new information into account as it arrives. Otherwise, participants would have to either wait till the last possible moment to begin their decision making processes or forego taking late-arriving information into account. However, when information arrives at an advanced stage of processing, the possibility of acting on it often conflicts with existing commitments which are already at an advanced stage of processing.
- *Division and specialization of labor and Multiple Authorities* can increase pluralism, diversity, and robustness. *Division of labor* can eliminate bottlenecks by physically distributing the work. *Specialization of labor* can enable participants to concentrate and focus their efforts on a narrow range of goals. However, these capabilities can produce conflict when the specialized commitments of multiple authorities are incompatible and come into conflict.
- *Arm's length relationships* enable participants to conceal their internal

[1] This paper uses capitalization to distinguish technical usage from ordinary usage.

activities from other participants, thereby facilitating recovery of investments in new products and the enforcement of policies by detecting violations before they can be covered up. This can increase the severity of conflict because other participants may develop entrenched incompatibile commitments before conflict is discovered.

Balancing the tradeoff between Self-reliance and Interdependence is one of the most fundamental issues in DAI. Powerful, well-understood methods are needed to help manage this tradeoff.

Since deduction is one of the most powerful and well-understood methods available for Information Systems, OIS Semantics needs to provide a good understanding of the role that deduction has in OIS.

2.2. Issues concerning the role of deduction in OIS

The DAI literature raises important unresolved issues on the use of deduction [53]. Not the least of these is providing a general definition of deduction! OIS Semantics provides a definition of Deduction that encompasses *N*th-Order Logics, Meta-theories, Modal Logics, Circumscription [37, 38], Default Logic [43], Autoepistemic Logic [40], Restricted Scope Nonmonotonic Logics [14], etc. Given this characterization of Deduction, what is its role in DAI? Can it be used as a universal systems implementation language as claimed by Kowalski [33]? Can Deduction be used as the foundation for representational work in OIS?

2.3. Issues in new foundations for DAI OIS

OIS Semantics addresses fundamental questions such as: What are the fundamental activities in OIS and how are they composed into larger activities? In particular, what is the exact nature of *commitment*? *Conflict* has been of great concern in DAI. Where and why does it arise and what is to be done about it? What role does *cooperation* play in OIS processes? The issue of *representation* has become even more thorny in DAI than classical AI! How does OIS Semantics provide a theory of meaning for OIS activities? What does it mean to be *robust* and how can it be achieved? How can *negotiation* be characterized and what role does it play?

3. The role of deduction in DAI OIS

OIS Semantics provides answers to important questions about the use of deduction in DAI [34, 53]. Attempts to use deduction in DAI raises whole new questions and issues beyond the well familiar ones of classical AI [39]. OIS Semantics provides a characterization of deduction as a pre-requisite to analyzing the role that it plays in OIS.

Microtheories are a way of formalizing declarative knowledge. A *Microtheory* is defined to be a Derivational calculus together with a prespecified operation that can check the correctness of any individual Derivation step given only the step and no additional information. In other words, an automaton only has to do one such checking operation for each step in a Derivation in order to check the entire Derivation for correctness. The checking operation is provided to the automaton in advance and no other computation is required other than to read the Derivation and apply the checking operation. Various constraints can be placed on the checking operation to make precise the resource constraints that are required for checking the correctness of Derivations. For example, a very tight constraint would be that the correctness must be decided in a time which is a fixed constant times the size of the Derivation step to be checked. Such a constraint would require Derivations to be very fine-grained with a multitude of explicit steps that would otherwise not have to be present.

Deduction is the presentation of Derivations and checking them for correctness. This definition of Deduction encompasses *N*th-Order Logics, Metatheories, Modal Logics, Circumscription [37, 38] Default Logic [43], Autoepistemic Logic [40], Restricted Scope Nonmonotonic Logics [14], etc. Microtheories are based on a closed-world assumption—using an automaton specified in advance, Derivations can be algorithmically checked for correctness without having to make any observations of the external world or to consult any external information sources. In fact, the Closed World assumption is just these commitments. The Closed World commitment is in fact the commitment for verifying the correct operation of such an automaton and verifying that its decision depends only on the Derivation being checked for correctness. Within various logics, additional commitments can be made to provide closed logical worlds such as those of Default Logic [43] and Circumscription [37, 38] in which the axiom systems are closed with respect to certain logical properties. So Default Logic and Circumscription are commitments that assume and go beyond the commitments of Deduction.

A spreadsheet is a good example of a Microtheory. The Derivation rules are the calculation procedures used for the cells of the spreadsheet. Given the current values in the cells and the checking operation derived from the formulas to compute the new cell values, an automaton can algorithmically check whether the new values are correct.

Microtheories have important strengths:

- Microtheories are highly portable (cf. [41]). They can be expressed as stable *inscriptions* (i.e. bit strings, cf. [35]) that can easily be stored, moved, and copied.
- The correctness of a Derivation in a Microtheory is algorithmically decidable solely from the text of the Derivation. An automaton can decide whether or not a Derivation is correct without having to make any external physical measurements or consult any external information systems.

In this way, OIS Semantics provides a general characterization of Deduction. Given this characterization, the next step is to analyze the scope and limits of the use of Deduction in OIS.

3.1. The use of Microtheories in OIS operations

Consider a shared financial account which is accessible from multiple sites using electronic funds transfer. Further suppose that two parties Ueda and Shapiro are concurrently attempting to withdraw funds from the account and there is insufficient money in the account to satisfy both withdraw requests. The issue is to decide which one of them succeeded in withdrawing the money which they requested.

For concreteness consider an implementation of a shared account expressed in the message passing programming language ACORE [36]. Each behavior in ACORE has structure expressed by a list of Handles of actors with which it can communicate and functionality expressed by a Script which has message handlers (indicated by –serial→ below); one of these handlers will be applicable to the incoming communication.

Changing behavior in actors is captured by the concept of *replacement behavior*. In our actor core language, a replacement behavior can be specified by a change in the parameters of the same behavior by using a Ready command.

The code for a Behavior to process withdraw requests in an account is as follows:[2]

```
(DefName Account
 (Behavior [balance owner] {Serializer}
       ;each account has a balance and owner
  (–serial→ (A WithdrawRequest amount)
       ;a withdrawal of amount is requested
   (If (≥ balance amount)
    (Then
     (Let {[newBalance = (– balance amount)]}
    ;Let newBalance be balance less amount
     (Ready Serializer [balance = newBalance])
    ;Account is ready for the next message with balance of newBalance
    (Return (A WithdrawReceipt amount owner newBalance))))
     (Else
      (Ready Serializer) the account is ready for the next message
     (Complain (An OverDraftNotice amount owner balance))))))
```

A new account can be created with balance $100M and owner Clark can be created and bound to an identifier named Account1 as follows:

[2] A communication handler is also called a *method* or *virtual procedure* in object-oriented languages.

```
(DefName Account1 (Create Account $100M Clark))
```

Suppose that Ueda and Shapiro need to share access to Clark's account. The following commands give them the ability to communicate with Account1:

```
(Send Ueda Account1)
(Send Shapiro Account1)
```

Now if Ueda attempts to withdraw $70M from Account1 using

```
(Send Account1 (A WithdrawRequest $70M))
```

while concurrently Shapiro attempts to withdraw $80M,

```
(Send Account1 (A WithdrawRequest $80M))
```

then the operation of using the account will be serialized so that one of them will get a withdraw receipt and the other an overdraft complaint.

However, it is Physically Indeterminate which will have their withdraw request honored. No amount of knowledge of the physical circumstances in which the withdraw requests are made determines the outcome. Therefore, the outcome cannot be Deductively Decided even from complete knowledge of all the circumstances at the time when Ueda and Shapiro sent their respective requests to withdraw funds. This is an instance of the *Deductive Indecision Problem*.

Deduction does not provide means adequate to decide important questions that arise in the course of operation of OIS because of the omnipresence of indeterminacy. Deductive Indecision has important operational consequences for the use of deduction for OIS. It refutes Kowalski's Thesis that Deductive Logic can be used as a universal systems implementation language [33]. Previously it has been almost universally assumed that Deductive Logic is a universal systems implementation language because it is universal for Closed Algorithmic Systems. Deductive Indecision about important operational questions (such as whether or not a withdrawal is being honored) is a fatal flaw in Kowalski's Thesis.

In addition to the operational role of Kowalski's Thesis, Deduction has also been proposed as the foundation for representational activities. The hope has been that given a nondeductive operational basis as a foundation, Deduction can be used as the foundation for the meaning of sentences.

3.2. The use of Microtheories in Representation

In checking the correctness of a Derivation, there are well-defined methods for dealing with any conflict that might arise. Negotiations are usually not very important because the correctness of Derivation can be decided an automaton specified in advance.

3.2.1. The Deductive Indecision Problem in Circumscription

In this section I present an example to show how the Deductive Indecision Problem arises in the use of Circumscription in OIS. Circumscription [37, 38] has been introduced as a way to close logical axiom systems to provide qualifications that are useful in compactly expressing axioms and their qualifications. This section of the paper uses Circumscription to illustrate some further points about Deductive Indecision in Microtheories. Circumscription makes it possible to analyze a small Microtheory at greater and greater levels of detail with respect to analyzing how rules can be circumscribed.

Consider the question of the safety of the Diablo Canyon nuclear power plant which came up as a crucial issue as part of the process of deciding whether or not it should be given an operating license.

Let's suppose that all participants accept the following propositions:

> trained-operators
> earthquake-zone

which state that the operators are trained and that the nuclear plant is in an earthquake zone:

> Axiom 1:
> If trained-operators, then safe-plant

which states that if the operators are trained, then the plant is safe.

> Axiom 2:
> If earthquake-zone, then not (safe-plant)

which states that if the plant is in an earthquake zone, then it is not safe.

The above propositions taken together are inconsistent in that they imply both safe-plant and not(safe-plant).

Using Circumscription, we can remove the contradiction by replacing each axiom A_i with a new axiom of the form

> If not(C_i), then A_i,

where C_i is a new unique propositional variable which I call a *Caveat* and which McCarthy calls a *Normality Condition*.

So Axiom 1 is transformed to Axiom 1′:

> Axiom 1′:
> If trained-operators and not(caveat-1), then safe-plant

and Axiom 2 is transformed to Axiom 2′:

Axiom 2′:
If earthquake-zone and not(caveat-2), then not(safe-plant)

Circumscription provides that conclusions can be drawn from the maximal consistent models of the axioms by varying which Caveats are taken to be true and false. In this way Circumscription eliminates the contradiction in the Microtheory obtained by joining the Microtheories of the proponents and opponents. However, note that the Deductive Indecision Problem has been enlarged by Circumscription because in addition to be being Undecided about safe-plant, the new Circumscription Microtheory is undecided about caveat-1 and caveat-2 as well. There are two inconsistent extensions: one in which caveat-2 is true along with safe-plant and vice versa. The Deductive Indecision reflects some of the actual Indeterminacy in plant safety.

In response to the above discussion, the utility proposes the following axiom:

Interaction Axiom 3:
If trained-operators, then caveat-2

because it maintains that its operators have been trained to deal with earthquakes and so the fact that the power plant is in an earthquake zone does not imply that it is not safe. If the above proposition is accepted and the discussion ends here, then by Circumscription we can conclude that the power plant is safe.

However, the opponents to the plant also have a new axiom to propose:

Interaction Axiom 4:
If earthquake-zone, then caveat-1

because they maintain that being in an earthquake zone implies that having trained operators does not imply that the plant is safe since the effects of a high intensity earthquake cannot be predicted.

The machinery that Circumscription establishes to join together two formally inconsistent microtheories has become part of the content of the dispute between the participants! Actually this is not too surprising given the entrenched nature of the conflict. Roughly the same phenomena should be expected regardless of whatever means are used to provide a forum for the participants.

Neither side is willing to accept each other's new proposals for axioms and so Circumscription is applied to produce Axioms 3′ and 4′:

Interaction Axiom 3′:
If trained-operators and not(caveat-Interaction-Axiom-3), then caveat-2

Interaction Axiom 4′:
If earthquake-zone and not(caveat-Interaction-Axiom-4), then caveat-1

There is no resolution and the Deductively Undecided atomic propositions have been enlarged to include caveat-Interaction-Axiom-3 and caveat-Interaction-Axiom-4.

But the discussion is not done yet! The utility proposes the following axiom:

Second-Order Interaction Axiom 5:
If trained-operators, then caveat-Interaction-Axiom-4

because it believes that if the operators are trained to handle earthquakes, then the power plant being in an earthquake zone does not imply that trained operators will not have a safe plant, while the opponents counter with:

Second-Order Interaction Axiom 6:
If earthquake-zone, then caveat-Interaction-Axiom-3

because they believe that if the power plant is in an earthquake zone, then having trained operators does not imply that the earthquake zone does not make the plant unsafe because even though the operators are trained, they will not be able to keep the plant safe.

The participants are arguing about the *process* of the forum in which they engage in representational activity couched in a logical language. The same kind of behavior should be expected in any other forum that is provided to the participants: they will use whatever machinery is available to them in order to further incompatible entrenched commitments.

Determination of the safety of the power plant is a very difficult issue. So it is not surprising that it cannot be solved using Deduction. However, the Deductive Indecision Problem can be made worse! Deduction is concerned exclusively with the *internal* structure of Microtheories. Its great power stems from the ability to analyze Microtheories from anywhere and from any context in which they might have arisen. However, it seems that it has left out something crucial by concentrating only on the *logical* relationships among Microtheories.

Deduction may still be of use even if it can't decide the issue of plant safety. Derivation of contradictions in Microtheories can be helpful in uncovering the assumptions on which the contradictions are based.

3.2.2. What is the use of Deduction to uncover assumptions?

> Deduction enables participants who contradict each other to unwind their assumptions and come to an agreement about the assumptions on which they differ.

Although the above claim is commonly made for Deduction, it has some severe shortcomings. Limitations of the above principle become apparent in cases like the dispute over the safety of the nuclear power plant in which participants *deliberately* present contradictory Microtheories as tools to further their conflicting commitments. In such cases, attempts to "unwind" contradictions usually result in the participants providing an increasing supply of new more detailed Microtheories that contradict each other point by point and introduce new issues into the debate whenever possible. Consequently, the "unwinding" process not only does not halt, but actually becomes larger and more intractable the more it is pursued. Furthermore, opponents of licensing the power plant might agree only in their conviction that the plant is unsafe. Their assumptions can otherwise be completely at odds with each other!

Previous sections of this paper have characterized the role of Deduction in operations, representation, and uncovering assumptions in OIS. All of these limitations arise from the Indeterminacy of conflicting commitments. Operationally, it is impossible to deduce the information needed to carry out operations because of the Indeterminacy of attempting to carry them out. Inscriptions deduced from a Microtheory are not responsive to the Indeterminate circumstances of the arena in which they are Represented. Microtheories put forth as justifying a commitment, are countered with conflicting Microtheories. Furthermore, all of these characterizations of Deduction become stronger as the scale of projects is increased.

With the above characterization of the scope and role of Deduction as background, OIS Semantics attempts to provide new scientific foundations for DAI OIS.

4. New foundations

OIS provides characterizations of Systems *Trials of Strength*, *Commitments*, *Cooperation*, and *Negotiation* as a step towards providing scientific foundations for DAI OIS. OIS Semantics for DAI integrates methods from Sociology [18, 19, 35, 50] with methods from Concurrent Systems Science [25]. The challenge is to provide suitable foundations for *both* disciplines with respect to OIS. This paper provides a snapshot of where we currently stand in the process of developing these foundations.

4.1. Trials of Strength

Any situation in which forces are pulling in different directions constitutes a *trial of strength*. *Trials of Strength* (cf. [35]) are the fundamental units of action in Open Systems. All Trials of Strength are local in the sense that they occur at a particular time and place among local *Participants*.

Below are some mechanisms for processing OIS Trials of Strength, in order of increasing complexity:

- *Arbiter*: An arbiter is an asynchronous gating device which selects one of two input signals. For example, two phone calls to a certain party might be placed concurrently. Arbiters in the telephone switching system decide which one of the two concurrent telephone calls gets through and which gets a busy signal, thus processing the Trial of Strength between the two calls.
- *Serializer*: A serializer is an Actor which processes messages in the order of their arrival. For example, two people sharing a bank account may make concurrent requests to withdraw funds from two different ATMs. A serializer for the accounts will process the withdraw requests in the arrival order thereby processing the Trial of Strength between the two withdraw requests.
- *Guardian*: A guardian is an Actor which accepts requests for a resource and manages the resource according to some procedures and policies. For example, requests to a printer may be managed by a guardian. The policy of the guardian may be to print short letters before long listings. Thus, a Trial of Strength between the print requests sent to the guardian will be processed according to the policies and procedures then in effect for the guardian. Policies for Use of the printer may change, e.g., by changing the policy to give first priority to the jobs for which the customers are waiting, and postpone other jobs to the evening.
- *Open Systems Interconnection* (*OSI*):[3] "OSI is a protocol suite that has the potential to provide both a political and technical solution to world-wide networking."

  "The Internet suite of protocols (commonly called TCP/IP) is the current solution of choice for achieving interoperability between machines and operating systems of different manufacture, networks of different technology, and communities of different administration. For various technical and political reasons, a new protocol suite, based on the OSI model, will join and eventually diplace the Internet protocol suite as the off-the-shelf commodity of choice with which to build open computer networks and user intrastructure in the office, laboratory, and factory floor. The possibilities of OSI are extremely attractive, given the wide range of applications and the far-reaching connectivity and interoperability that it can provide."

  "Work began on OSI in 1978. In 1989 the market is still waiting for OSI's promise. The Internet protocols have provided the user community with many of the technical benefits of Open Systems with few of the political problems. Nevertheless, the days of the Internet suite are numbered—perhaps they are numbered in years, but they *are* numbered. To rephrase a popular witicism about computer languages:

[3] The quotations are taken from [45].

I don't know what the computer-communication protocols of the 90s will consist of, but they will be called OSI."

Large-scale OIS have instances of all these and many more complex mechanisms for processing Trials of Strength that will be discussed below. In more complex cases, the alternatives are usually not static and clear cut, so more general mechanisms are required.

Sometimes a Trial of Strength occurs without manifest conflict. One Participant says, "Let's do it this way", and everybody agrees, so no Conflict is noticed, but there is always the *potential* for Conflict. No one can be certain in advance about the outcome, so any Trial of Strength introduces Indeterminacy.

Trials of Strength are useful in helping to analyze the scope and use of Deduction in OIS. Consider the case of the shared financial account which was presented above. The capability to process Trials of Strength in which multiple Participants concurrently withdraw and deposit funds goes beyond the capabilities of Deduction because the outcome is Indeterminate. Of course a record can be made of what happened, but this record is not the same as a Deduction step produced in advance of the Trail of Strength that can be checked for "correctness". For example a deposit slip sent to the owners of an account with the balance at the time the deposit was credited is such a historical record. On the other hand, producing a correct derivation in a Microtheory is a Trial of Strength! In some cases the Indeterminacy is quite small, but it is never altogether absent. By taking Trials of Strength to be fundamental units of action, OIS Semantics provides a foundation for understanding and implementing Indeterminate systems.

With a characterization of *Trials of Strength* in hand, OIS Semantics has the basis for analyzing larger activities.

4.2. Systems Commitments

Systems Commitments are *In Place* to the extent that the Participants are present and carry out their joint activities.

For example, a utility can have an organizational Commitment to build a new power plant. The utility's Finance department has the role of funding the cost of the plant, while its Engineering department has the role of design and construction. While Finance and Engineering must work closely together to build the plant, the utility has organizational Commitments and authority that go beyond just the individual ones of its departments and members.

Inanimate objects are often Participants in Systems Commitments. For example the Systems Commitments provided by a computerized double entry accounting system involve subsystems which are Participants in maintaining the Commitment even though they are inanimate.

Systems Commitments have the aspects of being *in place*, *providing closure*, and *being robust*. Being *In Place* emphasizes the reality of a joint course of action: that the Participants will indeed carry it out. In the construction project mentioned above, the Finance and Engineering departments are In Place, have done the prerequisite work, and not encumbered with other commitments that will prevent them from carrying out the project. Having *Closure* emphasizes that the systems in which the joint activity occurs is to that extent closed for Participants whose activities depend on it actually taking place. For example the utility has Closure on the financing for the construction to the extent provided by the Commitments of the Finance Department. Being *Robust* emphasizes the Systems Commitments in place for carrying out the joint activity in the face of conflict. The construction project is Robust to the extent that the Commitments involving the Finance Department provide the capability to overcome all kinds of conflicts and problems that can arise in funding the construction. For example, Finance can have access to funds that provide a large cushion in case the construction project turns out to cost more than expected.

Systems Commitments are said to be *Conflicting* if they give rise to a Trial of Strength which results in one of them not being kept. For example, the Commitment of a utility to operate a nuclear power plant can come into conflict with the Commitment of an environmental group to shut it down. These two Commitments are incompatible, and cannot both be kept. Conflict is a fundamental aspect of large-scale Open Systems for a variety of reasons.

Resources are finite and limited; choices must be made about how to use them. There are several kinds of resources: money, space/time/material, mechanism/technology, and sentiment. Money and space/time/material are self-explanatory. Mechanism/technology is anything that transforms the world: for example, a nuclear power plant transforms radioactive material into electricity. Sentiment deals with how various Participants feel about each other: goodwill, reputation, obligation, etc. For example, when a public utility says that its power plant is safe, it is staking part of its reputation on that statement. Also, when a utility asks for leniency on an issue from a regulatory board, it is putting to use some of its goodwill for the utility, which means that it is inhibited in its freedom later on.

The past is really gone and the future is never here. Both planning for the future and reflecting upon past experience are activities that take place in the present. Planning activities can create Commitments by allocating resources in one way instead of another. Creating financial records generates Commitments. When a utility creates an annual report, it makes a statement which says how much money it earned that year. Publishing the report creates Commitments. If the regulators investigate, the utility may have to substantiate its claim that it really did earn that much during the year.

4.3. Deduction as Systems Commitments

Once again consider the example presented above concerning the Derivation that the power plant is safe because the operators have been trained. The

Derivation can be expanded and presented as part of the decision process and this presentation can even influence the outcome. Deduction is concerned with the *logical* structure of the Derivations of a Microtheory. However, by focusing only on the logical relationships, it fails to address the large issues of the roles Derivations have in the licensing process. Deduction alone is inadequate to process Trials of Strength because the processes which actually produce the outcomes are *necessarily* left out. Deduction requires that the procedure for checking the correctness of Derivations in a Microtheory must be specified in advance of the Trials of Strength in which it is to be applied. Deduction cannot infer the outcome of these Trials of Strength because of the Indeterminacy inherent in them. The portability and context independence that make Deduction such a powerful tool for information systems, prohibits the use of Deduction to produce the outcomes of Trials of Strength. Thus, the very characteristics of a Microtheories that give them their great power turn out to also be their greatest limitations!

Of course Derivations can appear in a transcript of the hearings that were held concerning whether or not to grant an operating license for the power plant. But this transcript is not the same as a Derivation in a Microtheory produced in advance of the hearings. On the other hand, activities for producing, presenting, and processing Derivations in a Microtheory are Systems Commitments. In fact these Commitments embody the procedures for presenting and checking the correctness of Derivations in a Microtheory. Without these Commitments there would be *no* Microtheories!

If systems are continually potentially involved in Trials of Strength over conflicting Commitments, how do they every get anything accomplished? Won't bringing negotiation to human–telecomputer systems create even worse messes than in human systems? OIS Semantics helps analyze how Cooperation helps "grease the wheels" in large-scale projects.

4.4. Cooperation

Cooperation is the process by which Participants have mutually dependent roles in Systems Commitments. For example, both Finance and Engineering have important roles in building a new power plant. Finance has the role of providing the funds to build the plant, and Engineering has the role of constructing the plant. Finance relies on Engineering's role to build the plant on schedule in order to have credibility in the financial marketplace to raise funds—so the role of Finance supports the role Engineering. In a similar fashion, Engineering relies on Finance's ability to provide the money to pay the construction cost as it comes due so that construction can continue. So Engineering and Financing have mutually dependent roles which provide the basis for their cooperation.

Another example deals with a customer and vendor. The vendor generates a quotation for the product P representing that it will supply the product. The utility generates a purchase order for product *P* representing that it will pay for the product. The customer's role to pay for the product is dependent on the vendor's role to furnish the product as represented by its quotation. The vendor's role to ship the product is dependent on the customer's role to pay for the product—as represented by the purchase order. Thus the quotation and purchase order formalize the cooperation between customer and vendor.

This process of developing mutually dependent roles in commitments—cooperation—is of fundamental importance.

4.5. Representational Activity in OIS

OIS Semantics provides an account of the meaning of *Representational Activity* (i.e., conveying information about System Commitments that is accomplished using digital communications). Representational Activities entail changes in Systems Commitments, and that change is the *Meaning* of the activities.

This is an open-world characterization of meaning—as opposed to previous, closed-world attempts based on possible worlds in which the meaning of a set of sentences is defined to be the set of all possible worlds that satisfy the meaning conditions. In logical semantics, representation is the mapping between a sentence proposition and specified meaning conditions. Meaning is built on and grows out of representation. Two Participants agree about the meaning of a sentence when they agree about the meaning conditions.

An important difference between classical Deductive semantics and OIS is conveyed by the following slogan:

No Representation without communication!

The Meanings of Representational Activities are localized: they begin at particular times and places and then can propagate to wider contexts.

Whether or not particular Systems Commitments will be kept is indeterminate because they are composed of Trials of Strength. It follows that Participant Representational Activities will in general conflict because prior ones do not provide guarantee of absence of conflict with future ones. Moreover, an increase in the difference in space-time and Participants between such activities will in general increase the likelihood of conflict because of the accumulated increase of Indeterminacy. Therefore, in general, Representational Activities will not be the consequences of any Derivational System. Consequently, in general, it is not possible to Deductively determine what underlying factors are the sources of Participants conflicting Representational Activities.

Next, OIS Semantics turns to the question of how Systems Commitments, Representational Activities, Cooperation, and Robustness can be scaled. Perhaps not too surprisingly, it turns out that *negotiation* plays a central role.

4.6. *Negotiation*

Negotiation is a Trial of Strength that proceeds by Participants (who often are representatives of various systems with a stake in the issues under negotiation) participating by communicating Inscriptions held in common. For example, a debate between proponents and opponents of licensing the Diablo Canyon nuclear power plant constituted part of a negotiation. However, the special vibration stress tests that were performed on Diablo Canyon power plant components were not part of a negotiation because they were not carried out by communicating Inscriptions. Negotiation is *scalable* in that it takes place among *representatives* of other organizations which can themselves be large-scale.

An organizational Commitment of a utility to construct a nuclear power plant can lead to giving its Finance and Engineering departments more specialized Subcommitments. Engineering has the Subcommitment to build the plant and Finance has the Subcommitment to raise the money for construction, Negotiation gives both Participants an opportunity to negotiate how the utility can construct the plant in the face of unanticipated Conflict.

4.6.1. *What happens during a negotiation*

During a negotiation, the Participants engage in Representational Activities that change Systems Commitments. In this way, the various Participants can arrive at new mutual Systems Commitments.

4.6.2. *Microtheories in negotiations*

Microtheories play an important role in negotiations because they can be used as calculation tools to provide support for Commitments. For example, a utility's Finance and Engineering departments might each have a different spreadsheet model of the utility's financial condition with respect to the costs of a new plant, and can bring their Microtheories to the negotiation. Their respective conclusions about the cost of construction might be contradictory. Comparing their Microtheories can help to determine what some of the underlying conflicts might be about. They might discover that Finance claims that construction costs are greater than what Engineering reports because certain indirect costs should be included. On the other hand Engineering claims that these indirect costs are negligible because they are covered by other projects. Derivations of a Microtheory can be brought to bear as supporting arguments in the negotiation. In general, however, there will be many Microtheories including some new ones created on the spot when the cost discrepancy is noted. Microtheories are useful tools in negotiation. Having good Microtheories facilitates negotiation, but in general does not determine the outcome.

Many of the Microtheories embody aspects of various Systems Commitments. For example a spreadsheet Microtheory derived from the tax code can be used to deduce the tax consequences of differing proposals, and the Participant holding this Microtheory can claim the IRS as an ally (i.e., claiming that the IRS will support the conclusions drawn).

4.6.3. Outcomes of negotiation

Many kinds of outcomes are possible, but the following three often occur:

- A *resolution* which results in new Commitments.
- A *deadlock* in which the Participants at this particular negotiation cannot reach an agreement. Quite often as a result of deadlock, another negotiation is held with different representatives, and on a different issue: namely, the fact that the other negotiation deadlocked. "Those guys didn't work it out, what are we going to do about it?"
- An *appeal*. Some of the representatives might be unhappy about the outcome and appeal to other Participants—which might set up another negotiation to deal with the issue of what to do about the outcome of the previous negotiation.

In some cases, a negotiation ends when one Participant runs out of the resources needed to continue. In other cases, the process explicitly provides a backup procedure in the sense that it leaves the conflict potentially resumable, but ends the current negotiation. An example of this would be a state that is determined to oppose a public utility in its attempt to operate a nuclear powerplant. The state can oppose the utility at every stage of its attempt to get an operating license. Suppose that at each stage the negotiation is broken off when the Nuclear Regulatory Commission decides in favor of the utility. After each hearing the resources committed to the negotiation are allowed to go their own way, with the intention that a whole new negotiation might be convened at another time. Finally just before the nuclear power plant goes into operation, the state might "win" the negotiation by offering to compensate the utility for what it would earn by operating the nuclear plant *provided* that it agrees to sell the plant to the state for $1!

4.6.4. Negotiations create Commitments

Negotiations are important, even if no conflict emerges, because they create Systems Commitments that go beyond the individual commitments of the Participants involved. Negotiations always have multiple possible outcomes. Late-arriving information can cause Participants to change course in the middle of a negotiation. Actions are taken during negotiations which create new Systems Commitments. A negotiation might seem rather trivial because agreement is reached tacitly, but the outcomes are important Systems Commitments.

The significance of negotiations lies in their outcomes and the way those outcomes affect other Commitments. For example a nation will incrementally develop an electric power industry—and that industry will influence energy costs, pollution levels, generating capacity, etc. In the case of a utility constructing a nuclear power plant with two reactors, Engineering and Finance can have a dispute as to whether to construct both reactors concurrently, as opposed to finishing one before starting the next. Engineering advocates building both at once because it can overlap similar activities to bring down the cost. Finance advocates building them sequentially because the financial burden and risk is less. The dispute between Finance and Engineering will have an outcome in terms of the utility's profitability.

4.6.5. Negotiation is creative

Negotiation is intrinsically creative. Often, the outcome is not as predicted, or is unintended by Participants, or may even be unwanted by some Participants. On the other hand, an outcome may turn out to be better than expected. Even when a negotiation does not break new ground and the outcome is one of those initially sought by one or more Participants, the process used to reach that outcome is fundamentally creative in the sense that it creates new Systems Commitments.

As we have seen, Trials of Strength embody indeterminacy (because no Participant can be certain what the outcome will be). Trials of Strength are the fundamental unit of activity that we want to understand and explore. The actual unfolding of a Trial of Strength is a unique performance, so strictly speaking, a Trial of Strength can never be repeated. A similar one could be staged at a different place and time, but each performance is unique.

This cycle of undertaking Negotiations which create new Commitments, some of which conflict with other Commitments and thus lead to further Negotiations is the way the world works.

4.6.6. Rationales for Commitments

Rationales are Representational Activities for justifying Commitments. Sometimes they are created during negotiation processes. Often new Rationales are developed after the Commitments they justify. Rationales can be categorized in several ways. For in negotiation between Finance and Engineering about which kind of plant to build, rationales supporting the outcome are:

- *Predicted beneficial results*: A utility justifies the development of a new plant: "Nuclear power will cost less than burning fossil fuel."
- *Policies guiding conduct*: The management of a utility makes a policy: "We follow the regulations of the state public utility board in deciding what kind of plant to build."
- *Reasons tied to specific institutional roles or processes*: A utility sells a complete, ready to go, nuclear power plant for $1 to the state government

(which plans to demolish it) with the justification that the state has agreed to compensate the utility in other ways.

- *Precedent*: It is traditional to run diagnostics for the nuclear power plant on Monday morning.

Precedent may seem like a weak rationale. However, deciding according to precedent in the absence of strong alternatives has the consequences of predictability and stability. In the absence of strong alternatives, using precedent is usually less costly than constant redoing a decision process.

4.6.7. Negotiation and Deduction

Several different kinds of Microtheories are possible. One is to include all the *ifs*, *ands*, *buts* and *wherefores* that one can imagine. This creates cumbersome Microtheories that attempt to cover all possible special circumstances. For example, "If the utility uses more than 25% of its income for debt payment, *and if furthermore* it does not have lots of liquid assets, *and if furthermore* . . . , then the utility should not take on more debt."

Another possibility is to use Microtheories with simple rules and let it unfold in the ongoing negotiation whether any exceptions apply. So the Comptroller says: "If construction is delayed, then the utility will spend much more than 25% of its income for debt, so we shouldn't adopt the construction plan." And the other Participant replies, "Yes, but—Engineering has a good record for completing construction projects on schedule close to its estimated cost. Even though Engineering is building a new kind of plant which can burn either coal or gas, it is not very different from what it has built before." Having simple Microtheories that are parsimonious, easily understood, and clear in their causality is often better than having ones which try to stipulate in advance all of the conditions which govern the applicability of every rule.

Most organizations have built-in checks and balances which more or less deliberately generate the need to address conflicting Commitments by giving its Participants roles in Commitments that are commonly in conflict. For example in constructing a nuclear power plant, the Safety department has the role of insuring safety while the Project Expediter has the role of minimizing construction time. The general policies as well as the outcomes of particular Trials of Strength can be Negotiated by representatives of the Expediter, Safety Department, and other Participants.

5. Using the new foundations

Since OIS Semantics aims to provide an integrated foundation for Sociology and Concurrent Systems Science, it inherits methods from both disciplines. The question naturally arises whether it has any methods which go beyond those which it inherits. Part of this endeavor is attempting to use the foundations that we have developed so far as a test of their generality and precision.

5.1. Architecture for OIS

The central question for accomplishing large-scale projects is:

How to organize the work?

Scalability, Robustness, and Manageability are issues that must be addressed by any architecture for large-scale OIS. OIS Semantics calls for the development of an *architectural framework* which lays out the structure and functionality that address the needs of large-scale OIS DAI systems. Such an architecture should be *general-purpose* to address the requirements of the vast majority of future large-scale OIS applications and *ultraconcurrent* to permit implementations to take advantage of all the concurrency available in ultraconcurrent applications—i.e., the architectural framework should not limit the potential concurrency.

The Message Passing Semantics Group [25] is developing an architecture that specifically addresses the issues that arise in the development of OIS Semantics. The architecture provides for ORGs ("Organizations of Restricted Generality") that are composable, programming-language-independent units for building scalable, robust, manageable ultraconcurrent applications. OIS Semantics leads to the conclusion that ORGs must provide facilities to support the following requirements:

- *Operations requirements*: Effective applications require facilities providing efficient use of processors, communications and storage resources, as well as transportation (migration) and garbage collection built on these facilities.
- *Liaison requirements*: Modularizing tasks and mediating external influences require facilities for creating, maintaining, and evolving communications interfaces.
- *Record-keeping requirements*: Keeping track of work accomplished and resources used in large-scale work requires facilities to record when, where, how, and by whom work is accomplished.
- *Management requirements*: Accountability for the behavior of the ORG. It sets the policies and procedures for the ORG, controlling how its work is organized, divided up, and performed, and how resources are used.

The basic idea is that while Actors provide primitives for building concurrent, distributed, reconfigurable open information systems, ORGs provide the modularity and organizational facilities to *manage the complexity* of constructing and managing large-scale OIS for DAI. Our hypothesis is that by organizing large-scale systems into composable units, each of which provides support for operations, membership liaison, accounting, and management, we will be able to construct large-scale systems which are more *scalable*, *robust*, and *manageable*.

5.2. Controlling bureaucracy

OIS has the potential to help control bureaucratic behavior such as:

- the rigid application of rules;
- the arbitrary application of authority.

5.3. Mathematical foundations

We are still a considerable distance from being able to accomplish the task of providing adequate foundations for Sociology and Concurrent Systems Science of OIS. In fact our goal is to develop *mathematical* foundations that are suitable to the methods of both disciplines building on previously developed Actor Semantics [3, 25]. Ultimately, the foundations need to be represented in mathematical language because this is the most precise language that we have.

6. Conclusions

The new discipline of Open Information Systems Semantics provides foundations for Distributed Artificial Intelligence that are different from the foundations of classical Artificial Intelligence in several aspects:

- In OIS Semantics, the primary (nonnumerical) indicators are *Robustness* (Activities to keep commitments in the face of conflict) and *Scalability* (Activities to increase the scale of commitments). OIS Semantics is grounded in the information systems of large-scale projects. Classical AI is grounded in intelligent agents and robots.
- In OIS Semantics the *Meaning* of Representational Activities are the resulting changes in Activities. Without communication there is no Representational Activity. In classical Artificial Intelligence, representation is traditionally about the correspondence between a structure in an intelligent agent and a state of affairs in the world.

OIS Semantics for DAI integrates methods from Sociology with methods from Concurrent Systems Science, whereas classical Artificial Intelligence has traditionally turned to neurophysiology, psychology, and cognitive science. OIS Semantics provides increased understanding of important concepts such as systems *Conflicts*, *Joint Activities*, *Representational Activities*, *Robustness*, *Scalability*, *Cooperation*, and *Negotiations*. Also, it provides requirements for architectural foundations for constructing *scalable*, *robust*, *manageable* OIS. Thus, Open Information Systems Semantics provides a powerful foundation for the further development of DAI OIS.

7. Related work

For excellent collections of readings on Distributed Artificial Intelligence (henceforth DAI) and related topics see [9, 16, 28]. The literature of DAI speaks of many important concepts such as *commitment* (Bond [7]), *conflict* (Adler, Davis, Weihmeyer, and Worrest [1]), *negotiation* (Durfee and Lesser [13], Sathi and Fox [46], Sycara [53], Kuwabara and Lesser [34]), *cooperation* (Decker, Durfee and Lesser [11]), *distributed problem solving* (Hayes-Roth, M. Hewett, Washington, R. Hewett and Seiver [21]), *representation* (Gasser, Rouquette, Hill and Lieb [17]), *deduction* (Sycara [53], Kuwabara and Lesser [34]), etc.

Hewitt in [22] re-examined the issue of control structures in Artificial Intelligence. Control structures were previously defined as looking for the best choice in moving from the current global state to the next one. The control structure was supposed to accomplish this either by guiding the production system or by guiding a theorem prover that was attempting to search through the realm of possibilities. This paper pointed out that traditional programming language control structures (such as iteration and recursion) could be analyzed in terms of patterns: stereotypical or stylized patterns of communication among different participants. Instead of looking at the behavior of an *individual* intelligent agent as Newell and Simon did, this paper initiated the idea that communities of people are a primary existence proof and analog for how to extend these ideas.

Kornfeld and Hewitt introduced in [32] several important concepts into the Artificial Intelligence arena, and further developed the ideas Hewitt first discussed in [21]. They used the scientific community as a model for the problem-solving process, and speak generally about how principles and mechanisms of scientific communities might be incorporated into the problem-solving technology of Artificial Intelligence. Several fundamental properties of scientific communities have nice analogs for computing systems that aspire to intelligent behavior. Among these properties are monotonicity, commutativity, concurrency, and pluralism. The paper also introduces the notion of having skeptics as well as proponents of different kinds of ideas, and explains how those kinds of question can be investigated concurrently.

A further development of the work in [32] is given in [31]. Kornfeld here shows that by developing a concurrent process that has critics as well as proponents of ideas, the amount of resources consumed can, in some cases, be vastly reduced. This results in a kind of combinatorial implosion instead of the usual combinatorial explosion where the number of alternatives proliferate indefinitely. Such exponential proliferation of possibilities is typical of backward-chaining reasoning.

The negotiation described here is very primitive in form, and consists of entering absolute objections—a very cut-and-dried situation. We would like to apply this type of process in more relaxed situations where one has less hard knowledge, and the objections aren't guaranteed to be always fatal to what they're objecting to.

Barber shows in [5] how the viewpoint mechanism introduced by Kornfeld and Hewitt in [32] can be used to model changing situations in terms of multiple points of view. It also introduces some of the kinds of mechanisms for dealing with contradictory Microtheories.

A collection of articles which deal with the nature, design, description, implementation, and management of Open Information Systems appears in [28]. The articles are grouped in three major sections. Papers in the first section deal with general issues underlying OIS, studies of computational ecologies, and their similarities with social organizations. Papers in the second section deal with implementation issues of distributed computation, and those in the third section discuss the issues of developing suitable languages and information media for OIS. The papers provide a perspective on market mechanisms for computer systems that supplements the treatment in this paper. This paper treats markets only in a very general way as simple negotiation systems.

Stefik describes in [51] the growth and spread of cultural knowledge: the kinds of things that communities of humans do—and shows how the existence of a technical infrastructure (such as railroads) can greatly facilitate and accelerate cultural change. Stefik portrays active information systems that have the capability of taking action to interact with both its human users and other dynamic information systems.

Alvaredo, Dyer and Flowers show in [4] how arguments can be diagrammed in much the same way that debate contests are often diagrammed by their judges. Such diagramming examines the beliefs, the tree structure of the supporting beliefs, and the way one side can attack the other side's beliefs. (There are really two kinds of important relationships between the two sides: support relationships and attack relationships.) The paper presents an analysis that looks at both the achievement of plans and goals, and the development of editorials that critique other sides, showing how other sides have beliefs that are supporting to the opinion that's being reported. This is quite interesting work in terms of starting to build technology that can do argument analysis, because that's an important component of negotiation.

In [12], Devereux expands on something very similar to the argument units in [4]. Devereux takes the whole of the Lincoln–Douglas debates and attempts to identify both attacking statements between Douglas and Lincoln and supporting links within the individual arguments themselves.

Bond and Gasser analyze in [8] the DVT and Contact Net systems from the standpoint of commitments.

Bond, in [7], discusses the concept of commitment from the Symbolic Interactionist literature, and its potential relation to DAI.

Gibbs, Tsichritzis, Casais, Nierstrasz and Pintado discuss in [20] how to organize and manage object classes to support software sharing, selection, browsing and evolution. Object-oriented development promises important improvements in the development and maintenance of application systems in general, and office systems in particular, but requires that the right combination of mechanisms be available in the language and run-time system, and that advanced tools exist to support software development, reuse and evolution. Our research covers the following topics:

- oriented development based on reuse and evolution,
- information management to support sharing and reuse,
- how to support rapid and flexible construction of applications using a software base,
- language, run-time support and modeling of active objects.

Rein and Ellis have submitted their report [42], for the special issue in the IJMMS on CSCW. It scribes rIBIS, a real-time group hypertext system, which allows a distributed set of users to simultaneously browse and edit multiple views of a hypertext network. At any time, rIBIS users can switch back and forth between tightly coupled and loosely coupled interaction modes. The paper describes the high-level architecture, underlying object classes, and user interface of the rIBIS system. Early use of the rIBIS system by a software system design team suggests that users' acceptance increases as they continue to use the tool. We conclude that rIBIS effectiveness is affected by both people and implementation issues.

Kahn and Miller explore in [29] the properties a programming language needs to have, in order to support large-scale distributed computing in a uniform and transparent manner. A survey of various programming languages is presented from the perspective of their adequacy for open systems programming.

Acknowledgement

First, I wish to acknowledge the aid of Elihu Gerson in repeatedly pulling me out of intellectual quicksand and setting me back on fruitful paths. Also Les Gasser and David Kirsh contributed greatly by making extensive suggestions for reorganizing and refining the content of successive versions.

Distributed Artificial Intelligence is at a much earlier state of development compared with other foundations discussed in this special issue. Basic methods are not established nor is there agreement on issues and problems to be addressed in DAI. In view of these circumstances, Les Gasser and I previewed each other's contributions to this special volume to correct for these idiosyncrasies so that we could concentrate our discussion on larger issues of more central long-term interest. His analysis of issues from Sociology and DAI (of others as well as of his own work) provides a valuable critique of this paper and an important contribution to the foundations of DAI.

Second, I would like to acknowledge Wyn Snow for editorial assistance in removing "mindtraps" from early versions of this paper. Jeff Inman and Carl Manning and other members of the Message Passing Semantics Group made constructive suggestions for improvement in addition to pointing out errors and obscurities.

Third, I wish to acknowledge the help of Bruno Latour, John McCarthy, and Susan Leigh Star for pushing forward in new directions as well as helping to reconceptualize old ones. John McCarthy pointed out a fundamental misconception in my previous treatment of circumscription as well as providing a valuable critique of my approach vis-à-vis the other contributions in this special volume on Foundations of Artificial Intelligence.

Fourth (and perhaps most important), I wish to thank Randy Fenstermacher, Ron Flemming, Sue Gerson, Fanya Montalvo, John Stutz, and other close friends for providing support and helping me to continue to grow.

References

[1] Adler, A.B. Davis, R. Weihmeyer and F.W. Worrest, Conflict resolution strategies for non-hierarchical distributed agents, in: L. Gasser and M.N. Huhns, eds., *Distributed Artificial Intelligence* **2** (Pitman/Morgan Kaufmann, London, 1989) 139–162.

[2] G. Agha, Semantic considerations in the Actor paradigm of concurrent computation, in: *Proceedings NSF/SERC Seminar on Concurrency* (Springer, New York, 1984).

[3] G. Agha, *Actors: A Model of Concurrent Computation in Distributed Systems* (MIT Press, Cambridge, MA, 1986).

[4] S.J. Alvaredo, M.G. Dyer and M. Flowers, Editorial comprehension in OpEd through argument units, in: *Proceedings AAAI-86*, Philadelphia, PA (1986) 250–256.

[5] G.R. Barber, Office semantics, Ph.D. Thesis, Department of EECS, MIT, Cambridge, MA (1982).

[6] H.S. Becker, Notes on the concept of commitment, *Am. J. Sociol.* **66** (1960) 32–40.

[7] A.H. Bond, Commitment: A computational model for organizations of cooperating intelligent agents, in: *Proceedings 1990 Conference on Office Information Systems*, Cambridge, MA (1990).

[8] A.H. Bond and L. Gasser, Organizational analysis of distributed artificial intelligence systems, Tech. Rept. CRI-88-33, Computer Research Institute, University of Southern California, Los Angeles, CA (1988).

[9] A.H. Bond and L. Gasser, eds., *Readings in Distributed Artificial Intelligence* (Morgan Kaufmann, San Mateo, CA, 1988).

[10] W. Clinger, Foundations of Actor semantics, in: C. Hewitt, C. Manning, J. Inman and G. Agha, eds., *Towards Open Information Systems Science* (MIT Press, Cambridge, MA, 1990).

[11] K.S. Decker, E.H. Durfee and V.R. Lesser, Evaluating research in cooperative distributed problem solving.

[12] E.A. Devereux, Processing political debate: a methodology for data production with special application to the Lincoln–Douglas debates, B.S. Thesis, Department of Political Science, MIT, Cambridge, MA (1985).

[13] E.H. Durfee and V.R. Lesser, Negotiating task decomposition and allocation using partial global planning, in: L. Gasser and M.N. Huhns, eds., *Distributed Artificial Intelligence* **2** (Pitman/Morgan Kaufmann, London, 1989).

[14] D.W. Etherington, S. Kraus and D. Perlis, Nonmonotonicity and the scope of reasoning, Personal communication: Draft of November 1, 1989.
[15] E. Fikes, A commitment-based framework for describing informal cooperative work, *Cogn. Sci.* **6** (1982) 331–347.
[16] L. Gasser and M.N. Huhns, eds., *Distributed Artificial Intelligence* **2** (Pitman/Morgan Kaufmann, London, 1989) 229–244.
[17] L. Gasser, N.F. Rouquette, R.W. Hill and J. Lieb, Representing and using organizational knowledge in DAI systems, in: L. Gasser and M.N. Huhns, eds., *Distributed Artificial Intelligence* **2** (Pitman/Morgan Kaufmann, London, 1989) 55–78.
[18] E.M. Gerson, On the quality of life, *Am. Sociol. Rev.* **41** (1976) 793–806.
[19] E.M. Gerson and S.L. Star, Analyzing due process in the workplace, *ACM Trans. Off. Inform. Syst.* **4** (1986) 257–270.
[20] S. Gibbs, A.D. Tsichritzis, A.E. Casais, A.O. Nierstrasz and A.X. Pintado, Class management in software information systems, *Commun. ACM* (to appear).
[21] B. Hayes-Roth, M. Hewett, R. Washington, R. Hewett and A. Seiver, in: L. Gasser and M.N. Huhns, eds., *Distributed Artificial Intelligence* **2** (Pitman/Morgan Kaufmann, London, 1989) 385–412.
[22] C. Hewitt, Viewing control structures as patterns of passing messages, *Artif. Intell.* **8** (1977) 323–364.
[23] C. Hewitt, The challenge of open systems, *Byte* **10** (1985) 223–242.
[24] C. Hewitt, Organizations of restricted generality, in: *Proceedings 1989 IFIP Congress*, San Francisco, CA (1989).
[25] C. Hewitt, C. Manning, J. Inman and G. Agha, eds., *Towards Open Information Systems Science* (MIT Press, Cambridge, MA, 1990).
[26] C. Hewitt and R. Atkinson, Specification and proof techniques for serializers, *IEEE Trans. Softw. Eng.* **5** (1979) 10–23.
[27] C. Hewitt and H. Baker, Laws for communicating parallel processes, in: *Proceedings 1977 IFIP Congress* (1977) 987–992.
[28] B.A. Huberman, ed., *The Ecology of Computation* (North-Holland, Amsterdam, 1988).
[29] K.M. Kahn and M.S. Miller, Language design and open systems, in: B.A. Huberman, ed., *The Ecology of Computation* (North-Holland, Amsterdam, 1988).
[30] M.J. Katz and J.S. Rosenschein, Plans for multiple agents, in: L. Gasser and M.N. Huhns, eds., *Distributed Artificial Intelligence* **2** (Pitman/Morgan Kaufmann, London, 1989) 197–228.
[31] W.A. Kornfeld, Concepts in parallel problem solving, Ph.D. Thesis, Department of EECS, MIT, Cambridge, MA (1982).
[32] W.A. Kornfeld and C. Hewitt, The scientific community metaphor, *IEEE Trans. Syst. Man Cybern.* **11** (1981) 24–33.
[33] R.A. Kowalski, Logic programming, in: *Proceedings 1983 IFIP Congress* (1983).
[34] K. Kuwabara and V.R. Lesser, Extended protocol for multistage negotiations, in: L. Gasser and M.N. Huhns, eds., *Distributed Artificial Intelligence* **2** (Pitman/Morgan Kaufmann, London, 1989) 129–162.
[35] B. Latour, *Science in Action* (Harvard University Press, Cambridge, MA, 1987).
[36] C. Manning, Introduction to programming actors in Acore, in: C. Hewitt, C. Manning, J. Inman and G. Agha, eds., *Towards Open Information Systems Science* (MIT Press, Cambridge, MA, 1990).
[37] J. McCarthy, Circumscription: a form of non-monotonic reasoning, *Artif. Intell.* **13** (1980) 27–39.
[38] J. McCarthy, Applications of circumscription to formalizing common-sense knowledge, *Artif. Intell.* **28** (1986) 89–118.
[39] M. Minsky, *The Society of Mind* (Simon and Schuster, New York, 1985).
[40] R.C. Moore, Semantical considerations on nonmonotonic logic, *Artif. Intell.* **25** (1985) 75–94.
[41] N.J. Nilsson, Logic and artificial intelligence, *Artif. Intell.* **47** (1991) 31–56, this volume.
[42] G.L. Rein and C.A. Ellis, rIBIS: A real-time group hypertext system, Rept. STP-095-90, MCC Software Technology Program, Austin, TX (1990).
[43] R. Reiter, A logic for default reasoning, *Artif. Intell.* **13** (1980) 81–132.
[44] R. Reiter, A logic for default reasoning, *J. ACM* **27** (1988) 235–249.

[45] M.T. Rose, *The Open Book: A Practical Perspective on OSI* (Prentice Hall, Englewood Cliffs, NJ, 1990).
[46] A. Sathi and M.S. Fox, Constraint-directed negotiation of resource reallocations, in: L. Gasser and M.N. Huhns, eds., *Distributed Artificial Intelligence* **2** (Pitman/Morgan Kaufmann, London, 1989) 163–194.
[47] E. Shapiro, A subset of Concurrent Prolog and its interpreter, in: *Concurrent Prolog: Collected Papers* (MIT Press, Cambridge, MA, 1987) 27–83.
[48] R. Smith and R. Davis, Frameworks for cooperation in distributed problem solving, *IEEE Trans. Syst. Man Cybern.* **11** (1981) 61–70.
[49] S.L. Star, Simplification in scientific work: an example from neuroscience research, *Social Stud. Sci.* **13** (1983) 205–228.
[50] S.L. Star, The structure of ill-structured solutions: boundary objects and heterogeneous distributed problem solving, in: L. Gasser and M.N. Huhns, eds., *Distributed Artificial Intelligence* **2** (Pitman/Morgan Kaufmann, London, 1989) 37–54.
[51] M.J. Stefik, The next knowledge medium, *AI Mag.* **7** (1) (1986) 34–46.
[52] A. Strauss, *Negotiations* (Jossey-Bass, San Francisco, CA, 1978).
[53] K.P. Sycara, Multiagent compromise via negotiation, in: L. Gasser and M.N. Huhns, eds., *Distributed Artificial Intelligence* **2** (Pitman/Morgan Kaufmann, London, 1989) 119–138.
[54] E. Werner, Cooperating agents: a unified theory of communication and social structure in: L. Gasser and M.N. Huhns, eds., *Distributed Artificial Intelligence* **2** (Pitman/Morgan Kaufmann, London, 1989) 3–36.
[55] T. Winograd and F. Flores, *Understanding Computers and Cognition* (Addison-Wesley, Reading, MA, 1987).
[56] J. Palmucci and C. Hewitt, Organization of large-scale Open Information Systems, in: C. Hewitt, C. Manning, J. Inman and G. Agha, eds., *Towards Open Information Systems Science* (MIT Press, Cambridge, MA, 1990).

Note added in proof

After the Commentary which follows this paper was completed, I have come to appreciate that loaded expressions like "Systems Commitments" and "Trials of Strength" are undesirable for several reasons. One reason is that those who adhere to more loaded terminology will need to confront the issue of how the more loaded terminology goes beyond plain usage. In future publications (e.g. [25]) these expressions are being replaced as follows:

Systems Commitments → (Joint) Activities
Trials of Strength → Conflicts

The technical meaning of plain usage such as "Joint Activities" and "Conflicts" is going to be shaped by future development of Mathematics and Technology which provides context for their use.

I have retained the use of "Systems Commitments" and "Trials of Strength" throughout this paper, however, in order to preserve the original context for the Commentary which follows this paper.

Artificial Intelligence 47 (1991) 107–138
Elsevier

Social conceptions of knowledge and action: DAI foundations and open systems semantics

Les Gasser

Distributed Artificial Intelligence Group, Computer Science Department, University of Southern California, Los Angeles, CA 90089-0782, USA

Received January 1990
Revised July 1990

Abstract

Gasser, L., Social concepts of knowledge and action: DAI foundations and open systems semantics, Artificial Intelligence 47 (1991) 107–138.

This article discusses foundations for Distributed Artificial Intelligence (DAI), with a particular critical analysis of Hewitt's *Open Information Systems Semantics* (OISS). The article sets out to do five things:

- It presents a brief overview of current DAI research including motivations and concepts, and discusses some of the basic problems in DAI.
- It introduces several principles that underly a fundamentally multi-agent (i.e., *social*) conception of action and knowledge for DAI research. These principles are introduced to provide definitions, to delimit the discussion of OISS and as background against which to assess its contributions.
- It analyzes the main points of OISS in relation to these principles.
- It shows how attention to these principles can strengthen OISS approach to foundations for DAI.
- It traces some of the implications of this synthesis for theorizing and system-building in AI.

The OISS approach productively challenges some conceptions of knowledge, reasoning, and action in classical AI research. However, it sometimes ignores the sophistication and richness of contemporary DAI research. Several of the key concepts of OISS are not clearly enough defined or operationalized, and the article points out several ways to strengthen the OISS approach.

1. Introduction

All real systems are distributed
F. Hayes-Roth [20]

Artificial intelligence research is fundamentally concerned with the intelligent behavior of machines. In attempting to create machines with some degree

3. Social conceptions of knowledge and action for AI and DAI

DAI systems, as they involve multiple agents, are *social* in character; there are properties of DAI systems which will not be derivable or representable solely on the basis of properties of their component agents. We need to begin to think through and articulate the bases of knowledge and action for DAI in the light of their social character. Here, we suggest and briefly discuss several principles that ought to underly the scientific and conceptual foundations for DAI systems from a social perspective. Since theories that support the construction of DAI systems ought to follow these principles, we will use the principles as a framework for analyzing OISS claims.

Principle 1. AI research must set its foundations in ways that treat the existence and interaction of multiple actors as a fundamental category.

Since we observe and actually are building multi-agent systems, we should investigate how to conceive aspects of representation and reasoning as fundamentally grounded in multi-agent systems. This leads directly to a serious research question for AI, namely:

> How can we usefully conceptualize representation, reasoning, problem solving and action, when we begin with multiple participants?

A social perspective on the nature of intelligent behavior is not a new idea. For example, Mead stated [77]

> We are not, in social psychology, building up the behavior of the social group in terms of the behavior of the separate individuals composing it; rather we are starting with a given social whole of complex group activity, into which we analyze (as elements) the behavior of each of the separate individuals composing it. We attempt, that is, to explain the conduct of the individual in terms of the organized conduct of the social group, rather than to account for the organized conduct of the social group in terms of the conduct of the separate individuals belonging to it. For social psychology, the whole (society) is prior to the part (the individual), not the part to the whole; and the part is explained in terms of the whole, not the whole in terms of the parts.

The traditional set of analytical categories and implementation techniques used in AI does not include fundamentally social elements; the focus is on the individual actor as the locus of reasoning and knowledge and the individual proposition as the object of truth and knowing. For example, a number of researchers are studying *commitment*, a basic concept in OISS, as a foundation of many concepts in AI and DAI, including intentions and goals, negotiation, and knowledge [7, 14, 15, 30, 96]. The research literature most often portrays commitment as a kind of rational choice made by an individual actor. Along these lines, Cohen and Levesque [14, 15] have developed a notion of commitment based on what they call a *relativized persistent goal.* Some agent A relativizes its goal g to a predicate q, so that A gives up g only when A believes that either something has satisfied g, or nothing can satisfy g, or $\neg$q. To use one of Cohen and Levesque's examples, when rain is falling, A may reason that it will be committed to the goal of getting an umbrella unless it believes that (1) it has obtained an umbrella, or (2) it cannot get an umbrella, or (3) the rain has stopped and it no longer needs an umbrella. They state that "Persistence involves an agent's *internal* commitment over time to her choices. . . . This is not a *social* commitment; it remains to be seen *if the latter can be built out of the former*" [14, p. 410] (final italics mine).

Symbolic interactionist sociologists, and authors of recent investigations in the sociology of science, have begun to provide some conceptually fruitful, though not presently computational, approaches for understanding knowledge and action in social terms. (See [13] for an illuminating review, and [18, 87] for discussions directly related to AI.) In contrast to Cohen and Levesque, for example, Becker [4] and especially Gerson [41] develop commitment as the overall organization of an agent's participation in many settings simultaneously. For example, imagine that a Los Angeles industrialist takes off in an airplane from Narita airport, bound for California, after formulating preliminary business deals in Tokyo and telephoning her associates in Los Angeles. While flying, she is participating in many settings simultaneously: the activity in the plane, the ongoing business negotiations in Tokyo and in Los Angeles (where people are planning for her arrival and making business judgements while considering her views, even in her absence).[2] Her simultaneous involvement in interlocking courses of action in all of these situations provides the commitment to her arrival in California. Both she and others balance and trade off her involvement in joint courses of action in many different situations. Moreover, whether she makes a choice or not, she is committed to landing in LA because the plane is not in her control. Her commitments in any of these settings *amount to* the interaction of many activities of many agents in many other settings. Since this multi-setting participation occurs *simultaneously* in many places, it can't be located simply to where she physically "is". In other words, the notion of commitment is distributed because the agent of commitment—"she"—is a distributed entity.

This approach rests on a somewhat untraditional idea of what an agent is: in Gerson's formulation, an agent A is a reflexive collection of processes involved in many situations. To varying degrees, the agent—that is, some component

[2] Of course we leave out many, many others—her family, etc.—including some she may not be aware of.

process of the agent—can take on the viewpoint of any participant in those situations. Commitment of A (i.e., continued participation of A) in a course of action in any particular setting is a product of the interactions among its simultaneous participations in many other settings—*whether* A *explicitly "knows" fully about the other settings beforehand or not*. Thus, if A has goals, they can't be effectively "relativized" because the relativizing conditions that would make A's goals contingent can't necessarily be known beforehand (a version of the qualification problem [76]). Moreover, since continued participation is distributed and simultaneous, it isn't based on localized, individual choices and goals.

In the umbrella case, from the social perspective, an infinite variety of circumstances may arise under which A's participation in other settings could change A's participation in the umbrella-getting course of action; at any time, some other agent could act in a way such that A is no longer a participant in that course (in simple cases, A could get hit by a car or unplugged); this presents problems for Cohen and Levesque's notion of commitment. Commitment from the social perspective is grounded in the actions of many agents' activities *taken together*—it is not a matter of individual choice. It is A's actions in relation to those of others (and vice versa) that maintain A's participation in a course of action (e.g., by providing resources, etc.—see below). Commitment in this sense is the outcome of a web of activity, or in OISS terms, it is "systems commitment".

Moreover, this social notion of commitment doesn't rely upon a more-primitive mental concept such as "belief" or "goal" (this is how it unifies the individual and the social). In fact, this notion of commitment cannot be grounded on individual belief or choice, because it is not located "within" the individual. Because of this, it extends in varying degrees to objects as well as people as active participants in settings, and to multiple levels of analysis. For example, for the industrialist to call Los Angeles from a coin-operated telephone, both she and a telephone system must together enter into a course of action that involves consuming coins, providing dial tones, and so on. *They are mutually committed to doing those things in that way to make a phone call*, regardless of whether she or the telephone has any mental state such as a state of belief, or any shared view of the situation. (A self-dialing modem can make phone calls. Does a telephone have a viewpoint to share?). The industrialist's other commitments (e.g., in the business deals) are simultaneously mediated by the actions of the telephone—and of course of the whole telephone network and organizations behind it: waiting time, missed connections, etc. (cf. [75]).

Many other concepts which are basic to AI researchers and AI programs, and typically (in AI) associated with individual actors or problem solvers, are, in sociological terms, reifications, constructed through joint courses of action and *made* stable by webs of commitment [4, 41], or "alliances" [60, 61] among the actors using them. Some examples include concepts such as *problems* [32], *knowledge* [5, 13, 63], *facts* about the world [62], and even technical objects [53]. From this perspective, stable alliances or systems of commitment even produce the demarcation and ongoing existence of individual agents as units of knowledge and interaction. In the case of people, for example, alliances among cells, chemical processes, and the environment at the lowest levels and among social actors at the more macro levels (e.g., organizations such as hospitals) yield stable and ongoing individuals.[3] In a computational intelligent agent, such a web includes (at least) the structure of the computing system and all that keeps it running "properly", including the program, the evolving content of its data stuctures (e.g., a set of represented propositional beliefs), the language processor, the hardware and the resources and activity (electricity, maintenance, and so on) that keep it active over time (cf. [56]). This is as true of a connectionist system as of a symbolic one. Perhaps the nature of this idea of alliances, and the conception of both agents and knowledge as stable systems of alliance, are easier to see if we examine what it takes to remove an agent's influence in a situation (e.g., by disabling it or discrediting its knowledge). What alliances must be broken? Actually it can be fairly simple—unplug the machine; or change the operational semantics of its program e.g., by changing the operating system, language processor, or hardware [84]; or change the behavior of another agent upon which it critically relies; or change the definition of a set of possible worlds which establishes the semantics of a proposition in its belief set.

Treating problems, knowledge, and facts as webs of commitment is a fundamentally non-local, distributed conception. Like conventional AI conceptions, such distributed conceptions account for change in knowledge and world states. They have the additional advantage of accounting for the stability and robustness of facts or agents or procedures in the face of challenges posed by alternative viewpoints or discrediting activities (sometimes known as "brittleness"), and for what OISS calls the indeterminate nature of systems.

Certain existing approaches to overcoming brittleness are theoretically problematic. For example, TMS/ATMS systems and belief networks, which do locate belief in a network of supporting evidence, rely on unwinding of assumptions and the posing of incommensurate alternative worlds or contexts—but they cannot account for how to resolve inconsistency at the assumption levels; these are battles that agents resolve outside the system. They rely on the option of keeping alternatives separate, until some unifying viewpoint or discriminating facts appear from some external source. They also

[3] The issue is the nature of the individual as the locus of interaction and knowledge. Bentley [6] and Dewey [24] lay out the problems well; Buss [10] and Wimsatt [95] discuss evolutionary changes in biological units of selection from cells to higher-order aggregates and MacFarlane [71] discusses transformations of units of knowledge, action, and ownership from the social to the individual in English history.

don't allow for *n*th-order flexibility or robustness—e.g. in the choice of world representations, proof theories, etc., and they are subject to deductive indeterminacy, as the OISS proposal points out.

Principle 2. DAI theory and practice must address the basic tension between the local, situated, and pragmatic character of knowledge and action, and the ways in which knowledge and action necessarily implicate multiple contexts.

The notion that the meaning of a message is the response it generates in the system that receives it was introduced by Mead (see, e.g., [77, Chapter 11]) and was later used independently in the context of computing by Hewitt [45]. Using this conceptualization, a message that provokes no response has no meaning, and each message with impact has a *specific* meaning, played out as a set of specific response behaviors. In an asynchronous and open distributed system, no message can be guaranteed to lead to the same set of behaviors twice. Thus knowledge in an open system always means something local and situated. (See also [3, 63, 91].) As to the implications for action, actors take actions (including reasoning and planning actions) at specific times and places with specific (but of course possibly selective, incomplete, faulty, etc.) knowledge brought to bear. In a sense *action is a particular commitment to doing things a particular way*—a way conditional upon the actor's particular knowledge in and of the situation of the action (cf. [78]).

It seems, however, that some sort of generalization across situations is what makes knowledge useful and what ultimately makes knowledge knowledge. General knowledge makes possible *action-at-a-distance*:[4] reasoning about and taking control over activity located at some other place in space or time such as the future, another network site, or over actions taken by another agent—in other words, acting in a distributed fashion. There is, then, a basic tension between a local, "situated" conception of knowledge and action, and the non-local conception of action-at-a-distance. It appears that the ability to generalize across situations and the utility of doing so makes knowledge inherently *non*-local. The knowledge is derived from and can apply in many situations.

Still, any general knowledge, to be useful, has to *be applied* in a local setting, hence *made local* again. Generalization leads to transportability across contexts, and thus helps in achieving action-at-a-distance, but does not obviate the need for reintegration into a local context of use. A production rule with variables exemplifies transportability. Variables make the rule applicable in any setting where they can be bound. Such a rule is useless with variables unbound;[5] binding variables specializes the rule into a specific *rule instantia-*

[4] In general, "distance" here refers to some axis of distribution. Bond [8] discusses numerous axes of distribution in this sense, including space, time, and semantics.

[5] Except of course when used itself as an object of discourse; it then becomes a localized and concrete representation employed in a higher-order (meta) process.

tion, i.e. makes it local and specific again. Moreover, the localization process itself (e.g., the binding of variables) is another purely local and situated process.

Principle 3. Representation and reasoning approaches used in DAI must (1) assume that multiple representations are recursively possible at any level of analysis or action, (2) assume that actors will employ multiple representations individually and collectively, and (3) provide mechanisms for reasoning among multiple representations.

In order to understand fully the implications of the OISS analysis on the limits of deduction, we need to understand the character of what we usually view as "shared" knowledge. This is important, for example, in understanding the nature of contradiction, a concept crucial to several OISS arguments. Shared knowledge, as I think we normally conceive it,[6] is impossible; nonetheless, we have ways of pragmatically aligning our activities and acting *as though* we share knowledge (see, e.g., [91]). The difference becomes an issue precisely when conflict arises, and appeals to shared knowledge are inadequate both to explain the nature of and to resolve conflicts. Approaches to conflict that rely on logical formulations necessarily require a common semantics even to decide that conflict exists. Conflict means inconsistency and inconsistency is impossible without a common model. In an open DAI system without a priori assumptions of globality, we need another definition of conflict. The choices we have come down to conflict in action and more specifically conflict in the consumption of resources, not just conflict in representations.

Different actors necessarily have different sets of commitments, by virtue of their different histories, the different resources they use, different settings they participate in, and so on. Multiple perspectives are a fundamental feature of any multi-agent system, simply by virtue of differing commitment histories and local circumstances. The interesting phenomenon, then, would be any apparent *commonality of perspectives* or mutually aligned, mutually supportive commitments—how would they get and stay that way [35]?

If multiple perspectives are basic, disparities in perspectives are an issue. Elsewhere, we have posed this issue as a basic problem for DAI, because of its theoretical consequence and its ubiquity in DAI research [8, 37]. Moreover, multiplicity of perspectives raises the issue of the impossibility of global conceptions. As Star points out in her study of the development of a localization theory of the brain by a community of scientists [88, p. 193]:[7]

> The momentum of the theory, professional developments, turf battles between specialists and general practitioners, and the rise of

[6] I.e., as several agents knowing the *same fact* interpreted the *same way*—what would this mean, and how would the agents ever be able to verify it? Cf. Principle 5.

[7] For an analysis of multiple perspectives over time, as well as over agents, see also Lakatos' study of the reconstruction of mathematical theorems in [59].

> specialty hospitals with their separate domains of expertise made the theory impossible to comprehend from any single point.

In effect, what the scientists involved talked about as "a theory" was in fact multiple theories by virtue of the multiple perspectives brought to the activity of expressing and understanding it.

Principle 4. DAI theory and practice must account for resource-limited activity.

All resources are limited, and real agents act in finite circumstances. Resources used by a collection of agents can be arranged and allocated in numerous ways, but the resources used to allocate resources are also limited, and in the end agents do take particular actions. "Optimal" resource allocations are in general not possible, for at least four reasons: (1) computing an optimal allocation might require infinite resources, (2) allocation actions must be taken opportunistically in a dynamic world, (3) there is no limit to how completely an allocation decision situation can be specified, and (4) agents might not agree on criteria for optimality. Moreover, no agent supplies all of its own resources. Resource allocations are the *product* of interactions of many agents, and at the same time resources serve as a key *channel* of interaction among agents—as one agent uses up a resource, others' options are restricted. Thus a complete DAI theory must integrate a treatment of limited resources with a treatment of joint actions of multiple agents.

Principle 5. DAI theory and practice must provide accounts of and mechanisms for handling the three key problems of joint qualification, representation incommensurability and failure indeterminacy.

The impossibility of fully specifying the assumptions behind a characterization of any situation, has been termed the *qualification problem* by McCarthy [76]. Given this, DAI theories must account for how agents can come to have and to act upon *mutually compatible* sets of assumptions (e.g., common defaults) in the face of partial descriptions and no global semantics. That is, how can agents leave compatible aspects of a situation unquestioned or unsupported—what accounts for how they can "stay out of each others' way" when they do? No agent can fully describe its assumptions to another, yet they must mutually take some things for granted to act jointly without conflict (see, e.g., [91]). This can be called the *joint qualification problem*, and a full DAI theory must account for it.

In the face of the assumption incompleteness, no agent can fully specify the semantics of its representations. If this is so, how are two agents to determine if they have the basis for joint action, or if they are in conflict? This can be called the problem of *representational incommensurability*. Bond and Gasser [8] discussed three types of disparity among agents' knowledge: incompleteness, inconsistency, and incompatibility. The first two are conventionally defined, and incompatibility referred to agents' representing the same situation with different kinds of descriptions. With incompatibility disparity, consistency could not be assessed. Incommensurability is a still deeper problem. Two agents in principle cannot have *identical* representations—any pair of similar representations can always be differentiated by more complete description. So on what basis can agents be sure that they either (1) have common (e.g., Tarskian or possible worlds) semantics (since the definition of a model or possible worlds would have to be global), or (2) common semantics based on our earlier theory of meaning as response of the system (because response can only be assessed from some particular perspective)?

Finally, when there has been some disparity at some level between two agents with different representations of the same situation, and this conflict leads to a failure of action, how are they to determine where the cause of the failure lies? For example, both Agre and Gasser have discussed the nature of agents' behavioral *routines* (Agre in the single-agent case [2], and Gasser for organized activity [35]). Suppose an agent A has a theory $\mathcal{T}$ of the routine behavior of another agent B. For example, $\mathcal{T}$ might be:

(1) If I send B a task announcement then B will reply with a bid request

Since this is a theory of a routine, it is necessarily an idealization—no routine behavior is actually carried out in precisely the same way twice [35]. Now suppose that to reason about B's behavior in a particular situation s, A qualifies or specializes $\mathcal{T}$ with some additional observations $\mathcal{I}$. (Since $\mathcal{T}$ is in idealization, $\mathcal{I}$ is necessary to make it fit s.) For example, since today is Monday and communication is via email, $\mathcal{I}$ might be:

(2) If today is Monday and bids are to be sent via email then (1)

$\mathcal{T}$ with $\mathcal{I}$ will lead to some prediction q about B's behavior:

Today is Monday
Bids are to be sent via email
I sent a task announcement to B
Thus:
q: B will reply with a bid

But suppose that A's observation q′ of B's behavior is inconsistent with q?:

q′: B does not reply with a bid

Does the problem lie with $\mathcal{T}$ or with $\mathcal{I}$?[8] (Perhaps B doesn't send bids to every task announcement, or perhaps it doesn't read email on Monday). The problem may even lie with the way $\mathcal{T}$ or $\mathcal{I}$ are interpreted in the situation (e.g., A got a message but was it a bid?). (Since interagent interaction is involved, the joint qualification and representation incommensurability problems also enter into the interpretive question.) The unfortunate problem seems to be that unless we already know that both the interpretive scheme and A's theory of B's routine are correct, A can't tell how to make them so because it can't deduce what failed—at least not using its own knowledge. This problem can be called the "failure indeterminacy" problem. It is the problem faced in any scientific experiment or court of law: Since the acceptability of a scientific theory depends on the experiment, and the experiment depends upon the apparatus, and the nature of the apparatus depends upon the theory, where is the source of experimental conviction? In court, is the defendant guilty or is the prosecution's theory wrong? Of course in either domain, like good distributed reasoners, we rely on many experiments and agreement among many participants, not just one—but this raises the joint qualification and representation incommensurability problems again [17, 62].

Principle 6. Overall, DAI theory and practice must account for how aggregates of agents can achieve joint courses of action that are robust and continuable (ongoing) despite indeterminate foulups, inconsistency, etc. which may occur recursively at any level of the system.

OISS raises the issue of self-reliance for DAI systems: how can agents preserve local autonomy (i.e. become robust to failure and challenge) while still drawing from and providing resources to the larger community? The first five principles above point to numerous possible sources of failure, discrepancy, and potentially indeterminate states of knowledge in which any agent in a multi-agent system can find itself. Principle 6 takes note of the fact that robust DAI systems that handle all of these contingencies do *exist*: many human social organizations as well as deeply embedded information systems (e.g., [35, 56, 75]). Any complete DAI theory must account for how this is possible and what the limits are; a complete set of mechanisms for DAI ought to provide us the capability to construct such systems within the limits.

4. DAI foundations and open systems semantics

With these principles in mind, then, let us move ahead to consider OISS as a proposed foundation for DAI. The OISS viewpoint has two primary compo-

[8] This exposition makes use of Laymon's argument on the difficulties of using experiments for drawing conclusions about the truth of scientific theories [64].

nents. One is an investigation of the *deductive indecision problem*, and the other is a characterization of open systems, and the nature of problem solving in them. A style of reasoning that elsewhere has been called *due process* [47], built from concepts such as trials of strength, commitments, and negotiations, glues these two together. We shall first discuss the nature of the overall OISS argument. Then we shall investigate how effectively the OISS proposal addresses the six principles presented in Section 3, contrasting the utility of the OISS approach with that of existing DAI research. The thread of the OISS argument is as follows:

(1) DAI research is concerned with work in large-scale open systems, but DAI does not yet have a clearly articulated vocabulary or common conceptual machinery. Open information systems semantics (OISS) can provide a useful and coherent set of concepts, some tractable research issues, a methodology, and a comparative vocabulary for DAI.
(2) DAI systems trade off the costs and benefits of *self-reliance*—the ability to take effective local action and to become robust against indeterminacy and conflict, with *interdependence*—contributing to the performance of the overall aggregate and drawing from it.
(3) "Deductive microtheories" are the primary competing foundation for DAI. Logical semantics are sufficient for reasoning in closed systems, and hence can be used as a foundation for reasoning within deductive microtheories. Problem solving in open systems involves interacting proposals founded in different microtheories. Different microtheories are generated and modified asynchronously, and involve differing commitments among their participants. Thus, logical and representational conflict is endemic to open systems. Logic is insufficient for reasoning in the presence of conflict and meta-conflict (i.e., conflict over the boundaries of decision making—e.g., circumscription axioms in [48]) and therefore for conflict resolution. Thus,
Conclusion 1. Because conflict is endemic, and logic is insufficient for processing under conflict, deductive microtheories are insufficient as a foundation for large-scale DAI in open systems (though they may be useful components).
(4) Alternative and more powerful foundations can be built upon the notions of *trials of strength* and *systems commitments*. Commitments are commitments because they are relatively stable or *robust* in the face of challenge or conflict.
(5) Constructing and exchanging "representations" is a basic activity; representation is not possible without communication. The "meaning" of a representation is defined to be the ways in which it modifies systems commitments.
(6) *Negotiations* (and other trials of strength) are the tools by which conflict is processed. Negotiations can occur recursively at many levels of

analysis, have many potential outcomes, are inherently creative, and generate further commitments.

(7) *Conclusion* 2. Founding DAI in OISS is a different proposition from founding DAI in classical AI terms. OISS is inherently more "social", "grounded in large-scale information systems" rather than individual agents, and provides a different account of representation processes.

Up to Conclusion 1 the OISS argument is relatively strong, but within some narrow limits (which incidentally are left underspecified). It is not entirely true that DAI has failed to crystallize a common conceptual vocabulary, including a set of problems, methods, and terms. Section 2 presented a collection of these, gathered from a thorough examination of the DAI literature. Another very detailed proposal for a core set of DAI problems that coheres closely with those above can be found in [23]. With some exceptions the more basic principles presented in Section 3 above have not in general been fully artificulated or addressed in extant DAI research.

Some deeper questions are the extent to which DAI has been addressing the right set of problems at the right level of analysis, and how OISS may focus us on a different set of problems that is either more fundamental or that allows us to make better headway by changing our perspective. The implication of the OISS perspective seems to be that DAI has not chosen the appropriate set of problems. Deductive indeterminacy is clearly an issue that DAI research has certainly not openly considered until now, though other disciplines have addressed variants (see below). It is not properly subsumed in the six DAI problems of Section 2. The self-reliance/interdependence problem is a clearer and more encompassing notion than "global coherence with local control". But the only other problems posed (e.g., understanding negotiation, commitment, representation, etc.) are also precisely the set of concepts proposed as solutions, and the way they are to be woven together in a mutual foundation is unclear. There are several other key problems that must be addressed for a complete account of open DAI systems, including some of those discussed in several of the principles above. OISS actually does provide ways of thinking about them, but they are not clearly articulated as problems.

The observation that DAI is inherently concerned with work in large-scale open systems is only partially true; DAI certainly *should* be concerned with the question, but most contemporary researchers have had their hands full grappling with the (apparently) far simpler problems of coordination and performance of collections of agents under certain closure assumptions (see Section 2). An interesting open question, then, is what is the extent to which providing new foundations such as those of OISS will simplify the problems of knowledge and action in closed systems as well, and possibly go some distance toward eliminating the categories "open" and "closed".[9]

[9] Recent ferment in sociology, history, and philosophy of science is moving in precisely this direction. See, e.g., [17, 34, 42, 88, 93].

It is true that there has not been enough methodological clarity, debate or variety in DAI,[10] as has been pointed out in both [8] and [38]. But for many of the standard DAI problems, existing representation and experimentation methods have provided fruitful progress.[11] It is not entirely clear what the *methodology* of OISS is, or whether the OISS methodological focus is analytical or constructive. To what extent will it help us explain the behavior of existing DAI systems? How can a constructive methodology be built upon the explanatory theory? As an analytical theory, we are provided with a set of concepts but little guidance for how to go about finding instances, studying, comparing, or operationalizing them. Useful research methods for studying OISS questions analytically have been clearly articulated in sociology, upon which OISS has drawn for its concepts (e.g., [90]), but these or other such are not integrated into the current OISS approach as methods.

To the extent that OISS provides a mathematical or computational analysis, the Actor model for concurrent systems [1] is the chosen descriptive calculus, but at the moment, the connection is incomplete. There are three partially clear links from features of OISS to the descriptive machinery of the Actor model. *Actor configurations* are ways of providing local abstractions or closures, but are not clearly connected with OISS foundation concepts such as commitments or trials of strength. *Serializers* are one way of settling a trial of strength by arbitrating the handling of simultaneously arriving messages, and they do capture fundamental indeterminacy of open systems. *Replacement behaviors* give Actors both local autonomy and participation in joint enterprises, and thus help to address self-reliance issues. The relationship between the Actor model and other concepts such as negotiations, cooperation, commitments, etc. is not clear, and thus the formal descriptive power of OISS is currently limited.

In previous work, such features of open systems as arms-length relationships and asynchrony have been treated as the sources of difficult problems to be overcome. Now, from an OISS perspective, these also provide benefits for components of DAI systems. The notion of "self-reliance/interdependence" is used to capture the advantages and disadvantages of becoming more autonomous while somehow staying integrated with a larger community of agents. But the unit of analysis over which this self-reliance occurs is not clear—what is the self that is self-reliant? Is it a particular node in a system? If so, how are the boundaries of this node defined, by reference to a fundamentally distributed conception of knowledge and action? We can contrast the OISS notion of self-reliance to Gerson's concept of *sovereignty* which is [41, p. 798]:

> . . . the overall organization of commitments associated with any delimitable social object . . . the net balances of resources and

[10] Or in AI in general; see, e.g., [43].

[11] One notable exception is the issue of reflexive modeling and reasoning about DAI system behavior for development purposes and as a foundation for organization self-design. See [37, 52].

constraints available to a person, organization, or other demarcatable group across the full range of settings in which he (or she, or it) participates.

Sovereignty can be seen as the kinds and degrees of constraint an object faces, over all the situations in which it participates simultaneously, and resulting from its interactions in those settings. As Gerson points out, the locus of sovereignty is any particular social object it is convenient to use for analysis, and it also "removes the distinction between 'individual' and 'society' considered as abstract entities apart from their activities and each other" [41, p. 798]. An object has its particular type of sovereignty by relationship to those other entities and situations in which it participates; it never stands alone (cf. the discussion of commitment in Section 3 above). The self-reliance/interdependence framework maintains the distinction between the individual and the larger system in which it participates.

The question of the limitations of deductive microtheories for open systems reasoning is not a new one, though I have not seen it formulated in circumscriptive terms before. Gödel's second incompleteness theorem is based on a variant of it [80], as in Garfinkel's famous description experiment[12] [33]. The importance of the OISS account is that it draws our attention to a basic limitation of a tool drawn upon by DAI theorists, and because it stresses the need for other computational approaches.

OISS also presents a proposal for alternative foundations for DAI, based on the new lexicon of trials of strength, systems commitments, representations, negotiation, cooperation, etc. Our problem is to investigate how clearly and how completely the OISS proposal addresses each of the principles for DAI foundations. One difficulty of doing this is the vagueness of some definitions. The nature and scope of concepts such as "trial of strength", "commitment", "systems commitment", or "negotiation", are matters of inference from examples, not definition. Without greater background it is sometimes difficult to see which features of an example are relevant to the concept under elucidation. For example, does "in place" mean something like "continuable" or "ongoing" (i.e., not deadlocked or otherwise become impossible)? Or does it mean something like "robust" (able to face many different challenges and withstand them)? Part of the problem may be that some concepts have not yet reached conventionalized status (e.g., "negotiation", is a term that has been used in literally dozens of different ways in the DAI literature).

[12] Garfinkel asked students to explain the meaning of a conversation by annotating it, and ultimately to give a set of instructions for unambiguously describing the meaning. Students took this as a request for more complete description, but finally realized that the task was impossible. Further description only muddled the issue because the descriptions themselves were potential sources of ambiguity. There had to be some other way of achieving conversational coherence besides shared *a priori* assumptions. This idea underlies Suchman's discussion of human–machine communication in [91]. See also our discussion of Principle 2 above.

With the specter of misconceptions of definition looming over us, let us examine how OISS addresses the six principles of Section 3, how it extends current wisdom in the DAI literature, and how it is deficient.

4.1. Principle 1: Multiple actors

Some statements of fundamental AI problems have recognized that multiple actors with different viewpoints are an important part of AI (e.g., [31, 76]). Of course, DAI research by definition deals with multiple agents, but to date, DAI research has had only limited theories. What theories do exist take certain aspects of system closure for granted, as pointed out in Sections 2 and 3. Many OISS concepts have already been in widespread use in DAI systems. For example, Mason and Johnson have designed a Distributed ATMS system for nuclear seismic analysis [74]. In this application it is essential that each node avoid compromising its local set of beliefs and assumptions by integrating faulty or malicious messages from other sensing nodes—that is, each node must maintain local autonomy and arms-length relationships while incorporating useful information generated by others. Mason and Johnson's approach is to let each node use non-local information for local focus-of-attention decisions, but never to propagate it. Similarly, the DVMT of Lesser and Corkill [67] includes mechanisms to experimentally vary a node's degree of local autonomy and how greatly it can be "distracted" by information from others; they term this "internal versus external control," and note that positive and negative distractions are sometimes hard to distinguish with a local perspective. Their definition of organization as a set of well-defined problem-solving roles and communication patterns implemented by restrictions on agent capability can be interpreted as a collection of "systems commitments"—but they are commitments by virtue of nodes' lack of sovereignty over their own roles, which is to say by virtue of the actions of designers and reflexive limits of representational theories.

OISS provides a strong foundation for DAI to the extent that it provides an account of knowledge and action from the social level to the individual (which it begins to do), recognizes the possibilities for fundamental disparities in agents' views (which it clearly does), and presents a theory of how agents act despite these disparities and without global knowledge (which it does partially).

In another light, OISS attacks in some sense the wrong problems of multi-agent systems. The important issue is not necessarily the inadequacy of closed-system microtheory techniques for OS problems, (about which there is likely to be little debate) but instead the nature of the processes of "closure"—when and how it is appropriate to make and rely upon closures, and what to do when they break down. This is my reading of one intent of circumscription and other foundations for nonmonotonic reasoning—to provide a promising but necessarily incomplete theory of how to make useful closures in a local reasoning process.

4.2. *Principle 2: Tension between situated, pragmatic knowledge and action-at-a-distance*

In contemporary DAI research this principle is addressed by reference to the problem of "how to achieve global coherence with local control" [22, 68], which involves the first five of the six basic DAI problems discussed in Section 2 above. Typical analyses assume that global views are possible (e.g., by an observer or oracle, to measure global coherence), that disparities that impede global coherence occur only at one level of interaction, and that general knowledge can be applied in remote settings by communicating it. For example, representations and interaction protocols are generally assumed to be fixed within the system or theory, making performance *theory-relative* to the descriptive limits imposed by them (cf. [72, 86]). The local utility approaches of Rosenschein and colleagues probably come closest to accounting for locality of knowledge because they do not depend on shared notions of utility, but they are, again, single-level analytical schemes. Agre and Chapman's "indexical" approach has promise, but it is not clear how to scale it up to aggregate interaction, and they still take the individual agent and its relationship with the world as the locus of knowledge and activity—see, e.g., [12].

OISS concepts useful for addressing Principle 2 include the self-reliance/interdependence tradeoff, the reliance on local processing of representations and the notions of systems commitments. OISS proposes negotiation as a basic mechanism. In OISS, global coherence would be conceptualized as the situated outcome of a negotiation—as long as agents collectively reach agreement (and agree that they have), their actions are coherent. But because of indeterminacy and late arriving information, a preordained concept of global coherence doesn't make sense for OISS—it is necessarily a *post-hoc* notion.

Latour provides a partial and not computational answer to the problem posed by Principle 2, that has not been fully assimilated by OISS, but that is coherent with much DAI work. The way to achieve action-at-a-distance is ". . . by *somehow* bringing home these (distant) events, places, and people. . ." [60, p. 223]. How to do this? By turning the remote entities into "immutable mobiles" which are *mobile* (transportable across contexts), *stable* (so that they keep their useful qualities in new contexts) and *combinable* (so that they can be usefully entered into associations with other such things). That is, by either bringing back preserved, representative samples (e.g., collections of animals or plants) or by bringing back *representations* of distant terrain (e.g., maps, notes, descriptions) built in a systematic (combinable) language. As indicated above, much DAI research has investigated the problems of *building models of other agents*, and of using and exchanging these models as foundations for coordination [25, 39, 65, 81, 82, 92]; from an action-at-a-distance perspective, models of other agents are the crucial immutable mobiles.

However, the stability (immutability) of any of these "mobiles," reflected in their continued representativeness, is always problematic. Transporting plants, animals, and other exemplars necessarily strips them of their context, and may render them uncombinable (e.g., if they die in a new habitat). Transporting representations raises problems of completeness (is the map detailed enough?), and of interpretation in a new context. Others in AI have begun to deal with the problem of re-interpretation in new contexts, and have suggested that it be considered in the context of the hermeneutic problem [96]. Latour's account doesn't deal fully with the mechanisms for keeping mobiles stable. OISS addresses the concern with stability of representations, in part, by delimiting its scope to open *information* systems, which are defined to be systems which manipulate digital information. The advantage of digital information is precisely its stability over time and space, and (ideally) its combinability with other digital information. It is not clear to me, however, that digital information is inherently more or less combinable than any other information, except insofar as its combinability can be automated; some studies have shown the inherent difficulty of combining digital information [35]. Moreover, the stability of interpretation over context is still problematic for OISS. Conceptually the problem can be handled by better integrating the ideas of webs of commitment developed by Becker and Gerson, but it still needs to be made computational.

It doesn't seem sensible or complete, then, to take the OISS view and say simply that representations are "information conveyed using digital communications". Instead, it seems more accurate to characterize representations as artifacts ("inscriptions" [62]) that can be passed around and reinterpreted. Latour's point is that inscriptions are useful precisely because they are transportable across spatial or semantic contexts and they are combinable (cf. Star's discussion of boundary objects in [89]). To link representation and communication, therefore, we can say that any knowledge intended to be used non-locally must be converted into a stable mobile (represented) and (re)interpreted in the local context where it is delivered. In the light of the need to keep the mobile stable, communication can be seen as the maintenance of a collection of commitments across contexts. Communication takes place via the webs of commitment. Though in OISS communication takes place digitally, that is only possible within webs of commitment [35, 56, 75].

4.3. Principle 3: Multiple perspectives

The advantages and disadvantages of multiple perspectives are well known in contemporary DAI research. Multiple views can be used to improve robustness, and several techniques for reaching reliable joint conclusions using many bits of unreliable data from multiple perspectives have been proposed. These include the functionally accurate, cooperative (FA/C) problem-solving approach of Lesser and Corkill [66], the Distributed ATMS approach of Mason and Johnson [74], and the Ether problem-solving system of Kornfeld and Hewitt [57]. The disadvantages of multiple perspectives (e.g., for global coherence) are well recognized in DAI research, and many distributed coordination mechanisms are based on reducing disparities globally by exchanging self-descriptions among agents in a process often called negotiation (e.g., [21, 26, 58, 92]). But all current approaches rely on a global perspective on some level, whether it be semantics or communication protocols, and assume that the context of negotiation cannot itself be negotiated; thus DAI as yet has no complete theory. PGPs have been suggested as a foundation for multi-level negotiations, but not for reflexively negotiating communications protocols [26].

OISS provides a deeper understanding of the basic problems of multiple viewpoints than is currently extant in most DAI. In particular, OISS accounts for the fact that negotiations can be carried out at any level of the system, including negotiations about the appropriate context of negotiations. (Others share this view to various extents. See, e.g., [26, 29, 39]). But a primary difficulty is that, despite defining negotiations as "Trials of Strength carried out using Representations", OISS provides no mechanism for integrating negotiations and more primitive (i.e., implementable) trials of strength. We do have illustrations of trials of strength at several levels of complexity, but no guidance in constructing these into multi-level negotiation mechanisms.

A *perspective* can be seen as a local organization of commitments that takes some aspects of the situation as variable or negotiable and others as fixed (cf. [39]). Strong commitment webs are ways of making things seem invisible or taken for granted—unquestioned—in dealing with the world. For example, in a logic-based agent, a perspective is manifested as the choice of a set of predicates an agent uses to describe its world, and their truth values, which the agent then uses, in a taken-for-granted way, as a world representation. It is also manifested in the decision processes the agent uses to weigh control choices it makes; these are typically commitments that cannot be changed by the agent. We can view these as *commitments* because the agent—or its designer—*could* change its representation, but that would take shifting other commitments in other contexts, e.g., commitments to using some particular communication protocol, understood by others, that relies on those predicates, or to avoiding the effort of reprogramming. Thus, the advantage of meta-level control is that it allows an agent to take on different control perspectives reflexively, but at added cost [27, 44, 72].

Multiple perspectives can be seen as differences in commitments. Moving from one perspective to another, or aligning perspectives among agents involves changing some set of commitments—i.e., the commitments that define what the local perspectives are, e.g. commitments to what predicates to use, or what assumptions to allow, or what features of a situation are important, etc.

In this way, the OISS concepts of systems commitment, representation and negotiation can be brought together, and used as a foundation for conceiving problems of disparate perspectives.

4.4. Principle 4: Resource limitations

Lesser and Erman described the DAI problem as that of enabling a collection of problem solvers to exercise sufficient control to make use of available resources and knowledge to solve a problem, assuming that the knowledge and resources were adequate for some solution [69]. Some recent DAI work has turned to resource-bounded problem solving. The issue has been inherent if not explicit in DAI due to the ways global coherence has been measured. If work is divided among nodes with potential redundancy, then one node's activities must be temporally correlated with the responses of its associates. Otherwise, these nodes may perform necessary tasks themselves, believing that they haven't been done—leading to redundancy and lowered global performance. Thus time constraints can arise purely by the need for coordination. The primary distributed AI approach to explicit resource-bounded reasoning has been *approximate processing*, introduced by Lesser et al. [70].

Problem solving under resource constraints is not clearly accounted for in the OISS framework. Earlier notions of resource *sponsors* introduced by Kornfeld and Hewitt [57] have not been incorporated into OISS at this point. This naturally raises the question of how would OISS approaches fit in real-time settings? Resource limitations are not explicit in the OISS notion of systems commitments, though they could be made so.

The oversight of OISS with respect to Principle 4 is that commitments are ways of allocating resources, and any resource-bounded activity can be represented as negotiation among participants with conflicting commitments. As the availability of resources is always linked to the activities of other agents, it is clear that the commitments of the collection of agents are an influence on resource use. In fact, remaining consistent with the social notion of commitment introduced in Section 3, we can see a commitment as simply *the use of resources*. Commitment in this sense necessarily has future implications: actor A's use of resources for one purpose in the present constrains A's (and others') choices in the future. (The economic notion is "opportunity cost".) Commitments thus "flow" through resources. (OISS would say that resources participate in systems commitments.) Moreover, the possibilities for resource allocation now (e.g., the amount of resources available) is a result of other *prior* commitments of many agents, including those of A. Becker's notion of being committed to a course of action through a collection of "side bets"—other courses of action related through resource dependencies—also falls out of this conception [4]. So do the observations that resource constraint reduces the range of practical choice of a course of action, locking the agent in ("Beggars can't be choosers.") and slack resources reduce commitment by opening a greater number of practical courses of action ("The rich can do what they want.").

4.5. Principle 5: Joint qualification, representation incommensurability, failure indeterminacy

These three problems are simply designed out of contemporary DAI systems—or rather brittleness in the face of them is designed in. There has been little or no attempt to grapple with them, in large part, because there has been so little attention to the automated formulation of problems [8] or with collaborative learning. Computational approaches to the construction of scientific knowledge and scientific explanation have in general been quite naive about scientific practice and the nature of explanation [87], a multi-agent arena in which failure indeterminacy appears routinely. In general, joint qualification and representation incommensurability are handled by assuming a global semantics for a system, and working within the constraints of the theory-relativity of the semantics. Failure indeterminacy has been dealt with via generalization [54] and model-based reasoning [52], but these are not essentially distributed approaches, nor have they been implemented under assumptions of joint qualification problems and representational incommensurability.

OISS allows us to consider several of the concepts embodied in Principle 6. First, OISS takes for granted that participants have fundamentally local and separate representations, and thus are subject to each of these problems. OISS presents a single framework—conflicting systems commitments—that integrates representational incommensurability with other levels of discrepancy mentioned in the fifth DAI problem of Section 2. The OISS approach to the joint qualification problem is to negotiate qualification discrepancies when they become manifest. OISS embeds the qualification problem in a situated process, and makes its solution responsive to local contingencies. Since negotiations can set precedents, the foundation for stable joint qualifications is laid in OISS. The OISS definition of *cooperation*, "mutually dependent roles in a Systems Commitment", is also a statement of the joint qualification problem. It does make the link to mutually supportive commitments (i.e. those that allow resources to flow in both directions) which are the foundation of an approach to joint qualification (cf. the discussions of Principle 4 above). OISS deals with representation incommensurability through the mechanism of recursive negotiation, if at all. It is not clear that OISS recognizes representation incommensurability as a key problem, and any treatment it would have would be necessarily incomplete, because the treatments of commitment and action-at-a-distance are not well-integrated. Likewise, failure indeterminacy is not accounted for, again because the development and integration of commitment is weak.

4.6. *Principle 6: Robust joint courses of action and knowledge*

Current DAI systems and theories achieve robustness through several mechanisms, which primarily are founded on either triangulation of multiple perspectives, redundancy and slack resources, or pre-specification of the causes and possibilities of failure. Several methods for robust problem solving under uncertainty that exploit multiple perspectives have been discussed in Section 4.3 above. A number of DAI systems rely upon redundancy available through parallelism to guard against failure or overload, and these have proven robust in practice. There have been few tests of the performance and overload limits of various DAI approaches, or the limits of organizational and coordination forms. Malone has given a characterization of the susceptibility of various organizational structures to node failure [73] under particularly rigid interaction assumptions. Several approaches to multi-agent planning attempt to iron out the contingencies of interaction before plan execution by interleaving partial orders of concurrent actions [40]; these are not properly in the domain of open systems approaches.

One reason that multiple agents and openness matter to DAI is because of a basic difficulty in building reliable distributed decision-making systems, that is accounted for in the conceptual machinery of OISS, but not in conventional DAI. As the nationwide nine-hour telephone network service interruption of January 1990 illustrates [75], systems which depend upon shared knowledge, common semantics, and global conceptions of coherence (e.g., identical programs at each node of a network with identical decision rules) can be subject to cascading catastropic failures (see also [38, 51]). On the other hand, without common semantics and global conceptions, interoperability and reliability become difficult for other reasons. In OISS terms, greater self-reliance produces inherent conflicts of commitment, e.g, to decision rules or communication protocols. The OISS concepts of arms-length relationships, local and multiple authority, asynchrony, self-reliance and openness are useful conceptual tools here. The fact that the network service disruptions were never complete, and operations could be restored in nine hours (i.e. the network *was* a robust and continuable process) can only be explained by reference to the existence of multiple authorities and arms-length relationships, including at least the authority of telephone engineers at multiple sites over the behavior of network nodes, and their alternative decision-making activities. The network standing alone could not restore itself, and the OISS concepts help us to focus on the actual actors doing the job, not just the network itself as a unit of analysis.

The OISS perspective makes use of the concept "in place" but this is not well-enough defined to be sensible. The notion of robustness, defined as keeping commitments in the face of conflict, is coherent with a concept of a continuable joint action. Further elaboration and mechanisms, however, are lacking. Earlier we spoke of commitment as the outcome of joint courses of action woven together. The notion of systems commitments being in place could be defined by using meta-commitment (commitment to commitment) but this has not been done in OISS.

What OISS needs is a way of linking particular negotiation contexts and particular kinds of commitment to particular ways of achieving robust joint courses of action. Latour [61] uses the image of an army made invincible by association with numerous allies, as a way of explaining robust joint courses of action. OISS must integrate similar images with computational mechanisms.

5. A synthesis

A key missing link is OISS and the other new approaches discussed in this paper, at the moment, is how to make them computational. Because commitment has been posed as a foundational concept, let us briefly examine some of the computational questions surrounding it, to see the directions we might take to construct a more computational theory based on extensions to OISS. Cohen and Levesque's construction of commitment, which is to date the most sophisticated mathematical model, is based on representing commitment using notions of "belief" and "goal", and then computing whether an agent is committed based on the logical entailments of its beliefs. Their commitment is laced into a series of decisions, and at any one of them an agent has to deduce whether it is still committed to a goal. As we discussed in Section 3, this idea of being committed is something local to the agent, and local to its viewpoint. In contrast, the OISS notion of commitment as *Systems Commitment*, though ill-defined, has roots in a basically distributed framework of multiple agents being commited together. But how can such a notion be made both computational and non-local?

One way is to begin to develop theories that dissolve the distinction between open and closed systems, that consider all systems as fundamentally open ones, and that focus on mechanisms for weaving webs of commitment as ways of achieving robustness, joint action, and plausible knowledge. When an actor is committed in the social sense of Becker and Gerson it is constrained to a course of action because of its particular local sovereignty. Establishing commitments in a manner that is both social and computational means setting up numerous side bets that constrain an agent's field of choice. Computing commitment means setting up relationships of mutual influence with additional agents.[13] There are two ways to do this that are already familiar to the world of DAI: passing self-descriptions, and developing checks and balances. Currently, these are only minimal parts of the OISS analysis.

[13] It means also being honest about what those alliances are—whether they're property of the programmer of the physical world, or of the "knowledge" in the system.

A promising approach to distributed computational commitment is based on agents modeling one another and exchanging *self-descriptions*. This approach is a foundation of the MACE system, has been exploited in DATMS [74], PGPs [26], and various network protocols, and has foundations in what Mead [77] saw as a concept that could unify concepts of the self and of society: the process of "taking the role of the other". Self-descriptions can be as simple as an address at which to receive messages, or as complex as a rich knowledge model of an agent. Variance in the ability to self-describe and to incorporate self-descriptions into action differentiate the interactive power of participants.

The flexible composition mechanism of *actor configurations* introduced by Agha and Hewitt [1], is based on actors' ability to pass self-descriptions—their mail addresses. The boundaries of a configuration are defined purely in terms of various actors' access to the addresses of other actors within and outside the configuration; this makes a configuration both flexible and distributed, and in a sense defines limits of interaction and thus provides commitment.

Self-descriptions are also ways of embedding participants in many situations simultaneously. Commitment is generated to the extent that those self-descriptions actually become a part of the calculus of action in those situations. If one agent takes another's self-description into account, it becomes committed to action in a more constrained way. For example, in the network service interruption case, most nodes' decision algorithms did react to the overload indications in passed self-descriptions, which involved them all in joint courses of action that, on the whole, interrupted service. Passing self-descriptions and meta-self-descriptions can also increase sovereignty in distributed ways, by increasing local awareness of how to adapt (e.g., [27, 67]); this was the aim of the phone network self-descriptions but there was a missing link: checks and balances.

Including a collection of checks and balances (plurality) in a DAI system, so that different participants have control over different resources in critical interactions and no participant can be ignored, is another computational approach to OISS. To some extent this notion has already been built into the convergent multi-perspective approaches such as FA/C problem solving, PGPs, and the DATMS. Building in plurality also means that self-descriptions are necessarily involved in joint courses of action. This gives us preliminary tools for implementing a balance between skepticism and involvement or self-reliance and interdependence.

Finally, by creating system-building mechanisms that treat the nature of systems as fundamentally open, we construct for ourselves another paradox—namely, do we really need new mechanisms? Suppose we change focus from problems of reasoning *across* participants with their own microtheories (which is the focus of OISS) to instead understanding the *processes of establishing and changing the boundaries of microtheories* (e.g., by understanding how to change the mix of actors participating in pragmatically common viewpoints, or by understanding how to effect closure by building denser webs of commitment). Then we have also removed the distinction between two approaches to system building (i.e. using microtheories or using OISS methods), and replaced it with a distinction in points of view toward *any* systems we build. Said another way, a viewpoint based on OISS and social foundations for DAI will provide new ways of explaining how and why *existing* reasoning paradigms work, and how they rethink their boundaries and the participants and work they leave out. In effect, we will be saying that we don't necessarily need new programming foundations, but we do need new theoretical foundations for explaining how and why existing programming foundations have the effects they do.

6. Conclusions

It is clear and not completely surprising that there are several problems with using deductive logic as a foundation for problem solving in open systems; these include Hewitt's deductive indeterminacy problem, as well as others such as the failure indeterminacy, representational incommensurability, and joint qualification problems. Since any deductive theory depends upon precursors such as a universe of discourse, a model, etc. it doesn't seem unreasonable to say that when multiple viewpoints are at stake, logic may fail.

Defining and exemplifying the problems of deduction, open systems, or DAI is an exercise—finding solutions appears to require some new foundations for knowledge and interaction, if deductive logic can't be used. OISS tells us to build our analytical foundations on trials of strength, and systems commitments. But it doesn't tell us how to win particular trials or how to organize particular sets of systems commitments, and this is typically what engineers want. OISS and others do tell us that we cannot hope to be sure of organizing and winning some of them.

Neither this paper nor OISS is trying to criticize useful reasoning mechanisms that work within bounded microtheories. It does appear to me that OISS, coupled with some of the conceptions outlined in this paper, can begin account for both the processes of delimiting microtheories in practice and the processes of reasoning employed within them, while the converse is not the case. Our major focus is upon open large-scale multi-agent systems. Both OISS and I propose approaches based upon commitments, resource allocations and interaction, and a notion of meaning independent of Tarskian semantics or possible worlds. Though thoughtful, the proposal is just that. Nonetheless, we must make a start somewhere, and the place to begin again seems to be an examination of the processes of human interaction, social organization, and concurrent systems—and thus the distributed foundations of knowledge and interaction.

Acknowledgement

Continuing discussions over many years with Elihu Gerson of the Tremont Research Institute have been invaluable in formulating the ideas in this paper. Carl Hewitt was generous enough to provide a number of clarifications of his work and critical comments on mine. I am also grateful for the comments of Phil Agre, Alan Bond, Geoff Bowker, Phil Cohen, Kari T. Eloranta, Rick Hull, Dean Jacobs, Izhar Matzkevitch, and Nick Rouquette for helping to improve the presentation of several concepts, and to David Kirsh for gently shepherding the process. I thank Susan Williams for her comments and for vigorous, unflinching editing, and M. Sue Gerson for her great herb tea at key moments. This research is partially supported by a grant from the AT&T Affiliates Program.

References

[1] G. Agha, *Actors: A Model of Concurrent Computation in Distributed Systems* (MIT Press, Cambridge, MA, 1986).

[2] P.E. Agre, Routines, AI Lab Memo 828, MIT, Cambridge, MA (1985).

[3] P.E. Agre, The dynamic structure of everyday life, Ph.D. Thesis, Department of Electrical Engineering and Computer Science, MIT, Cambridge, MA (1988).

[4] H.S. Becker, Notes on the concept of commitment, *Am. J. Sociol.* **66** (1960) 32–40.

[5] H.S. Becker, *Doing Things Together* (University of Chicago Press, Chicago, IL, 1986).

[6] A.F. Bentley, The human skin: Philosophy's last line of defense, in: S. Ratner, ed., *Inquiry into Inquiries* (Beacon Press, Boston, MA, 1954) Chapter 10, 195–211.

[7] A.H. Bond, Commitment: A computational model for organizations of cooperating intelligent agents, in: *Proceedings 1990 Conference on Office Information Systems*, Cambridge, MA (1990).

[8] A.H. Bond and L. Gasser, An analysis of problems and research in Distributed Artificial Intelligence, in: A.H. Bond and L. Gasser, eds., *Readings in Distributed Artificial Intelligence* (Morgan Kaufmann, San Mateo, CA, 1988).

[9] A.H. Bond and L. Gasser, eds., *Readings in Distributed Artificial Intelligence* (Morgan Kaufmann, San Mateo, CA, 1988).

[10] L.W. Buss, *The Evolution of Individuality* (Princeton University Press, Princeton, NJ, 1987).

[11] B. Chandrasekaran, Natural and social system metaphors for distributed problem solving: Introduction to the issue, *IEEE Trans. Syst. Man Cybern.* **11** (1) (1981) 1–5.

[12] D. Chapman and P.E. Agre, Abstract reasoning as emergent from concrete activity, in: M.P. Georgeff and A.L. Lansky, eds., *Reasoning about Actions and Plans: Proceedings of the 1986 Timberline Workshop* (Morgan Kaufmann, San Mateo, CA, 1987) 411–424.

[13] A.E. Clarke and E.M. Gerson, Symbolic interactionism in social studies of science, in: H.S. Becker and M. McCall, eds., *Symbolic Interactionism and Cultural Studies* (University of Chicago Press, Chicago, IL, 1990).

[14] P.R. Cohen and H.J. Levesque, Intention = Choice + Commitment, in: *Proceedings AAAI-87*, Seattle, WA (1987) 410–415.

[15] P.R. Cohen and H.J. Levesque, Intention is choice with commitment, *Artif. Intell.* **42** (1990) 213–261.

[16] P.R. Cohen and C.R. Perrault, Elements of a plan-based theory of speech acts, *Cogn. Sci.* **3** (3) (1979) 177–212.

[17] H.M. Collins, *Changing Order: Replication and Induction in Scientific Practice* (Sage, Beverly Hills, CA, 1985).

[18] H.M. Collins, *Artificial Experts: Social Knowledge and Intelligent Machines* (MIT Press, Cambridge, MA, 1990).
[19] D.D. Corkill, K.Q. Gallagher and K.E. Murray, GBB: A generic blackboard development system, in: *Proceedings AAAI-86*, Philadelphia, PA (1986) 1008–1014.
[20] R. Davis, Report on the workshop on distributed AI, *SIGART Newslett.* **73** (1980) 42–52.
[21] R. Davis and R.G. Smith, Negotiation as a metaphor for distributed problem solving, *Artif. Intell.* **20** (1) (1983) 63–109.
[22] K.S. Decker, Distributed problem-solving techniques: A survey, *IEEE Trans. Syst. Man Cybern.* **17** (5) (1987) 729–740.
[23] K.S. Decker, E.H. Durfee and V.R. Lesser, Evaluating research in cooperative distributed problem solving, in: L. Gasser and M.N. Huhns, eds., *Distributed Artificial Intelligence* **2** (Pitman/Morgan Kaufmann, London, 1989) 487–519.
[24] J. Dewey, The reflex arc concept in psychology, *Psychol. Rev.* **3** (1986) 357–370.
[25] E.H. Durfee and V.R. Lesser, Using partial global plans to coordinate distributed problem solvers, in: *Proceedings IJCAI-87*, Milan, Italy (1987) 875–883.
[26] E.H. Durfee and V.R. Lesser, Negotiating task decomposition and allocation using partial global planning, in: L. Gasser and M.N. Huhns, eds., *Distributed Artificial Intelligence* **2** (Pitman/Morgan Kaufmann, London, 1989) 229–244.
[27] E.H. Durfee, V.R. Lesser and D.D. Corkill, Coherent cooperation among communicating problem solvers, *IEEE Trans. Comput.* **36** (1987) 1275–1291.
[28] L.D. Erman, J.S. Lark and F. Hayes-Roth, ABE: an environment for engineering intelligent systems, *IEEE Trans. Softw. Eng.* **14** (2) (1988) 1758–1770.
[29] J. Ferber and J.-P. Briot, Design of a concurrent language for distributed artificial intelligence, Tech. Rept. LITP-88-57-RXF, Laboratoire Informatique, Theorique, et Programmation (LITP), Université Pierre et Marie Curie, Paris (1988).
[30] R.E. Fikes, A commitment-based framework for describing informal cooperative work, *Cogn. Sci.* **6** (4) (1982) 331–347.
[31] R.E. Fikes, P.E. Hart and N.J. Nilsson, Some new directions in robot problem solving, in: B. Meltzer and D. Michie, eds., *Machine Intelligence* **7** (Wiley, New York, 1972) 405–430.
[32] J.H. Fujimura, Constructing doable problems in cancer research: Articulating alignment, *Social Stud. Sci.* **17** (1987) 257–293.
[33] H. Garfinkel, *Studies in Ethnomethodology* (Prentice-Hall, Englewood Cliffs, NJ, 1967).
[34] H. Garfinkel, M. Lynch and E. Livingston, The work of a discovering science construed with materials from the optically discovered pulsar, *Philos. Social Sci.* **11** (1981) 131–158.
[35] L. Gasser, The integration of computing and routine work, *ACM Trans. Off. Inf. Syst.* **4** (3) (1986) 205–225.
[36] L. Gasser, C. Braganza and N. Herman, MACE: a flexible testbed for distributed AI research, in: M.N. Huhns, ed., *Distributed Artificial Intelligence* (Pitman/Morgan Kaufmann, San Mateo, CA, 1987) 119–152.
[37] L. Gasser and R.W. Hill, Engineering coordinated problem solvers, in: *Annual Reviews of Computer Science* **4** (Annual Reviews, Palo Alto, CA, 1990).
[38] L. Gasser and M.N. Huhns, eds., *Distributed Artificial Intelligence* **2** (Pitman/Morgan Kaufmann, London, 1989).
[39] L. Gasser, N.F. Rouquette, R.W. Hill and J. Lieb, Representing and using organizational knowledge in DAI systems, in: L. Gasser and M.N. Huhns, eds., *Distributed Artificial Intelligence* **2** (Pitman/Morgan Kaufmann, London, 1989) 55–78.
[40] M.P. Georgeff, Planning, in: *Annual Reviews of Computer Science* **2** (Annual Reviews, Palo Alto, CA, 1987) 359–400.
[41] E.M. Gerson, On quality of life, *Am. J. Sociol.* **41** (1976) 793–806.
[42] E.M. Gerson, Scientific work and social worlds, *Knowledge* **4** (1977) 357–377.
[43] R.P. Hall and D. Kibler, Differing methodological perspectives in artificial intelligence research, *AI Mag.* **6** (3) (1985) 166–178.
[44] B. Hayes-Roth, A blackboard architecture for control, *Artif. Intell.* **26** (1985) 251–321.
[45] C.E. Hewitt, Viewing control structures as patterns of passing messages, *Artif. Intell.* **8** (1977) 323–364.

[46] C.E. Hewitt, The challenge of open systems, *Byte* **10** (4) (1985) 223–242.
[47] C.E. Hewitt, Offices are open systems, *ACM Trans. Off. Inf. Syst.* **4** (3) (1986) 271–287; also in: B.A. Huberman, *The Ecology of Computation* (Elsevier Science Publishers, Amsterdam, 1988).
[48] C.E. Hewitt, Open Information Systems Semantics for Distributed Artificial Intelligence, *Artif. Intell.* **47** (1991) 79–106, this volume.
[49] C.E. Hewitt and P. de Jong, Open systems, in: M. Brodie et al., *On Conceptual Modeling* (Springer, New York, 1984) 147–164.
[50] T. Hinke, Query by committee: distributed, data-driven problem elaboration, Ph.D. Thesis, Department of Computer Science, University of Southern California, Los Angeles, CA (in preparation).
[51] B. Huberman, ed., *The Ecology of Computation* (Elsevier Science Publishers, Amsterdam, 1988).
[52] E. Hudlicka and V.R. Lesser, Modeling and diagnosing problem solving system behavior, *IEEE Trans. Syst. Man Cybern.* **17** (3) (1987) 407–419.
[53] T. Hughes P., *Networks of Power: Electric Supply Systems in the US, England and Germany* (Johns Hopkins University Press, Baltimore, MD, 1983).
[54] M.N. Huhns, U. Mukhopadhyay, L.M. Stephens and R.D. Bonnell, DAI for document retrieval: the MINDS project, in: M.N. Huhns, ed., *Distributed Artificial Intelligence* (Pitman/Morgan Kaufmann, San Mateo, CA 1987) 249–284.
[55] J.L. King and S.L. Star, Conceptual foundations for the development of organizational decision support systems, in: J.F. Nunamaker Jr, ed., *Proceedings Twenty-Third Annual Hawaii International Conference on System Sciences* **3**, Los Alamitos, CA (1990) 143–151.
[56] R. Kling and W.S. Scacchi, The web of computing: computer technology as social interaction, in: M.C. Yovits, ed., *Advances in Computers* (Academic Press, New York, 1982) 1–89.
[57] W.A. Kornfeld and C.E. Hewitt, The scientific community metaphor, *IEEE Trans. Syst. Man Cybern.* **11** (1) (1981) 24–33.
[58] K. Kuwabara and V.R. Lesser, Extended protocol for multistage negotiations, in: M. Benda, ed., *Proceedings 9th Workshop on Distributed Artificial Intelligence*, Bellevue, WA (1989) 129–162.
[59] I. Lakatos, *Proofs and Refutations: The Logic of Mathematical Discovery* (Cambridge University Press, New York, 1976).
[60] B. Latour, *Science in Action* (Harvard University Press, Cambridge, MA, 1987).
[61] B. Latour, *The Pasteurization of France, with Irreductions* (Harvard University Press, Cambridge, MA, 1988).
[62] B. Latour and S. Woolgar, *Laboratory Life: The Social Construction of Scientific Facts* (Sage, Beverly Hills, CA, 1979).
[63] J. Lave, *Cognition in Practice* (Cambridge University Press, New York, 1988).
[64] R. Laymon, Idealization and the testing of theories by experimentation, in: P. Achinstein and O. Hannaway, eds., *Observation, Experiment, and Hypothesis in Modern Physical Science* (Bradford Books/MIT Press, Cambridge, MA, 1985) Chapter 6, 147–173.
[65] D.B. Lenat, Beings: knowledge as interacting experts, in: *Proceedings IJCAI-75*, Tblisi, USSR (1975) 126–133.
[66] V.R. Lesser and D.D. Corkill, Functionally accurate, cooperative distributed systems, *IEEE Trans. Syst. Man Cybern.* **11** (1) (1981) 81–96.
[67] V.R. Lesser and D.D. Corkill, The distributed vehicle monitoring testbed: a tool for investigating distributed problem solving networks, *AI Mag.* **4** (1983) 15–33.
[68] V.R. Lesser and D.D. Corkill, Distributed problem solving, in: S.C. Shapiro, ed., *Encyclopedia of Artificial Intelligence* (Wiley, New York, 1987) 245–251.
[69] V.R. Lesser and L.D. Erman, Distributed interpretation: A model and experiment, *IEEE Trans. Comput.* **29** (12) (1980) 1144–1163.
[70] V.R. Lesser, J. Pavlin and E.H. Durfee, Approximate processing in real time problem solving, *AI Mag.* **9** (1) (1988) 49–61.
[71] A. MacFarlane, *The Origins of English Individualism* (Cambridge University Press, New York, 1978).

[72] P. Maes, Computational reflection, *Knowl. Eng. Rev.* **3** (1) (1988) 1–19.
[73] T.W. Malone, Modeling coordination in organizations and markets, *Manage. Sci.* **33** (10) (1987) 1317–1332.
[74] C.L. Mason and R.R. Johnson, DATMS: a framework for distributed assumption-based reasoning, in: L. Gasser and M.N. Huhns, eds., *Distributed Artificial Intelligence* **2** (Pitman/Morgan Kaufmann, London, 1989) 293–318.
[75] T. McCarroll and P.A. Witteman, Ghost in the machine, *Time Mag.* **135** (5) (1990) 58–59.
[76] J. McCarthy, Epistemological problems of artificial intelligence, in: *Proceedings IJCAI-77*, Cambridge, MA (1977) 1038–1044; reprinted in: R. Brachman and H.J. Levesque, eds., *Readings in Knowledge Representation* (Morgan Kaufmann, Los Altos, CA, 1985).
[77] G.H. Mead, *Mind, Self, and Society* (University of Chicago Press, Chicago, IL, 1934).
[78] R.C. Moore, Reasoning about knowledge and action, in: *Proceedings IJCAI-77*, Cambridge, MA (1977) 223–227.
[79] H.P. Nii, N. Aiello and J. Rice, Experiments on CAGE and POLIGON: measuring the performance of parallel blackboard systems, in: L. Gasser and M.N. Huhns, eds., *Distributed Artificial Intelligence* **2** (Pitman/Morgan Kaufmann, London, 1989) 319–384.
[80] W.V. Quine, *Theories and Things* (Harvard University Press, Cambridge, MA, 1981).
[81] J.S. Rosenschein, Synchronization of multi-agent plans, in: *Proceedings AAAI-82*, Pittsburgh, PA (1982) 115–119.
[82] J.S. Rosenschein and M.R. Genesereth, Deals among rational agents, in: *Proceedings IJCAI-85*, Los Angeles, CA (1985) 91–99.
[83] A. Sathi and M.S. Fox, Constraint-directed negotiation of resource reallocations, in: L. Gasser and M.N. Huhns, eds., *Distributed Artificial Intelligence* **2** (Pitman/Morgan Kaufmann, London, 1989) 163–194.
[84] R. Sethi, *Programming Languages: Concepts and Constructs* (Addison Wesley, Reading, MA, 1989).
[85] R.G. Smith, The Contract Net protocol: high-level communication and control in a distributed problem solver, *IEEE Trans. Comput.* **29** (12) (1980) 1104–1113.
[86] B.C. Smith, Varieties of self-reference, in: J.Y. Halpern, ed., *Proceedings 1986 Conference on Theoretical Aspects of Reasoning about Knowledge* (1986) 19–43.
[87] Special issue: Symposium on "Computer Discovery and the Sociology of Scientific Knowledge", *Social Stud. Sci.* **19** (4) (1989) 563–695.
[88] S.L. Star, *Regions of the Mind: Brain Research and the Quest for Scientific Certainty* (Stanford University Press, Stanford, CA, 1989).
[89] S.L. Star, The structure of ill-structured solutions: boundary objects and heterogeneous distributed problem solving, in: L. Gasser and M.N. Huhns, eds., *Distributed Artificial Intelligence* **2** (Pittman/Morgan Kaufmann, London, 1989) 37–54.
[90] A.L. Strauss, *Qualitative Analysis for Social Scientists* (Cambridge University Press, New York, 1987).
[91] L. Suchman, *Plans and Situated Actions: The Problem of Human-Machine Communication* (Cambridge University Press, New York, 1987).
[92] K.P. Sycara, Multiagent compromise via negotiation, in: L. Gasser and M.N. Huhns, eds., *Distributed Artificial Intelligence* **2** (Pitman/Morgan Kaufmann, London, 1989) 119–138.
[93] G. Teil, M. Akrich, B. Michelet and B. Latour, The Hume machine: can association networks do more than formal rules?, Centre de Sociologie de l'Innovation, École Nationale Supérieure des Mines de Paris (submitted).
[94] R.B. Wesson, F.A. Hayes-Roth, J.W. Burge, C. Stasz and C.A. Sunshine, Network structures for distributed situation assessment, *IEEE Trans. Syst. Man Cybern.* **11** (1) (1981) 5–23.
[95] W. Wimsatt, Reductionist research strategies and their biases in the units of selection controversy, in: T. Nickles, ed., *Scientific Discoveries: Case Studies* (Reidel, Boston, MA, 1980) 213–259.
[96] T. Winograd and F. Flores, *Understanding Computers and Cognition* (Ablex, Norwood, NJ, 1986).

Artificial Intelligence 47 (1991) 139–159
Elsevier

Intelligence without representation*

Rodney A. Brooks

MIT Artificial Intelligence Laboratory, 545 Technology Square, Rm. 836, Cambridge, MA 02139, USA

Received September 1987

Abstract

Brooks, R.A., Intelligence without representation, Artificial Intelligence 47 (1991) 139–159.

Artificial intelligence research has foundered on the issue of representation. When intelligence is approached in an incremental manner, with strict reliance on interfacing to the real world through perception and action, reliance on representation disappears. In this paper we outline our approach to incrementally building complete intelligent Creatures. The fundamental decomposition of the intelligent system is not into independent information processing units which must interface with each other via representations. Instead, the intelligent system is decomposed into independent and parallel activity producers which all interface directly to the world through perception and action, rather than interface to each other particularly much. The notions of central and peripheral systems evaporate—everything is both central and peripheral. Based on these principles we have built a very successful series of mobile robots which operate without supervision as Creatures in standard office environments.

1. Introduction

Artificial intelligence started as a field whose goal was to replicate human level intelligence in a machine.

Early hopes diminished as the magnitude and difficulty of that goal was appreciated. Slow progress was made over the next 25 years in demonstrating isolated aspects of intelligence. Recent work has tended to concentrate on commercializable aspects of "intelligent assistants" for human workers.

* This report describes research done at the Artificial Intelligence Laboratory of the Massachusetts Institute of Technology. Support for the research is provided in part by an IBM Faculty Development Award, in part by a grant from the Systems Development Foundation, in part by the University Research Initiative under Office of Naval Research contract N00014-86-K-0685 and in part by the Advanced Research Projects Agency under Office of Naval Research contract N00014-85-K-0124.

No one talks about replicating the full gamut of human intelligence any more. Instead we see a retreat into specialized subproblems, such as ways to represent knowledge, natural language understanding, vision or even more specialized areas such as truth maintenance systems or plan verification. All the work in these subareas is benchmarked against the sorts of tasks humans do within those areas. Amongst the dreamers still in the field of AI (those not dreaming about dollars, that is), there is a feeling that one day all these pieces will all fall into place and we will see "truly" intelligent systems emerge.

However, I, and others, believe that human level intelligence is too complex and little understood to be correctly decomposed into the right subpieces at the moment and that even if we knew the subpieces we still wouldn't know the right interfaces between them. Furthermore, we will never understand how to decompose human level intelligence until we've had a lot of practice with simpler level intelligences.

In this paper I therefore argue for a different approach to creating artificial intelligence:

- We must incrementally build up the capabilities of intelligent systems, having complete systems at each step of the way and thus automatically ensure that the pieces and their interfaces are valid.
- At each step we should build complete intelligent systems that we let loose in the real world with real sensing and real action. Anything less provides a candidate with which we can delude ourselves.

We have been following this approach and have built a series of autonomous mobile robots. We have reached an unexpected conclusion (C) and have a rather radical hypothesis (H).

(C) When we examine very simple level intelligence we find that explicit representations and models of the world simply get in the way. It turns out to be better to use the world as its own model.

(H) Representation is the wrong unit of abstraction in building the bulkiest parts of intelligent systems.

Representation has been the central issue in artificial intelligence work over the last 15 years only because it has provided an interface between otherwise isolated modules and conference papers.

2. The evolution of intelligence

We already have an existence proof of the possibility of intelligent entities: human beings. Additionally, many animals are intelligent to some degree. (This is a subject of intense debate, much of which really centers around a definition of intelligence.) They have evolved over the 4.6 billion year history of the earth.

It is instructive to reflect on the way in which earth-based biological evolution spent its time. Single-cell entities arose out of the primordial soup roughly 3.5 billion years ago. A billion years passed before photosynthetic plants appeared. After almost another billion and a half years, around 550 million years ago, the first fish and vertebrates arrived, and then insects 450 million years ago. Then things started moving fast. Reptiles arrived 370 million years ago, followed by dinosaurs at 330 and mammals at 250 million years ago. The first primates appeared 120 million years ago and the immediate predecessors to the great apes a mere 18 million years ago. Man arrived in roughly his present form 2.5 million years ago. He invented agriculture a mere 19,000 years ago, writing less than 5000 years ago and "expert" knowledge only over the last few hundred years.

This suggests that problem solving behavior, language, expert knowledge and application, and reason, are all pretty simple once the essence of being and reacting are available. That essence is the ability to move around in a dynamic environment, sensing the surroundings to a degree sufficient to achieve the necessary maintenance of life and reproduction. This part of intelligence is where evolution has concentrated its time—it is much harder.

I believe that mobility, acute vision and the ability to carry out survival-related tasks in a dynamic environment provide a necessary basis for the development of true intelligence. Moravec [11] argues this same case rather eloquently.

Human level intelligence has provided us with an existence proof but we must be careful about what the lessons are to be gained from it.

2.1. A story

Suppose it is the 1890s. Artificial flight is the glamor subject in science, engineering, and venture capital circles. A bunch of AF researchers are miraculously transported by a time machine to the 1980s for a few hours. They spend the whole time in the passenger cabin of a commercial passenger Boeing 747 on a medium duration flight.

Returned to the 1890s they feel vigorated, knowing that AF is possible on a grand scale. They immediately set to work duplicating what they have seen. They make great progress in designing pitched seats, double pane windows, and know that if only they can figure out those weird "plastics" they will have their grail within their grasp. (A few connectionists amongst them caught a glimpse of an engine with its cover off and they are preoccupied with inspirations from that experience.)

3. Abstraction as a dangerous weapon

Artificial intelligence researchers are fond of pointing out that AI is often denied its rightful successes. The popular story goes that when nobody has any good idea of how to solve a particular sort of problem (e.g. playing chess) it is known as an AI problem. When an algorithm developed by AI researchers successfully tackles such a problem, however, AI detractors claim that since the problem was solvable by an algorithm, it wasn't really an AI problem after all. Thus AI never has any successes. But have you ever heard of an AI failure?

I claim that AI researchers are guilty of the same (self) deception. They partition the problems they work on into two components. The AI component, which they solve, and the non-AI component which they don't solve. Typically, AI "succeeds" by defining the parts of the problem that are unsolved as not AI. The principal mechanism for this partitioning is abstraction. Its application is usually considered part of good science, not, as it is in fact used in AI, as a mechanism for self-delusion. In AI, abstraction is usually used to factor out all aspects of perception and motor skills. I argue below that these are the hard problems solved by intelligent systems, and further that the shape of solutions to these problems constrains greatly the correct solutions of the small pieces of intelligence which remain.

Early work in AI concentrated on games, geometrical problems, symbolic algebra, theorem proving, and other formal systems (e.g. [6, 9]). In each case the semantics of the domains were fairly simple.

In the late sixties and early seventies the blocks world became a popular domain for AI research. It had a uniform and simple semantics. The key to success was to represent the state of the world completely and explicitly. Search techniques could then be used for planning within this well-understood world. Learning could also be done within the blocks world; there were only a few simple concepts worth learning and they could be captured by enumerating the set of subexpressions which must be contained in any formal description of a world including an instance of the concept. The blocks world was even used for vision research and mobile robotics, as it provided strong constraints on the perceptual processing necessary [12].

Eventually criticism surfaced that the blocks world was a "toy world" and that within it there were simple special purpose solutions to what should be considered more general problems. At the same time there was a funding crisis within AI (both in the US and the UK, the two most active places for AI research at the time). AI researchers found themselves forced to become relevant. They moved into more complex domains, such as trip planning, going to a restaurant, medical diagnosis, etc.

Soon there was a new slogan: "Good representation is the key to AI" (e.g. *conceptually efficient programs in* [2]). The idea was that by representing only the pertinent facts explicitly, the semantics of a world (which on the surface was quite complex) were reduced to a simple closed system once again. Abstraction to only the relevant details thus simplified the problems.

Consider a chair for example. While the following two characterizations are true:

(CAN (SIT-ON PERSON CHAIR)), (CAN (STAND-ON PERSON CHAIR)),

there is much more to the concept of a chair. Chairs have some flat (maybe) sitting place, with perhaps a back support. They have a range of possible sizes, requirements on strength, and a range of possibilities in shape. They often have some sort of covering material, unless they are made of wood, metal or plastic. They sometimes are soft in particular places. They can come from a range of possible styles. In particular the concept of what is a chair is hard to characterize simply. There is certainly no AI vision program which can find arbitrary chairs in arbitrary images; they can at best find one particular type of chair in carefully selected images.

This characterization, however, is perhaps the correct AI representation of solving certain problems; e.g., a person sitting on a chair in a room is hungry and can see a banana hanging from the ceiling just out of reach. Such problems are never posed to AI systems by showing them a photo of the scene. A person (even a young child) can make the right interpretation of the photo and suggest a plan of action. For AI planning systems however, the experimenter is required to abstract away most of the details to form a simple description in terms of atomic concepts such as PERSON, CHAIR and BANANAS.

But this abstraction is the essence of intelligence and the hard part of the problems being solved. Under the current scheme the abstraction is done by the researchers leaving little for the AI programs to do but search. A truly intelligent program would study the photograph, perform the abstraction and solve the problem.

The only input to most AI programs is a restricted set of simple assertions deduced from the real data by humans. The problems of recognition, spatial understanding, dealing with sensor noise, partial models, etc. are all ignored. These problems are relegated to the realm of input black boxes. Psychophysical evidence suggests they are all intimately tied up with the representation of the world used by an intelligent system.

There is no clean division between perception (abstraction) and reasoning in the real world. The brittleness of current AI systems attests to this fact. For example, MYCIN [13] is an expert at diagnosing human bacterial infections, but it really has no model of what a human (or any living creature) is or how they work, or what are plausible things to happen to a human. If told that the aorta is ruptured and the patient is losing blood at the rate of a pint every minute, MYCIN will try to find a bacterial cause of the problem.

Thus, because we still perform all the abstractions for our programs, most AI work is still done in the blocks world. Now the blocks have slightly different shapes and colors, but their underlying semantics have not changed greatly.

It could be argued that performing this abstraction (perception) for AI programs is merely the normal reductionist use of abstraction common in all good science. The abstraction reduces the input data so that the program experiences the same perceptual world (*Merkwelt* in [15]) as humans. Other (vision) researchers will independently fill in the details at some other time and place. I object to this on two grounds. First, as Uexküll and others have pointed out, each animal species, and clearly each robot species with their own distinctly non-human sensor suites, will have their own different *Merkwelt*. Second, the *Merkwelt* we humans provide our programs is based on our own introspection. It is by no means clear that such a *Merkwelt* is anything like what we actually use internally—it could just as easily be an output coding for communication purposes (e.g., most humans go through life never realizing they have a large blind spot almost in the center of their visual fields).

The first objection warns of the danger that reasoning strategies developed for the human-assumed *Merkwelt* may not be valid when real sensors and perception processing is used. The second objection says that even with human sensors and perception the *Merkwelt* may not be anything like that used by humans. In fact, it may be the case that our introspective descriptions of our internal representations are completely misleading and quite different from what we really use.

3.1. A continuing story

Meanwhile our friends in the 1890s are busy at work on their AF machine. They have come to agree that the project is too big to be worked on as a single entity and that they will need to become specialists in different areas. After all, they had asked questions of fellow passengers on their flight and discovered that the Boeing Co. employed over 6000 people to build such an airplane.

Everyone is busy but there is not a lot of communication between the groups. The people making the passenger seats used the finest solid steel available as the framework. There was some muttering that perhaps they should use tubular steel to save weight, but the general consensus was that if such an obviously big and heavy airplane could fly then clearly there was no problem with weight.

On their observation flight none of the original group managed to get a glimpse of the driver's seat, but they have done some hard thinking and think they have established the major constraints on what should be there and how it should work. The pilot, as he will be called, sits in a seat above a glass floor so that he can see the ground below so he will know where to land. There are some side mirrors so he can watch behind for other approaching airplanes. His controls consist of a foot pedal to control speed (just as in these newfangled automobiles that are starting to appear), and a steering wheel to turn left and right. In addition, the wheel stem can be pushed forward and back to make the airplane go up and down. A clever arrangement of pipes measures airspeed of the airplane and displays it on a dial. What more could one want? Oh yes. There's a rather nice setup of louvers in the windows so that the driver can get fresh air without getting the full blast of the wind in his face.

An interesting sidelight is that all the researchers have by now abandoned the study of aerodynamics. Some of them had intensely questioned their fellow passengers on this subject and not one of the modern flyers had known a thing about it. Clearly the AF researchers had previously been wasting their time in its pursuit.

4. Incremental intelligence

I wish to build completely autonomous mobile agents that co-exist in the world with humans, and are seen by those humans as intelligent beings in their own right. I will call such agents *Creatures*. This is my intellectual motivation. I have no particular interest in demonstrating how human beings work, although humans, like other animals, are interesting objects of study in this endeavor as they are successful autonomous agents. I have no particular interest in applications; it seems clear to me that if my goals can be met then the range of applications for such Creatures will be limited only by our (or their) imagination. I have no particular interest in the philosophical implications of Creatures, although clearly there will be significant implications.

Given the caveats of the previous two sections and considering the parable of the AF researchers, I am convinced that I must tread carefully in this endeavor to avoid some nasty pitfalls.

For the moment then, consider the problem of building Creatures as an engineering problem. We will develop an *engineering methodology* for building Creatures.

First, let us consider some of the requirements for our Creatures.

- A Creature must cope appropriately and in a timely fashion with changes in its dynamic environment.
- A Creature should be robust with respect to its environment; minor changes in the properties of the world should not lead to total collapse of the Creature's behavior; rather one should expect only a gradual change in capabilities of the Creature as the environment changes more and more.
- A Creature should be able to maintain multiple goals and, depending on the circumstances it finds itself in, change which particular goals it is actively pursuing; thus it can both adapt to surroundings and capitalize on fortuitous circumstances.
- A Creature should do *something* in the world; it should have some purpose in being.

Now, let us consider some of the valid engineering approaches to achieving these requirements. As in all engineering endeavors it is necessary to decompose a complex system into parts, build the parts, then interface them into a complete system.

4.1. Decomposition by function

Perhaps the strongest traditional notion of intelligent systems (at least implicitly among AI workers) has been of a central system, with perceptual modules as inputs and action modules as outputs. The perceptual modules deliver a symbolic description of the world and the action modules take a symbolic description of desired actions and make sure they happen in the world. The central system then is a symbolic information processor.

Traditionally, work in perception (and vision is the most commonly studied form of perception) and work in central systems has been done by different researchers and even totally different research laboratories. Vision workers are not immune to earlier criticisms of AI workers. Most vision research is presented as a transformation from one image representation (e.g., a raw grey scale image) to another registered image (e.g., an edge image). Each group, AI and vision, makes assumptions about the shape of the symbolic interfaces. Hardly anyone has ever connected a vision system to an intelligent central system. Thus the assumptions independent researchers make are not forced to be realistic. There is a real danger from pressures to neatly circumscribe the particular piece of research being done.

The central system must also be decomposed into smaller pieces. We see subfields of artificial intelligence such as "knowledge representation", "learning", "planning", "qualitative reasoning", etc. The interfaces between these modules are also subject to intellectual abuse.

When researchers working on a particular module get to choose both the inputs and the outputs that specify the module requirements I believe there is little chance the work they do will fit into a complete intelligent system.

This bug in the functional decomposition approach is hard to fix. One needs a long chain of modules to connect perception to action. In order to test any of them they all must first be built. But until realistic modules are built it is highly unlikely that we can predict exactly what modules will be needed or what interfaces they will need.

4.2. Decomposition by activity

An alternative decomposition makes no distinction between peripheral systems, such as vision, and central systems. Rather the fundamental slicing up of an intelligent system is in the orthogonal direction dividing it into *activity* producing subsystems. Each activity, or behavior producing system individually connects sensing to action. We refer to an activity producing system as a *layer*. An activity is a pattern of interactions with the world. Another name for our activities might well be *skill*, emphasizing that each activity can at least post facto be rationalized as pursuing some purpose. We have chosen the word activity, however, because our layers must decide when to act for themselves, not be some subroutine to be invoked at the beck and call of some other layer.

The advantage of this approach is that it gives an incremental path from very simple systems to complex autonomous intelligent systems. At each step of the way it is only necessary to build one small piece, and interface it to an existing, working, complete intelligence.

The idea is to first build a very simple complete autonomous system, and *test it in the real world*. Our favourite example of such a system is a Creature, actually a mobile robot, which avoids hitting things. It senses objects in its immediate vicinity and moves away from them, halting if it senses something in its path. It is still necessary to build this system by decomposing it into parts, but there need be no clear distinction between a "perception subsystem", a "central system" and an "action system". In fact, there may well be two independent channels connecting sensing to action (one for initiating motion, and one for emergency halts), so there is no single place where "perception" delivers a representation of the world in the traditional sense.

Next we build an incremental layer of intelligence which operates in parallel to the first system. It is pasted on to the existing debugged system and tested again in the real world. This new layer might directly access the sensors and run a different algorithm on the delivered data. The first-level autonomous system continues to run in parallel, and unaware of the existence of the second level. For example, in [3] we reported on building a first layer of control which let the Creature avoid objects and then adding a layer which instilled an activity of trying to visit distant visible places. The second layer injected commands to the motor control part of the first layer directing the robot towards the goal, but independently the first layer would cause the robot to veer away from previously unseen obstacles. The second layer monitored the progress of the Creature and sent updated motor commands, thus achieving its goal without being explicitly aware of obstacles, which had been handled by the lower level of control.

5. Who has the representations?

With multiple layers, the notion of perception delivering a description of the world gets blurred even more as the part of the system doing perception is spread out over many pieces which are not particularly connected by data paths or related by function. Certainly there is no identifiable place where the "output" of perception can be found. Furthermore, totally different sorts of processing of the sensor data proceed independently and in parallel, each affecting the overall system activity through quite different channels of control.

In fact, not by design, but rather by observation we note that a common theme in the ways in which our layered and distributed approach helps our Creatures meet our goals is that there is no central representation.

- Low-level simple activities can instill the Creature with reactions to dangerous or important changes in its environment. Without complex representations and the need to maintain those representations and reason about them, these reactions can easily be made quick enough to serve their purpose. The key idea is to sense the environment often, and so have an up-to-date idea of what is happening in the world.
- By having multiple parallel activities, and by removing the idea of a central representation, there is less chance that any given change in the class of properties enjoyed by the world can cause total collapse of the system. Rather one might expect that a given change will at most incapacitate some but not all of the levels of control. Gradually as a more alien world is entered (alien in the sense that the properties it holds are different from the properties of the world in which the individual layers were debugged), the performance of the Creature might continue to degrade. By not trying to have an analogous model of the world, centrally located in the system, we are less likely to have built in a dependence on that model being completely accurate. Rather, individual layers extract only those *aspects* [1] of the world which they find relevant—projections of a representation into a simple subspace, if you like. Changes in the fundamental structure of the world have less chance of being reflected in every one of those projections than they would have of showing up as a difficulty in matching some query to a central single world model.
- Each layer of control can be thought of as having its own implicit purpose (or goal if you insist). Since they are *active* layers, running in parallel and with access to sensors, they can monitor the environment and decide on the appropriateness of their goals. Sometimes goals can be abandoned when circumstances seem unpromising, and other times fortuitous circumstances can be taken advantage of. The key idea here is to be using the world as its own model and to continuously match the preconditions of each goal against the real world. Because there is separate hardware for each layer we can match as many goals as can exist in parallel, and do not pay any price for higher numbers of goals as we would if we tried to add more and more sophistication to a single processor, or even some multi-processor with a capacity-bounded network.
- The purpose of the Creature is implicit in its higher-level purposes, goals or layers. There need be no explicit representation of goals that some central (or distributed) process selects from to decide what is most appropriate for the Creature to do next.

5.1. No representation versus no central representation

Just as there is no central representation there is not even a central system. Each activity producing layer connects perception to action directly. It is only the observer of the Creature who imputes a central representation or central control. The Creature itself has none; it is a collection of competing behaviors. Out of the local chaos of their interactions there emerges, in the eye of an observer, a coherent pattern of behavior. There is no central purposeful locus of control. Minsky [10] gives a similar account of how human behavior is generated.

Note carefully that we are not claiming that chaos is a necessary ingredient of intelligent behavior. Indeed, we advocate careful engineering of all the interactions within the system (evolution had the luxury of incredibly long time scales and enormous numbers of individual experiments and thus perhaps was able to do without this careful engineering).

We do claim however, that there need be no explicit representation of either the world or the intentions of the system to generate intelligent behaviors for a Creature. Without such explicit representations, and when viewed locally, the interactions may indeed seem chaotic and without purpose.

I claim there is more than this, however. Even at a local level we do not have traditional AI representations. We never use tokens which have any semantics that can be attached to them. The best that can be said in our implementation is that one number is passed from a process to another. But it is only by looking at the state of both the first and second processes that that number can be given any interpretation at all. An extremist might say that we really do have representations, but that they are just implicit. With an appropriate mapping of the complete system and its state to another domain, we could define a representation that these numbers and topological connections between processes somehow encode.

However we are not happy with calling such things a representation. They differ from standard representations in too many ways.

There are no variables (e.g. see [1] for a more thorough treatment of this) that need instantiation in reasoning processes. There are no rules which need to be selected through pattern matching. There are no choices to be made. To a large extent the state of the world determines the action of the Creature. Simon [14] noted that the complexity of behavior of a system was not necessarily inherent in the complexity of the creature, but perhaps in the complexity of the environment. He made this analysis in his description of an Ant wandering the beach, but ignored its implications in the next paragraph when he talked about humans. We hypothesize (following Agre and Chapman) that much of even human level activity is similarly a reflection of the world through very simple mechanisms without detailed representations.

6. The methodology in practice

In order to build systems based on an activity decomposition so that they are truly robust we must rigorously follow a careful methodology.

6.1. *Methodological maxims*

First, it is vitally important to test the Creatures we build in the real world; i.e., in the same world that we humans inhabit. It is disastrous to fall into the temptation of testing them in a simplified world first, even with the best intentions of later transferring activity to an unsimplified world. With a simplified world (matte painted walls, rectangular vertices everywhere, colored blocks as the only obstacles) it is very easy to accidentally build a submodule of the system which happens to rely on some of those simplified properties. This reliance can then easily be reflected in the requirements on the interfaces between that submodule and others. The disease spreads and the complete system depends in a subtle way on the simplified world. When it comes time to move to the unsimplified world, we gradually and painfully realize that every piece of the system must be rebuilt. Worse than that we may need to rethink the total design as the issues may change completely. We are not so concerned that it might be dangerous to test simplified Creatures first and later add more sophisticated layers of control because evolution has been successful using this approach.

Second, as each layer is built it must be tested extensively in the real world. The system must interact with the real world over extended periods. Its behavior must be observed and be carefully and thoroughly debugged. When a second layer is added to an existing layer there are three potential sources of bugs: the first layer, the second layer, or the interaction of the two layers. Eliminating the first of these source of bugs as a possibility makes finding bugs much easier. Furthermore, there is only one thing possible to vary in order to fix the bugs—the second layer.

6.2. *An instantiation of the methodology*

We have built a series of four robots based on the methodology of task decomposition. They all operate in an unconstrained dynamic world (laboratory and office areas in the MIT Artificial Intelligence Laboratory). They successfully operate with people walking by, people deliberately trying to confuse them, and people just standing by watching them. All four robots are Creatures in the sense that on power-up they exist in the world and interact with it, pursuing multiple goals determined by their control layers implementing different activities. This is in contrast to other mobile robots that are given programs or plans to follow for a specific mission.

The four robots are shown in Fig. 1. Two are identical, so there are really three designs. One uses an offboard LISP machine for most of its computations, two use onboard combinational networks, and one uses a custom onboard parallel processor. All the robots implement the same abstract architecture, which we call the *subsumption architecture*, which embodies the fundamental ideas of decomposition into layers of task achieving behaviors, and incremental

Fig. 1. The four MIT AI laboratory Mobots. Left-most is the first built Allen, which relies on an offboard LISP machine for computation support. The right-most one is Herbert, shown with a 24 node CMOS parallel processor surrounding its girth. New sensors and fast early vision processors are still to be built and installed. In the middle are Tom and Jerry, based on a commercial toy chassis, with single PALs (Programmable Array of Logic) as their controllers.

composition through debugging in the real world. Details of these implementations can be found in [3].

Each layer in the subsumption architecture is composed of a fixed-topology network of simple finite state machines. Each finite state machine has a handful of states, one or two internal registers, one or two internal timers, and access to simple computational machines, which can compute things such as vector sums. The finite state machines run asynchronously, sending and receiving fixed length messages (1-bit messages on the two small robots, and 24-bit messages on the larger ones) over *wires*. On our first robot these were virtual wires; on our later robots we have used physical wires to connect computational components.

There is no central locus of control. Rather, the finite state machines are data-driven by the messages they receive. The arrival of messages or the expiration of designated time periods cause the finite state machines to change state. The finite state machines have access to the contents of the messages and might output them, test them with a predicate and conditionally branch to a different state, or pass them to simple computation elements. There is no possibility of access to global data, nor of dynamically established communications links. There is thus no possibility of global control. All finite state machines are equal, yet at the same time they are prisoners of their fixed topology connections.

Layers are combined through mechanisms we call *suppression* (whence the name subsumption architecture) and *inhibition*. In both cases as a new layer is added, one of the new wires is side-tapped into an existing wire. A pre-defined time constant is associated with each side-tap. In the case of suppression the side-tapping occurs on the input side of a finite state machine. If a message arrives on the net wire it is directed to the input port of the finite state machine as though it had arrived on the existing wire. Additionally, any new messages on the existing wire are suppressed (i.e., rejected) for the specified time period. For inhibition the side-tapping occurs on the output side of a finite state machine. A message on the new wire simply inhibits messages being emitted on the existing wire for the specified time period. Unlike suppression the new message is not delivered in their place.

As an example, consider the three layers of Fig. 2. These are three layers of control that we have run on our first mobile robot for well over a year. The robot has a ring of twelve ultrasonic sonars as its primary sensors. Every second these sonars are run to give twelve radial depth measurements. Sonar is

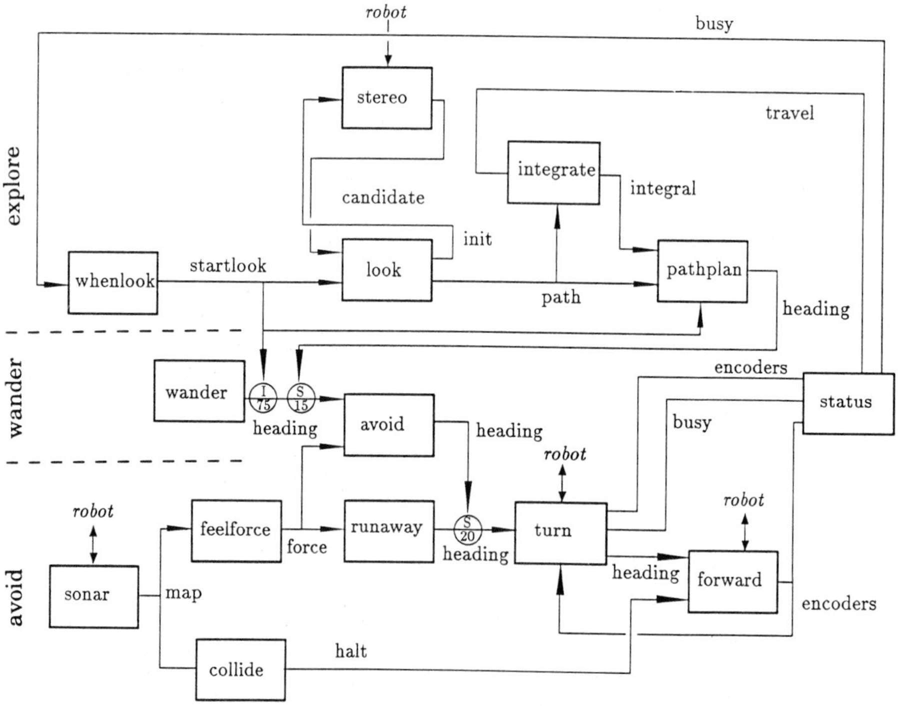

Fig. 2. We wire finite state machines together into layers of control. Each layer is built on top of existing layers. Lower level layers never rely on the existence of higher level layers.

extremely noisy due to many objects being mirrors to sonar. There are thus problems with specular reflection and return paths following multiple reflections due to surface skimming with low angles of incidence (less than thirty degrees).

In more detail the three layers work as follows:

(1) The lowest-level layer implements a behavior which makes the robot (the physical embodiment of the Creature) avoid hitting objects. It both avoids static objects and moving objects, even those that are actively attacking it. The finite state machine labelled *sonar* simply runs the sonar devices and every second emits an instantaneous map with the readings converted to polar coordinates. This map is passed on to the *collide* and *feelforce* finite state machine. The first of these simply watches to see if there is anything dead ahead, and if so sends a *halt* message to the finite state machine in charge of running the robot forwards—if that finite state machine is not in the correct state the message may well be ignored. Simultaneously, the other finite state machine computes a repulsive force on the robot, based on an inverse square law, where each sonar return is considered to indicate the presence of a repulsive object. The contributions from each sonar are added to produce an overall force acting on the robot. The output is passed to the *runaway* machine which thresholds it and passes it on to the *turn* machine which orients the robot directly away from the summed repulsive force. Finally, the *forward* machine drives the robot forward. Whenever this machine receives a halt message while the robot is driving forward, it commands the robot to halt.

This network of finite state machines generates behaviors which let the robot avoid objects. If it starts in the middle of an empty room it simply sits there. If someone walks up to it, the robot moves away. If it moves in the direction of other obstacles it halts. Overall, it manages to exist in a dynamic environment without hitting or being hit by objects.

(2) The next layer makes the robot wander about, when not busy avoiding objects. The *wander* finite state machine generates a random heading for the robot every ten seconds or so. The *avoid* machine treats that heading as an attractive force and sums it with the repulsive force computed from the sonars. It uses the result to suppress the lower-level behavior, forcing the robot to move in a direction close to what *wander* decided but at the same time avoid any obstacles. Note that if the *turn* and *forward* finite state machines are busy running the robot the new impulse to wander will be ignored.

(3) The third layer makes the robot try to explore. It looks for distant places, then tries to reach them. This layer suppresses the wander layer, and observes how the bottom layer diverts the robot due to obstacles (perhaps dynamic). It corrects for any divergences and the robot achieves the goal.

The *whenlook* finite state machine notices when the robot is not busy moving, and starts up the free space finder (labelled stereo in the diagram) finite state machine. At the same time it inhibits wandering behavior so that the observation will remain valid. When a path is observed it is sent to the *pathplan* finite state machine, which injects a commanded direction to the *avoid* finite state machine. In this way, lower-level obstacle avoidance continues to function. This may cause the robot to go in a direction different to that desired by *pathplan*. For that reason the actual path of the robot is monitored by the *integrate* finite state machine, which sends updated estimates to the *pathplan* machine. This machine then acts as a difference engine forcing the robot in the desired direction and compensating for the actual path of the robot as it avoids obstacles.

These particular layers were implemented on our first robot. See [3] for more details. Brooks and Connell [5] report on another three layers implemented on that particular robot.

7. What this is not

The subsumption architecture with its network of simple machines is reminiscent, at the surface level at least, with a number of mechanistic approaches to intelligence, such as connectionism and neural networks. But it is different in many respects for these endeavors, and also quite different from many other post-Dartmouth traditions in artificial intelligence. We very briefly explain those differences in the following sections.

7.1. It isn't connectionism

Connectionists try to make networks of simple processors. In that regard, the things they build (in simulation only—no connectionist has ever driven a real robot in a real environment, no matter how simple) are similar to the subsumption networks we build. However, their processing nodes tend to be uniform and they are looking (as their name suggests) for revelations from understanding how to connect them correctly (which is usually assumed to mean richly at least). Our nodes are all unique finite state machines and the density of connections is very much lower, certainly not uniform, and very low indeed between layers. Additionally, connectionists seem to be looking for explicit distributed representations to spontaneously arise from their networks. We harbor no such hopes because we believe representations are not necessary and appear only in the eye or mind of the observer.

7.2. It isn't neural networks

Neural networks is the parent discipline of which connectionism is a recent incarnation. Workers in neural networks claim that there is some biological significance to their network nodes, as models of neurons. Most of the models seem wildly implausible given the paucity of modeled connections relative to the thousands found in real neurons. We claim no biological significance in our choice of finite state machines as network nodes.

7.3. *It isn't production rules*

Each individual activity producing layer of our architecture could be viewed as an implementation of a production rule. When the right conditions are met in the environment a certain action will be performed. We feel that analogy is a little like saying that any FORTRAN program with IF statements is implementing a production rule system. A standard production system really is more—it has a rule base, from which a rule is selected based on matching preconditions of all the rules to some database. The preconditions may include variables which must be matched to individuals in the database. Our layers run in parallel and have no variables or need for matching. Instead, aspects of the world are extracted and these directly trigger or modify certain behaviors of the layer.

7.4. *It isn't a blackboard*

If one really wanted, one could make an analogy of our networks to a blackboard control architecture. Some of the finite state machines would be localized knowledge sources. Others would be processes acting on these knowledge sources by finding them on the blackboard. There is a simplifying point in our architecture however: all the processes know exactly where to look on the blackboard as they are hard-wired to the correct place. I think this forced analogy indicates its own weakness. There is no flexibility at all on where a process can gather appropriate knowledge. Most advanced blackboard architectures make heavy use of the general sharing and availability of almost all knowledge. Furthermore, in spirit at least, blackboard systems tend to hide from a consumer of knowledge who the particular producer was. This is the primary means of abstraction in blackboard systems. In our system we make such connections explicit and permanent.

7.5. *It isn't German philosophy*

In some circles much credence is given to Heidegger as one who understood the dynamics of existence. Our approach has certain similarities to work inspired by this German philosopher (e.g. [1]) but our work was not so inspired. It is based purely on engineering considerations. That does not preclude it from being used in philosophical debate as an example on any side of any fence, however.

8. Limits to growth

Since our approach is a performance-based one, it is the performance of the systems we build which must be used to measure its usefulness and to point to its limitations.

We claim that as of mid-1987 our robots, using the subsumption architecture to implement complete Creatures, are the most reactive real-time mobile robots in existence. Most other mobile robots are still at the stage of individual "experimental runs" in static environments, or at best in completely mapped static environments. Ours, on the other hand, operate completely autonomously in complex dynamic environments at the flick of their on switches, and continue until their batteries are drained. We believe they operate at a level closer to simple insect level intelligence than to bacteria level intelligence. Our goal (worth nothing if we don't deliver) is simple insect level intelligence within two years. Evolution took 3 billion years to get from single cells to insects, and only another 500 million years from there to humans. This statement is not intended as a prediction of our future performance, but rather to indicate the nontrivial nature of insect level intelligence.

Despite this good performance to date, there are a number of serious questions about our approach. We have beliefs and hopes about how these questions will be resolved, but under our criteria only performance truly counts. Experiments and building more complex systems take time, so with the caveat that the experiments described below have not yet been performed we outline how we currently see our endeavor progressing. Our intent in discussing this is to indicate that there is at least a plausible path forward to more intelligent machines from our current situation.

Our belief is that the sorts of activity producing layers of control we are developing (mobility, vision and survival related tasks) are necessary prerequisites for higher-level intelligence in the style we attribute to human beings.

The most natural and serious questions concerning limits of our approach are:

- How many layers can be built in the subsumption architecture before the interactions between layers become too complex to continue?
- How complex can the behaviors be that are developed without the aid of central representations?
- Can higher-level functions such as learning occur in these fixed topology networks of simple finite state machines?

We outline our current thoughts on these questions.

8.1. How many layers?

The highest number of layers we have run on a physical robot is three. In simulation we have run six parallel layers. The technique of completely debugging the robot on all existing activity producing layers before designing and adding a new one seems to have been practical till now at least.

8.2. How complex?

We are currently working towards a complex behavior pattern on our fourth robot which will require approximately fourteen individual activity producing layers.

The robot has infrared proximity sensors for local obstacle avoidance. It has an onboard manipulator which can grasp objects at ground and table-top levels, and also determine their rough weight. The hand has depth sensors mounted on it so that homing in on a target object in order to grasp it can be controlled directly. We are currently working on a structured light laser scanner to determine rough depth maps in the forward looking direction from the robot.

The high-level behavior we are trying to instill in this Creature is to wander around the office areas of our laboratory, find open office doors, enter, retrieve empty soda cans from cluttered desks in crowded offices and return them to a central repository.

In order to achieve this overall behavior a number of simpler task achieving behaviors are necessary. They include: avoiding objects, following walls, recognizing doorways and going through them, aligning on learned landmarks, heading in a homeward direction, learning homeward bearings at landmarks and following them, locating table-like objects, approaching such objects, scanning table tops for cylindrical objects of roughly the height of a soda can, serving the manipulator arm, moving the hand above sensed objects, using the hand sensor to look for objects of soda can size sticking up from a background, grasping objects if they are light enough, and depositing objects.

The individual tasks need not be coordinated by any central controller. Instead they can index off of the state of the world. For instance the grasp behavior can cause the manipulator to grasp any object of the appropriate size seen by the hand sensors. The robot will not randomly grasp just any object however, because it will only be when other layers or behaviors have noticed an object of roughly the right shape on top of a table-like object that the grasping behavior will find itself in a position where its sensing of the world tells it to react. If, from above, the object no longer looks like a soda can, the grasp reflex will not happen and other lower-level behaviors will cause the robot to look elsewhere for new candidates.

8.3. Is learning and such possible?

Some insects demonstrate a simple type of learning that has been dubbed "learning by instinct" [7]. It is hypothesized that honey bees for example are pre-wired to learn how to distinguish certain classes of flowers, and to learn

Artificial Intelligence 47 (1991) 161–184
Elsevier

Today the earwig, tomorrow man?

David Kirsh

Department of Cognitive Science C-015, University of California, San Diego, La Jolla, CA 92093, USA

Received November 1987
Revised January 1988

Abstract

Kirsh, D., Today the earwig, tomorrow man?, Artificial Intelligence 47 (1991) 161–184.

A startling amount of intelligent activity can be controlled without reasoning or thought. By tuning the perceptual system to task relevant properties a creature can cope with relatively sophisticated environments without concepts. There is a limit, however, to how far a creature without concepts can go. Rod Brooks, like many ecologically oriented scientists, argues that the vast majority of intelligent behaviour is concept-free. To evaluate this position I consider what special benefits accrue to concept-using creatures. Concepts are either necessary for certain types of perception, learning, and control, or they make those processes computationally simpler. Once a creature has concepts its capacities are vastly multiplied.

Introduction

Is 97% of human activity concept-free, driven by control mechanisms we share not only with our simian forbears but with insects? This is the challenge proposed by Rod Brooks and fellow moboticists to mainstream AI. It is not superficial. Human activities fall along a continuum. At one extreme are highly reactive, *situationally determined* activities: walking, running, avoiding collisions, juggling, tying shoelaces. At the other extreme are highly *cerebral* activities: chess, bridge playing, mathematical problem solving, replying to non-obvious questions, and most discursive activities found in university research laboratories. It is an open question just where to draw the line between situationally determined activity—activity that can be initiated and regulated by smart perception-action systems—and activity that requires thought, language-like conceptualization, and internal search.

Brooks' position is that if we consider precisely what sensing is required to intelligently control behaviour in specific tasks, we make the startling discovery that in most cases there is no need, or next to no need, for symbolic

0004-3702/91/$03.50

information. Smart perception can index into the world cleverly, extracting exactly what is needed for task control without solving the general vision problem.[7]

(5) the hardest problems of intelligent action are related to the control issues involved in coordinating the various behavioural abilities so that the world itself and a predetermined dominance or preference ordering will be sufficient to decide which activity layer has its moment in the sun.

In short, the theme of this alternative theory is that representation can be exchanged for control. If a creature knows where to look and when to look, and knows what activities to activate and deactivate, then it can approximate arbitrarily rational agents.

To take a rather simple example consider an insect which feeds off of sugar, and lives in an environment of wily but slow predators. Such a creature must be able to sense sugars or the probability of sugars at a small distance, "Feed" on those sugars when possible, "Move", in a specified direction, "Run Away" when it gets too close to certain objects—particularly predators, "Stop Short" if it is about to hit an object directly in front of it, and be able to perform compounds of these low level abilities such as "Wander" so that it might improve its probability of finding food, "Avoid Obstacles" and "Follow Freeways" so that it may move through irregular terrain or flee predators without stumbling. Each of these activities is tuned to certain environmental conditions, such that the activity is turned on or off, amplified or diminished according to locally detectable conditions in conjunction with the internal switching circuitry. If all works well, the net effect is that as the world changes, either because the robot itself is moving through it, or because of external events, the robot will behave as if it is choosing between many goals. Sometimes it runs, sometimes it wanders, sometimes it feeds.

Obviously, the trick in making a mobot behave in a way that looks like it is choosing between many goals without it explicitly predicting the effects which the various behaviours would have on the world, is to design the right pattern of control into the circuitry. Certain pathways will carry messages which dominate the normal input to a module or which suppress the normal output. Accordingly, one goal of research is to find a way of minimizing the amount of this control. Each FSM should be tuned to the *right* stimuli so as to let the world force choice whenever possible.

Thus, for example, when the senses register a looming stimulus, the Stop Short module, takes command. Stop short was primed; it was in a state which acts on a looming stimulus and is hooked up to output so that its signal overrides any others that may also be transmitted. Similarly, if a system were

[7] Again compare [4, 5]. In Gibson's view the senses are not passive receptors of information; they are active seeking mechanisms, searching out the information—often minimal information—required for effective action and avoidance of physical harm.

on a coke can collecting mission, the Move Hand module might take over as soon as the system sensed a halt in optical flow and a streak of red. A complex cooperative behaviour might emerge, therefore, simply because each component activity becomes primed for particular changes in the state of the world that matter to it. Hence, coordination is achieved automatically without posting requests on some central blackboard or relying on some active arbitrator to pass control to slave activities because the preference relations among activities have been built into the switching network of the system.

Let us call behaviour that is controlled by the situation in this way, *situation-determined behaviour*. Situation-determined behaviour can be considerably more complex than the stimulus driven behaviour found in behaviourist theory. For instance, humans, when putting together jig saw puzzles, may be said to be situationally determined if there is enough joint constraint in the tiles and assembled layout to ensure that they can complete the puzzle without wasted placements. No behaviourist theory can explain jig saw performance, however, because there is no readily definable set of structural properties—i.e. stimulus conditions—that are the causes of jig saw placements—i.e. responses. The agent is too active in perceptually questioning the world. On two confrontations with the same world the same agent might perceive different situations as present because it asked a different set of perceptual questions. These questions are a function of the state of the agent and its most recent interactions with the world.

We can say that jig saw puzzles are perceptually hard but intellectually simple. The actions are intentional but under perceptual rather than conceptual guidance. Thus it is the eye, not the thinking center, which must be trained to look for the salient corners that differentiate tiles and signal proper fit. It is a problem of perceptual search.

Viewing situation-determined behaviour to be a solution to a perceptual problem points out several worthwhile aspects of situationally determined tasks.

First, there is enough local constraint in the world to "determine" successful placement despite there being several tiles that can be successfully played at any moment. In a sense each move is underdetermined, hence no deterministic behaviourist theory can explain placement behaviour. Nonetheless, given a tile and an existing layout, the situation wholly determines whether or not the tile can be correctly placed at that time and where. There is no need to check downstream effects. In the jig saw game, successful placements are additive. Good moves do not interact hostilely with other good moves. There are no traps, dead ends, or loops that may stymie a player. The situation contains enough information to pre-empt the need for lookahead. This is the main point of assumption three.

Second, the perceptual problem is tractible in the sense that only a fraction of the visible world state must be canvassed to determine where to move. The point of sensing is to provide enough information to permit a creature to choose between the actions it can perform next. In the case of jig saw it is conceivable that to solve the puzzle one must identify the overall shape of all the pieces first. If this were true, a jig saw puzzle would be a tedious game indeed, for either it would require collosal visual processing each move, or it would require tremendous visual memory of shapes. How much easier if complete shape identification is unnecessary.

Is this possible? Is it possible to decide which tile to place next by using a strategy of visually questioning the board that does not require computing the overall shape of each tile? The question is important because if perceptual questioning can be confined to simple features there will be no need for higher level intermediate representations.

Imagine a case where a player cannot decide which of five tiles to play in a particular opening. Each tile seems like it might be a proper fit, but it is hard to tell. An obvious aid to the problem is to have the player try to fit one of the tiles in the opening to let the world highlight the crucial feature that differentiates the proper tile from the near misses. The function of this test move is to focus the player's attention on the situationally *salient* features of the tiles. It is to identify the crucial differentiating features. Now a true expert of the game might not need this help; his perceptual system may be so tuned to the task that he can home right in on the relevant differentiating features. If so, this possibility affirms the point of assumption four: that if one knows what to look for, there is a fairly local feature which correlates with correct moves. Not only does the situation contain enough local constraint to determine good moves, these constraints are highly specific to the task and learnable.

It is worth dwelling on this issue for it emphasises the truth of assumption five: that control is the hard problem, and the methodological importance of assumption one: that behaviour can be partitioned into task oriented activities. These, I take it, are the backbone of this alternative approach to action.

It is standard in decision theory to treat perception as a bounded resource that must be guided in order to be used to its fullest. The problem which decision-theoretic accounts encounter, however, is that to know what question it is best to ask next, or which test it is best to perform next, the agent must know all the sources of information available now and in the future, all the decisions that might be taken now and in the future, their consequences, utilities, etc. To achieve optimality is clearly impossible in practice, for it requires knowing where you are most likely to get the information you want before you know exactly which decisions you must make. If one restricts the horizon of one's decisions to specific task-oriented activities the problem is simpler. Must I halt now? Can I proceed in that direction? Is there a predator nearby? For each of these questions there may be a straightforward test which is decisive, or nearly decisive, or indicative of what to test next. Once again the question is whether the test (or perceptual query) is computationally cheap.

In a situationally determined context such questions are necessarily cheap.

The environment can be factored into a set of partial states or *indicators* which correlate well with the presence or absence of the larger environmental factors which affect task performance. Thus for a robot whose environment contains doors with right angles it may be possible to discover an invariant *microfeature* of doors which under normal conditions can be seen from all angles. Relative to door entering activity, this invariant may be all that need be sought. Moreover, it may be simple—a top right and bottom left corner in suitable opposition for example. This fraction of doorness is sufficient for door recognition in this environment, as long as the robot remains upright, as long as no new doors are introduced, and so forth. It correlates with all and only doors. Consequently, one of the hardest problems for mobot designers is to discover these indicators, and the perceptual queries that best identify them. For each activity the designer must determine which possible indicators correlate well with the likelihood of success or failure of the activity given the current state of the world. This is a hard problem for most activities. But the key point is that without the assumption that behaviour can be partitioned into task-oriented activities, it would be impossible to discover these indicators at all.

This introduces the third and final respect situationally determined tasks are illustrative of the alternative theory of action: what is most salient in the environment is usually discernable and economically detectable from the *agent's perspective*. Most task indicators are egocentrically definable. This is a crucial factor in deciding how much of activity can be intelligently controlled without concepts because concepts are often held to be non-egocentric, public or quasi-public entities.

Developmental psychologists draw a distinction between the *egocentric space* of an agent and the *public space*, which as observers we see the agent performing in. The distinction is intuitive. In egocentric space, the agent is always at the spatio-temporal origin of its world. It sees the environment from its own perspective. Indexical terms such as beside-me, to my right, in front, on top, nearby, occluded-right-now, are all well defined, and depend essentially on the agent's location. They shift as it moves about.

In public space, by contrast, the world is understood almost as if viewed from nowhere. If the agent is included in the world at all it is included objectively as another entity in relation with objects in the world. This is done to facilitate useful generalization. Two people can see the same ball; a ball remains the same ball despite its currently being outside the agent's visual field; and it remains beside a companion ball whether partly occluded or not. Because we can count on the permanence of objects and on a consensual understanding of space-time we can usefully organize our experience of the world by appeal to public objects, public space, and public time. We can describe actions and strategies in a manner which allows people in different circumstances to use them; and we can talk about consequences of actions as if we were not there to see them. Thus, in describing the action of lifting a box five feet in the air it is usually irrelevant whether the agent approaches the box from the right or left. Where the agent was positioned in the situation is less important than what it did to make the box go up. This can be stated in terms of the lawful changes which the objects in the environment undergo.

In the classical theory of action, the beliefs that were thought causally important in determining action were stated in the language of public objects and properties. Actions were defined as situation-action rules—transformations between pre and postconditions, and were understood as transformations over public states.

The practice of enumerating the troubles of situation action rules based on public concepts is by now a familiar pastime in discussions of AI planning. It is therefore regarded a virtue of the situationally determined account that the indicators which matter to situationally determined task performance are definable from an egocentric perspective.

J.J. Gibson, for example, argued at length that the genuine environment of action is not a world of objects and objective relations but a world of surfaces and textural flows as seen by the agent. Gibson, in his ecological approach to perception, emphasised that action and perception are not distinct processes. Animals and people do not passively perceive the world. They move about in it actively, picking up the information needed to guide their movement. This information is always available in an egocentric form, because as a result of the interlocking between perception and action, certain egocentric invariants emerge. Flies can find landing sites by detecting wiping of texture in the optic flow [17, pp. 215–218], chicks and babies can avoid precipices by detecting motion parallax and texture gradients [17, pp. 234–235]. These invariants can be picked up early. They do not require the level of visual processing involved in creating a full 3-D representation. The same it seems holds for most situationally determined tasks: the indicators which matter can be gleaned by relatively early attention to egocentric invariants, or properties.

The upshot is that for situationally determined activity, perception, particularly egocentric perception, rather than conceptual reasoning is the determining factor of success. This holds because there is a reliable correlation between egocentrically noticeable properties of the environment and actions that are effective.[8]

Now, from both a scientific and engineering standpoint nothing but good can come from exploring in silicon and metal how much of intelligent activity can be duplicated following the principles of this alternative theory of action. Until

[8] The conception of situation determinedness I offer is stipulative. Others can be proposed. For instance, one could propose that a context situationally determines an action for an agent if the situation in conjunction with the inner state of the agent determines what he will do next. But to stretch the definition in that direction is to give up the distinction between situation determinedness and determinedness simplicitur. Agents are usually determined by the union of mental state and local environment. The noteworthy condition of true situation determinedness is that reasoning is not required for action.

we construct creatures which can have hundreds of procedures turned on and waiting, we cannot know how effective the world might possibly be in deciding the sequence of the procedures to use. There may be far more indicators in the world that are able to bias performance than we would have dreamed possible prior to designing creatures to run in the real world.

Nevertheless, as with most nascent areas of AI, it is easy to see early results as compelling evidence for strong conclusions. In Brooks' case, the success of this design strategy for simple insect-like creatures is meant to justify a host of methodological directives and criticisms for design strategies of far more complex creatures and behaviours.

Accordingly, let us consider some of the limits of situationally determined actions, and the attendant reasons higher-level creatures are likely to use concepts and representations in action, perception, and control.

3. The limits of situationally determined action

Situationally determined activity has a real chance of success only if there are enough egocentrically perceptible cues available. There must be sufficient local constraint in the environment to determine actions that have no irreversibly bad downstream effects. Only then will it be *un*necessary for the creature to represent alternative courses of actions to determine which ones lead to dead ends, traps, loops, or idle wandering.

From this it follows that if a task requires knowledge about the world that must be obtained by reasoning or by recall, rather than by perception, it cannot be classified as situation determined. Principle candidates for such tasks are:

- Activities which involve other agents, since these often will require making *predictions* of their behaviour.
- Activities which require response to events and actions beyond the creature's current sensory limits, such as taking precautions now for the future, avoiding future dangers, contingencies, idle wandering—the standard motive for internal lookahead.
- Activities which require understanding a situation from an objective perspective such as when a new recipe is followed, advice is assimilated, a strategy from one context is generalized or adapted to the current situation. All these require some measure of conceptualization.
- Activities which require some amount of problem solving, such as when we wrap a package and have to determine how many sheets of paper to use, or when we rearrange items in a refrigerator to make room for a new pot.
- Activities which are creative and hence stimulus free, such as much of language use, musical performance, mime, self-amusement.

These activities are not isolated episodes in a normal human life. Admittedly, they are all based on an underlying set of reliable control systems; but these control systems are not sufficient themselves to organize the *global* structure of the activity.

Thus, to prepare tea requires coordinating both global and local constraints. At the global level, teamakers must be sensitive to the number of people they are serving, ensuring there is enough water, tea, cups, saucers and biscuits. Once these items are laid out more mobot-like control systems may take over, pouring the water, stirring etc. But the initial resource allocation problems are hard to solve. Animals are notoriously ineffective at them. Moreover, can we expect mobots to intelligently arrange plates on the tray? Arrangement or bin packing requires attention to a number of non-local factors, such as how many items remain to be placed, how well they can be expected to stack, and how stable the overall configuration must be, given the path to the parlor. Anticipation of the future is required. Hence, whenever global considerations enter the control of action, the creature must either be pre-tuned to the future, or it must be able to call on memories, reason about contingencies, ask for advice, and so forth.

In short, the world of human action regularly falls short of total situation determinedness. Most of our life is spent managing locally constrained choice.[9] It is at this management level that we can best appreciate the virtue of concepts and representations.

4. The virtues of concepts and representations

Concepts are involved in the management of action because they serve at least three organizing functions in cognitive economies. At the *perceptual* level, concepts unify perceptions into equivalence classes. An agent possessing the concept of a dog, for instance, should be able to recognize dogs from different points of view. A dog is an invariant across images. It is also an object for the visual system in the sense that the visual field will be segmented into dog images and non-dog images, offering whatever attentional mechanisms reside in the perceptual system to be directed at specifics of dog images. Accordingly, one aspect of saying that a creature has a concept of dog is to say that he or she can identify dogs perceptually. This means that a vast array of perceptual circumstances can be simplified and reasoned about economically, and that a host of perceptual mechanisms are coordinated around the perceptual object dog.

At a more *conceptual* level, concepts license inferences. A dog is *not* identical with the set of its possible appearances. It is a spatially extended temporally enduring entity that can enter into causal relations with other

[9] For an outline of the virtues and problems with local choice, see [6].

objects. It is a possible subject of predication. Hence much of what is true of other objects—other possible subjects of predication—will be true of dogs. Many of these *inheritable* truths constitute the *presuppositions* which a creature able to have beliefs and thoughts about dogs will hold. In thinking about dogs, then, the creature will have in mind an entity that is alive, breathes, normally has four legs, and so on. This information is readily accessible, but of course need not be conscious. It enables the creature, however, to intelligently respond to invisible properties of dogs [18]. Thus, a child may resist striking a dog because it knows it would hurt the dog, despite the fact that the property of being open to hurt is not a perceptually present property of dogs.[10]

At a *linguistic* level, a concept is the meaning of a term. To know the meaning of 'dog' in English is to have the concept of dog, and to know that the English word signifies that concept. The concept dog is a semantic value; in the Fregean system, when coupled with another appropriate semantic value it constitutes a proposition, or truth bearer.

Now, when an agent has a concept it can do things and think thoughts it could not otherwise. As developmentalists have pointed out, once a child has the concept of an object, it can know that the same object can present different appearances. It can decide that what looks like a dog is not really a dog, but a misleading image of a bear. It can infer that your image of this dog is different than mine, but that we both know it is the same dog [14]. And it can infer that dogs feel pain because they are alive. Concept users understand a great deal about their environment when they conceptualize it.

There can be no doubt that the skills we identify with possession of concepts are of great value for certain forms of intelligent behaviour. But how widespread is this behaviour? Can we approximate most intelligent behaviour without concepts? This is Brooks' challenge.

One of the most important uses of concepts is to organize memory. Whether or not a system has limited memory, it has a need to index memories in a manner that facilitates recall. In action management, an effective creature will benefit from its performances in the past. It will remember dangers, failures, helpful tricks, useful sub-goals. It may recall unexpected consequences of its previous performances. These memory accesses need not be conscious. Nor need they be complete. Someone describing a particular pet dog may not have accessed all the related information he or she knows about the animal. Some information lies untouched. But this information is *primed* in the sense that retrieving that related information in the near future takes less time than had the topic never been discussed [10].

[10] Gibson argues that sentience and the like are perceivable properties of an animal. But in his system, there is almost no action-relevant property that is not perceivable. Thus, post boxes have the perceivable property of affording letter posting. Just how many non-obvious properties can be perceived or registered is a deep question which the alternative theory of action raises. But I think we may safely say that the line must be drawn short of *all* action-relevant properties. Default reasoning will be valuable for these.

[4] J.J. Gibson, *The Senses Considered as Perceptual Systems* (Houghton Mifflin, Boston, MA, 1966).

[5] J.J. Gibson, *The Ecological Approach to Visual Perception*, (Houghton Mifflin, Boston, MA, 1979).

[6] D. Kirsh, Managing local choice, in: *Proceedings AAAI Workshop on AI and Rational Choice* (1989).

[7] D. Kirsh, When is information explicitly represented?, in: P. Hanson, ed., *Information, Content and Meaning* (UBC Press, Vancouver, BC, 1990).

[8] N.J. Mackintosh, *Conditioning and Associative Learning* (Oxford University Press, Oxford, 1983).

[9] G. Mandler, *Cognitive Psychology* (Erlbaum, Hillsdale, NJ, 1985).

[10] G. Mandler, Memory: Conscious and unconscious, in: P.R. Solomon, G.R. Goethals, C.M. Kelley and B.R. Stephens, eds., *Memory: Interdisciplinary Approaches* (Springer, New York, 1989).

[11] J. Mandler, How to build a baby: on the development of an accessible representational system, *Cogn. Dev.* **3** (1988) 113–136.

[12] M. Minsky, *The Society of Mind* (Simon and Schuster, New York, 1986).

[13] V. Reynolds, The origins of a behavioural vocabulary: The case of the rhesus monkey, *J. Theor. Social Behav.* **6** (1976) 105–142.

[14] M. Siegel, *Knowing Children: Experiments in Conversation and Cognition* (Erlbaum, Hillsdale, NJ, 1990).

[15] E.S. Spelke, Where perceiving ends and thinking begins: the apprehension of objects in infancy, in: A. Yonas, ed., *Perceptual Development in Infancy* (Erlbaum, Hillsdale, NJ, 1988).

[16] R. Sternberg, ed., *Advances in the Psychology of Intelligence* **4** (Erlbaum, Hillsdale, NJ, 1988).

[17] B. Vicki, and P. Green, *Visual Perception, Physiology, Psychology and Ecology* (Erlbaum, Hillsdale, NJ, 1985).

[18] H.M. Wellman and S.A. Gelman, Children's understanding of the nonobvious, in: R. Sternberg, ed., *Advances in the Psychology of Intelligence* **4** (Erlbaum, Hillsdale, NJ, 1988).

Artificial Intelligence 47 (1991) 185–250
Elsevier

On the thresholds of knowledge*

Douglas B. Lenat
MCC, 3500 W. Balcones Center, Austin, TX 78759, USA

Edward A. Feigenbaum
Computer Science Department, Stanford University, Stanford, CA 94305, USA

Received September 1987
Revised November 1989

Abstract

Lenat, D.B. and E.A. Feigenbaum, On the thresholds of knowledge, Artificial Intelligence 47 (1991) 185–250.

We articulate the three major findings and hypotheses of AI to date:
(1) The Knowledge Principle: If a program is to perform a complex task well, it must know a great deal about the world in which it operates. In the absence of knowledge, all you have left is search and reasoning, and that isn't enough.
(2) The Breadth Hypothesis: To behave intelligently in unexpected situations, an agent must be capable of falling back on increasingly general knowledge and analogizing to specific but superficially far-flung knowledge. (This is an extension of the preceding principle.)
(3) AI as Empirical Inquiry: Premature mathematization, or focusing on toy problems, washes out details from reality that later turn out to be significant. Thus, we must test our ideas experimentally, *falsifiably*, on large problems.

We present evidence for these propositions, contrast them with other strategic approaches to AI, point out their scope and limitations, and discuss the future directions they mandate for the main enterprise of AI research.

1. Introduction

For over three decades, our field has pursued the dream of the computer that competently performs various difficult cognitive tasks. AI has tried many approaches to this goal and accumulated much empirical evidence. The evidence suggests the need for the computer to have and use domain-specific knowledge. We shall begin with our definition of intelligence:

* This article was originally prepared in May 1987 for the MIT Workshop on Foundations of AI the following month, and issued then as MCC Technical Report AI-126-87. A very much shortened version was given as an invited paper at IJCAI-87 in Milan, August 1987. It was edited in 1989 in preparation for this publication.

Definition. *Intelligence* is the power to rapidly find an adequate solution in what appears a priori (to observers) to be an immense search space.

So, in those same terms, we can summarize the empirical evidence: "Knowledge is Power" or, more cynically "Intelligence is in the eye of the (uninformed) beholder". The *knowledge as power* hypothesis has received so much confirmation that we now assert it as:

Knowledge Principle (KP). A system exhibits intelligent understanding and action at a high level of competence primarily because of the *knowledge* that it can bring to bear: the concepts, facts, representations, methods, models, metaphors, and heuristics about its domain of endeavor.

The word *knowledge* in the KP is important. There is a tradeoff between knowledge and search; that is, often one can either memorize a lot of very detailed cases, or spend time applying very general rules. Neither strategy, carried to extremes, is optimal. On the one hand, *searching* is often costly, compared to the low cost of just not forgetting—of preserving the knowledge for future use. Our technological society would be impossible if everyone had to rediscover everything for themselves. On the other hand, even in a relatively narrow field, it's impractical if not impossible to have a pre-stored database of all the precise situations one will run into. Some at least moderately general knowledge is needed, rules which can be applied in a variety of circumstances. Since *knowledge* includes control strategies and inference methods, one might ask what is *excluded* by the KP. The answer is that we exclude unbalanced programs: those which do not contain, and draw power from, a mixture of explicit and compiled knowledge, and we advocate programs in which the balance is tipped toward the explicit, declarative side. Section 2 discusses the Knowledge Principle in more detail, and Section 3 provides experimental evidence for it.

The KP suggests that any system which is to perform intelligently incorporate both particular facts and heuristic rules. But how far-ranging must such knowledge be? Consider the brittleness of current knowledge-based systems. They have a plateau of competence, but the edges of that plateau are steep descents into complete incompetence. Evidence for how *people* cope with novelty is sparse and unreliable. Still, there is suggestive evidence supporting their reliance on general "commonsense" knowledge, and their reliance on partial or analogical matching. This leads us to a plausible extension of the Knowledge Principle:

Breadth Hypothesis (BH). Intelligent performance often requires the problem solver to fall back on increasingly general knowledge, and/or to analogize to specific knowledge from far-flung domains.

Are we, of all people, advocating the use of weak methods? Yes, but only in the presence of a breadth of knowledge far afield of the particular task at hand. We are adding to the KP here, not contradicting it. Much of the power still derives from a large body of task-specific expertise (cases and rules). We are adding to the KP a new speculation, namely that intelligent problem solvers cope with novel situations by analogizing and by drawing on "common sense". Section 4 examines the brittleness of current expert systems, and Section 5 presents evidence in support of the Breadth Hypothesis. That evidence comes from considering the limits of what AI can do today, in areas such as natural language understanding and machine learning.

The natural tendency of any search program is to slow down (often combinatorially explosively) as additional assertions are added and the search space therefore grows. All our real and imagined intelligent systems must, at some level, be *searching* as they locate and apply general rules and as they locate and perform analogical (partial) matches. Is it inevitable, then, that programs must become less intelligent in their previously-competent areas, as their KBs grow? We believe not. The key to avoiding excess search is to have a little meta-knowledge to guide and constrain the search. Hence, the key to preserving effective intelligence of a growing program lies in judicious adding of meta-knowledge along with the addition of object-level knowledge. Some of this meta-knowledge is in the form of meta-rules, and some of it is encoded by the ontology of the KB; these are, respectively, the dynamic and static ways of effectively preserving whatever useful bundlings already existed in the KB. (Of course, meta-rules can and should be represented explicitly, declaratively, as well as having a procedural form. That way, meta-meta-knowledge can apply to *them*; and so on.) This is a prescription for one to gradually add and refine categories and predicates (types of slots) as one grows the KB. This is why we believe the KP works "in the large", why we can scale up a KB to immense size without succumbing to the combinatorial explosion.

There is an additional element in our paradigm of AI research, which says that intelligence is still so poorly understood that Nature still holds most of the important surprises in store for us. This leads, in Section 6, to our central *methodological* tenets:

Empirical Inquiry Hypothesis (EH). The most profitable way to investigate AI is to embody our hypotheses in programs, and gather data by running the programs. The surprises usually suggest revisions that start the cycle over again. Progress depends on these experiments being able to *falsify* our hypotheses. Falsification is the most common and yet most crucial of surprises. In particular, these programs must be capable of behavior not expected by the experimenter.

Difficult Problems Hypothesis. There are too many ways to solve simple problems. Raising the level and breadth of competence we demand of a system makes it *easier* to test—and raise—its intelligence.

The Knowledge Principle is a mandate for humanity to concretize the knowledge used in solving hard problems in various fields.[1] This *might* lead to faster training based on explicit knowledge rather than apprenticeships. It has *already* led to thousands of profitable expert systems.

The Breadth Hypothesis is a mandate to spend the resources necessary to construct one immense knowledge base spanning human consensus reality, to serve as scaffolding for specific clusters of expert knowledge.

The Empirical Inquiry Hypothesis is a mandate to actually try to build such systems, rather than theorize about them and about intelligence. AI is a science when we use computers the way Tycho Brahe used the telescope, or Michaelson the interferometer—as a tool for looking at Nature, trying to test some hypothesis, and quite possibly getting rudely surprised by finding out that the hypothesis is false. There is quite a distinction between using a tool to gather data about the world, and using tools to, shall we say, merely fabricate ever more beautiful crystalline scale models of a geocentric universe.

In Section 7, the various principles and hypotheses above combine to suggest a sweeping three-stage research program for the main enterprise of AI research:

(1) Slowly hand-code a large, broad knowledge base.
(2) When enough knowledge is present, it should be faster to acquire more from texts, databases, etc.
(3) To go beyond the frontier of human knowledge, the system will have to rely on learning by discovery, to expand its KB.

Some evidence is then presented that stages (1) and (2) may be accomplished in approximately this century; i.e., that artificial intelligence is within our grasp. Lenat's current work at MCC, on the CYC program [28], is a serious effort to carry out the first stage by the mid-1990s.

We are betting our professional lives—the few decades of useful research we have left in us—on KP, BH, and EH. That's a scary thought, but one has to place one's bets somewhere, in science. It's especially scary because:

(a) the hypotheses are not obvious to most AI researchers,
(b) they are unpalatable in many ways even to us, their advocates!

Why are they not obvious? Most AI research focuses on very small problems, attacking them with machinery (both hardware and search methods) that overpower them. The end result is a program that "succeeds" with very little

[1] Russell and others started a similar codification in the 1920s, but that movement was unfortunately led astray by Wittgenstein (see [41]).

knowledge, and so KP, BH, and EH *are irrelevant*. One is led to them only by tackling problems in difficult "real" areas, with the world able to surprise and falsify.

Why are our three hypotheses (KP, BH, EH) not particularly palatable? Because they are unaesthetic! And they entail person-centuries of hard knowledge-entry work. Until we are forced to them, Occam's Razor encourages us to try more elegant solutions, such as training a neutral net "from scratch"; or getting an infant-simulator and then "talking to it". Only as these fail do we turn, unhappily, to the "hand-craft a huge KB" tactic.

Section 8 summarizes the differences between our position and that of some other schools of thought on AI research. Section 9 lists several limitations and problems. We do not see any of them as insurmountable. Some of the problems seem at first blush to be "in-principle limitations", and some seem to be pragmatic engineering and usability problems. Yet we lump them side by side, because our methodology says to approach them all as symptoms of gaps in our (and our programs') knowledge, which can be identified and filled in incrementally, by in-context knowledge acquisition. Several of these problems have, in the two years since the first draft of this paper was prepared, been adequately "solved". The quote marks around "solved" mean that we have found adequate ways of handling them, typically by identifying a large collection of special-case solutions that cover the vast majority of occurrences in actuality.

The biggest hurdle of all has already been put well behind us: the enormous local maximum of building and using *explicit-knowledge-free* systems. On the far side of that hill we found a much larger payoff, namely expert systems. We have learned how to build intelligent artifacts that perform well, using knowledge, on specialized tasks within narrowly defined domains. An industry has been formed to put this technological understanding to work, and widespread transfer of this technology has been achieved. Many fields are making that transition, from data processing to knowledge processing.

And yet we see expert systems technology, too, as just a local maximum. AI is finally beginning to move on beyond that threshold. This paper presents what its authors glimpse on the far side of the expert systems local-maximum hill: the promise of a large, broad KB serving as the nucleus of crystallization for programs which respond sensibly to novel situations because they can reason more by analogy than by perfect matching, and, ultimately, because, like us, they understand the meanings of their terms.

2. The Knowledge Principle

There is a continuum between the power of already knowing and the power of being able to search for the solution. In between those two extremes lie, e.g., generalizing and analogizing and plain old observing (for instance, noticing that your opponent is Castling). Even in the case of having to search for a solution, the *method* to carry out the search may be something that you already know, or partial-match to get, or search for in some other way. This recursion bottoms out in things (facts, methods, etc.) that are *already known*. Though the knowledge/search tradeoff is often used to argue for the primacy of search, we see by this line of reasoning that it equally well argues for the primacy of knowledge.

2.1. Thresholds of competence

Before you can apply search *or* knowledge to solve some problem, though, you need to already know enough to at least state the problem in a well-formed fashion. For each task, there is some minimum knowledge needed for one to even formulate it—that is, so that one can recognize when one has solved the problem.

Beyond this bare minimum, today's expert systems also include enough knowledge to reach the level of a typical practitioner performing the task. Up to that "competence" level, the knowledge/search tradeoff is strongly tipped in favor of knowledge. That is, there is an ever greater "payoff" to adding each piece of knowledge, up to some level of competence (e.g., where a useful subset of the original NP-complete problem becomes polynomial). Some of the knowledge that competent practitioners have is the knowledge of which distinctions to make and which ones to ignore. As shown by Polya [39] and Amarel [2], the space one needs to search for a solution to a problem can become smaller and smaller as one incorporates more and more such knowledge into the representation.

Beyond that "practitioner" level is the "expert" level. Here, each piece of additional knowledge is only infrequently useful. Such knowledge deals with rare but not unheard-of cases. In this realm, the knowledge/search tradeoff is fairly evenly balanced. Sometimes it's worth knowing all those obscure cases, sometimes it's more cost-effective to have general models and "run" them.

Notice that we have not yet considered "the rest of human knowledge", all the facts, heuristics, models, etc., that are not known to be relevant to this particular task. This does not mean that all other knowledge is truly irrelevant and useless to the task; perhaps it will one day be seen to be relevant through new discoveries, perhaps it will be useful to analogize from (and thereby lead to a novel solution to some tough situation), etc. Of course, putting this into an expert system for just one particular task is even *less* cost-effective, per piece of knowledge added, so no one seriously considers doing it.

2.2. Why the Knowledge Principle works so frequently

The above arguments describe how the KP *might* work; but why *does* it work so frequently? In other words, why is building even conventional expert systems a powerful and useful thing to do?

(1) Many useful real-world tasks are sufficiently narrow that the "practitioner level" and even some degree of "expert level" can be achieved by a system containing only, say, several hundred if/then rules—hence requiring only a few person-years of effort.
(2) These systems often embody only the delta, the *difference* between expert and non-expert. MYCIN may outperform general practitioners at deciding which kind of meningitis a patient has, but that's because the GPs have to know about thousands of varieties of medical problems, and relatively rarely encounter meningitis, while the program can assume that the other 99% of medicine has been judged to be irrelevant, and is free to focus on how to differentiate one type of meningitis from another.
(3) Conventional programs that perform a similar task lack most of the "if" parts of the corresponding expert system's rules. That is, they have compiled away much of the knowledge, in order to gain efficiency. The price they pay for this, though, is the high cost of integrating a new piece of knowledge into their program once it exists. To put this the other way, you can never be sure, in advance, how the knowledge already in the system is going to be used, or added to, in the future. Therefore, much of the knowledge in an intelligent system needs to be represented explicitly, declaratively, although compiled forms of it may of course also be present. We might call this the "Explicit Knowledge Principle". In other words, the experts in a field often do not yet have all the required knowledge explicitly codified (otherwise anyone could be proficient, and there wouldn't *be* recognized experts). Therefore, standard software design methodology may fail to build a program "in one pass" to perform the task. However, as the developing expert system makes mistakes, the experts can correct them, and those corrections incrementally accrete the bulk of the hitherto unexplicated rules. In this manner, the system incrementally approaches competence, and even expertise, where no traditional software solution would work.
(4) There is another benefit that accrues when knowledge—including procedural knowledge—is represented declaratively, as explicit objects, following the "Explicit Knowledge Principle", above. Namely, *meta*-rules can apply to it, e.g., helping to acquire, check, or debug other rules. Structured objects that represent knowledge can be more easily analogized to, and can enable generalizations to be structurally induced from them. So while we concede to procedural attachment (having opaque lumps of code here and there in the system) for efficiency reasons, we argue that there should be a declarative version of that also (i.e., a declarative structure containing the information which is encoded in the procedure).

2.3. Control in knowledge-based systems

What about the control structure of an intelligent system? Even granted that lots of knowledge is necessary, might we not need sophisticated as-yet-unknown reasoning methods?

Knowledge Is All There Is Hypothesis. No sophisticated, as-yet-unknown control structure is required for intelligent behavior.

On the one hand, we already understand deduction, induction, analogy, specialization, generalization, and so on, well enough to have *knowledge* be our bottleneck, not control strategies. This does not mean that we fully understand such processes, of course. To be sure, additional work still needs to be done there. But we have examined them enough to eliminate the gross inefficiencies in their execution, to devise data structures and algorithms for efficiently performing them in the most commonly occurring cases. (For instance, consider Stickel's non-clausal connection graph resolution theorem prover [44], which was a response to the known inefficiency of deduction.)

On the other hand, all such strategies and methods are themselves just pieces of knowledge. The control structure of the intelligent system can be *opportunistic*: select one strategy, apply it for a while, monitor progress, and perhaps decide to switch to another strategy (when some other piece of knowledge suggests it do so).

Carefully reading our wording in this section will reveal that we are making a pragmatic argument, involving choices for where to focus current AI research, rather than making a hypothesis we expect to hold true forever. We don't understand induction, analogy, etc., perfectly, but further progress on understanding them needs to be done in the context of a large knowledge base. So let's worry about getting that built, and then return to study these phenomena. Perhaps at that time we will see the need to develop some useful new control scheme.

2.4. The manner in which knowledge boosts competence

Can we be more specific about the manner in which knowledge boosts competence? Can we give, say, an equation for how to measure the effective power of the knowledge in a system, when it's applied to a problem P? It is premature to even attempt to do so—it may *never* be possible to do so. It may never even be possible to give precise definitions for terms like "useful" and "competence". Nevertheless, this section speculates on what some of the terms in that equation would be.

Factor 1. Consider a heuristic H; e.g., "Drive carefully late at night". It has a characteristic curve of how powerful or useful it is, as a function of what problem it's applied to. As detailed in [25], the area under this curve is often constant across heuristics. In simpler and more familiar terms, this is just the generality/power tradeoff: the more powerful a heuristic's "peak power" is, the narrower its domain of applicability is likely to be. A heuristic that only applies to driving on Saturday nights, in Austin, might be far more powerful than H, but its range of applicability is correspondingly narrower. As a first approximation to the power of the knowledge in the system, we might simply superpose all the "power curves" of the heuristics (and algorithms) that comprise the knowledge. That would give us an overall idea of the power of the system as a function of what problem it was applied to. If we're interested in applying the system to a particular problem P, we could then read off the value of this curve at point P. If we're going to apply the system to several problems, so that P is a large distribution, then we would weight the result by that distribution.

Factor 2. As a correction to this first rough guess, attempt to factor out some of the redundancy and dependence among the pieces of knowledge.

Factor 3. Weight each heuristic by how costly it is to run. "Cost" here includes literal CPU and memory resources used, and also includes the less tangible cost of asking questions of slow and busy human beings. Also included in this factor would be the downside risks of what might happen if the heuristic gave incorrect advice.

Factor 4. To be fair to the less-knowledge-based approaches, we should also deduct some amount which amortizes the effort we spent *acquiring* that rule or method.

Those represent just four of the factors in measuring the effective power of the knowledge in a system. We encourage further investigation in this direction. Recent work in nonmonotonic logic may bear on Factors 1 and 3; and [46] may bear on Factor 2.

3. Evidence for the Knowledge Principle

Half a century ago, before the modern era of computation began, Turing's theorems and abstract machines gave a hint of the fundamental idea that the computer could be used to model the symbol-manipulating processes that make up that most human of all behaviors: thinking.

Thirty years ago, following the 1956 Dartmouth Summer Conference on AI, the work began in earnest. The founding principle of the AI research paradigm is really an article of faith, first concretized by Newell and Simon: (See [35] for more details.)

Physical Symbol System Hypothesis. The digital computer has sufficient means for intelligent action; to wit: representing real-world objects, actions, and relationships internally as interconnected structures of symbols, and applying symbol manipulation procedures to those structures.

The early dreaming included intelligent behavior at very high levels of competence. Turing speculated on wide-ranging conversations between people and machines, and also on expert-level chess playing programs. Newell and Simon also wrote about champion chess programs, and began working with Cliff Shaw toward that end. McCarthy wrote about the Advice Taking program. Gelernter, Moses, Samuel, and many others shared the dream.

Lederberg and Feigenbaum chose, in 1964, to pursue the AI dream by focusing on scientific reasoning tasks. With Buchanan and Djerassi, they built Dendral, a program that solved structure elucidation problems at a high level of competence. Many years of experimenting with Dendral led to some hypotheses about what its source of power might be, how it was able to solve chemical structure problems from spectral data. Namely, the program worked because it had enough knowledge of basic and spectral chemistry.

Table 1 shows that as each additional source of chemical knowledge was added, the Dendral program proposed fewer and fewer candidates (topologically plausible structures) to consider (see [7]). The fifth and final type of rule of thumb were rules for interpreting nuclear mass resonance (NMR) data. With all five types of rule in the program, many problems—such as the one illustrated—resulted in only a single candidate isomer being proposed as worth considering! Threatened by an a priori huge search space, Dendral managed to convert it into a tiny search space. That is, Dendral exhibited intelligence.

When searching a space of size 1, it is not crucial in what order you expand the candidate nodes. If you want to speed up a blind search by a factor of 43 million, one could perhaps parallelize the problem and (say, by 1995) employ a 43-mega-processor; but even back in 1965 one could, alternatively, talk with the human experts who routinely solve such problems, and then encode the knowledge they bring to bear to avoid searching. There is a cost associated with making the generator "smarter" in this fashion (i.e., there is inferencing

Table 1
Dendral at work: Finding all atom-bond graphs that could have the formula $C_{20}H_{43}N$. The sources given are cumulative; thus, the final "1" refers to Dendral with all five types of rules running in it.

Information source	Number of structures generated
Topology (limits of 3D space)	42,867,912
Chemical topology (valences)	14,715,814
Mass spectrography (heuristics)	1,284,792
Chemistry (first principles)	1,074,648
NMR (interpretation rules)	1

going on inside the generator, to utilize the knowledge it now contains) but that cost is insignificant compared to the seven orders of magnitude reduction in the size of the search space it permits.

Obvious? Perhaps, in retrospect. But at the time, the prevailing view in AI ascribed power to the reasoning processes, to the inference engine and not to the knowledge base. (E.g., consider LT and GPS and the flurry of work on resolution theorem provers.) The *knowledge as power* hypothesis, supported by Feigenbaum (Dendral), McCarthy (Advice Taker), and a few others, stood as a *contra*-hypothesis. It stood awaiting further empirical testing to either confirm it or falisfy it.

The 1970s were the time to start gathering evidence for or against the Knowledge Principle. Medical and scientific problem solving provided the springboard.

- Shortliffe's MYCIN program formed the prototype for a large suite of expert-level advisory systems which we now label "expert systems" [12]. Its reasoning system was simple (exhaustive backward chaining) and ad hoc in parts.
- DEC has been using and extending R1 program (EXCON) since 1981; its control structure is also simple: exhaustive forward chaining [32].
- Over a period of two decades, Bledsoe was led to incorporate more and more heuristics into his theorem provers, ultimately rejecting resolution entirely and opting for knowledge-guided natural deduction [3, 4].
- The INTERNIST program [40] got underway at nearly the same time as MYCIN. By now it has grown to a KB of 572 diseases, 4500 manifestations, and many hundreds of thousands of links between them.
- The AM [9] and EURISKO [25] programs, 15 years old by now, demonstrated that several hundred heuristic rules, of varying levels of generality and power, could adequately begin to guide a search for plausible (and often interesting) new concepts in many domains, including set theory, number theory, naval wargaming tactics, physical device design, evolution, and programming. These experiments showed how scientific discovery—a very different sort of intelligent behavior from most expert systems' tasks—might be explained as rule-guided, knowledge-guided search. Not all of the AM experiments were successful; indeed, the ultimate limitations of AM as it was run longer and longer finally led to EURISKO, whose ultimate empirical limitations [27] led to CYC, of which more later.

In the past decade, thousands of expert systems have mushroomed in engineering, manufacturing, geology, molecular biology, financial services, machinery diagnosis and repair, signal processing, and in many other fields. From the very beginning, these expert systems could interact with professionals in the jargon of the specialty; could explain their line of reasoning by displaying annotated traces of rule-firings; and had subsystems (such as

MYCIN's TEIRESIAS [9] and XCON's SALT [29]) which aided the acquisition of additional knowledge by guiding the expert to find and fix defects in the knowledge (rule) base.

Very little ties these areas together, other than that in each one, some technical problem solving is going on, guided by heuristics: experimental, qualitative rules of thumb—rules of good guessing. Their reasoning components are weak and simple; in their knowledge bases lies their power. The evidence for the various propositions we made in Section 2 lies in their details—in the details of their design, development, and performance.

In the 1980s, many other areas of AI research began making the shift over to the knowledge-based point of view. It is now common to hear that a program for understanding natural language must have extensive knowledge of its domain of discourse. Or, a vision program must have an understanding of the "world" it is intended to analyze scenes from. Or even, a machine learning program must start with a significant body of knowledge which it will expand, rather than trying to learn from scratch.

4. The Breadth Hypothesis

A limitation of past and current expert systems is their brittleness. They operate on a high plateau of knowledge and competence until they reach the extremity of their knowledge; then they fall off precipitously to levels of ultimate incompetence. People suffer the same difficulty, too, but their plateau is much broader and their slope is more gentle. Part of what cushions the fall are layer upon layer of weaker, more general models that underlie their specific knowledge.

For example, if engineers are diagnosing a faulty circuit they are unfamiliar with, they can bring to bear: circuit analysis techniques; their experiences with the other products manufactured by the same company, published handbook data for the individual components, and commonsense rules of thumb for water circuits (looking for leaks, or breaks), for electrical devices (turn it off and on a few times), and for mechanical devices in general (shake it or smack it a few times). Engineers might analogize to the last few times their automobile engine failed, or even to something as distant as a failed love affair. Naturally, the more different the causality of the thing they analogize to, the less likely it will be to apply in the electronic circuit diagnosis situation.

Domain-specific knowledge represents the distillation of experience in a field, nuggets of compiled hindsight. In a situation similar to the one in which they crystallized, they can powerfully guide search. But when confronted by a *novel* situation, human beings turn to reasoning strategies like generalizing and analogizing in real time and (even better) *already having* more general rules to fall back on. This leads to the Breadth Hypothesis (BH), which we stated in Section 1.

4.1. *Falling back on increasingly general knowledge*

Each of us has a vast storehouse of general knowledge, though we rarely talk about any of it explicitly to one another; we just assume that other people already know these things. If they're included in a conversation, or an article, they confuse more than they clarify. Some examples are:

- water flows downhill,
- living things get diseases,
- doing work requires energy,
- people live for a single, contiguous, finite interval of time,
- most cars today are riding on four tires,
- each tire a car is riding on is mounted on a wheel,
- if you fall asleep while driving, your car will start to head out of your lane pretty soon,
- if something big is between you and the thing you want, you probably will have to go around it.

It is *consensus reality* knowledge. Lacking these simple commonsense concepts, expert systems' mistakes often appear ridiculous in human terms. For instance, when a car loan authorization program approves a loan to a teenager who put down he'd worked at the same job for twenty years; or when a skin disease diagnosis program concludes that my rusted out decade-old Chevy has measles; or when a medical system prescribes an absurd dosage of a drug for a maternity patient whose weight (105) and age (35) were accidentally swapped during the case's type-in.

As we build increasingly complex programs, and invest them with increasing power, the humor quickly evaporates.

4.2. *Reasoning by analogy*

Reasoning by analogy involves *partial*-matching from your current situation to another one. There are two independent dimensions along which analogizing occurs, vertical (simplifying) and horizontal (cross-field) transformation.

- *Vertical*: When faced with a complex situation, we often analogize to a much simpler one. Of course simplification can be overdone: "the stock market is a seesaw"; "medication is a resource" (this leads many patients to overdose).
- *Horizontal*: Cross-field mapping is rarer but can pay off: "curing a disease is like fighting a battle" may help doctors devise new tactics to try (e.g., viruses employed to perform the analogue of propaganda) and may help soldiers devise new military tactics (e.g., choosing missions which function like vaccination).

Successful analogizing often involves components of both vertical and horizontal transformation. For instance, consider reifying a country as if it were an individual person: "Russia is angry". That accomplishes two things: it simplifies dealing with the other country, and it also enables our vast array of first-hand experiences (and lessons learned) about inter-personal relations to be applied to international relations.

Do not make the mistake we did, of thinking of this reasoning method as little more than a literary device, used for achieving some sort of emotional impact. It can be used to help discover solutions to problems, and to flesh out solutions; and it can be argued that analogy pervades human communication and perhaps almost all of human thought! (see [22]). Even conceding that analogy is powerful, and often applies, still two questions linger: "*Why* does such an unsound problem-solving method work well?", and "Why does it work so often?"

There is much common causality in the world; that leads to similar events A and B; people (with our limited perception) then notice a little bit of that shared structure; finally, since we *know* that human perception is often limited, people come to rely on the following rule of thumb:

Analogical Method. If A and B appear to have some unexplained similarities, then it's worth your time to hunt for additional shared properties.

This rule is general but inefficient. There are many more specialized versions for successful analogizing in various task domains, in various user-modes (e.g., by someone in a hurry, or a child), among analogues with various epistemological statuses, depending on how much data there is about A and B, and so on. These are some of the n dimensions of analogy space; we can conceive having a special body of knowledge—an expert system—in each cell of that n-dimensional matrix, to handle just that sort of analogical reasoning.

Why focus on causality? If cause(A) and cause(B) have no specific common generalization, then similarities between A and B are more likely to be superficial coincidences, a metaphor useful perhaps as a literary device but not as a heuristic one.

Analogy in mathematics, where there is no clear notion of causality, operates similarly to "genuine" analogy, with the weaker relation of material implication substituting for causality. In that case, what one is often finding is a connection between two instances of a not-yet-conceptualized generalization. Also, much of analogizing in the doing of mathematics [39] is analogizing between the current problem-solving situation and a past one, i.e., between two search processes, not between two mathematical entities. And the act of trying to solve math problems is indeed frought with causality and, hence, opportunities for the above sort of "genuine" analogizing.

The above paragraphs are really just a rationalization of how analogy *might* work. The reason this unsound reasoning method *frequently* succeeds has to do with three *moderation properties* that happen to hold in the real world:

(1) The moderate distribution of causes with respect to effects. If there were a vast number of unrelated kinds of causes, or if there were only one or two distinguishable causes, then analogy would be less useful.
(2) The moderately high frequency with which we must cope with novel situations, and the moderate degree of novelty they present. Lower frequency, or much higher (volatility of the world in which the problem solver must perform), would decrease the usefulness of trying to analogize. Why? In a world with essentially no surprises, memory is all you need; and in volatile world, matching to past occurrences is more of a hindrance than a help.
(3) The obvious metric for locating relevant knowledge—namely, "closeness of subject matter"—is just a moderately good predictor of true relevance. Far-flung knowledge and imagery *can* be useful. If we already understood all the connections, we'd always know when *X* was relevant; and if we had no attributes of knowledge to match to, we'd have no idea of how to generate (let alone flesh out) an analogy.

Analogizing broadens the relevance of the entire knowledge base. It can be used to construct interesting and novel interpretations of situations and data; to retrieve knowledge that has not been stored the way that it is now needed; to guess values for attributes; to suggest methods that just might work; and as a device to help students learn and remember. It can provide access to powerful methods that might work in this case, but which might not otherwise be perceived as "relevant". E.g., Dirac analogized between quantum theory and group theory, and very gingerly brought the group theory results over into physics for the first time, with quite successful results.

Today, we suffer with laborious manual knowledge entry in building expert systems, carefully codifying knowledge and placing it in a data structure. Analogizing may be used in the future not only as an inference method inside a program, but also as an aid to adding new knowledge to it.

5. Evidence for the Breadth Hypothesis

If we had as much hard evidence about the BH as we do for the KP, we would be calling it the Breadth *Principle*. Still, the evidence is there, if we look closely at the limits of what AI programs can do today. Most of the current AI research we've read about is currently stalled. As Mark Stefik recently remarked in a note to us, "*Progress will be held back until a sufficient corpus of knowledge is available on which to base experiments.*" For brevity, we will focus on natural language understanding (NL) and machine learning (ML), but similar results are appearing in most other areas of AI as well.

5.1. The limits of natural language understanding

To understand sentences in a natural language, one must be able to disambiguate which meaning of a word is intended, what the referent of a pronoun probably is, what each ellipsis means, and so on. These are knowledge-intensive skills.

---

1. I saw the Statue of Liberty flying over New York.
2. The box is in the pen. The ink is in the pen.
3. Mary saw a dog in the window. She wanted it.
4. Napolean died on St. Helena. Wellington was saddened.

Fig. 1. Sentences presume world knowledge furiously.

Consider the first sentence in Fig. 1. Who's flying, you or the statue? Clearly we aren't getting any clues from English to do that disambiguation; we must know about people, statues, passenger air travel, the size of cargo that is shipped by air, the size and location of the Statue of Liberty, the ease or difficulty of seeing objects from a distance, and numerous other consensus reality facts and heuristics. What if we'd said "I saw the Statue of Liberty standing in New York Harbor." It's not fair to say the verb (flying *versus* standing) decides it for you; consider, e.g., "I saw the Statue of Liberty standing at the top of the Empire State Building." See [45] for similar examples.

On line 2, in Fig. 1, the first "pen" is a corral, the other is a writing implement. But how do you know that? It has to do with storage of solids and liquids, of how big various objects are, with your ability to almost instantly and subconsciously consider *why* one might place a box in each kind of pen, *why* one might put ink inside each kind of pen, and choose the plausible interpretation in each case. This ability can of course be misled, as for example in one category of jokes.

On line 3, does "it" refer to the dog or the window? What if we'd said "She *smashed* it", or "She pressed her nose up against it"?

A program which *understood* line 4 should be able to answer "Did Wellington hear of Napoleon's death?" Often, we communicate by what *isn't* said, in between one sentence and the next one. And of course we should then be able to draw the obvious conclusions from those inferred assertions; e.g., being able to answer the question "Did Wellington outlive Napoleon?"

For any particular chosen text, an NL program can incorporate the small set of necessary twentieth century Americana, the few commonsense facts and scripts that are required for semantic disambiguation, question answering, anaphoric reference, and so on. But then one turns to a new page, and the new text requires more semantics (pragmatics) to be added.

In a sense, the NL researchers *have* cracked the language understanding problem. But to produce a general Turing-testable system, they would have to provide more and more domain-specific information, and the program's semantic component would more and more resemble the immense KB mandated by the Breadth Hypothesis. As Norvig [38] concludes: "the complexity [has been shifted] from the algorithm to the knowledge base, to handle examples that other systems could do only by introducing specialized algorithms."

Have we overstated the argument about how NL programs must ultimately have a large, real-world knowledge base to draw upon? Hardly; if anything we have drastically *under*stated it! Look at almost any newspaper story, e.g., and attend to how often a word or concept is used in a clearly metaphorical, non-literal sense. Once every few minutes, you might guess? No! Reality is full of surprises. The surprise here is that almost every sentence is packed with metaphors and analogies [22]. An unbiased sample: here is the first article we saw today (April 7, 1987), the lead story in the *Wall Street Journal* [50]:

> Texaco lost a major ruling in its legal battle with Pennzoil. The Supreme Court dismantled Texaco's protection against having to post a crippling $12 billion appeals bond, pushing Texaco to the brink of a Chapter 11 filing.

Lost? Major? Battle? Dismantled? Posting? Crippling? Pushing? Brink? The example drives home the point that, far from overinflating the need for real-world knowledge in language understanding, the usual arguments about disambiguation barely scratch the surface. (Drive? Home? The point? Far? Overinflating? Scratch? Surface? oh no, I can't call a halt to this! (call? halt?)) These layers of analogy and metaphor eventually "bottom out" at physical—*somatic* – primitives: up, down, forward, back, pain, cold, inside, seeing, sleeping, tasting, growing, containing, moving, making noise, hearing, birth, death, strain, exhaustion, . . . , and calling and halting.

NL researchers—and dictionaries—usually get around analogic usage by allowing several meanings to a word. Definition #1 for "war", say, is the literal one, and the other definitions are various common metaphorical uses of "war" (such as "an argument", "a commercial competition", "a search for a cure for", etc.).

There are many millions (perhaps a few hundred million) of things we authors can assume you readers know about the world: the number of tires an auto has; who Ronald Reagan is; what happens if you fall asleep when driving—what we called consensus reality. To use language effectively, we select the best consensus image to quickly evoke in the listener's mind the complex thought we want to convey. If our program doesn't already know most of those millions of shared concepts (experiences, objects, processes, patterns, . . .), it will be awkward for us to communicate with it in NL.

It is common for NL researchers to acknowledge the need for a large semantic component nowadays; Schank and others were saying similar things a decade ago! But the first serious efforts have only recently begun to try to actually build one: at MCC (in conjunction with CYC), and at EDR, the Japanese Electronic Dictionary Research project [10]. We shall have to wait a few more years until the evidence is in.

5.2. The limits of machine learning (induction)

Machine learning is a second area where research is stalled owing to insufficiently broad knowledge bases. We will pick on AM and EURISKO because they exemplify the extreme knowledge-rich end of the current ML spectrum. Many experiments in machine learning were performed on them. We had many surprises along the way, and gained an intuitive feel for how and why heuristics work, for the nature of their power and their brittleness. Lenat and Brown present many of those surprises in [27]; some are listed in Fig. 2.

1. It works. Several thousand concepts, including some novel concepts and heuristics, from several domains, were discovered.
2. Most of the interesting concepts could be discovered in several different ways.
3. Performing the top *N* tasks on the Agenda in simulated-parallel provided only about a factor of 3 speedup even when *N* grew as large as 100.
4. Progress slows down unless the program learns new heuristics (compiles its hindsight) often.
5. Similarly, progress slowed down partly because the programs could not competently learn to choose, switch, extend, or invent different representations.
6. These programs are sensitive to the assumptions woven into their representations' semantics; e.g., "What does it *mean* for Jane to appear as the value on the spouse slot of the Fred frame?"
7. Some of their apparent power is illusory, only present in the mind of the intelligent observer who recognizes concepts which the program defines but does not properly appreciate.
8. Structural mutation works iff syntax mirrors semantics: represent heuristics using many small if- and many small then-parts, so the results of point mutation can be more meaningful.
9. In each new domain, there would be a flurry of plausible activities, resulting in several unexpected discoveries, followed by a period of decreased productivity, and finally lapsing into useless thrashing. The above techniques (e.g., 4, 5, 8) only delayed this decay.

Fig. 2. Some of the major surprises of the "discovery guided by heuristic rules" experiments performed with the AM and EURISKO programs, during the decade 1975–1984.

Despite their relative knowledge-richness, the ultimate limitations of these programs derived from their small size. Not their small number of methods, which were probably adequate, but the small initial knowledge base they had to draw upon. One can analogize to a campfire that dies out because it was too small, and too well isolated from nearby trees, to start a major blaze. The heuristics, the representations chosen, etc., provide the kindling and the spark, but the real fuel must come from without.

In other words, AM and other machine learning programs "ran down" because of insufficient knowledge. EURISKO partially solved this, by having new heuristics be learned simultaneously with the object-level learning, but this merely delayed the inevitable. The point here is that one can only learn something—by discovery or by being told—if one almost knows it already. This leads to Piagetian stages in young children, courses of study in young adults, and suggests the need for large knowledge bases in AI programs.

Marvin Minsky cites a variant of this relationship in his afterword to *True Names* [49]: "The more you know, the more (and faster) you can learn." The inverse of this enabling relationship is a disabling one, and that's what ultimately doomed AM and EURISKO:

Knowledge Facilitates Learning (Catch 22). If you don't know very much to begin with, don't expect to learn a lot quickly.

This is the standard criticism of pure Baconian induction. As philosophers are wont to say, "To get ahead, get a theory." Without one, you'll be lost. It will be difficult (or time-consuming) to determine whether or not each new generalization is going to be useful. In hindsight, perhaps we shouldn't have been surprised at this. After all, learning can be considered a task; and, like other tasks, it is subject to the Knowledge Principle.

This theme (knowledge facilitates learning) is filtering into ML in the form of explanation-based generalization (EBG) and goal-based learning. Unfortunately, EBG requires well-defined theories (too strong a requirement) and works by logically deducing (too restrictive a process) the explanandum. Hence we would expect this method of getting machines to learn to have some— but limited—success, which seems to be empirically what ML researchers report. E.g., Mostow [34] concludes that "scaling up for harder learning problems . . . is likely to require integrating [additional] sources of knowledge."

Don't human beings violate this Catch, starting as we do "from nothing"? Maybe, but it's not clear *what* human infants start with. Evolution has produced not merely physically sophisticated structures, but also brains whose architecture make us well suited to learning many of the simple facts that are worth learning about the world. Other senses, e.g., vision, are carefully tuned as well, to supply the brain with data that is already filtered for meaning (edges, shapes, motion, etc.) in the world in which we do happen to live. The exploration of those issues is beyond the scope of this paper, and probably beyond the scope of twentieth century science, but one thing is clear: neonatal brains are far from *tabula rasae*.

Besides starting from well-prepared brain structures, humans also have to spend a lot of time learning. It is unclear what processes go on during infancy. Once the child begins to communicate by speaking, *then* we are into the symbolic sort of learning that AI has traditionally focused on. One theory of why it's difficult to remember one's infancy and young childhood is that we radically reorganize our knowledge once or twice during our early life, and the memory structures we built as infants are not interpretable by the retrieval and reasoning methods we use as an adult [33].

6. The Empirical Inquiry Hypothesis

We scientists have a view of ourselves as terribly creative, but compared to Nature we suffer from a poverty of the imagination; it is thus much easier for us to uncover than to invent. As we state elsewhere in this paper, experimentation must be hypothesis-driven; we are not advocating the random mixture of chemicals in the hope that lead transmutes to gold. But there is a difference between having theories as one's guide versus as one's master. Premature adherance to a theory keeps Nature's surprises hidden, washing out details that later turn out to be significant (i.e., either not perceiving them at all, or labeling them as anomalies [20] and then not attending to them). E.g., contrast the astonishing early empirical studies by Piaget (*Stages of Development*) with his subsequent five decades of barren attempts to mathematize them.

This attitude leads to our central methodological hypothesis, our paradigm for AI research: the Empirical Inquiry Hypothesis (EH). We stated it in Section 1, and repeat it here:

Empirical Inquiry Hypothesis (EH). Intelligence is still so poorly understood that Nature still holds most of the important surprises in store for us. So the most profitable way to investigate AI is to embody our hypotheses in programs, and gather data by running the programs. The surprises usually suggest revisions that start the cycle over again. Progress depends on these experiments being able to *falsify* our hypotheses. Falsification is the most common and yet most crucial of surprises! In particular, these programs must be capable of behavior not expected by the experimenter.

What do we mean by "a surprise"? Surely we wouldn't want to increase surprises by having more naive researchers, less careful thought and planning of experiments, sloppier coding, unreliable machines, etc. We have in mind astronomers getting surprised by what they see (and "see") through telescopes; i.e., things surprising to the professional. Early AI programs often surprised their builders in this fashion; e.g., Newell, Simon, and Shaw's LT program [36] and Gelernter's geometry program [15]. Then fascination with axiomatizing and proving set in, and surprises from "the real world" became rare.

We have no objection to experimentation and theorizing proceeding hand in hand, we object only to the nearly exclusive doing of one of those activities and ignoring the other. As Genesereth and Nilsson argue in the preface of [17], having a good understanding of the theoretical issues can enable one to be a better experimenter.

The inverse to the EH is cruel:

Inverse to the Empirical Inquiry Hypothesis. If one builds programs which cannot possibly surprise him/her, then one is using the computer either
(a) as an engineering workhorse, or
(b) as a fancy sort of word processor (to help articulate one's hypothesis), or
(c) as a (self-)deceptive device masquerading as an experiment.

Most expert systems work falls into the first category; DART's use of MRS exemplifies the middle [16]; PUP5 (by the young Lenat [24]) and HACKER (by the young Sussman [47]) exemplify the latter category.

6.1. PUP5: a bad example

To illustrate this point, we will use some of our own earlier work. The PUP5 program [24] used a community of about one hundred Beings (similar to what have since been called actors and blackboard knowledge sources) to cooperate and synthesize a long LISP program, namely a variant of the Arch-learning program that Patrick Winston had written for his thesis a few years earlier.

That was the program that PUP5 was built to synthesize, the target it was to hit. We chose that target first, and wrote a clean version of the program in INTERLISP. Next, we wrote down an English dialogue in which a user talked to an idealized automatic program synthesis program which then gradually wrote the target program. Next, we analyzed the script of that dialogue, writing down the specific knowledge needed on the part of the synthesizer to handle each and every line that the user typed in. Finally, we encoded each of those pieces of knowledge, and bundled up the related ones into little actors or Beings.

Given this methodology, it should come as no surprise that PUP5 was then able to carry on that exact dialogue with a user, and synthesize that exact Arch program. We still firmly believe in the paradigm of multiple cooperating knowledge sources, it's just that our methodology ensured that there wouldn't be any surprises when we ran PUP5. Why? All along the way, there were numerous chances to cut corners, to consciously or unconsciously put down knowledge in a very specific form: just the knowledge that was needed, and in just the form that it would be needed during the dialogue we know was going to be run. There wasn't much else PUP5 could do, therefore, besides hit its target, and there wasn't much that we learned about automatic programming or intelligence from that six-month exercise.

There was one crucial *meta*-level lesson we did learn: You can't do science if you just use a computer as a word processor, to illustrate your ideas rather than test them. That's the coarse form of the Empirical Inquiry Hypothesis. We resolved, in late 1974, to choose a task that eliminated or minimized the chance of building a wind-up toy like PUP5. We did not want a program whose target behavior was so narrow, so precisely defined, that it could "succeed" and yet teach us nothing. The AM program, written during 1975, was the direct result of Lenat's violent recoil from the PUP5 project.

There was no particular target behavior that AM was designed with; rather, it was an experiment: What would happen if a moderate-sized body of a few hundred math heuristics (about what were plausible directions to go in, about when something was and wasn't interesting) were applied in an agenda-managed best-first search, given an initial body of a hundred or so simple math concepts. In this sense, AM's task was less constrained than any program's had ever been: to explore areas of mathematics and do interesting things (gather data, notice regularities, etc.), with no preconceptions about what it might find or by what route it would find it. (Actually, we did have a few examples in mind for what AM might do, involving simple lattice theory and abstract algebra, but it never did those!)

Unlike PUP5, AM provided hundreds of surprises, including many experiments that led to the construction of EURISKO. EURISKO ran for several thousand CPU hours, in half a dozen varied domains (see Fig. 2, above). And again the ultimate limitation was not what we expected (CPU time), or hoped for (the need to learn new representations of knowledge), but rather something at once surprising and daunting: the need to have a large fraction of consensus reality already in the machine. In this case, the data led Lenat to the next project to work on—CYC—an undertaking we would have shied away from like the plague if the empirical evidence hadn't forced us to it. It has similarly led Feigenbaum to undertake his current line of research, namely building a large KB of engineering and scientific knowledge.

Thus, progress along our personal "paths of evolution" was due to running large experiments. As the Difficult Problems Hypothesis said in Section 1, *There are too many ways to solve simple problems. Raising the level and breadth of competence we demand of a system makes it* easier *to test and raise its intelligence.*

Much research in cognitive psychology, e.g., traditionally sidesteps hard-to-quantify phenomena such as scientific creativity or reading and comprehending a good book, in favor of very simple tasks such as remembering nonsense syllables. If a "messy" task *is* studied, then usually either (1) it is abstracted and simplified almost beyond recognition [23], or (2) the psychologist focuses on (and varies) one specific variable, so "respectable" statistical tests for significance can be run.

6.2. Paradigms for AI research

Much of the confusion about AI methodology may be due to our casual mixing together of two quite different things: AI *goals* and AI *strategies* for achieving those goals. The confusion arises because many entries appear on both lists. Almost any strategy can apply toward any goal. Consider just one example: (1) An *expert system strategy* for a *language understanding goal* might be to build a rule-based system containing rules like "If a person gets excited, they break more grammatical rules than usual." By contrast: (2) A *language understanding strategy* for an *expert system goal* might be to build a restricted-English front end that helps an expert enter and edit rules.

All scientific disciplines adopt a paradigm: a list of the problems that are acceptable and worthwhile to tackle, a list of the methods that can and should be tried, and the standards by which the results are judged. Adopting a paradigm is done for reasons of cognitive economy, but each paradigm is one narrow view. Adding to the confusion, some paradigms in AI have grown up both around the various goals *and* around the various strategies! See Appendix A for a more detailed look into AI goals and strategies.

Finer distinctions can be drawn, involving the *tactical* choices to be made, but this turns out to be misleading. In what way misleading? Tactics that appear to be superficially different may share a common source of power: E.g., predicate calculus and frames both rely on a judicious dividing up of the world. Much of the "scruffies' " recent work on plausible reasoning by heuristic rules overlaps (but with very little shared vocabulary!) the "neats' " recent work on nonmonotonic reasoning and circumscription.

The KP and BH and EH are all *strategic* statements. Each could be prefaced by the phrase "*Whichever of the ultimate goals for AI you are pursuing . . .*". The strategic level is, apparently, the level where one needs to take a stand. This is rarely stated explicitly, and it is rarely taken into account by news media or by conference organizers.

We have an abiding trust in our chosen paradigm—empirical inquiry—in doing science the same way as the early Piaget, Newell, Simon, and Gelernter. The number of states that a brain or a computer can be in is immense; both those numbers are so huge as to be almost unimaginable. Turing's Hypothesis likens them to each other; the only other system we're familiar with with that degree of complexity is Nature itself. Mankind has made progress in studying natural phenomena only after centuries of empirically studying those phenomena; there is no reason to expect intelligence to be exempt. Eventually, many of the natural sciences advanced to the point that theory now often precedes experiment by years or decades, but we have far to go in AI before reaching that stage.

James Wilkinson was asked in 1974 why *he* was the first to discover the truncation errors of early twentieth century integration methods. After all, Wilkes at Cambridge, and others, had access to equal or better machines at the same time. He replied that at the National Physical Laboratory, the Pilot Ace machine was sitting out, available to all to use and to watch. He was fascinated by the rows of blinking lights, and often stood mesmerized by them while his programs ran. Soon he began to recognize patterns in the lights—patterns where there should *not* have been patterns! By contrast, the Cambridge computer was screened off from its users, who got one-day turnaround on their card decks, but who were denied access to the phenomenon that Wilkinson was allowed to observe.

The point is that while having a theory is essential, it is equally important to examine data and be driven by exceptions and anomalies to revise, criticize, and if necessary reject one's theory. To take one last example: a computer-simulated Newtonian world really would *be* Newtonian; only by hooking up actual telescopes and interferometers and such (or the data from them) can the non-Newtonian nature be perceived.

7. A mandate for AI research: mapping the human memome

AI must somehow get to that stage where—as called for by KP and BH—learning begins to accelerate due to the amount already known. Induction will not be an effective means to get to that stage, unfortunately; we shall have to hand-craft that large "seed" KB one piece at a time. In terms of the graph in Fig. 3, all the programs that have ever been written, including AM and EURISKO, lie so far toward the left edge of the x-axis that the learning rate is more or less zero. Several of the more successful recent additions to the suite of ML techniques can be interpreted as pushes in the direction of adding more knowledge from which to begin the learning.

The graph in Fig. 3 shows learning by induction (DISCOVERY) constantly accelerating: the more one knows, the faster one can discover still more. Once you speak fluently, learning by talking with other people (LANGUAGE) is more efficient than rediscovery, until you cross the frontier of what humanity already knows (the vertical line at $x = F$), at which point there is no one to tell you the next piece of knowledge.

"Learning by discovery" is meant to include not only scientific research (e.g., cancer research), but also the many smaller-scale events in which someone formulates a hypothesis, gathers data to test it, and uses the results to adjust their "theory". That small-scale case can occur in a (good) classroom; or just by driving the same route to work over various different times of the day

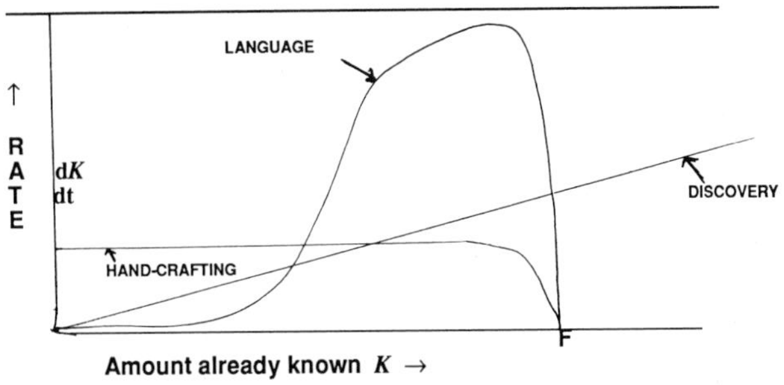

Fig. 3. The rate at which one can learn new knowledge. One can also integrate these three curves with respect to time, to see how the total amount known might grow over time.

(and hypothesizing on rush hour patterns). It involves defining new concepts (at least in principle), formulating new heuristics, and even adjusting or changing one's representation of knowledge. Figure 3 illustrates two more things. Learning by discovery is much *slower* than other forms of learning—such as being told something in natural language—but it is the chief method that extends the boundary F of human knowledge.

By contrast, the rate of hand-coding of knowledge is fairly constant, though it, too, drops to zero once we cross the boundary of what is already known by humanity. The hand-coding rate may slope down a bit, since the time to find related concepts will increase perhaps as the log of the size of the KB. Or, instead, the hand-coding rate may slope *up* a bit, since copy and edit is a powerful technique for knowledge entry, and, as the KB grows, there will be more chance that some very similar concept is already present.

This is an example of EH (the Empirical Inquiry Hypothesis which was presented in Section 1): Only by trying to hand-code the KB will we see which of those two counteracting factors outweighs the other, and by how much. Only by continued work on NL and ML will we determine whether or not there is a region, near where all three curves meet, where ML temporarily surpasses NL as a way to grow the KB. And only much further in the future, after our program crosses the frontier F will we find out if the discovery curve begins to slope up or down.

Figure 3 suggests a sweeping three-stage research program for the coming three decades of AI research:

- Slowly hand-code a large, broad knowledge base.
- When enough knowledge is present, it will be faster to acquire more through reading, assimilating databases, etc.
- To go beyond the frontier of human knowledge, the system will have to rely on learning by discovery, carrying out research and development projects to expand its KB.

Three decades? What are the scales on the axes of Fig. 3? Why do we think it's not a three-*century* or three-*millenia* program? Even if the vague shapes of the curves are correct, and even if we are near the left edge, how far over to the right is that place where language understanding meets and then surpasses the hand-coding level? Might we need a trillion things in our knowledge base, in order to get analogy and generalization to pay off? The usefulness and timeliness of the Breadth Hypothesis rest on the following quantitative assumption:

Breadth Is within Our Grasp. A KB of about a million "frames" will provide a significant performance increase, due to generalization and analogy; this will consume ~2 person-centuries of time, ~$50 million, and ~1 decade. Why such a "small size"? That's about all that people know!

"Just one million 'frames'! Where did that number come from? What an insult!" you may say. "You just argued that the world is a complicated place. Surely we human beings each know an effectively infinite number of things! It's hopeless to try to represent an appreciable fraction of that, so we may as well settle on writing programs that know only 10–1000 specific things."

What goes on during the 200,000 hours between birth and age 21? Certainly most of it is spent gathering experiences, building up long-term memories; some conscious time (and perhaps some sleep time) is spent generalizing and organizing one's memories. Much of what we're learning is quite specific to ourselves, our home, our family, our friends, and our culture. The result of thrusting someone into a different culture is often tragic or comic; consider, e.g., Crocodile Dundee, A Connecticut Yankee, The Beverly Hillbillies, and The Gods Must Be Crazy.

Three recent estimates of the number of concepts (frames) needed for full breadth of knowledge all came up with a figure of approximately one million:

(1) Alan Kay: 30,000 articles × 30 frames per article.[2]
(2) EDR: 200k words × 1 frame for each of a few languages.[3]
(3) Marvin Minsky: 4 LTM entries/hour from birth to adulthood.[4]

Two other ways for bounding the "bits" a human brain can store lead to much larger numbers: (1) counting neurons and synapses; but it's unclear how memories are stored in them; (2) counting pixels in our "mental images"; but controversy rages in cognitive psychology over whether mental imagery is just an illusion caused by the consistency and regularity in the world that lets us fill in missing pieces of memories—and of dynamic sensory experiences—with

[2] Based on research performed at Atari Research Labs, in conjunction with *Encyclopaedia Britannica*, during 1983.

[3] Reported at the First Workshop on Electronic Dictionaries, Tokyo, November 1988; proceedings available.

[4] Back of the envelope calculation performed for Bob Kahn, at NRI planning meeting, 1985.

default values (see, e.g., [13]). And humans who are blind from birth are not particularly less intelligent for want of those terrabytes of stored mental images. So it's unclear what those larger numbers signify. (Also, though it's clearly an over-simplification, having a million entries means that there can be a trillion one-step inferences involving pairs of them. And it would surprise no one to discover that one-step inference is going on unconsciously in our minds constantly.)

Here again is a situation in which one should apply the EH. Various theories give various estimates, and the way to settle the issue—and, perhaps, much more importantly, achieve the goal of having the KB we want—is to go off and try to build the large KB. Along the way, it will no doubt become clear how big it is growing and what the actual obstacles are that must be overcome.

Lenat started the CYC project in late 1984 for this very purpose. It is now halfway through its ten-year time frame, and, most surprisingly, it is still on schedule. A book describing the project and its philosophy has been published [28], and the interested reader is referred there for details. Here, we shall just very briefly list a few of the surprises that actually trying to build this immense KB has engendered:

(1) The need for more formality, for a more principled representation language. In a typical expert system application, much of the meaning of an entry on a slot of a frame can be idiosyncratic to that particular application; but CYC, which might be used for any application, cannot afford such sloppiness. E.g., consider placing "IceCream" on the "likes" slot of the "Fred" frame. Does this mean that that's all he likes? Does he like all ice cream? In what sense does he like it? Has he liked it from birth onward (and does it mean he'll like it until he dies), or is there some temporal sub-abstraction of Fred that likes it? etc.

(2) The search for a use-neutral control structure and use-neutral representation is not unlike the search for a single universal carpenter's tool. The pragmatic global *effect* of use-neutrality arises by having a large set of tools that complement each other (and sometimes overlap) and easily work together to get most common jobs done. On very, very rare occasions, a new tool may have to get invented; use the existing ones to fabricate it then.

(3) In the case of control structure, CYC has by now amassed two dozen separate inference engines: inheritance, inverse slots, automatic classification, Horn clause rules, transfersThrough, etc. One lesson is that it is cost-effective to write and fine-tune a separate truth (actually, justification) maintenance system (TMS) for each feature, rather than relying on any one general (but of necessity inefficient) TMS algorithm.

(4) In the case of representation, besides frames, we now have numerous other "tools". One of them is a powerful constraint language which is

essentially predicate calculus. This is because much of the knowledge in the system is inherently constraint-like. Consider "The number of children that Joe and Sam have are equal." We could define a new slot sameNumberOfChildrenAs, and such tactics might well get us through any one application, but that's hardly a scalable solution. In general, though, we wanted, needed, and developed a general constraint language. The constraint language is superficially second-order; in almost all real uses, any quantification over predicates (slot names) can be mechanically reduced to first-order. Several dozen of the most common sorts of constraints (e.g., the domain and range of slots) have been "slotized"; i.e., special slots (in this case, makesSenseFor and entryIsA) have been created and optimized, but still the general language is there to fall back on when needed. From time to time, when numerous constraints of the same form have been entered, we "slotize" that form by defining a new slot. For instance, we could create sameNumberOfChildrenAs if there were really heavy use of that sort of constraint.

(5) There are almost ten times as many "frames" required as we had originally expected; luckily, our rate of knowledge entry is also that much faster, so we still hope to "finish" by 1994. In the search for eliminating ambiguity, the knowledge being entered must be more precise than we are used to being in everyday conversation. E.g., the meaning of "Japan" or "water" varies depending on the context of the conversation. Each separate meaning (e.g., political Japan during the 1890s) has its own frame, which is why there are more than we expected. But balancing that, it is relatively easy to build a knowledge entry tool which assists the user in copying and editing an entire cluster of related frames at once. So the two order-of-magnitude increases are not unrelated. By the way, "finishing by 1994" means approaching the crossover point (see Fig. 3), where it will be more cost-effective to continue building CYC's KB by having it read online material, and ask questions about it, than to continue the sort of manual "brain-surgery" approach we are currently employing.

8. Differences with other positions

8.1. Our position regarding the aesthetes

There is a *methodological* difference between our "scruffy" way of doing AI and the aesthetes' "neat" way. This in turn stems from a difference of opinion about whether the world must admit an elegant and simple formalization of intelligence.

If only there were a *secret ingredient* for intelligence—Maxwell's equations of thought. If only we could axiomatize the world in a small set of axioms, and deduce everything. If only our learning program could start from scratch. If only our neural nets were big or cerebellar or hyperlinear enough. If only the world were like that. But it isn't. The *evidence indicates* that almost all the power is in the bulk knowledge. As Whitehead remarked, "God is in the details."

Following the Difficult Problems Hypothesis, we are firmly convinced that the AI researcher must make a major time commitment to the domain(s) in which his/her programs are to be competent; e.g., the two years that Stefik and Friedland spent to learn about molecular biology before doing MOLGEN [14]; the decade-long time frame for CYC. This is in contrast to, e.g., research that uses the Fifteen Puzzle, or cryptarithmetic, as its domain. Even in physics, where Nature so far *has* been remarkably elegant, it is still strongly cost-effective to expend the enormous time and money to build and use a SLAC or a CERN or a superconducting super-collider.

We may be exhausting the range of potent experimental AI theses that can be carried out in two years, by a student starting more or less from scratch; witness the trend to give the Computers and Thought Award to increasingly less recent graduates. The presence of a large, widely-accessable "testbed" KB should enable a new round of important theses.

People do prefer—and *should* prefer—the simplest consistent hypothesis about any phenomenon. That doesn't make the hypotheses correct, of course [20]. A few examples:

- Early astronomers with poor instruments had no problem with a geocentric model. When one friend of Wittgenstein's ridiculed them for making this error, he replied "Ah, yes, how foolish. But I wonder what it would have looked like if the sun *did* go around the earth?"
- Biologists, who are unable to perform experiments on evolution, or even get precise data on it, can still believe it operates so quickly as it does, using nothing more than random mutation, random generate-and-test—a simple, elegant, appealing, but (as we in AI found out empirically) woefully inadequate problem-solving method.
- James Wilkinson, a fellow of the Royal Society and one of the world's leading numerical analysts, spoke at Stanford in 1974 about bugs in early twentieth century methods of numerical integration. These algorithms had "proofs", and were used (to a couple iterations only) by human beings armed only with pencil and paper. Those people, by the way, were called "computers". The introduction of the high-speed electronic digital computer provided the next round of "criticism"—namely, truncation errors made the algorithms unstable—which led to the next round of improvement in that field.
- Lakatos [21] presents the historical series of mathematicians' retreats from

slots to make it compactly representable. In extreme cases, add a whole new representation language to the toolkit. Besides frames and "rules" and our formal constraint language (described above), we use stored images and neural nets as representation schemes. Images are useful for users to point at; e.g., to say something about the strike plate of a door lock—if you don't happen to know what it's called, but you could pick it out instantly given a photo of a door lock. Statistical space partitioning (neural nets) may be useful for certain kinds of user modeling (e.g., gesture level), and the CYC group is currently training one on examples of good analogizing, so as to suggest promising "hunches" of new analogies to investigate, an activity which CYC will then do symbolically.

The quality of the solutions to many of these "Problems", including this one, depend on the quality of our system's emerging ontology. What category boundaries are drawn; what individuals get explicitly represented; what is the vocabulary of predicates (slots) with which to describe and interrelate them, etc.? Much of the 1984–89 work on CYC has been to get an adequate global ontology; i.e., has been worrying about ways to represent knowledge; most of the 1990–94 work will be actually representing knowledge, entering it into CYC. That is why we have "only" a million entries of CYC's KB today, but expect dozens of times that many in 1994.

Problem 4. *How will inference be done in CYC?* The representation chosen will of course impact on what inference methods are easy or difficult to implement. Our inclination was, once again, to apply EH: when we encountered some kind of operation that needed to be performed often, but it was very inefficient, then we adjusted the representation or the inference methods available, or both. As with Problem 3, there is a temptation to early specialization: it is a local optimum, like swerving around a mattress in the road. Pulling this mattress aside means assembling a large repertoire of reasoning methods, and heuristics for choosing, monitoring, and switching among them. When we first prepared this article, such a toolkit of methods was merely an expectation; today (as described earlier), we have two dozen such inference engines, each with its own optimized justification maintenance system (and each capable of running "forward" or "backward").

To illustrate one of those inference methods briefly, consider "transfers-Through". If I tell you that Michael's last name is Douglas, and Michael's father is Kirk, then you infer that Kirk's last name is Douglas. If you see a car with snazzy wire wheels, and I tell you that Fred owns that car, then you infer that Fred owns those wheels. One could represent such inferencing by general if–then rules; for instance, "If x's last name is y, and x's father is z, then guess that z's last name is y." So many such rules were added to CYC, though, that we defined a new inference template (predicate, slot, . . .) called "transfers-Through". There is a frame representing the transfersThrough relationship, and one of its slots contains a definition in our constraint language, of the form:

(ForAll slots s1, s2) ((transfersThrough s1 s2) ⇔

[(ForAll x, y, z) (s1 x y) and (s2 x z) ⇒ (s1 x z)])

We're often asked how we expect to efficiently "index"—find relevant partial matches—as the KB grows larger and larger. The implicit assumption behind that question is that the problem gets worse and worse as the KB size grows. Our answer therefore often appears startling at first glance: wait until our programs *are* finding many, far-flung analogies, but inefficiently, i.e. only through large searches. Then investigate what additional knowledge *people* bring to bear, to eliminate large parts of the search space in those cases. Codify the knowledge so extracted, and add it to the system. This is a combined application of the Difficult Problems Hypothesis and the EH. It is a claim that the true nature of the indexing problem will only become apparent—and solvable—in the context of a large problem running in an already very large KB.

Earlier, we sketched an opportunistic (nonmonolithic) control structure which utilizes items in the control-strategy region of the KB. As with partial matching, we expect that meta-level control mechanism to be more, and more easily, fleshed out as the system grows.

In other words, the large and increasing size of the KB makes certain tasks less difficult, due to having a large and representative sample of cases one ought to try to make efficient. That holds for choosing specialized inference engines, for meta-level control, and for partial matching.

Problem 5. *How can someone interact "naturally" with KB systems?* Knowledge-based systems built so far share with their knowledge-free predecessors an intolerant rigidity of stylistic expression, vocabulary, and concepts. They rarely accept synonyms and pronouns, never metaphors, and only acknowledge users willing to wear a rigid grammatical straitjacket. The coming few years should witness the emergence of systems which begin to overcome this problem. As is only fitting, they will overcome it with knowledge: knowledge of the user, of the system's domain, of discourse, of metaphor. They will employ pictures, gestures, and sound as well as text, as means of input and output. Many individual projects (such as CYC) and expert system tools (such as KEE) are already moving in this direction.

Problem 6. *How can you combine several enterers'/systems' knowledge?* One solution is to sequentialize the entry, but it's not a good solution. Many EMYCIN-based programs designated someone to be the knowledge base czar, with whom all the other experts would discuss the knowledge to be entered.

EURISKO, built on RLL, tried *explicitly* enforced semantics. Each slot was given a description of its intended use, constraints that could be checked statically or dynamically (e.g., each rule's If-maybe-relevant slot should take less CPU time to execute than its If-truly-relevant slot). When someone enters rules that violate that constraint, the system can complain to them, to get everyone back on track using the same semantics again. CYC extends this to *implicitly* enforced semantics: having such a large existing KB that copy and edit is the clearly favorite way of entering new knowledge. When one copies and edits an existing frame, virtually all of its slots' semantics (and even most of their values!) carry right over.

We are not talking about just text-editing here, but rather a problem-solving process in its own right, which CYC should monitor and assist with. Already, CYC makes guesses about which "slots" will exist on the new "frame", which entries on the value will carry over, which will need to be changed, if they're to be changed then will the new entries be idiosyncratic (e.g., monarch) or predictable based on other information about this new frame (e.g., majorExports).

Although this discussion has assumed that inconsistency should be detected and stamped out, there is a much more fundamental long-range solution to the problem of inconsistent KBs: live with them! Problem 7 describes this position:

Problem 7. *How should the system cope with inconsistency?* View the knowledge space, and hence the KB, not as one rigid body, but rather as a set of independently supported buttes. Each butte should be locally consistent, and neighboring buttes should be maximally coherent. These terms are described in Section 8.2. The power of such systems should derive, then, not from perfect matching, but rather from partial matching, heuristic guidance, and (ultimately) confirming empirical evidence. Systems such as we are describing must encompass several points of view; they are "open" in the sense of Hewitt [18]. It should be possible for new knowledge to compatibly and safely flow among them. At a much more exotic level, one can imagine mental immune systems providing (in the background) constant cross-checking, healthy skepticism, advice, and criticism.

Problem 8. *How can the system builder, and the system user, not get lost?* "Getting lost" is probably the right metaphor to extend here, because what they need to do is to successfully navigate their way through knowledge space, to find and/or extend the relevant parts. Many systems, including CYC, are experimenting with various exploration metaphors and orientation tools: helicoptering through semantic nets; exploring a museum with Alician entry into display cases and posters, etc. Both of these are physical spatial metaphors, which allow us to use kinesthetic memory to some extent, as the enterer or user gets more and more familiar with the layout of the KB.

On a typical day in mid-1989, ten to thirty people are logged into CYC's Knowledge Server, all actively adding to its KB simultaneously. Thus, one's world sometimes changes out from under one a bit, adding to the relevance of the (dis)orientation metaphor. For more elaborately scripted interface metaphors, see *True Names* [49], *Riding the Torch* [42], or *Knoesphere* [26]. For instance, the latter suggests clip-on filters to shade or highlight certain aspects of what was seen; models of groups and each individual user; and simulated tour-guides with distinct personalities.

Problem 9. *How big a fraction of "consensus reality" do you need to represent, before the "crossover" occurs and language understanding is a better knowledge entry paradigm?* We believe the answer is around 30–50%. Why? When communicating with an intelligent entity, having chosen some concept X, we would expect the "listener" to be familiar with X; if it fails several times in a row—often!—then it is missing too much of consensus reality. A similar argument applies to analogizing, and to generalizing. Now to have a 30% chance for the chosen analogue to be already known by the listener, he/she/it might have to know 30% of the concepts that are analogized to. But how *uniformly* are good analogues distributed in concept space? Lacking more data, we assume that they are uniformly distributed, which means the system should embody 30% of the full corpus of consensus reality. The distribution is quite possibly *not* uniform, which is why (the EH again) we need to build the KB and see.

10. Conclusion: Beyond local maxima

Our position includes the statements:

- One must include *domain-specific* knowledge to solve difficult problems effectively.
- One must also include both *very general* knowledge (to fall back on) and very *wide-ranging* knowledge (to analogize to), to cope with novel situations.
- We already have plenty of theories about mechanisms of intelligence; we need to proceed empirically: go off and build large testbeds for performing, analogizing, ML, NL, ...
- Despite the progress in learning, language understanding, and other areas of AI, *hand-crafting* is still the fastest way to get the knowledge into the program for at least the next several years.
- With a large KB of facts, heuristics, and methods, the fastest way will, after some years, tip toward NL (reading online textual material), and then eventually toward ML (learning by discovery).

article written about Alan Kay's Knoesphere project (which in some ways was the precursor to CYC), our position was already clear:

> Something which is absent for a typical encyclopedia but must be present in the Knoesphere KB is commonsense knowledge. This includes everyday physics, models of human interaction . . . as well as facts and heuristics about teaching, question-answering, imagery, analogy, etc. We intend to spend much of the coming decade in research trying to build such a core [of everyday concepts] [10].

In that same long footnote, Smith accuses us of being "considerably more optimistic" four years ago than today, about the chances for success in getting something like CYC to succeed. Although we don't discuss such things in our article, quite the reverse trend has occurred. When CYC began, back in late 1984, we estimated it had a low (less than one in ten) chance of succeeding. Year by year, our optimism has grown; we now put its chances at better than 50–50. Yes, we spent most of the early years in thrashing out a representation language and ontology, and now we're spending most of the effort using that (rather than fighting it) to do knowledge entry. Smith interprets that as a negative indicator, but we interpret it as an extremely positive and encouraging pattern. The time for pessimism—or perseverence—was 5 years ago, not today. We chose perseverence, and it has paid off.

In that same footnote, Smith claims our estimate of the size of the required KB has increased over the years. That's true (it correlates with our decreasing naivete), but even back in 1983 [10] our estimate was 300k frames for factual knowledge, and a similar volume for commonsense knowledge. Assuming about 100 individual assertions per concept, that number (600k frames, 60 million assertions) is not so far away from our best guess today (1 million frames, 100 million assertions). Perhaps some of the confusion came from mixing the two units of measure: concepts (frames) and individual assertions.

Again in that footnote, Smith confuses the pragmatic necessity of having several inference engines (to do efficient justification maintenance) with the theoretical "plank" of ours which continues to state that sophisticated inference procedures alone won't solve all your problems (literally and figuratively) if you lack knowledge.

We're almost ready to leave Smith's footnote 2. Smith implies, near the end of it, that we believe that all the theoretical foundations of AI will be complete by 1994. We certainly do not believe that. In fact, a host of fundamental research questions may be uncovered by this work, and become seen as important. E.g., one can successfully build a bridge over a stream without much theoretical understanding of engineering and physics, and the enterprise of doing so is quite likely to reveal many new issues to begin to investigate, issues that eventually lead to the development of a theory. The same situation occurs when high energy experimental physicists gather data about collisions at new energy levels, etc., etc. It's foolish never to theorize, but it's commonplace for empirical experiments and constructions to outstrip (and drive) the development of theory, especially in a field's first few centuries of life. In its early stages, a theory may be little more than a plausible generalization of a class of recently observed phenomena. Theory building must—and does—go on in the absence of complete sets of data to characterize; and experiments must—and do—go on in the absence of complete theories.

Finally, we can leave footnote 2! A few lines later, Smith mistakenly attributes to us the absurd claim that "just a million frames . . . could intelligently manifest the sum total of human knowledge". That is most definitely not what we believe, or claim, or hope. Rather, our hope is that that order of magnitude (i.e., about 1 million "frame-fulls" or about 100 million assertions) will suffice for crossing the point where knowledge acquisition could be more profitably done by natural language understanding (reading online texts and "discussing" the difficult parts) rather than continuing to build the KB manually, one assertion at a time. We may span much of the breadth of human knowledge, but of course not the depth—one of the main uses of such a KB will be as a substrate on which to build the next generation of knowledge-based systems which do go into depth in particular areas.

Moreover, we certainly don't restrict ourselves to frames, though the majority of the assertions can be cast as simple $P(x, y)$ statements. Our philosophy is to not flinch from building special-purpose machinery (for representation, for control, for interfacing, etc.) to handle the most commonly occurring cases, and to thus have a series of increasingly general (and inefficient) mechanisms even though most of the very general ones are rarely used.

In the case of representation, we use frames for most of the assertions in the KB, but we of course have to have a way to represent disjunctions, set-theoretic constraints, quantified statements, etc., and so we have a constraint language (similar to predicate calculus with equality) as well.

For most human users browsing through the KB and editing it, it's proven useful to present assertions $P(u, v, \ldots)$ which share a common first argument u clumped together—i.e., to have what appears to be a frame-based interface. There are by now half a dozen different editing and browsing tools, some of them quite un-framelike (built around semantic nets, or a metaphor to a museum floorplan, or predicate calculus). While many humans prefer frame-like anchorings, the most common interface to/from other (non-CYC-based) application programs has been straight constraint language expressions. Although this is not the place to discuss "standards" for knowledge representation, we expect that whatever interlingua develops and becomes adopted will likely be based around something which is similar to that. See, e.g., Genesereth's proposal for KIF [1].

In the case of control structure, we again see a series of increasingly general (and inefficient) rules of inference—inference engines—and once again the most specific ones are the most efficient and the most frequently used. E.g., we could express the fact that "children(x, y) iff parents(y, x)" using general if–then rules, Horn clause rules, . . . , all the way down to the special-purpose mechanism "inverse" (i.e., by asserting inverse(children, parents)). The latter is not just shorter to state, it is much faster to "run" (e.g., to later retract, to not show up later in irrelevant situations while searching for a proof, etc.) because the maintenance of inverse(r, s) assertions has been thoroughly worked out ahead of time in CYC.

1.b. Genuine disagreements[2]

We do believe that clever control structures *alone* are no substitute for large amounts of cached knowledge. Of course some amount of effort—perhaps as high as 20% of the two person-centuries of effort in getting CYC to its mid-1990's "crossover point" must deal with inference—with symbol manipulating methods to do deduction and induction (including abduction, analogy, and so on).

We do believe that a decade of flat-out work will get us through "stage 1" in our research program. Smith is welcome to begin his "decades of debate"; meanwhile, we are happy to announce that CYC is halfway through its one decade lifetime and still on schedule. Yes, of course there is "a middle realm", Brian, but it is immense. A brief paper can do little more than tantalize, and we encourage the reader to go through [12] for a several hundred page foray into that middle realm.

2. Conceptual tunneling

2.a. Mistakenly attributed beliefs

We are as aware as anyone of the range of application of expert system technology today—and its limitations. We have written about that in numerous books and articles over the past fifteen years. An expert system can't be a nurse because of the heavy reliance on sight, hearing, etc., the need for frequent and subtle motor activity and hand–eye coordination, the need to provide inter-personal warmth and support, etc. Could an expert system in principle one day write a good textbook on nursing, or design a new device used in nursing? To that we would answer affirmatively, and astonishingly enough so would Smith. We are pleased in a way that Smith views our general principles as tautologous. Not so many years ago, and still today in many academic circles, they would be quite controversial.

His attributing a trivial Analogical Method to us is a bit unfair. Immediately

[2] As explained earlier, this section—1.b—discusses the genuine disagreements that we have with Section 1 of Smith, answers some of his objections to our position, and presents our disagreements with his position as stated therein.

after we state it, we explain why it's too general and weak to be useful, and how it can and should be specialized. We have a useful specification of the notion of causality, a family of "causes" relations, and a calculus for using them to predict (deductively), to explain (abductively), and to help us epistemologically to favor one explanation over another.

Yes, we know "these issues have been investigated for years". We've been doing some of the investigating! He accuses us of not being aware that "analogy requires a notion of relevant similarity", which is odd given the detail with which we discussed that in [9]. And as the previous paragraph indicated, we've proceeded a long way further than that in the intervening years.

2.b. Genuine disagreements

The need for formulation: Simple problems can of course be solved without explicitly formulating them—else the meta-meta-····-level recursion would never end. But difficult ones require formulation. You may grasp your coffee mug unconsciously, but you probably don't design an airplane that way. At least not a plane I'd care to be the first to fly in. Raw perception and low-level muscle coordination are not part of what we were calling knowledge, though of course propositions about what you have perceived, about the act of your perceiving it, etc., are knowledge.

This ties in to his remark about children not having explicit mental models (formulations, representations). Two remarks are in order here. First, although Smith (and the colleagues he cites) tell us we don't need such things, they don't propose any alternative. Second, we don't care whether that's "really" how people solve problems and get around in the real world—we're AI scientists, not cognitive psychologists. And we feel that, in limited domains, the best computational scheme to get programs to duplicate human-level problem-solving behavior is through explicit formulation (and logical manipulation of same).

How dare we try to build this KB: We are not so pessimistic (or perhaps so perfectionistic) as Smith. In our opinion, AI has progressed to the point where it's worth trying to build the large, broad KB: we do know ways to adequately represent a vast variety of knowledge, we do know enough about ontology and ontological engineering to choose and debug an adequate set of collections, predicates (slots), and so on. If we fail, then the next set of important lessons for AI are likely to emerge by tackling this large empirical task, rather than by micro-experiments or sterile philosophical argument.

Are we sure about the one million frame number (100 million assertions)? Of course not. But we have lots of supportive evidence, based not just on the three estimates we gave in our article, but also based on the thousands of man-years of effort spent on building knowledge-based systems in the past fifteen years. Yes, by now we feel we do have the right to estimate how many "frames" it will take.

Smith chooses visual imagery as his examples (recognizing faces; the expression on a person's face gradually changing)—even though we explicitly claimed we would not tackle perception head-on. On the other hand, knowledge *about* facial expressions can and should be part of the large KB, and it is easy to see that a small number of assertions suffices to predict the change in expression when one goes from glee to horror, and a moderate number of assertions to predict the change in emotional state as one loses control of one's vehicle. Yes, one can sit around for decades and bemoan the impenetrable mystique of the human intellect, and make grand arguments for why it is unknowable, or one can sit down and try to penetrate it.

The heart of this disagreement is made clear over the issue of whether we in AI should use computers to test (i.e., verify or falsify) our hypotheses and surprise us (our view), versus merely as fancy word processors to articulate and clarify one's hypothesis (his view).

As Guha[3] reminds us,

> One of the things we have learnt from so many years of science is that given any hard problem it is wise to break it down into separate pieces, solve these, and put the solutions together. But for Brian Smith, perception, inference, representation are all one complex integrated (nondecomposable) problem that has to be dealt with at one shot. The idea that he (or anyone else) can do this seems rather optimistic. Divide and conquer is really a pretty good idea.

It's a bit much for Smith to presume that he knows what discouraged Winograd and we don't; but granting for the sake of argument it was the problem of "genuine semantics", we claim that this problem gets easier, not harder, as the KB grows. In the case of an enormous KB, such as CYC's, for example, we could rename all the frames and predicates as G001, G002, . . . , and—using our knowledge of the world—reconstruct what each of their names must be. While this does not guarantee that the genuine meanings of the concepts have been captured, it's good enough for us. After all, how does one guarantee that one's neighbor shares the same meanings for terms? The answer is that one doesn't, at least not formally or exhaustively. Rather, in practice, one defeasably assumes by default that everyone agrees, but one keeps in reserve the ubiquitous conflict resolution method that says "one may call into question whether they and their neighbor are simply disagreeing over the meaning of some terms".

Near the end of Section 2, Smith raises the question of how a set of symbols relates to the world. He, better than most people, knows how many person-centuries have been lost on this issue. Programmers were writing working programs long before people developed fancy semantics for programming

[3] Personal communication.

languages. Surely he drives a car and uses other devices without "really knowing" how they work. In a similar fashion, we hope to use symbol structures to represent things without "really knowing" the answer to this question.

There are two issues, then, as regards our disagreement with Smith about how "solved" the problems are about deduction and control. The first issue is how to—and whether to—come up with a formalism in which to state relevant information. The second issue is how to actually use these formalisms to state the axioms. We are claiming that AI has found at least reasonable candidates for the former, and that it's finally time to really start doing the latter. Another way to look at what we are saying is that at the current state of the field, the maximum gain/improvement can be obtained by building KBs. Not that we are going to have a fully human-level intelligent agent in 1994, but that better AI—a whole new and qualitatively different set of experiments—can be done in 1995, using as a substrate the large KBs constructed between now and then.

3. The structure of the middle realm

3.a. Mistakenly attributed beliefs

Question 1: Explicit representation

Smith seems to massively misunderstand what we meant by "explicit". E.g., he says "L&F are even more committed to explicit representation than adherents of logic", which to us is a non-sequitor. What we mean by "explicit" is a representation with a declarative semantics. Thus, we might say a program P represents X even if there is no data structure in P that means exactly X, so long as X follows from other data structures (where "follows from" is given shape by the declarative semantics).

We are pragmatists and engineers; tradesmen, not philosophers. We are happy to use any tool that helps us in some specialized ways, and that includes implicitly represented knowledge. Despite myriad examples of such (which Smith mentions in his footnote 13) that we use in our programs, the evidence still supports our expectation that the vast majority of the contents of CYC *will* be declarative, and we view the gradual translation of knowledge into increasingly declarative form as both inevitable and desirable. (There is also often an extra level of translation, from declarative into efficient "compiled" form, and this final stage is also probably inevitable and futile.)

Question 5: Multiple representations of knowledge

We are of course not arguing that any one narrow representation (such as frames and slots) is enough; see our earlier comments about our formal constraint language, etc. Nevertheless, it's important to remark that binary predicates (slots on frames) are—surprisingly often—quite adequate, and such awkwardnesses as arise in trying to represent some new situation *can* often be remedied just by slotizing (creating specialized new slots). E.g., there are now about 50 slotized forms of constraints on slots—what sort of frames can legally have them, what sort of entries can legally fill them, how many entries they can have, and so on—and we almost never have to resort to writing a full-fledged constraint language expression. Indeed, most of those slotized constraints were introduced (as new slots) to eliminate the need for the various constraint language expressions we had to write. Smith might say that all this is still just one "grammar" for representation—that the frames and slots are a special case of the constraint language. In that case, we count this as a genuine disagreement rather than a mistakenly attributed belief.

Question 7

We could not understand Smith's words here (his use of "traditional" early on in this discussion, his use of "non-representational experience" late in the discussion, his "LISP" example about (LENGTH '(A B C)) which seems to be just a discourse example, etc.). So we're not sure if he misunderstood us or genuinely disagrees.

Resource-limited computation is an important part of our systems' design (e.g., the different GET levels in CYC), and we also rely on explicit meta-level reasoning about strategies, progress being made, time of day, models of the particular people using the system at present, etc.

Question 8

Smith cites Rosenschein's system as an example of "moving beyond logic's familiar representational assumptions". Our understanding of that system, though, is that it is built solidly on modal logic. It illustrates our assumption that one can reason adequately, using propositions, even about phenomena which people intuitively feel are somehow gestalt, mysterious, non-decomposable.

Question 9

A 200% incorrect misreading by Smith. Of course inference is important—it lets you just represent log n of the KB you'd otherwise have to represent if you tried to cache everything (n is the average depth of reasoning chain your system goes through). As mentioned in our article, CYC has dozens of specialized inference procedures, not just one (as do most AI programs) or zero (as Smith seems to think it does). Our point was not to advocate a 100-million-assertion KB in lieu of a small one plus some inference method—rather, it's to advocate a 100-million-assertion KB plus dozens of inference methods as being just barely enough to get us from stages 1 to 2 in our three-stage research program. It does appear, by the way, that most commonsense inference is rather shallow—2–6 "rule firings" deep—shallow compared to, say, playing master-level chess or proving a difficult theorem. Still, $n = 3$ means $\log^3$(total assertions) = 100 million. So it would be absurd to even consider an equivalent $n = 0$ KB (it would have to have $10^{10^{10^{10^8}}}$ assertions in it!)

Why did we say 200% instead of 100%? Because he is also wrong in saying that reasoning is central to the logicist position. Some mathematical logicians might say it is, but most computer science logicians would say that knowledge is (see, e.g., McCarthy's Missouri Program; Pat Hayes' Second Naive Physics Manifesto [7]; and so on).

Question 10: Does meaning bottom out?

There are at least two senses in which we shout a negative answer; and one way in which we murmur an affirmative one. First, we have a very strong belief in the "gray box" view of knowledge and—hopefully—our large KB. "Gray box" means that one typically treats the thing as black box, as primitive, but when confronted by some novel problem, or the need to analogize, etc., one can open the black box and examine, modify, etc., the substructure that comprises it. A simple example of "gray boxing" is what we do with cars—we treat them as black boxes so long as they work. Other examples include the route we take to work every day; our use of an English dictionary which is itself written in English; etc. Of course, in practice, CYC and any such KB is of necessity finite. This does not concern us overmuch. Why? Sometimes, there are boxes which are (*currently*) still black to all of humanity—such as when we delve down to physical phenomena whose mechanisms are not yet understood; and most of us get by in the world quite well with a much larger fraction of black boxes than that.

The second way in which we claim meaning doesn't bottom out in an atomic base is illustrated by CYC's use of metaphorical sensibility. There are caches of popular metaphors, and in addition each slot P has a measure of how sensible (or common) it would be to say X when one actually meant $P(X)$. E.g., agent and physicalExtent have high metaphorical sensibility; one often says "The US did such and so" when they mean "Some agent of the US did such and so"; and one often says "Joe is huge" when one means "Joe's body—his physical extent—is huge." So one can state assertions like "Russia is angry", "Granadas guzzle gasoline" or "the relentless sun", and have them disambiguated and interpreted as (albeit much longer) legal (nonmetonomous) expressions.

The third way of looking at this issue, the one in which we murmur an affirmative answer to the question "Does meaning bottom out?", is to say that at any fixed level of abstraction, yes it does bottom out. We effectively drew on compositional semantics, above, to change this superficial Yes answer into a No, but we suspect that Smith does not believe in compositional semantics.

Question 11: Autonomous semantics

To the extent permitted by current sensors and effectors, the knowledge in CYC has autonomous semantics. CYC explicitly represents itself as a Program, its current "run" as an Event, the users logged onto it as Human, their activity as KnowledgeEntering, etc. The frames about computer mice, mousing, and so on, tie in to actual events (as when a user moves their mouse or clicks a button; in such cases, CYC frames get created and/or modified). The user's actions cause revisions in the user's model (CYC frames), and that user model determines in a great many situations how CYC treats the user. The knowledge in the KB about people—such as eating and sleeping—is used to help guess why a user isn't responding at 12:30 pm or 12:30 am. And so on.

In areas where there is no meaningful overlap—such as ChurningCream IntoButter—the semantics are of necessity not autonomous. We do not believe that they need to be in order to understand and reason intelligently about those concepts (how many of us have ever made butter, after all?), and perhaps that is the crux of a genuine disagreement between Smith and us on this issue.

Question 12: Representing "as"

Far from ignoring the " 'as' questions", the basic motivation for our paper and our current research (Feigenbaum's LSKB for engineering, and Lenat's CYC) is very much the brittleness of current systems. And much of that brittleness is due to what we have called the representation trap: using variable names pregnant with meaning—pregnant to the user, but barren to the system.

We choose to solve the "as" question empirically, by having our systems incrementally approach understanding. For instance, when a new piece of text is digested into CYC, a set of questions is raised, questions which "anyone ought to be able to answer." If CYC gets wrong answers, its KB is augmented. And the cycle repeats. Eventually, $DETENTE will not mean any less for the computer than "detente" means to us.

The final part of question 12 is the necessity of representing several different points of view for, say, the concept of detente. In CYC, we have a scheme for handling recursively nested propositional attitudes (e.g., Israel is afraid that Iran believes that Iraq expects that the USA will soon want to provoke a conflict with Russia in the Mid-East). To do this efficiently, we represent various sub-abstractions of the actors (e.g., Iran as Israel believes it to be) and have rules for projecting knowledge and beliefs, goals and dreads and expectations, from the "outer" world to the next "inner" world. One need only explicitly store the exceptions to what these projection rules would conclude. These rules are typically only run in a backwards direction, for efficiency reasons (this makes it increasingly costly to accurately simulate an actor with vastly different knowledge and reasoning methods than you have. Luckily, or perhaps by choice, we rarely have to deal with intelligent entities that don't share a large amount of knowledge with us.) And the various sub-abstractions are only created if we have something special to say about them, only if they have lasting importance. (Below, we discuss *temporal* sub-abstractions of actors and other objects.)

As stated in our general remark, above, this is the generous interpretation of his question 12. The less generous one would say that this is a genuine disagreement, and an irreconcilable one based on differences of faith. Even should we succeed in producing a generally acknowledged intelligent artifact, he might still refuse to acknowledge it on the grounds of this dimensional disagreement.

3.b. Genuine disagreements

We begin with a few basic problems with the material he presents before he begins discussing the various dimensions. The EC perspective Smith presents is too fuzzy to launch an attack against, so we shall restrict ourselves to particular "local" disagreements.

First of all, before he can criticize us or any AI paradigm for not having an adequate theory of representation, Smith has to define adequate. We claim that it's enough to have model theory, the theory of descriptions, etc.

The remark about "researchers rallying" around EC signifies nothing; we recall similar rallies in AI (e.g., around resolution), not to mention the numerous fads in philosophy. Actually, it signifies something a bit worse, given that the EC fad has been around longer than the CYC project, and has consumed a vastly larger annual budget. To wit, shouldn't they have something to show for all those years of work by now (i.e., some theoretical foundations built on a computational framework, embodied in programs)?

Smith seems to assume that the right way to go about developing a field (especially something like a logic) is to sit down, get all the foundations straight, and then start using it. (In this case, he's groping to try to erect a foundation that would compete with logic.) But that's not how the game is played. Consider what happened with logic. The big advance came with the *Principia Mathematica*, which was nothing but the CYC for mathematics. Building it exercised and honed logic. Tarski, Gödel et al. could then—a couple of decades later—set the foundations. So the best bet for Smith, and for what he calls EC, is to try something real with it. Forget the "decades of debate".

Question 1: Explicit representation

A trend that Smith begins here, and that we see throughout most of the twelve questions, is his equating us with the logic position, as if that somehow shows something bad about us. But there is nothing at odds between, say CYC and the proposed Advice Taker (as articulated in McCarthy's classic paper over thirty years ago; for a more recent update on this point of view, see [14]). The difference between the logic position and ours is principally one of focus: we think that our research time can best be spent actually trying to build big commonsense KBs, and they think it's not time yet, and so they continue building tools which eventually will be used to that end.

Another trend that keeps recurring in his treatment of these twelve questions, and which is first illustrated here, is the following. Smith mentions some very general and also very well-known problem (e.g., that explicit representation may result in unwarranted definiteness and premature categorization), and then slips in (as it were) the EC view toward eventually attacking that problem. The unstated parts of such an "argument" are (a) L&F have an approach to attacking it as well, and (b) the EC view is just that—one untried, fuzzy proposal which may or may not solve the problem. To the extent that the EC view is defined as "something which solves this problem", it's no wonder it's still unarticulated.

A third trend, which we will stoop to illustrate here, is ironically the sort of "tunneling" that he accuses us of. E.g., he goes from a true assertion ("interpreted code runs slower than compiled code") to an unfair generalization ("explicit representation leads to programs that are poor in general") and then back down to a few downright false specializations ("such programs are less effective"). But "effectiveness" means what can (ultimately) be derived from a program; if explicit representation has any effect on this attribute, it is to improve it, not decrease it! Similarly with his next target, "control flow". This means something like "how easy is it to decide, and include information affecting, what to do next, at each moment". Again, if explicit representation has any effect on this attribute, it is to improve it, not decrease it! His third target here is the negative effect this has on "overall system architecture". But that involves things like what knowledge the program can use, for what purposes. Given a fixed representation, an explicit one is likely to be usable by more types of architectures than an implicit one.

We shall give here just one more example of Smith's tunneling, and then try to restrict our attention to more substantive issues: Late in the question 8 discussion, Smith discusses the fact that traditional logic does not deal with certain issues (how to think creatively about the world, etc.). He then concludes that the problem is uncorrectable (we disagree), and logic is therefore woefully all wrong (we disagree), and therefore EC must be the answer (even if logic were wrong, this does not follow).

Question 2: Contextual content

Smith confuses the common practice of natural languages to economize (the meaning of "1989" or "tomorrow" is of course context-dependent) with the necessity of a KB to have this confusion. In CYC, e.g., there is a separate frame for 1987 in the Gregorian and Hebrew calendars, and a third frame for the word (so to speak) "1987", whose referents include both of those Event frames. There is little need, or benefit, in having the system itself confused about the meanings of "1987", any more than it's useful for a person not to understand the meanings—even if that person uses the word "1987" to mean one thing at one time and another thing at another time. So CYC in a way appears to have "situated" knowledge, but that is—thankfully!—just a superficial phenomenon.

This is in a way Smith's main point, so let's restate the part of his position that we agree with. Consider linguistic utterances (such as "the time is 4 p.m."). The "meaning" of such utterances is highly dependent on context. I.e., one cannot expect the truth of the sentence (by itself) to be preserved if you transplant it from one conversation to another. So if our representation were going to consist of such (natural) linguistic utterances, we would need some notion of context in ascribing meaning to our utterances.

That much we agree with. But then comes a huge jump in the argument: from such natural language utterances, Smith concludes that the same will apply to utterances (propositions) in logic. I.e., he jumps to the conclusion that one cannot ascribe meaning to a logical assertion independent of context.

The main argument for this is that utterances in logic are, after all, in some sense linguistic statements. The flaw in this argument is that there is a crucial difference between sentences in logic and sentences in natural language. Natural language sentences presume common sense, user modeling, etc., on the part of the listener, and utilize this to become relatively (compared to our corresponding logical encoding) terse—at the price of introducing ambiguities in word sense, ambiguities in pronominal referents, ambiguities in metaphorical and analogical references, and ambiguities in the interpretation of ellipses. By contrast, our sentences in logic have been "universalized" [16] to the extent humanly possible (but see the next paragraph): including explicit clauses that refer to the sorts of contextual information that would be omitted in natural language utterances. So Smith's argument for why non-situated representations are meaningless is just sophism, i.e. relies on a confusion between a natural language utterance and a logic utterance. If exactly the same notion of meaning etc. held in both, we wouldn't need to invent the formal languages of logic, would we?

There was an important clause in the previous paragraph: ". . . to the extent humanly possible. . .". Can we truly "universalize" a sentence? Is it really possible for us to unearth all the contextual information and make it explicit (without possibly introducing new implicit contextual assumptions?). The answer (both from the work of Carnap et al. and from results such as Gödel's theorem) is that this is indeed very very hard.[4]

Not one place did Smith make it clear what exactly this beast "context" is. The moment Smith lapses into what the EC position is, we get lots of fancy words used in a very fuzzy sense. E.g., "the egocentricity obtains in virtue of the machine's existence, not in virtue of any self-reference." Being that "fuzzy" is not bad science—it's simply not science at all. It might be foolhardy

[4] Basically, we have eliminated contextual information when only a single model (up to isomorphism) satisfies our axioms.

for Lenat and Feigenbaum to be ambitious, but we are at least precise in what we say. Mystifying contexts is of no use. Much better is to try to come to grips with it, and we know of no better tool for this purpose than logic. Just because we can't 100% universalize a statement in logic does not mean it is inadequate and should be abandoned.

So, alright, we need to deal with this contextual effect. What this means is that we should go and make this concept explicit in our representations and this is exactly the stance being pursued today by John McCarthy (what he calls "contexts"), Guha (what he calls "microtheories"), and others.

In a way, Smith's "computational examples" of context-assuming programs argue against his position, not for it. When someone at MCC sends a mail message to DOUG, it reaches me. Why? Because the operating system accesses a file which quite clearly defines how to disambiguate such partial addresses. I.e., it contains a simple yet adequate explicit model of context.

A similar response applies to his remark that CYC "wouldn't know what time it was." Natural language interfaces, or other programs written on top of CYC, would have the job of answering such questions. They in turn would call on the CYC KB to do various sorts of disambiguation. The KB in turn has explicit models of its being used (in this case, the particular conversation going on at a certain date and time, on a certain terminal, what has been said so far, etc.) and from that it is straightforward to disambiguate references to "today" and "next year". This is not much different from the way the e-mail program disambiguates what DOUG means.

If you broaden Smith's first two objections (about "explicit representation" and "not being situated") to the levels that he and his references typically intend—namely that a program cannot possibly be intelligent unless it "lives" in the real world and has direct sensory experiences—then we patently disagree with such mysticism. To dip our toe into Smith's metaphysical swamp, we might say "Yes, our KBs are indeed 'somewhere': they are where they are being used." That in turn would suggest that they should contain explicit models of situations where we expect them to be used, not used, etc., i.e. a rich explicit meta-theory about the scope and limitations of use of our systems. Just such a scheme was discussed in detail in [11].

Question 3: Content depending on use

We definitely hold that we can and are constructing knowledge bases whose content means something; i.e., KBs which have meaningful content independent of any particular use of that knowledge. We are unhappy with the somewhat vicious tone that Smith uses in his review about this issue; and we find it surprising that he believes in the negation of such a possibility. E.g., if you consider some of the facts ("George Washington was the first President of the USA") and heuristics ("If it's raining, then the ground is probably getting wet") in our large KB, it seems to us that we have precise, commonly agreed upon meanings for each of them, and for each of the terms they mention. We may use the second piece of knowledge to answer a variety of questions, such as deciding if we should watch where we're walking, or to guess whether or not the concrete mason will bother showing up to try to work on our driveway today, or to guess at why there is a large puddle of ammonia today in front of our spaceship (landed last week on some moon of Jupiter).

Of course the kind of uses of a proposition may be limited and biased by the way we choose to represent it, and we as reasoners are limited by what knowledge we choose to represent in the first place. The net effect of this is to make there be a pragmatic limit on the multiple uses of the knowledge in a KB. There aren't an infinite variety, there is a bias making some more natural or efficient, and the choice of contents of the KB limits the in-principle macro-level uses (problems tacklable). The net effect is at least multiple-use, if not truly use-neutral, knowledge.

Use-dependent meaning ("Is there water in the refrigerator?") does not imply we have to abandon the computational framework of logic. It might mean not insisting on an absolute account of the world. In fact we (and symbolic AI in general) don't even take a stance on the existence of such an absolute account. On the other hand, Smith seems to be insisting that there indeed exists such an "all independent" notion of meaning. Yes, of course the meaning of the English word "water" depends on the discourse in which it is used. This does not imply that we abandon explicit representation. It simply argues—and we would agree—that we should represent knowledge about discourses (common types, communication conventions, etc.). A large task? Yes. A theoretical impossibility? Hardly. The concept of use-dependent meaning only undermines the concept of soundness if one is reckless in introducing it.

Smith presumes much too direct a translation between the English word "water" and the term Water in the KB. He is assuming that we opt for a close connection, so that the natural language/logic translation is easy. However, we opt for as "deep" a representation as possible, one that often is quite far removed from the accidents and surface phenomena of English or any natural language.

Smith then goes on to point out some of the assumptions made in our research program—such as compositional semantics. We point them out, too [6, 12]. Every research program must have, and does have, numerous assumptions behind it. Not being prepared to make any assumptions leads only to apathy or to sterile argument. His approach implies that every problem in AI is "AI-complete"; perhaps this explains his hesitation to decompose problems.

Smith appears to be confusing the role of logic in mathematics (where it was used not as a real computational tool but as a precise language in which to state a minimal set of axioms from which everything else would follow) and the role of logic in AI. Precision (or rather a lack of it) is not even an issue that computer scientists can choose sides on: programs are precise, period. Logic is used in AI for its other properties such as having a denotational semantics, modularity, etc.

He frets that "nothing in the KB means anything". Well, there are a lot of expert systems out there built on logic that are very useful—their users would not care that Smith feels that they don't "mean" anything. Then, at the very end of the question 3 tirade, Smith asks us to rely on his "experience". If he has scientific evidence as to why we won't succeed, he needs to be more precise than just saying "it is simply my experience".

Incidentally, a rich and quite readable account of the "bottoming out" of metonomy into somatic metaphors is given by Lakoff and Johnson [8]; we encourage Smith and other interested readers to examine it.

Question 4: Consistency mandated?

We disagree with Smith's comment that logic hates and avoids inconsistency. That is a rather dated point of view. Inconsistency at some point is the hallmark of any nonmonotonic system, and a vast amount of attention has been focused recently on how to deal with this. Perhaps this is again a case of his equating logic in math with logic in AI.

Questions 6 and 8: Only discrete propositions?

We do believe that discrete propositions can arbitrarily closely model continuous phenomena. More importantly, they can do it adequately and efficiently for real-world problem solving. And they can capture whatever is worth capturing about a situation. That is, one need never *in principle* throw up one's hands and say "you just had to be there, I can't describe it!"

There is nothing to prevent one from adequately describing the terror and confusion at a theater fire, or the trials of committee work (here "adequate" means that conclusions could be drawn about something involving, say, a theater fire, conclusions which enable the problem solver to correctly predict victims' reactions and memories, media coverage, pre-catastrophe fire codes, etc.).

Smith's very example disarms him: the implicit assumptions that writers build their text upon. We have looked at thousands of such snippets, and continue to look at them, chosen from such diverse sources as encyclopedias, novels, and newspaper advertisements. Of course there is a tremendous amount of unstated assumptions, presumed shared experiences and knowledge—indeed, that is precisely what we hope to capture and represent in CYC. But as for implicit *nonconceptual* inferences, we have yet to run across one. All such apparent references have so far been successfully reduced to discrete concepts and propositions involving them.

Smith seems to be confusing the underlying computational formalism (a digital one) and a representation built on top of that. That the former is digital does not much impact on the latter. Does he want us all to go and build analog computers?

He then complains about the limitations of bivariance (having just True and False and perhaps a few other symbolic truth values). Our defense is twofold: First, the observation that the world is not vague (though language is); and second, we symbolic-AI'ers can get far enough with just what we have (far enough to, say, one day pass the Turing test).

As for his abjuration that we must provide more details on what our notion of inference is . . . we agree. Besides [2–5, 12], we are preparing an article dealing specifically with that issue.

Question 7: Do representations capture all that matters?

Earlier, in Section 3.a, we discussed our confusion over Smith's use of several terms and examples. There are some disagreements here as well, but we shall only call attention to the final line of this section: "there is no way in which L&F's system would ever be able to understand the difference between right and left."

We're rather puzzled by this. CYC can know about right and left propositionally, the same way it knows about hunger and democracy and computers and ownership. The assertional right/left knowledge can be related to digitized images, room floor plans, asymmetric particle physics phenomena, etc., but this is more of an affectation, a luxury, than a necessity. If a program uses "right" and "left" properly in sentences, answers queries involving it (e.g., "Which particular muscles does Connors use in his backhand?"), and acts appropriately (e.g., "Please open the rightmost pod door, HAL"), what more could be required in order to warrant our admitting that it understands the right versus left distinction?

Question 9: Participation and action crucial?

Of course participation often helps one understand a situation—especially in a field which is pre- or non-theoretical. But even in moderately well-understood fields it is "optional" (e.g., men can be gynecologists; non-criminals can be lawyers; and so on). And what does it mean for a college student to "participate" in Einstein's equations or other areas of math and theoretical physics?

Smith seems to believe there must be some fundamental reason we could never handle "See you tomorrow", or knowing that "tomorrow, today will be yesterday". Our response is essentially to repeat the above cry that such reasoning can easily be formalized and automated. We shall treat this example in a bit more detail, to convey the flavor of how we actually handle this sort of reasoning in CYC.

We handle the uttering of "See you tomorrow" by creating a 'frame' E_1 in CYC to represent that uttering event (E_1 is an instance of the set of all events).

Each event is grounded in time (whether or not the absolute time is known), and the meaning of "tomorrow" is clearly the day after this event E_1 takes place. A CYC "frame" E_2 would be created, representing a second event. E_2's temporal grounding would be "the day following the day E_1 takes place", and E_2 would be a seeing or meeting type of event.

This technique has been known to logicians since 1924. They (as does CYC) use an abstract (non-situated) notion of time. Smith claims you can't really compare 5 minutes of CPU time and 5 minutes of waiting at a train station. They (because of different situations) are simply different, incommensurable things. It is difficult for us to take his point of view seriously.

His more complicated example—and many much more complicated ones—are also straightforwardly handled in CYC. To see how, we must first discuss in a bit more detail how CYC handles time.

There is a pragmatically adequate language for describing pieces of time (unifying both set- and point-based abstractions of time), and fifty temporal relations—predicates (slots) which relate one piece of time to another. Although we originally kept separated (a) events and (b) the time intervals over which they occur, several years of experience at knowledge entering convinced us to combine those, so that each "frame" representing an event may have those fifty temporal relation "slots". One important class of events are *objects* (i.e., each object has a starting and ending time, can end-at-the-same-time-as another object, and so on). Another important class—a superset of the previous one—is *temporal sub-abstractions of objects*. Only those objects which are useful or required are created and represented explicitly; even more importantly for finiteness, only required sub-abstractions of objects are represented explicitly (typically, new sub-abstractions are created dynamically as required during the solving of a problem).

Now we can explain how CYC handles the effects of actions occurring and time passing: the basic idea is that each (frame representing an) event has actors (before, during, and after the event) which are temporal sub-abstractions of objects. Rules can thus be stated as to, e.g., the effect of taking a time-delay poison; they effect a particular sub-abstraction of the victim which is related to the present event's actor (the present event is the taking of the poison) in a clearly expressed fashion (expressed using the vocabulary of temporal relations).

4. The logical point of view

Here again we see Smith confusing the Nilsson kind of logic approach to AI (where all that's done with a KB is to prove sentences) and the McCarthy kind of logic approach to AI (where a declarative KB is used by all kinds of programs).

Yes, we are in many ways just a variation on that second "logicist" theme. The main difference is that we think it's high time to start trying for "a competent axiomatization", that additional work on reasoning is either unnecessary or, more likely, should be guided by the difficulties encountered in such an attempt. The "dig" about the expressiveness of our language is of course unwarranted, as this was a position paper and not an account of our current research projects. The dig is also, as so much of his review, simply false. See, for example, [12] for a several hundred page account of our representation language, inference engines, ontology, and yes, even some remarks on our paradigm.

5. Conclusion

Smith seems to be saying that AI can't move forward until we solve all the problems that have been haunting philosophers for centuries. We have tried to clarify why we disagree.

Just because "wheel-barrows are inadequate to try crossing Europe" does not mean that our existing representation technology is inadequate to try representing world knowledge: Analogies can of course be false. As we discussed, coincidentally, in our paper, this is especially likely if (as in the wheel-barrow case) there is no causal basis whatsoever for it, if it was chosen merely for dramatic impact on the reader.

We are hopefully more at the "age of discovery" stage in AI, where attempted ocean crossings will at least point out the inadequacies in our current vehicles and lead to improvements, and may lead to some surprising discoveries as well, even if we fail to reach our ultimate goal. Of course "work lies ahead of us", but let necessity and utility guide that work, not aesthetism and faith. Let's grope towards being Newton, not Aristotle.

Smith has us pegged correctly at the end, as disagreeing with Yeats' romantic but pessimistic mumbo-jumbo. We would say that inanimate objects and lower animals can embody truth, but Man (and one day AI) are distinguished because they *can* know it.

Acknowledgement

Discussions of the Smith piece which we have had with R.V. Guha and John McCarthy have provided many useful insights and examples, which we have included in this reply.

References

[1] M.R. Genesereth and N.P. Singh, Knowledge interchange format, Logic Group Rept. 89-13, Stanford University, Stanford, CA (1989).

[2] R.V. Guha and D.B. Lenat, The CycL representation language—Part 2, Tech. Rept. ACT-AI-452-89, MCC, Austin, TX (1989).

[3] R.V. Guha and D.B. Lenat, The world according to Cyc—Part 2, Tech. Rept. ACT-AI-453-89, MCC, Austin, TX (1989).

[4] R.V. Guha and D.B. Lenat, The world according to Cyc—Part 3, Tech. Rept. ACT-AI-455-89, MCC, Austin, TX (1989).

[5] R.V. Guha and D.B. Lenat, The CycL representation language—Part 3, Tech. Rept. ACT-AI-454-89, MCC, Austin, TX (1989).

[6] R.V. Guha and D.B. Lenat, Cyc: a midterm report, *AI Mag.* **11** (3) (1990) 30–59.

[7] P.J. Hayes, The second naive physics manifesto, in: R.J. Brachman and H.J. Levesque, eds., *Readings in Knowledge Representation* (Morgan Kaufmann, Los Altos, CA, 1985) 467–485.

[8] G. Lakoff and M. Johnson, *Metaphors We Live By* (University of Chicago Press, Chicago, IL, 1980).

[9] D.B. Lenat, Software for intelligent systems, *Sci. Am.* **251** (1984) 204–213.

[10] D.B. Lenat, A. Borning, D. McDonald, C. Taylor and S. Weyer, Knoesphere, in: *Procceedings IJCAI-83*, Karlsruhe, FRG (1983) 167–169.

[11] D.B. Lenat, R. Davis, J. Doyle, M.R. Genesereth, I. Goldstein and H. Schrobe, Reasoning about reasoning, in: F. Hayes-Roth, D. Waterman and D.B. Lenat, eds., *Building Expert Systems* (Addison-Wesley, Reading, MA, 1983) 219–240.

[12] D. Lenat and R.V. Guha, *Building Large Knowledge Based Systems* (Addison-Wesley, Reading, MA, 1990).

[13] D.B. Lenat, M. Prakash and M. Shepherd, CYC; Using common sense knowledge to overcome brittleness and knowledge acquisition bottlenecks, *AI Mag.* **7** (1986) 65–85.

[14] J. McCarthy, Some expert systems need common sense, *Ann. New York Acad. Sci.* **426** (1983) 129–137.

[15] J. McCarthy and P.J. Hayes, Some philosophical problems from the standpoint of AI, in: H.J. Levesque and R.J. Brachman, eds., *Readings in Knowledge Representation* (Morgan Kaufmann, San Mateo, CA, 1987) 335–343.

[16] W.V. Quine, Natural kinds, in: *Ontological Relativity* (Columbia University Press, New York, 1969) Chapter 5.

The owl and the electric encyclopedia*

Brian Cantwell Smith

Xerox Palo Alto Research Center, 3333 Coyote Hill Road, Palo Alto, CA 94304, USA; and Center for the Study of Language and Information, Stanford University, Stanford, CA 94305, USA

Received January 1989
Revised February 1990

Abstract

Smith, B.C., The owl and the electric encyclopedia, Artificial Intelligence 47 (1991) 251–288.

A review of "On the thresholds of knowledge", by D.B. Lenat and E.A. Feigenbaum.

1. Introduction

At the 1978 meeting of the Society for Philosophy and Psychology,[1] somewhat to the audience's alarm, Zenon Pylyshyn introduced Terry Winograd by claiming that his pioneering work on natural language processing had represented a "breakthrough in enthusiasm". Since those heady days, AI's hubris has largely passed. Winograd himself has radically scaled back his estimate of the field's potential (see, in particular [70, 72]), and most other practitioners are at least more sober in their expectations. But not to worry. Unbridled enthusiasm is alive and well, living in points South and West.[2]

* Thanks to David Kirsh, Ron Chrisley, and an anonymous reviewer for helpful comments on an earlier draft, and to Randy Davis for slowing down its original presentation.

[1] Tufts University, Medford, MA.

[2] Or at least it is alive. The original version of Lenat and Feigenbaum's paper (the one presented at the Foundations of AI conference, in response to which this review was initially written) was considerably more optimistic than the revision published here some four years later. For one thing, their estimate of the project's scale has grown: whereas in 1987 they suggested the number of things we know to be "many hundreds of thousands—perhaps a few million", that estimate has now increased to "many millions (perhaps a few hundred million)". In addition, whereas their original paper suggested that inference was essentially a non-problem (a sentiment still discernible in their "Knowledge Is All There Is Hypothesis", p. 192), the project is now claimed to incorporate at least "two dozen separate inference engines", with more on the way. Again, not

that there is no obvious model-theoretic analysis, since it is unclear what model-theoretic structure would be assigned to the term "water". Or even, setting model theory aside, that it is unclear what a well-defined semantical value for such a term could be. More seriously, soundness is fundamentally a claim that the use of a term or predicate has respected its independently given semantical value. Making interpretation dependent on use, at least at first blush, therefore gives one every reason to suppose that the notion of soundness is rendered circular, hence vacuous.[19]

Second, it is a likely consequence of this view that the meaning or significance of a complex representational structure won't be able to be derived, systematically, from the "bottom up", but will instead have to be arrived at in some more holistic way. It challenges, in other words, the traditional view that semantics can be "compositionally" defined on top of a base set of atomic values.[20] I.e., the point isn't just that the interpretation of a sentence (its propositional value) is sometimes determined by mutually interlocking constraints established by various sentential constituents (as suggested in indexical cases, such as for the pronoun structure in "though Jim didn't like her, Mary was perfectly happy with him"), say by some sort of relaxation method. Rather, a deeper claim is being made: that the very meaning of the parts of a discourse can depend on the interpretation of the whole. For example, suppose the clouds clear, and you make a comment about the relentless sun. It is easy to imagine that I understand the meaning of "relentless"[21] in virtue of knowing what you're talking about, rather than the other way around. And if it is whole sentences that connect with situations, this may have to be done not bottom-up in terms of the representational constituents, but if anything top-down.

None of this suggests that representation, or interpretation, is impossible.

[19] See the discussion of *coordination conditions* in [65] for one suggestion as to how to retain the integrity of intentional analysis (better: integrity to the notion of intentionality) in the face of this radical a theoretical revision.

[20] To make this precise, you have to rule out cheats of encoding or implementation, of the following sort: Suppose there is some holistic regularity $\mathscr{H}$, a function of all kinds of contextual aspects $\mathscr{C}_i$, whereby complete intentional situations take on a meaning or significance $\mathscr{M}$, and suppose that $\mathscr{H}$ is in some way parameterized on the constituent words w_1, w_2, etc. (which of course it will be—on even the most situated account it still matters what words you use). By a kind of inverted currying process, this can be turned into a "bottom-up" analysis, based on a meaning of the form $\lambda\mathscr{C}_1, \mathscr{C}_2, \ldots, f_k(\mathscr{H})$ for each word w_k, so that when it is all put together $\mathscr{M}$ results, rather in the way in which control irregularities in programming languages (like QUIT, THROW, and ERROR) are handled in denotational semantics of programming languages by treating the continuation as a component of the context. The problem with such deviousness is that it essentially reduces compositionality to mean no more than that there exists *some* systematic overall story.

[21] Or, again, the meaning of the internal data structure or mental representation to which the word "relentless" corresponds. Nothing I am saying here (or anywhere else in this review) hinges on *external* properties of language. It's just simpler, pedagogically, to use familiar examples from natural language than to construct what must inevitably be hypothetical internal cases. As pointed out a few paragraphs back, of all the sorts of referential indefiniteness under review, only genuine ambiguity can be resolved during the parsing phase.

What it does bring into question are the assumptions on which such a system should be built, including for example the inferential viability of a system without any access to the interpretation of its representational structures—without, that is to say, *participating* in the subject matters about which it *reasons* (one way in which to resolve the obvious difficulty raised by the statement just made: that an agent know what is being said other than through the vehicle of the saying). But I'll leave some of these speculations until a later question.

For the time being, note merely that logic avoids this "meaning-depends-on-use" possibility like the plague. In fact the "use = representation + inference" aphorism reflects exactly the opposite theoretical bias: that representation (hence meaning) is an independent module in the intentional whole.

Once again, L&F's position is similar: nothing in their paper suggests they are prepared to make this radical a move. At one point they do acknowledge a tremendous richness in lexical significance, but after claiming this is all metaphor (which typically implies there is a firm "base case"), they go on to assert, without argument, that "these layers of analogy and metaphor eventually 'bottom out' at physical—somatic—primitives: up, down, forward, back, pain, cold, inside, seeing, sleeping, tasting, growing, containing, moving, making noise, hearing, birth, death, strain, exhaustion, ..." It's not a list I would want to have responsibility for completing.

More seriously, the integrity of L&F's project *depends* on avoiding use-dependent meaning, for the simple reason that they don't intend to consider use (their words: "you can never be sure in advance how the knowledge already in the system is going to be used, or added to, in the future", which they take as leading directly to the claim that it must be represented explicitly). If we were to take the meaning-depends-on-use stance seriously, we would be forced to conclude that *nothing in their knowledge base means anything*, since no one has yet developed a theory of its use.

I.e., L&F *can't* say yes to this one; it would pull the rug out from under their entire project.

In contrast (and as expected), the embedded view embraces the possibility. Perhaps the best way to describe the tension is in terms of method. A liberal logicist might admit that, in natural language, meaning is sometimes use-dependent in the ways described, but he or she would go on to claim that proper scientific method requires idealizing away from such recalcitrant messiness. My response? That such idealization throws the baby out with the bathwater. Scientific idealization is worth nothing if in the process it obliterates the essential texture of what one hopes to understand. And it is simply my experience that much of the structure of argument and discourse—even, the *raison d'être* of rationality—involves negotiating in an intentional space where meanings are left fluid by our linguistic and conceptual schemes, ready to be grounded in experience.

Question 4. Is consistency mandated?

Logic	L&F	EC
yes	no	no

L&F are quite explicit in rejecting an absolute dependence on consistency, to which traditional logical systems are so famously vulnerable. As indicated in the table, this is the first of the dozen questions where they and the embedded view align. That much said, however, it's not clear how deep the similarity goes. In particular, I'm unsure how much solace can be found in their recommendation that one carve the "knowledge base" into separate "buttes", and require each to be locally consistent, with neighbouring buttes maximally coherent. At least it's not clear, once again, without a much better intermediate theory.[22]

Fundamentally, the problem is that consistency is a relational property—the consistency of a set of sentences stands or falls on the set as a whole, not on an individual basis. This means that some relations between or among sentences (or frames) will have to be used as a basis for the partition (and to tie the resulting "buttes" together). Call these the system's *organizational principles*. Without them (on any remotely reasonable assumptions of error rates, dependence, etc.) the number of possible different configurations meeting their structural requirements would be intractably immense.

Furthermore, the organizational principles can't themselves be defined in terms of consistency; organizing a database *by* internal consistency would be crazy. Rather, I take it that what L&F really want is to be able to demonstrate (local) consistency for a database organized according to some other metric. What other metric? Surely only one makes sense: according to similarity or integrity of subject matter. *X* should be stored next to *Y*, in other words, because of the presence of (semantic) compatibility, not just the absence of (syntactic) incompatibility. Otherwise, descriptions of national politics might nestle up to lists of lemon meringue pie ingredients, but be kept separated from other statements about Washington policy making—so that things ended up together not because they agreed, but because they didn't have anything to do with one another.

So adequate organization will need to be defined in terms of a notion of subject matter. But where are we to find a theory of that? The problem is similar to that of representation in general: no one has one. The issue comes up in natural language attempts to identify topic, focus, etc. in theories of discourse (see, e.g., [30]), and in some of the semantical work in situation

[22] There's one problem we can set aside. As it happens, the very notion of consistency is vulnerable to the comments made in discussing question 3 (about use-dependent meaning). Like soundness and completeness, consistency, at least as normally formulated, is founded on some notion of semantic value *independent* of use, which an embedded view may not support (at least not in all cases). This should at least render suspicious any claims of *similarity* between the two positions. Still, since they stay well within the requisite conceptual limits, it's kosher to use consistency to assess L&F on their own (not that that will resolve them of all their troubles).

theory [3, 5]. But these are at best a start. Logic famously ducks the question. And informal attempts aren't promising: if my experience with the KRL project can be taken as illustrative [10], the dominant result of any such attempt is to be impressed with how seamlessly everything seems to relate to everything else.

When all is said and done, in other words, it is unclear how L&F plan to group, relate, and index their frames. They don't say, of course, and (in this case) no implicit principles can be inferred. But the answer is going to matter a lot—and not just in order to avoid inconsistency, but for a host of other reasons as well, including search, control strategy, and driving their "analogy" mechanism. Conclusion? That viable indexing (a daunting problem for any project remotely like L&F's), though different from consistency, is every bit as much in need as anything else of "middle-realm" analysis.

And as for consistency itself, we can summarize things as follows. Logic depends on it. L&F retain it locally, but reject it globally, without proposing a workable basis for their "partitioning" proposal. As for the embedded view (as mentioned in footnote 22) the standard notion of consistency doesn't survive its answer to question 3 (about use-dependent meaning). That doesn't mean, however, that I won't have to replace it with something analogous. In particular, I have no doubt that *some* notion of semantic viability, integrity, respect for the fact that the world (not the representation) holds the weight—something like that will be required for any palatable intentional system. Important as contextual setting may be, no amount of "use", reasoning processes, or consensual agreement can rescue a speaker from the potential of being wrong. More seriously, I believe that what is required are global *coordination conditions*—conditions that relate thinking, action, perception, the passing of the world, etc., in something of an indissoluble whole. To say more now, however—especially to assume that logic's notion can be incrementally extended, for example by being locally proscribed—would be to engage in tunneling of my own (but see [65]).

Question 5. Does the system use a single representational scheme?

Logic	L&F	EC
yes	yes	no

Tucked into a short paragraph of L&F's Section 9 is their response to the charge that one might encounter representational difficulties in trying to capture all of human knowledge. Their strategy is simple: "when something proves awkward to represent, add new kinds of slots to make it compactly representable". In fact they apparently now have over 5000 kinds. If only representation were so simple.

Several issues are involved. To start with, there is the question of the expressive adequacy of their chosen representational system—frames, slots, and values. Especially in advance, I see no reason to believe (nor argument to convince me) that mass nouns, plurals, or images should succumb to this scheme in any straightforward way—or, to turn it upside down, to suppose that, if an adequate solution were worked out within a frame-and-slot framework, that the framework would contribute much to the essence of the solution. Frames aren't rendered adequate, after all, by encoding other representational schemes within them.[23]

Furthermore, one wonders whether any single representational framework—roughly, a representation system with a single structural grammar and interpretation scheme—will prove sufficient for all the different kinds of representation an intelligent agent will need. Issues range from the tie-in to motor and perceptual processing (early vision doesn't seem to be frame-like, for example; is late vision?) to the seeming conflict between verbal, imagistic, and other flavours of memory and imagination. You might view the difficulties of describing familiar faces in words, or of drawing pictures of plots or reductio arguments, as problems of externalizing a single, coherent, mentalese, but I suspect they really indicate that genuine intelligence depends on multiple representations, in spite of the obvious difficulties of cross-representational translation.

Certainly our experience with external representations supports this conclusion. Consider architecture: it is simply impossible not to be impressed with the maze of blueprints, written specifications, diagrams, topological maps, pictures, icons, annotations, etc., vital to any large construction project. And the prospect of reducing them all to any single representational scheme (take your choice) is daunting to the point of impossibility. Furthermore, there are reasons for the range of type: information easily captured in one (the shape of topological contours, relevant to the determination of building site, e.g.) would be horrendously inefficient if rendered in another (say, English).[24]

The same holds true of computation. It is virtually constitutive of competent programming practice to be able to select (from a wide range of possibilities) a particular representational scheme that best supports an efficient and consistent implementation of desired behaviour. Imagine how restrictive it would be if, instead of simply enumerating them in a list, a system had to record N user names in an unordered conjunction of N^2 first-order claims:

[23] As indicated in their current comments, L&F have apparently expanded their representational repertoire in recent years. Instead of relying solely on frames and slots, they now embrace, among other things: blocks of compiled code, "unparsed" digitized images, and statistical neural networks. But the remarks made in this section still largely hold, primarily because no mention is made of how these different varieties are integrated into a coherent whole. The challenge—still unmet, in my opinion—is to show how the "contents" contained in a diverse set of representational schemes are semantically commensurable, in such a way as to support a generalized, multi-modal notion of inference, perception, judgment, action. For some initial work in this direction see [6] for a general introduction, and [7] for technical details.

[24] Different representational types also differ in their informational prerequisites. Pictures and graphs, for example, *can't* depict as little information as can English text—imagine trying to draw a picture of "either two adults or half a dozen children".

$$(\exists x_1 \mid \text{user}(x_1)) \wedge (\exists x_2 \mid \text{user}(x_2)) \wedge \cdots \wedge (\exists x_n \mid \text{user}(x_n))$$
$$\wedge ((x_1 \neq x_2) \wedge (x_1 \neq x_3) \wedge \cdots \wedge (x_1 \neq x_n))$$
$$\wedge ((x_2 \neq x_3) \wedge \cdots) \wedge \cdots \wedge ((x_{n-1} \neq x_n))$$

Or how equally untenable it would be to prohibit a reasoning system from using existentials, or to limit it to domains where uniqueness of names could always be assumed. Yet one or other options would be forced by commitment to a "single scheme". Similarly, it's as unthinkable to prohibit display hardware from using bitmaps, in favour of frame-and-slot representations of each illuminated spot, as to force all representation into a bit-per-pixel mold.

Against all such considerations, however, logic and L&F are once again similar in pledging allegiance to a single representational scheme. As representative of the embedded view, I'll vote for variety.

Question 6. Are there only discrete propositions (no continuous representation, images, . . .)?

Logic	L&F	EC
yes	yes	no

If pressed to represent continuous phenomena, L&F would presumably entertain real numbers as slot values, but that barely scratches the surface of the differences between discrete representations like formulae in a formal language, and various easily imagined forms of continuity, vagueness, indeterminacy, analogues, etc. And it is not just that we can imagine them; anything like real intelligence will have to deal with phenomena like this. We have the whole messy world to capture, not just the distilled, crystalline structure of Platonic mathematics.

In assessing the typology of representation, the distinction between discrete (digital) and continuous (analogue[25]) representations is sometimes given pride of place, as if that were the ultimate division, with all other possibilities subcategorized below it. But other just as fundamental divisions cross-cut this admittedly important one. For example, there is a question of whether a representation rests on a conception or set of formulated categories, or is in some way pre- or non-conceptual (terminology from [15]). The natural tendency, probably because of the prevalence of written language, is to assume that discrete goes with conceptual, continuous with non-conceptual, but this isn't true. The use of ocean buoys to demarcate treacherous water, for example, is presumably discrete but non-conceptual; intonation patterns to adjust the

[25] Calling continuous representations "analogue" is both unfortunate and distracting. "Analogue" should presumably be a predicate on a representation whose structure corresponds to that of which it represents: continuous representations would be analogue if they represented continuous phenomena, discrete representations analogue if they represented discrete phenomena. That continuous representations should historically have come to be called analogue presumably betrays the recognition that, at the levels at which it matters to us, the world is more foundationally continuous than it is discrete.

meanings of words ("what an *extraordinary* outfit") are at least plausibly both continuous and conceptual. Or consider another distinction: whether the base or "ur-elements" on which a representation is founded have determinate edges or boundaries. Both discrete and continuous objects of the sort studied in mathematics (the integers, the real line, and even Gaussian distributions and probability densities) are determinate, in the sense that questions about them have determinate answers. It's unclear, however, in questions about when tea-time ends, or about what adolescence is, or about exactly how many clouds there were when you poked your head out of your tent and said, with complete confidence, "there are lots of clouds today"—it's unclear in such cases whether there are determinate answers at all. The problem isn't an epistemic one, about incomplete knowledge, or a linguistic one, about the exact meanings of the words. The point is that the metaphysical facts just aren't there—nor is there any reason to suppose they should be there—to support a clean, black-and-white distinction. The competent use of the English plural, that is to say, doesn't require the existence of a denumerable base set of discrete elements. I am convinced that this distinction between phenomena that have sharp boundaries (support determinate answers) and those that don't is more profound and more consequential for AI than the distinction between discrete and continuous instances of each variety.

Modern logic, needless to say, doesn't deal with foundational indeterminacy. Nor are we given any reason to suppose that L&F want to take it on. One wonders, however, whether our lack of understanding of how relative certainty can arise on top of a foundationally vague base (no one would deny that there were lots of clouds outside that tent, after all) may not be the most important obstacle to the development of systems that aren't brittle in the way that even L&F admit we're limited to today.

Question 7. Do the representations capture all that matters?

Logic	L&F	EC
yes	yes	no

The situated view of representation cited earlier rests on the tenet that language, information, and representation "bridge the gap", in Perry's terms,[26] between the state of the user(s) of the representation, and the state of the world being referred to. It's a position that accords with a familiar view of language as dynamic action, rather than simply as static description. And it has among its more extreme consequences the realization that not all of what matters about a situation need be captured, at least in the traditional sense, in the meanings of its constituent representations.

For example, if someone simply yells "fire!", then some of what matters, including your understanding of what fire is, may be contributed by the surrounding situation, possibly even including the impinging thermal radiation. Call this totality of what matters—i.e., everything relevant to an assessment of

[26] The phrase is from various of John Perry's lectures given at CSLI during 1986–88.

whether the communication worked properly—its *full significance*. The claim, then, is that *the full significance of an intentional action can outstrip its content*. Facts of embodiment, of being there, of action, of experience, can, along with the content, influence the net or intended result.

To understand what this means, consider three things that it doesn't. First, it isn't merely a repetition of the claim made in discussing question 2: that conceptual content isn't uniquely determined by the type of representation used, but is partially determined by the context of its use. Nor, second, is it a replay of the stronger claim made in discussing question 3: that even the meanings—not just contents! (see footnote 17)—of words or internal structures may depend on their actual use. Although both of these involve use and context in a variety of ways, they remain claims about the relation between a representation and its semantic value. The current claim is stronger: that the full significance of an intentional act will outstrip even the situated semantic value of the representational ingredients constitutive of it, no matter how indexical, use-dependent, or situated a notion of content you care to come up with.

Even this last way of putting it, however, isn't strong enough, because it allows room for a third possible stance, stronger than the previous two (i.e., stronger than the embedded responses to questions 2 and 3), but still weaker than I have in mind here. In particular, someone might agree that an intentional action's full significance lies outside the content of the particular act itself, but go on to look for that additional contribution in the content of other representational structures. Thus, in determining the significance of "fire", you might look to other representations already present in the agent's head, or to conclusions that could be (quickly) drawn from things already represented. For example, you might expect to find the escape heuristic (that if someone shouts "fire!" it's good to get out of the way) represented in a previously stored internal frame.

I don't disagree that this can happen; in fact I take it as almost obvious (what else is inference for, after all?). However, I intend with this seventh question to get at a stronger position yet: that the full significance of an intentional action (not just a communicative one) can crucially involve *non-representational* phenomena, as well as representational ones. I.e., it is a claim that the millennial story about intelligence won't consist solely of a story about representation, but will inevitably weave that story together with analyses of other, non-representational aspects of an intentional agent. Some of these other ingredient stories will describe salient facts of embodiment (possibly even including adrenaline levels), but they will talk about other things as well, including genuine *participation* in represented subject matters,[27] and the internal *manifestation* (rather than *representation*) of intentionally important prop-

[27] The foundational notion underlying the view of embedded computation, in particular, is one of *partially disconnected participation*; see [65].

erties. Some modern roboticists, for example, argue that action results primarily from the dynamical properties of the body; the representational burden to be shouldered by the "mind", as it were, may consist only of adjustments or tunings to those non-representational capacities (see, e.g., [55, 56]). Rhythm may similarly as much be exhibited as encoded in the intelligent response to music. Or even take a distilled example from LISP: when a system responds with the numeral "3" to the query "(LENGTH '(A B C))", it does so by interacting with non-representational facts, since (if implemented in the ordinary way) the list '(A B C) will *have* a cardinality, but not one that is *represented*.

Distinguishing representational from non-representational in any careful way will require a better theory of representation than any we yet have.[28] Given such a story, it will bcome possible to inquire about the extent to which intelligence requires access to these non-formulated (non-formulable?) aspects of the subject matter. Although it's premature to take a definite stand, my initial sense is that there is every reason to suppose (at least in the human case) that it does. Introspection, common sense, and even considerations of efficient evolutionary design would all suggest that inferential mechanisms should avail themselves of any relevant available resources, whether those have arisen through representational channels, or otherwise. If this is true, then it follows that a system lacking any of those other channels—a system without the right kind of embodiment, for example—won't be able to reason in the same way we do. And so much the worse, I'd be willing to bet, for it.

How do our three players stand on this issue? I take it as obvious that L&F require what logic assumes: that representation has to capture all that matters, for the simple reason that there isn't anything else around. For L&F, in other words, facts that can't be described might as well not be true, whether about fire, sleep, internal thrashing, or the trials of committee work. They are forced to operate under a maxim of "inexpressible → irrelevant".

In contrast, as I've already indicated, I take seriously the fact that we are beaten up by the world—and not only in intentional ways. I see no reason to assume that the net result of our structural coupling to our environment—even that part of that coupling salient to intelligent deliberation—is exhausted by its representational record. And if that is so, then it seems overwhelmingly likely that the full structure of intelligence will rely on that residue of maturation and embodiment. So I'll claim no less for an embedded computer.

Here's a way to put it. L&F believe that intelligence can rest entirely on the meaning of *representations*, without any need for correlated, *non-representational experience*. On the other hand, L&F also imagine their system starting to read and distill things on its own. What will happen, however, if the writers

[28] Though some requirements can be laid down: such as that any such theory have enough teeth so that not *everything* is representational. That would be vacuous.

tacitly rely on non-representational actions on the part of the reader? The imagined system wouldn't be able to understand what it was reading. For example, there is no way in which L&F's system would ever be able to understand the difference between right and left.[29]

Question 8. Are reasoning and inference central?

Logic	L&F	EC
yes	yes	yes

When logicians develop axiomatic accounts of set theory, criteria of elegance and parsimony push towards a minimal number of axioms—typically on the order of a dozen—from which an infinite number of truths follow. It's a general truth: economy of statement is often a hallmark of penetrating insight.

No one, however, expects distilled scientific theories alone to sustain complete, workaday, general-purpose reasoning. It is obvious that any reasonable problem solver (like any imaginable person), rather than deriving all its conclusions from first principles, will depend on a rich stock of facts and heuristics, derived results and rules of thumb—to say nothing of a mass of a-theoretic but relevant particulars (such as who it's talking to). So we should expect general intelligence to rest on a relatively high ratio of relevant truths to foundational axioms, especially in the face of resource-bounded processing, complex or just plain messy subject matters, and other departures from theoretical purity.

Nonetheless, you can't literally know everything. No matter how knowledgeable, an agent will still have to think in order to deal with the world *specifically*—to conclude that if today is Tuesday then tomorrow must be Wednesday, for example (derived from the general fact that Wednesdays follow Tuesdays), or to figure out whether your friend can walk from Boston to Cambridge, not otherwise having heard of your friend. Universal instantiation and modus ponens may not be all there is to thought, but without some such faculty a system would be certifiably CPU-dead.[30] And instantiating universals

[29] All the remarks made in footnote 16 apply here: it won't do to reply that L&F could build a model of right and left inside the system, or even attach a camera, since that would fall outside their stated program for representing the world. I too (i.e., on the embedded view) would attach a camera, but I want a *theory* of what it is to attach a camera, and of some other things as well—such as how to integrate the resulting images with conceptual representations, and how envisionment works, and how this all relates to the existence of "internal" sensors and effectors, and how it ties to action, and so on and so forth—until I get a theory that, as opposed to slots-and-frames, really does do justice to full-scale participation in the world. Cameras, in short, are just the tip of a very large iceberg.

[30] To imagine the converse, furthermore, would be approximately equivalent to the proposal that programming languages do away with procedures and procedure calls, in favour of the advance storage of the sum total of all potentially relevant stack frames, so that any desired answer could merely be "read off", without having to do any work. This is no more plausible a route to intelligence than to satisfactory computation more generally. And it would raise daunting issues of indexing and retrieval—a subject for which, as discussed under question 4 (on consistency), there is no reason to suppose that L&F have any unique solution.

is only the beginning. "Inference" includes not only deduction, but induction, abduction, inference to the best explanation, concept formation, hypothesis testing—even sheer speculation and creative flights of fancy. It can hardly be argued that some such semantically coordinated processing[31] is essential to intelligence.

It shouldn't be surprising, then, that inference is the one issue on which all three positions coincide—logic, L&F, and EC. But superficial agreement doesn't imply deep uniformity. There are questions, in each case, as to what that commitment means.

To see this, note that any inference regimen must answer to at least two demands. The first is famous: though mechanically defined on the form or structure of the representational ingredients,[32] inference must make semantic sense (that's what makes it *inference*, rather than ad hoc symbol mongering). There simply must be some semantic justification, that is to say—some way to see how the "formal" symbol manipulation coordinates with semantic value or interpretation. Second, there is a question of finitude. One cannot forget, when adverting to inference as the mechanism whereby a finite stock of representations can generate an indefinite array of behaviour, that the inference mechanism iself must be compact (and hence productive). The deep insight, that is to say, is not that reasoning allows a limited stock of information to generate an unlimited supply of answers, but that a synchronously finite system can manifest diachronically indefinite semantic behaviour.

Logic, of course, supplies a clear answer to the first demand (in its notion of soundness), but responds only partially to the second (hence the dashed lines around its positive answer). A collection of inferential schemata are provided—each demonstrably truth-preserving (the first requirement), and each applicable to an indefinite set of sentences (the second). But, as AI knows so well, something is still missing: the higher-level strategies and organizational principles necessary to knit these atomic steps together into an appropriate rational pattern.[33] Being able to reason, that is to say, isn't just the ability to take the right atomic steps; it means knowing how to think in the large—how to argue, how to figure things out, how to think creatively about the world. Traditional logic, of course, doesn't address these questions. Nor—and this is the important point—is there any a priori reason to believe that that larger inferential demand can be fully met within the confines of logic's peculiar formal and semantic conventions.

[31] By "semantically coordinated" I mean only to capture what deduction, induction, reasoning, contemplation, etc., have in common: roughly, some kind of coordination between what is done to (or happens because of, or whatever) a representation and its semantic value or content. Soundness, completeness, and consistency are particularly disconnected species; I suspect much more complicated versions will ultimately be required.

[32] Or so, at least, it is traditionally argued. This is not a view I am ultimately prepared to accept.

[33] For simplicity, I'm assuming that rational belief revision will consist of a pattern of sound inference steps—almost certainly not true. See e.g. [38].

On the other hand—and this takes us to the embedded view—once one moves beyond logic's familiar representational assumptions (explicit, a-contextual representation, and so forth), no one has yet presented an inferential model that meets the first demand. To accept the embedded answers to questions 1–7 is thus to take on a substantial piece of homework: developing, from the ground up, a semantically coordinated and rationally justifiable notion of inference itself. This is just one of the reasons why the embedded perspective is still emerging.

Nonetheless, important steps are being taken in this direction. The development of a contextually sensitive model of inference (based on a semantic notion of information, rather than symbolic form) is constitutive of Barwise and Etchemendy's work on situation theory, for example [6, 7]. Similarly, in the situated automata work of Rosenschein, a similarly non-syntactic notion of inference is analyzed in terms of a machine's carrying information relative to the structure of its embedding environment[34]. In a somewhat different vein, I have argued that an embedded notion of inference will ultimately be as relevant to clocks and other transducers as to sentential transformation [64]. It is also becoming clear that even more traditional (i.e., linguistic) forms of inference will as much involve the preservation of reference across a change in context, as the more familiar preservation of truth across a change in subject matter.[35] Important as these new thrusts are, however, they are still just early steps.

What about L&F? They have two options. To the extent that they agree with the present characterization of their position, vis-à-vis questions 1–7, they would probably want to avail themselves of logic's notion of inference. For reasons discussed earlier, however, this isn't enough: they would still have to take a stand on the relationship between truth-preserving logical entailment and the appropriate structure of rational belief revision, for example (see footnote 33), to say nothing of providing a finite account of an appropriate set of high-level control strategies, in order to provide a complete answer to the second demand. On the other hand, to the extent that they feel confined by logic's stringent representational restrictions (as they admit they do, for example, at least with respect to its insistence on full consistency—see question 4), and want to embrace something more like the embedded view, then they too must answer to the much larger demand: of not simply presenting their inferential mechanism (let alone claiming to have embraced 20 different ones), but of explaining what their very notion of inference is.

[34] Where information is approximately taken as counterfactual supporting correlation, in the spirit of Dretske [19] and Barwise and Perry [8]. See also Rosenschein [57].

[35] For the application of some of these ideas to the design of an embedded programming language, see [18].

Question 9. Are participation and action crucial?

Logic	L&F	EC
no	no	yes

Reasoning is a form of action. Earlier I commented on L&F's relegation of reasoning to a secondary status by their treatment of it as search, their suggestion that the "control" problem is largely solved, and their claim that with enough "knowledge" deep reasoning will be largely unnecessary.

But reasoning isn't the only kind of action that (at least in humans) has to be coordinated with representation. If you wander around Kyoto for the first time, poking your head into small shops, stopping for tea on the Philosopher's Walk, and gradually making your way back to the ryokan by something like dead reckoning, then your emergent conceptual understanding of the layout of the city must be constantly coordinated with your on-going but non-conceptual bodily movements. For example, if you remember that the hotel is somewhere off to your right, and then turn in that direction, you need to know that it is now roughly in front of you. In a similar way, we all need to know that tomorrow today will be "yesterday". Representations that lead to action often have to be revised in light of that very action's being taken.

Coordination management, as I will call this indissoluble blend of adjustment, feedback, action, belief revision, perception, dance, etc., arises in many corners of AI, ranging from planning and robotics to systems dealing with their own internal state (reflection and meta-level reasoning). Nor is AI the first discipline to recognize its importance: philosophers of science, and theorists of so-called "practical reasoning", have always realized the importance—and difficulty—of connecting thinking and doing. Students of perception, too, and of robotics, wrestle with their own versions of the coordination problem.

Curiously enough, even L&F, although they don't embrace a participatory stance, won't entirely be able to avoid it. Though their system will clearly shun the external world as much as possible,[36] it will still have to grapple with internal participation, if they go ahead with their proposal to encode (at the meta-level) such control knowledge as turns out genuinely to be needed. For example, suppose someone adds the following rule: that if the system uses any search strategy for more than 10 seconds without making definite progress, it should abandon that approach and try an alternative. Obeying this injunction requires various kinds of participation: recognizing that you have wasted 10 seconds (perception); stopping doing so (action); registering what it was that you were doing (perception); selecting a plausible alternative (inference); setting that new goal in motion (action); "letting go" of the meta-level deliberations (action on inference). Introspection and reflection might be better

[36] One thing it won't be able to shun, presumably, will be its users. See footnote 37.

described as varieties of self-*involvement* than of self-*reference* (in spite of my "Varieties of Self-Reference" [63]; see also [65]).[37]

So we end this one with a curious tally. In virtue of its utterly disconnected stance, and of *not being a computational system*, logic is singularly able to ignore action and subject matter participation. On the embedded side, I take participatory connections with the world as not just important, but as essential. In fact the embedded view could almost be summed up in the following claim:

> *Participation in the subject matter is partially constitutive of intelligence.*

When all is said and done, in other words, I believe the term "intelligent" should be predicated of an integrated way of being that includes both thought and action, not simply an abstract species of disconnected symbol manipulation. This may contravene current theoretical assumptions, but I suspect it is consonant with ordinary common sense. Frankly, I don't see how you could believe a system could comprehend all of consensus reality without being able to understand "See you tomorrow!".[38]

Between these two, L&F occupy a somewhat unstable middle ground. I have listed them with logic, since that's where their claims go; there is no hint that they envisage tackling issues of coordination. On the other hand, they will have to confront coordination management merely in order to get their system to turn over, quite apart from whether it manifests anything I would call intelligence.

Question 10. Is physical embodiment important?

Logic	L&F	EC
no	no	yes

The authors of the mathematical theory of computability claimed as a great victory their elevation of the subject of computation from messy details of physical implementation and fallible mechanism onto a pure and abstract plane. And the prime results of recursive function theory, including the famous

[37] This paragraph makes explicit something I have otherwise tried, in this article, to sidestep: the fact that (at least on my analysis) L&F's theoretical framework is not only inadequate for understanding *intelligence*, but is also inadequate for understanding *their own system* (which, I am claiming, won't be *intelligent*, but will still *exist*). Driving a wedge between what computation is actually like and how we think of it is a primary brief of [65]; for the moment, simply assume that L&F, if they proceed with their project, will have to resort to a-theoretical programming techniques to handle this and other such issues. Control structure is only one example; another is user interaction. To the extent computers carry on conversations, after all, they actually *carry them on*, rather than merely representing them as being carried on (though they may do that as well).

[38] Again, as I said in footnote 16, it won't do to reply that they could simply add a counter to mark the passage of time. For one thing (or at least so I claim) this example, although simple, is symptomatic of a deep problem; it's not a surface nuisance to be programmed around. Furthermore, even if it were simply disposed of, for L&F to treat it in an ad hoc, procedural way would be to part company with their own analysis.

proofs of undecidability, genuinely didn't seem to rely on any such implementational details. Modern programmers don't typically traffic in recursive function theory in any very conscious way, but they still accept the legacy of a computational level of analysis separate from (and possibly not even theoretically reducible to[39]) the physical level at which one understands the underlying physical substrate.

More recently, however, especially with the increasing realization that relative computability is as important as (if not more important than) the absolute computability of the 1930s, the story is growing murkier. Though it treats its subject matter abstractly, complexity theory still deals with something called time and space; it's not entirely clear what relation those rather abstract notions bear to the space and time of everyday experience (or even to those of physics). At least with regard to time, though, real (non-abstract) temporal properties of computation are obviously important. Whether differences among algorithms are measured in minutes, milliseconds, or abstract "unit operations", the time they take when they run is the same stuff that I spend over lunch. And the true spatial arrangement of integrated circuits—not just an abstracted notion of space—plays an increasing role in determining architectures.

Although it isn't clear where this will all lead, it does allow the question to be framed of whether considerations of physical embodiment impinge on the analysis of a given computational system. For traditional logic, of course, the answer is *no*; it is as pure an exemplar as anything of the abstract view of computation and representation. And once again L&F's stance is similar: nothing suggests that they, along with most of the formal tradition, won't ignore such issues.

Again the embedded view is different. I am prepared to argue that physical constraints enter computational thinking in a variety of familiar places. For one thing, I have come to believe that what (in a positive vein[40]) we call the "formality" of computation—the claim, for example, that proof procedures rely solely on the formal properties of the expressions they manipulate—amounts in the end to neither more nor less than "whatever can be physically realized in a causally efficacious manner".[41] But this is not the only place where

[39] *Reducibility*, as the term is normally used in the philosophy of science, is a relation between *theories*; one theory is reducible to another if, very roughly, its predicates and claims can be translated into those of another. In contrast, the term *supervenience* is used to relate phenomena themselves; thus the strength of a beam would be said to supervene on the chemical bonds in the constitutive wood. The two relations are distinguished because people have realized that, somewhat contrary to untutored intuition, supervenience doesn't necessarily imply reducibility (see [27, 33, 40, 41]).

[40] As opposed to the "negative" reading: namely, that a formal computational process proceed independently of the semantics. That the two readings are *conceptually* distinct is obvious; that they get at different things is argued in [65].

[41] I am not asking the reader to agree with this statement, without more explanation—just to admit that it is conceptually coherent.

physical realization casts its shadow. Consider one other example: the notion of locality that separates doubly-linked lists from more common singly-linked ones, or that distinguishes object-oriented from function-based programming languages. Locality, fundamentally, is a physical notion, having to do with genuine metric proximity. The question is whether the computational use is just a metaphor, or whether the "local access" that a pointer can provide into an array is metaphysically dependent on the locality of the underlying physics. As won't surprise anyone, the embedded viewpoint endorses the latter possibility.

Question 11. Does the system support "original" semantics?

Logic	L&F	EC
no	no	yes

It has often been pointed out that books and encyclopedias derive their semantics or connection to what they're about from the people that use them. The analogous question can be asked about computers: whether the interpretations of the symbol structures they use are in any sense "authentic" or "original" to the computers themselves, or whether computational states have their significance only through human attribution (see, e.g., [17; 31, pp. 32ff; 60].

The question is widely accepted, but no one has proposed a really good theory of what is required for semantical originality, so not a whole lot more can be said. Still, some of the themes working their way through this whole set of questions suggest that this issue of originality may be relevant not only for philosophical reasons but also for purposes of adequate inference and reasoning. In particular, if the only full-blooded connection to subject matter is through external users, then it follows that a system won't be able to avail itself of that connection in carrying out its processes of symbol manipulation, reasoning, or inference. If, on the other hand, the semantic connection is autonomous (as one can at least imagine it is, for example, for a network mail system that not only represents facts about network traffic, but also sends and receives real mail), then the chances of legitimate inference may go up.[42]

So the question should be read as one of whether the way of looking at the system, in each case, points towards a future in which systems begin to "own" their semantic interpretations—if still in a clunky and limited way, then at least with a kind of proto-originality.

Even that vague a formulation is sufficient to corral the votes—and to

[42] I am not suggesting that physical involvement with the subject matter is sufficient for original intentionality; that's obviously not true. And I don't mean, either, to imply the strict converse: that anything like simple physical connection is *necessary*, since we can obviously genuinely refer to things from which we are physically disconnected in a variety of ways—by distance, from other galaxies; by fact, from Santa Claus; by possibility, from a round square; by type, from the number 2. Still, I am hardly alone in thinking that *some kind of causal connectivity* is at least a constituent part of the proper referential story. See e.g. Kripke [43], Dretske [19], and Fodor [28].

produce another instance of what is emerging as the recurring pattern. Like logic, L&F neither address nor imagine their system possessing anything like the wherewithal to give its frames and slots autonomous referential connection with the world. In fact something quite else suggests itself. Given the paucity of inference they imagine, the heavy demands on indexing schemes, and the apparent restriction of interaction to console events, L&F's system is liable to resemble nothing so much as an electric encyclopedia. No wonder its semantics will be derivative.

Now it's possible, of course, that we might actually want an electric encyclopedia. In fact it might be a project worth pursuing—though it would require a major and revealing revision of both goals and procedure. Note that L&F, on the current design, retain only the formal data structures they generate, discarding the natural language articles, digests, etc., used in its preparation. Suppose, instead, they were to retain all those English entries, thick with connotation and ineffable significance, *and use their data structures and inference engines as an active indexing scheme*. Forget intelligence completely, in other words; take the project as one of constructing the world's largest hypertext system, with CYC functioning as a radically improved (and active) counterpart for the Dewey decimal system. Such a system might facilitate what numerous projects are struggling to implement: reliable, content-based searching and indexing schemes for massive textual databases. CYC's inference schemes would facilitate the retrieval of articles on related topics, or on the target subject matter using different vocabulary. And note, too, that it would exploit many current AI techniques, especially those of the "explicit representation" school.

But L&F wouldn't be satisfied; they want their system itself to know what those articles mean, not simply to aid us humans. And it is against that original intention that the embedded view stands out in such stark contrast. With respect to owls, for example, an embedded system is more likely to resemble the creatures themselves than the *Britannica* article describing them. And this, I submit, to return to the question we started with, is the direction in which semantical originality lies.

Question 12. Is room made for a divergence between the representational capacities of theorist and agent?

Logic	L&F	EC
no	no	yes

The final question has to do with the relation between the representational capacities of a system under investigation, and the typically much more sophisticated capacities of its designer or theorist. I'll get at this somewhat indirectly, through what I'll call the *aspectual* nature of representation.

It is generally true that if X represents Y, then there is a question of *how* it represents it—or, to put it another way, of how it represents it *as being*. The two phrases "The Big Apple" and "the hub of the universe" can both be used to represent New York, but the latter represents it as something that the former does not. Similarly, "the MX missile" and Reagan's "the Peacemaker".

The "represent *as*" idiom is telling. If we hear that someone knew her brother was a scoundrel, but in public *represented him as* a model citizen, then it is safe for us to assume that she possessed the representational capacity to represent him in at least these two ways. More seriously—this is where things can get tricky—we, *qua* theorists, who characterize her, *qua* subject, know what it is to say "as a scoundrel", or "as a citizen". We know because we too can represent things as scoundrels, as citizens, and as a myriad other things as well. And we assume, in this example, that our conceptual scheme and her conceptual scheme overlap, so that we can get at the world in the way that she does. So long as they overlap, trouble won't arise.[43]

Computers, however, generally don't possess anything remotely like our discriminatory capacities,[44] and as a result, it is a very substantial question for us to know how (from their point of view) they are representing the world as being. For example (and this partly explains McDermott's [49] worries about the wishful use of names), the fact that we use English words to name a computer system's representational structures doesn't imply that the resulting structure represents the world for the computer in the same way as that name represents it for us. Even if you could argue that a KRYPTON node labeled $DETENTE genuinely represented detente, it doesn't follow that it represents it as what we would call detente. It is hard to know how it does represent it as being (for the computer), of course, especially without knowing more about the rest of its representational structures.[45] But one thing seems likely: $DETENTE will mean less for the computer than "detente" means for us.

I suspect that the lure of L&F's project depends in part on their ignoring "as" questions, and failing to distinguish theorists' and agents' conceptual schemes. Or at least this can be said: that they are explicitly committed to not making a distinction between the two. In fact quite the opposite is presumably their aim: what they want, of the system they propose to build, is something

[43] In logic, this required overlap of registration scheme turns up in the famous mandate that a metalanguage used to express a truth theory must *contain* the predicate of the (object) language under investigation (Tarski's convention T). Overlap of registration scheme, however, is at least potentially a much more complex issue than one of simple language subsumption.

[44] Obviously they are simpler, but the differences are probably more interesting than that. The individuation criteria for computational processes are wildly different from those for people, and, even if AI were to succeed up to if not beyond its wildest dreams, notions like "death" will probably mean something rather different to machines than to us. Murder, for example, might only be a misdemeanor in a society with reliable daily backups.

[45] It would also be hard (impossible, in fact) for us to say, exactly, what representing something as detente would mean for *us*—but for a very different reason. At least on a view such as that of Cussins [15], with which I am sympathetic, our *understanding* of the concept "detente" is not itself a conceptual thing, and therefore can't necessarily be captured in words (i.e., concepts aren't conceptually constituted). Cf. the discussion of formulation in Section 2.

point of view, knowledge and intelligence require participation in the world. Lenat and Feigenbaum, apparently, think not. I can only conclude that they would not agree with Yeats, who I think said it well:

> I have found what I wanted—to put it all in a phrase, I say, "Man can embody the truth, but cannot know it."[46]

References

[1] P.E. Agre, Routines, AI Memo 828, MIT, Cambridge, MA (1985).

[2] P.E. Agre, The dynamic structure of everyday life, Ph.D. Thesis, Tech. Rept., MIT, Cambridge, MA (1989).

[3] J. Barwise, The situation in logic II: conditionals and conditional information, in: E.C. Traugott, C.A. Ferguson and J.S. Reilly, eds., *On Conditionals* (Cambridge University Press, Cambridge, 1986); also: Rept. No. CLSI-85-21, Stanford, CA (1985); reprinted in: J. Barwise, *The Situation of Logic*, CLSI Lecture Notes **17** (University of Chicago Press, Chicago, IL, 1989) Chapter 5.

[4] J. Barwise, *The Situation of Logic*, CLSI Lecture Notes **17** (University of Chicago Press, Chicago, IL, 1989).

[5] J. Barwise and J. Etchemendy, Model-theoretic semantics, in: M. Posner, ed., *Foundations of Cognitive Science* (MIT Press, Cambridge, MA, 1989).

[6] J. Barwise and J. Etchemendy, Visual information and valid reasoning, in: W. Zimmermann, ed., *Visualization in Mathematics* (Mathematical Association of America, to appear).

[7] J. Barwise and J. Etchemendy, Information, infons, and inference, in: R. Cooper, K. Mukai and J. Perry, eds., *Situation Theory and Its Applications* I, CLSI Lecture Notes (University of Chicago Press, Chicago, IL, 1990) 33–78.

[8] J. Barwise and J. Perry, *Situations and Attitudes* (MIT Press, Cambridge, MA, 1983).

[9] D.G. Bobrow, ed., *Qualitative Reasoning about Physical Systems* (North-Holland, Amsterdam, 1984).

[10] D.G. Bobrow, T. Winograd et al., Experience with KRL-0: one cycle of a knowledge representation language, in: *Proceedings IJCAI-77*, Cambridge, MA (1977) 213–222.

[11] R. Boyd, Metaphor and theory change: what is "metaphor" a metaphor for?, in: A. Ortony, ed., *Metaphor and Thought* (Cambridge University Press, Cambridge, 1979).

[12] R.A. Brooks, A robust layered control system for a mobile robot, *IEEE J. Rob. Autom.* **2** (1986) 14–23.

[13] D. Chapman and P.E. Agre, Abstract reasoning as emergent from concrete activity, in: M.P. Georgeff and A.L. Lansky, eds., *Reasoning about Action and Plans: Proceedings of the 1986 Workshop* (Morgan Kaufmann, Los Altos, CA, 1987) 411–424.

[14] W.J. Clancey, The frame of reference problem in the design of intelligent machines, in: K. VanLehn, ed., *Architectures for Intelligence* (Erlbaum, Hillsdale, NJ, to appear).

[15] A. Cussins, The connectionist construction of concepts, in: M. Boden, ed., *The Philosophy of Artificial Intelligence*, Oxford Readings in Philosophy Series (Oxford University Press, Oxford, 1990) 368–440.

[16] R. Davis, ed., *Expert Systems: How Far Can They Go? AI Mag.* **10** (1–2) (1989).

[17] D.C. Dennett, *The Intentional Stance* (MIT Press, Cambridge, MA, 1987).

[18] M.A. Dixon, Open semantics and programming language design (working title), Doctoral Dissertation, Computer Science Department, Stanford University, Stanford, CA (to appear).

[46] Taken from a letter Yeats wrote to a friend shortly before his death. Dreyfus cites the passage at the conclusion of the introduction to the revised edition of his *What Computers Can't Do* [21, p. 66]; it has also been popularized on a poster available from Cody's Books in Berkeley.

[19] F. Dretske, *Knowledge and the Flow of Information* (MIT Press, Cambridge, MA, 1981).
[20] F. Dretske, *Explaining Behavior: Reasons in a World of Causes* (MIT Press/Bradford Books, Cambridge, MA, 1988).
[21] H.L. Dreyfus, *What Computers Can't Do: The Limits of Artificial Intelligence* (Harper Row, New York, rev. ed., 1979).
[22] H.L. Dreyfus, From micro-worlds to knowledge representation: AI at an impasse, in: J. Haugeland, ed., *Mind Design: Philosophy, Psychology, Artificial Intelligence* (MIT Press, Cambridge, MA, 1981) 161–205.
[23] H.L. Dreyfus, ed., *Husserl, Intentionality, and Cognitive Science* (MIT Press, Cambridge, MA, 1982).
[24] H.L. Dreyfus and S.E. Dreyfus, *Mind over Machine: The Power of Human Intuition and Expertise in the Era of the Computer* (Macmillan/Free Press, New York, 1985).
[25] G. Evans, *The Varieties of Reference* (Oxford University Press, Oxford, 1982).
[26] R. Fagin and J.Y. Halpern, Belief, awareness, and limited reasoning, in: *Proceedings IJCAI-85*, Los Angeles, CA (1985) 491–501.
[27] J.A. Fodor, Special sciences (or: the disunity of science as a working hypothesis), *Synthese* **28** (1974) 97–115; reprinted in: N. Block, ed., *Readings in the Philosophy of Psychology* (Harvard University Press, Cambridge, MA, 1980) 120–133.
[28] J.A. Fodor, *Psychosemantics* (MIT Press/Bradford Books, Cambridge, MA, 1987).
[29] D. Gentner and D. Gentner, Flowing waters or teeming crowds: Mental models of electricity, in: D. Gentner and A. Stevens, eds., *Mental Models* (Erlbaum, Hillsdale, NJ, 1983).
[30] B.J. Grosz and C.L. Sidner, Attention, intentions, and the structure of discourse, *Comput. Linguistics* **12** (3) (1986) 175–204.
[31] J. Haugeland, Semantic engines: introduction to mind design, in: J. Haugeland, ed., *Mind Design: Philosophy, Psychology, Artificial Intelligence* (MIT Press, Cambridge, MA, 1981) 1–34.
[32] J. Haugeland, ed., *Mind Design: Philosophy, Psychology, Artificial Intelligence* (MIT Press, Cambridge, MA, 1981).
[33] J. Haugeland, Weak supervenience, *Am. Philos. Q.* **19** (1) (1982) 93–103.
[34] P.J. Hayes, The second naive physics manifesto, in: J.R. Hobbs and R.C. Moore, eds., *Formal Theories of the Commonsense World* (Ablex, Norwood, NJ, 1985) 1–36.
[35] P.J. Hayes, Naive physics I: ontology for liquids, in: J.R. Hobbs and R.C. Moore, eds., *Formal Theories of the Commonsense World* (Ablex, Norwood, NJ, 1985) 71–107.
[36] J.R. Hobbs and R.C. Moore, eds., *Formal Theories of the Commonsense World* (Ablex, Norwood, NJ, 1985).
[37] J.R. Hobbs et al., Commonsense summer: final report, Tech. Rept. CSLI-85-35, Stanford University, Stanford, CA (1985).
[38] D.J. Israel, What's wrong with non-monotonic logic?, in: *Proceedings AAAI-80*, Stanford, CA (1980).
[39] L. Kaelbling, An architecture for intelligent reactive systems, in: M.P. Georgeff and A.L. Lansky, eds., *Reasoning about Action and Plans: Proceedings of the 1986 Workshop* (Morgan Kaufmann, San Mateo, CA, 1987) 395–410.
[40] J. Kim, Supervenience and nomological incommensurables, *Am. Philos. Q.* **15** (1978) 149–156.
[41] J. Kim, Causality, identity, and supervenience in the mind-body problem, *Midwest Stud. Philos.* **4** (1979) 31–49.
[42] D. Kirsh, When is information explicitly represented?, in: P. Hanson, ed., *Information, Language, and Cognition*, Vancouver Studies in Cognitive Science **1** (University of British Columbia Press, Vancouver, BC, 1990) 340–365.
[43] S.A. Kripke, *Naming and Necessity* (Harvard University Press, Cambridge, MA, 1980).
[44] J. Lave, *Cognition in Practice: Mind, Mathematics, and Culture in Everyday Life* (Cambridge University Press, Cambridge, 1988).
[45] H.J. Levesque, A logic of implicit and explicit belief, in: *Proceedings AAAI-84*, Austin, TX (1984) 198–202.
[46] D.M. Levy, D.C. Brotsky and K.R. Olson, Formalizing the figural, in: *Proceedings ACM Conference on Document Processing Systems*, Santa Fe, NM (1988) 145–151.

capable of such action. Human intelligence—which stands before us like a holy grail—shows to first observation what can only be termed *general intelligence*. A single human exhibits a bewildering diversity of intelligent behavior. The types of goals that humans can set for themselves or accept from the environment seem boundless. Further observation, of course, shows limits to this capacity in any individual—problems range from easy to hard, and problems can always be found that are too hard to be solved. But the general point is still compelling.

Work in AI has already contributed substantially to our knowledge of what functions are required to produce general intelligence. There is substantial, though certainly not unanimous, agreement about some functions that need to be supported: symbols and goal structures, for example. Less agreement exists about what mechanisms are appropriate to support these functions, in large part because such matters depend strongly on the rest of the system and on cost-benefit tradeoffs. Much of this work has been done under the rubric of AI tools and languages, rather than AI systems themselves. However, it takes only a slight shift of viewpoint to change from what is an aid for the programmer to what is structure for the intelligent system itself. Not all features survive this transformation, but enough do to make the development of AI languages as much substantive research as tool building. These proposals provide substantial ground on which to build.

The Soar project has been building on this foundation in an attempt to understand the functionality required to support general intelligence. Our current understanding is embodied in the Soar architecture [22, 26]. This article represents an attempt at describing and analyzing the structure of the Soar system. We will take a particular point of view—the description of Soar as a hierarchy of levels—in an attempt to bring coherence to this discussion.

The idea of analyzing systems in terms of multiple levels of description is a familiar one in computer science. In one version, computer systems are described as a sequence of levels that starts at the bottom with the device level and works up through the circuit level, the logic level, and then one or more program levels. Each level provides a description of the system at some level of abstraction. The sequence is built up by defining each higher level in terms of the structure provided at the lower levels. This idea has also recently been used to analyze human cognition in terms of levels of description [38]. Each level corresponds to a particular time scale, such as ~100 msec. and ~1 sec., with a new level occurring for each new order of magnitude. The four levels between ~10 msec. and ~10 sec. comprise the cognitive band (Fig. 1). The lowest cognitive level—at ~10 msec.—is the symbol-accessing level, where the knowledge referred to by symbols is retrievable. The second cognitive level—at ~100 msec.—is the level at which elementary deliberate operations occur; that is, the level at which encoded knowledge is brought to bear, and the most elementary choices are made. The third and fourth cognitive levels—at ~1 sec.

Rational Band	...	
	~10 sec.	Goal attainment
Cognitive Band	~1 sec.	Simple operator composition
	~100 msec.	Elementary deliberate operations
	~10 msec.	Symbol accessing
Neural Band	...	

Fig. 1. Partial hierarchy of time scales in human cognition.

and ~10 sec.—are the simple-operator-composition and goal-attainment levels. At these levels, sequences of deliberations can be composed to achieve goals. Above the cognitive band is the rational band, at which the system can be described as being goal oriented, knowledge-based, and strongly adaptive. Below the cognitive band is the neural band.

In Section 2 we describe Soar as a sequence of three cognitive levels: the memory level, at which symbol accessing occurs; the decision level, at which elementary deliberate operations occur; and the goal level, at which goals are set and achieved via sequences of decisions. The goal level is an amalgamation of the top two cognitive levels from the analysis of human cognition.

In this description we will often have call to describe mechanisms that are built into the architecture of Soar. The architecture consists of all of the fixed structure of the Soar system. According to the levels analysis, the correct view to be taken of this fixed structure is that it comprises the set of mechanisms provided by the levels underneath the cognitive band. For human cognition this is the neural band. For artificial cognition, this may be a connectionist band, though it need not be. This view notwithstanding, it should be remembered that it is the Soar architecture which is primary in our research. The use of the levels viewpoint is simply an attempt at imposing a particular, hopefully illuminating, theoretical structure on top of the existing architecture.

In the remainder of this paper we describe the methodological assumptions underlying Soar, the structure of Soar, an illustrative example of Soar's performance on the task of multi-column subtraction, and a set of preliminary analyses of Soar as an architecture for general intelligence.

1. Methodological assumptions

The development of Soar is driven by four methodological assumptions. It is not expected that these assumptions will be shared by all researchers in the field. However, the assumptions do help explain why the Soar system and project have the shapes that they do.

The first assumption is the utility of focusing on the cognitive band, as opposed to the neural or rational bands. This is a view that has traditionally been shared by a large segment of the cognitive science community; it is not, however, shared by the connectionist community, which focuses on the neural band (plus the lower levels of the cognitive band), or by the logicist and expert-systems communities, which focus on the rational band. This assumption is not meant to be exclusionary, as a complete understanding of general intelligence requires the understanding of all of these descriptive bands.[1] Instead the assumption is that there is important work to be done by focusing on the cognitive band. One reason is that, as just mentioned, a complete model of general intelligence will require a model of the cognitive band. A second reason is that an understanding of the cognitive band can constrain models of the neural and rational bands. A third, more applied reason, is that a model of the cognitive band is required in order to be able to build practical intelligent systems. Neural-band models need the higher levels of organization that are provided by the cognitive band in order to reach complex task performance. Rational-band models need the heuristic adequacy provided by the cognitive band in order to be computationally feasible. A fourth reason is that there is a wealth of both psychological and AI data about the cognitive band that can be used as the basis for elucidating the structure of its levels. This data can help us understand what type of symbolic architecture is required to support general intelligence.

The second assumption is that general intelligence can most usefully be studied by not making a distinction between human and artificial intelligence. The advantage of this assumption is that it allows wider ranges of research methodologies and data to be brought to bear to mutually constrain the structure of the system. Our research methodology includes a mixture of experimental data, theoretical justifications, and comparative studies in both artificial intelligence and cognitive psychology. Human experiments provide data about performance universals and limitations that may reflect the structure of the architecture. For example, the ubiquitous power law of practice—the time to perform a task is a power-law function of the number of times the task has been performed—was used to generate a model of human practice [39, 55], which was later converted into a proposal for a general artificial learning mechanism [27, 28, 61]. Artificial experiments—the application of implemented systems to a variety of tasks requiring intelligence—provide sufficiency feedback about the mechanisms embodied in the architecture and their interactions [16, 51, 60, 62, 73]. Theoretical justifications attempt to provide an abstract analysis of the requirements of intelligence, and of how various architectural mechanisms fulfill those requirements [38, 40, 49, 54, 56]. Comparative studies, pitting one system against another, provide an evaluation of how well the respective systems perform, as well as insight about how the capabilities of one of the systems can be incorporated in the other [6, 50].

[1] Investigations of the relationship of Soar to the neural and rational bands can be found in [38, 49, 56].

The third assumption is that the architecture should consist of a small set of orthogonal mechanisms. All intelligent behaviors should involve all, or nearly all, of these basic mechanisms. This assumption biases the development of Soar strongly in the direction of uniformity and simplicity, and away from modularity [10] and toolkit approaches. When attempting to achieve a new functionality in Soar, the first step is to determine in what ways the existing mechanisms can already provide the functionality. This can force the development of new solutions to old problems, and reveal new connections—through the common underlying mechanisms—among previously distinct capabilities [53]. Only if there is no appropriate way to achieve the new functionality are new mechanisms considered.

The fourth assumption is that architectures should be pushed to the extreme to evaluate how much of general intelligence they can cover. A serious attempt at evaluating the coverage of an architecture involves a long-term commitment by an extensive research group. Much of the research involves the apparently mundane activity of replicating classical results within the architecture. Sometimes these demonstrations will by necessity be strict replications, but often the architecture will reveal novel approaches, provide a deeper understanding of the result and its relationship to other results, or provide the means of going beyond what was done in the classical work. As these results accumulate over time, along with other more novel results, the system gradually approaches the ultimate goal of general intelligence.

2. Structure of Soar

In this section we build up much of Soar's structure in levels, starting at the bottom with memory and proceeding up to decisions and goals. We then describe how learning and perceptual-motor behavior fit into this picture, and wrap up with a discussion of the default knowledge that has been incorporated into the system.

2.1. Level 1: Memory

A general intelligence requires a memory with a large capacity for the storage of knowledge. A variety of types of knowledge must be stored, including declarative knowledge (facts about the world, including facts about actions that can be performed), procedural knowledge (facts about how to perform actions, and control knowledge about which actions to perform when), and episodic knowledge (which actions were done when). Any particular task will require some subset of the knowledge stored in the memory. Memory access is the process by which this subset is retrieved for use in task performance.

The lowest level of the Soar architecture is the level at which these memory phenomena occur. All of Soar's long-term knowledge is stored in a single production memory. Whether a piece of knowledge represents procedural, declarative, or episodic knowledge, it is stored in one or more productions. Each production is a condition-action structure that performs its actions when its conditions are met. Memory access consists of the execution of these productions. During the execution of a production, variables in its actions are instantiated with values. Action variables that existed in the conditions are instantiated with the values bound in the conditions. Action variables that did not exist in the conditions act as generators of new symbols.

The result of memory access is the retrieval of information into a global working memory. The working memory is a temporary memory that contains all of Soar's short-term processing context. Working memory consists of an interrelated set of objects with attribute-value pairs. For example, an object representing a green cat named Fred might look like (object o025 ^name fred ^type cat ^color green). The symbol o025 is the identifier of the object, a short-term symbol for the object that exists only as long as the object is in working memory. Objects are related by using the identifiers of some objects as attributes and values of other objects.

There is one special type of working memory structure, the preference. Preferences encode control knowledge about the acceptability and desirability of actions, according to a fixed semantics of preference types. Acceptability preferences determine which actions should be considered as candidates. Desirability preferences define a partial ordering on the candidate actions. For example, a better (or alternatively, worse) preference can be used to represent the knowledge that one action is more (or less) desirable than another action, and a best (or worst) preference can be used to represent the knowledge that an action is at least as good (or as bad) as every other action.

In a traditional production-system architecture, each production is a problem-solving operator (see, for example, [42]). The right-hand side of the production represents some action to be performed, and the left-hand side represents the preconditions for correct application of the action (plus possibly some desirability conditions). One consequence of this view of productions is that the productions must also be the locus of behavioral control. If productions are going to act, it must be possible to control which one executes at each moment; a process known as conflict resolution. In a logic architecture, each production is a logical implication. The meaning of such a production is that if the left-hand side (the antecedent) is true, then so is the right-hand side (the consequent).[2] Soar's productions are neither operators nor implications. Instead, Soar's productions perform (parallel) memory retrieval. Each produc-

[2] The directionality of the implication is reversed in logic programming languages such as Prolog, but the point still holds.

tion is a retrieval structure for an item in long-term memory. The right-hand side of the rule represents a long-term datum, and the left-hand side represents the situations in which it is appropriate to retrieve that datum into working memory. The traditional production-system and logic notions of action, control, and truth are not directly applicable to Soar's productions. All control in Soar is performed at the decision level. Thus, there is no conflict resolution process in the Soar production system, and all productions execute in parallel. This all flows directly from the production system being a long-term memory. Soar separates the retrieval of long-term information from the control of which act to perform next.

Of course it is possible to encode knowledge of operators and logical implications in the production memory. For example, the knowledge about how to implement a typical operator can be stored procedurally as a set of productions which retrieve the state resulting from the operator's application. The productions' conditions determine when the state is to be retrieved—for example, when the operator is being applied and its preconditions are met. An alternative way to store operator implementation knowledge is declaratively as a set of structures that are completely contained in the actions of one or more productions. The structures describe not only the results of the operator, but also its preconditions. The productions' conditions determine when to retrieve this declarative operator description into working memory. A retrieved operator description must be interpreted by other productions to actually have an affect.

In general, there are these two distinct ways to encode knowledge in the production memory: procedurally and declaratively. If the knowledge is procedurally encoded, then the execution of the production reflects the knowledge, but does not actually retrieve it into working memory—it only retrieves the structures encoded in the actions. On the other hand, if a piece of knowledge is encoded declaratively in the actions of a production, then it is retrievable in its entirety. This distinction between procedural and declarative *encodings* of knowledge is distinct from whether the knowledge is declarative (represents facts about the world) or procedural (represents facts about procedures). Moreover, each production can be viewed in either way, either as a procedure which implicitly represents conditional information, or as the indexed storage of declarative structures.

2.2. Level 2: Decisions

In addition to a memory, a general intelligence requires the ability to generate and/or select a course of action that is responsive to the current situation. The second level of the Soar architecture, the decision level, is the level at which this processing is performed. The decision level is based on the memory level plus an architecturally provided, fixed, decision procedure. The operator is available, then these lower operators may implement the operator by interpreting its declarative description (as was demonstrated in work on task acquisition in Soar [61]). Otherwise the operator can be implemented by decomposing it into a set of simpler operators for which operator implementation knowledge is available, or which can in turn be decomposed further.

When an operator is implemented in a subgoal, the combination of the operator and the subgoal correspond to the type of deliberately created subgoal common in AI problem solvers. The operator specifies a task to be performed, while the subgoal indicates that accomplishing the task should be treated as a goal for further problem solving. In complex problems, like computer configuration, it is common for there to be complex high-level operators, such as Configure-computer which are implemented by selecting problem spaces in which they can be decomposed into simpler tasks. Many of the traditional goal management issues—such as conjunction, conflict, and selection—show up as operator management issues in Soar. For example, a set of conjunctive subgoals can be ordered by ordering operators that later lead to impasses (and subgoals).

As described in [54], a subgoal not only represents a subtask to be performed, but it also represents an introspective act that allows unlimited amounts of meta-level problem-space processing to be performed. The entire working memory—the goal stack and all information linked to it—is available for examination and augmentation in a subgoal. At any time a production can examine and augment any part of the goal stack. Likewise, a decision can be made at any time for any of the goals in the hierarchy. This allows subgoal problem solving to analyze the situation that led to the impasse, and even to change the subgoal, should it be appropriate. One not uncommon occurrence is for information to be generated within a subgoal that instead of satisfying the subgoal, causes the subgoal to become irrelevant and consequently to disappear. Processing tends to focus on the bottom-most goal because all of the others have reached impasses. However, the processing is completely opportunistic, so that when appropriate information becomes available at a higher level, processing at that level continues immediately and all lower subgoals are terminated.

2.4. Learning

All learning occurs by the acquisition of chunks—productions that summarize the problem solving that occurs in subgoals [28]. The actions of a chunk represent the knowledge generated during the subgoal; that is, the results of the subgoal. The conditions of the chunk represent an access path to this knowledge, consisting of those elements of the parent goals upon which the results depended. The results of the subgoal are determined by finding the elements generated in the subgoal that are available for use in subgoals—an element is a result of a subgoal precisely because it is available to processes outside of the subgoal. The access path is computed by analyzing the traces of the productions that fired in the subgoal—each production trace effectively states that its actions depended on its conditions. This dependency analysis yields a set of conditions that have been implicitly generalized to ignore irrelevant aspects of the situation. The resulting generality allows chunks to transfer to situations other than the one in which it was learned. The primary system-wide effect of chunking is to move Soar along the space-time trade-off by allowing relevantly similar future decisions to be based on direct retrieval of information from memory rather than on problem solving within a subgoal. If the chunk is used, an impasse will not occur, because the required information is already available.

Care must be taken to not confuse the power of chunking as a learning mechanism with the power of Soar as a learning system. Chunking is a simple goal-based, dependency-tracing, caching scheme, analogous to explanation-based learning [4, 36, 50] and a variety of other schemes [55]. What allows Soar to exhibit a wide variety of learning behaviors are the variations in the types of subgoals that are chunked; the types of problem solving, in conjunction with the types and sources of knowledge, used in the subgoals; and the ways the chunks are used in later problem solving. The role that a chunk will play is determined by the type of subgoal for which it was learned. State-no-change, operator-tie, and operator-no-change subgoals lead respectively to state augmentation, operator selection, and operator implementation productions. The content of a chunk is determined by the types of problem solving and knowledge used in the subgoal. A chunk can lead to skill acquisition if it is used as a more efficient means of generating an already generatable result. A chunk can lead to knowledge acquisition (or knowledge level learning [5]) if it is used to make old/new judgments; that is, to distinguish what has been learned from what has not been learned [52, 53, 56].

2.5. Perception and motor control

One of the most recent functional additions to the Soar architecture is a perceptual-motor interface [75, 76]. All perceptual and motor behavior is mediated through working memory; specifically, through the state in the top problem solving context. Each distinct perceptual field has a designated attribute of this state to which it adds its information. Likewise, each distinct motor field has a designated attribute of the state from which it takes its commands. The perceptual and motor systems are autonomous with respect to each other and the cognitive system.

Encoding and decoding productions can be used to convert between the high-level structures used by the cognitive system, and the low-level structures used by the perceptual and motor systems. These productions are like ordinary

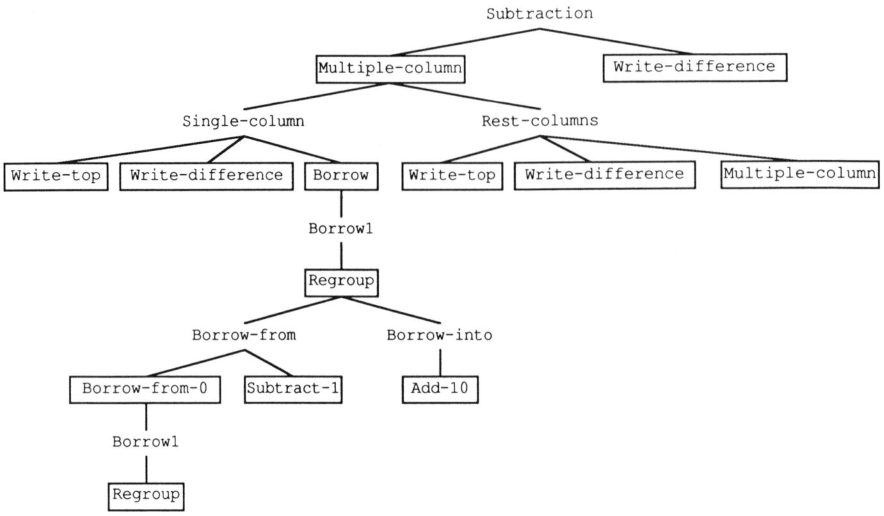

Fig. 3. A goal hierarchy for multi-column subtraction.

hierarchy that is similar to the one learned by Sierra.[3] Under each goal are shown the subgoals that may be generated while trying to achieve it. This Sierra goal hierarchy is mapped onto a hierarchy of operators and problem spaces in Soar (as described in Section 2). The boxed goals map onto operators and the unboxed goals map onto problem spaces. Each problem space consists of the operators linked to it from below in the figure. Operators that have problem spaces below them are implemented by problem solving in those problem spaces. The other operators are implemented directly at the memory level by productions (except for multiple-column and regroup, which are recursive). These are the primitive acts of subtraction, such as writing numbers or subtracting digits.

The states in these problem spaces contain symbolic representations of the subtraction problem and the scratch marks made on the page during problem solving. The representation is very simple and direct, being based on the spatial relationships among the digits as they would appear on a page. The state consists of a set of columns. Each column has pointers to its top and bottom digits. Additional pointers are generated when an answer for a column is produced, or when a scratch mark is made as the result of borrowing. The physical orientation of the columns on the page is represented by having "left" and "right" pointers from columns to their left and right neighbors. There is no inherent notion of multi-digit numbers except for these left and right relations between columns. This representation is consistent with the operators, which

[3] Sierra learned a slightly more elaborate, but computationally equivalent, procedure.

treat the problem symbolically and never manipulate multi-digit numbers as a whole.

Using this implementation of the subtraction procedure, Soar is able to solve all multi-column subtraction problems that result in positive answers. Unfortunately, there is little role for learning. Most of the control knowledge is already embedded in the productions that select problem spaces and operators. Within each problem space there are only a few operators from which to select. The preconditions of the few operators in each problem space are sufficient for perfect behavior. Therefore, goals arise only to implement operators. Chunking these goals produces productions that are able to compute answers without the intermediate subgoals.[4]

3.2. A single-space approach

One way to loosen up the strict control provided by the detailed problem-space/operator hierarchy in Fig. 3, and thus to enable the learning of the control knowledge underlying the subtraction procedure, is to have only a single subtraction problem space that contains all of the primitive acts (writing results, changing columns, and so on). Figure 4 contains a description of the

- *Operators*:
  - **Write-difference:** If the difference between the top digit and the bottom digit of the current column is known, then write the difference as an answer to the current column.
  - **Write-top:** If the lower digit of the current column is blank, then write the top digit as the answer to the current column.
  - **Borrow-into:** If the result of adding 10 to the top digit of the current column is known, and the digit to the left of it has a scratch mark on it, then replace the top digit with the result.
  - **Borrow-from:** If the result of subtracting 1 from the top digit in the current column is known, then replace that top digit with the result, augment it with a scratch mark and shift the current column to the right.
  - **Move-left:** If the current column has an answer in it, shift the current column left.
  - **Move-borrow-left:** If the current column does not have a scratch mark in it, shift the current column left.
  - **Subtract-two-digits:** If the top digit is greater than or equal to the lower digit, then produce a result that is the difference.
  - **Subtract-1:** If the top digit is not zero, then produce a result that is the top digit minus one.
  - **Add 10:** Produce a result that is the top digit plus ten.
- *Goal Test*: If each column has an answer, then succeed.

Fig. 4. Primitive subtraction problem space.

[4] This work on subtraction was done in an earlier version of Soar that did not have the perceptual-motor interface described in Section 2. In that version, these chunks caused Soar to write out all of the column results and scratch marks in parallel—not very realistic motor behavior. To work around this problem, chunking was disabled for goals in this task during which environmental interactions occurred.

problem space operators and the goal test used in this second implementation. The operators can be grouped into four classes: the basic acts of writing answers to a single column problem (write-difference, write-top); borrow actions on the upper digits (borrow-into, borrow-from); moving from one column to the next (move-left, move-borrow-left); and performing very simple arithmetic computations (subtract-two-digits, subtract-1, add-10). With this simple problem space, Soar must learn the subtraction procedure by acquiring control knowledge that correctly selects operators.

Every operator in the subtraction problem space is considered for every state in the space. This is accomplished by having a production for each operator that generates an acceptable preference for it. The conditions of the production only test that the appropriate problem space (subtraction) is selected. Similar productions existed in the original implementation, except that those productions also contained additional tests which ensured that the operators would only be considered when they were the appropriate ones to apply.

In addition to productions which generate acceptable preferences, each operator has one or more productions which implement it. Although every operator is made acceptable for every state, an operator will actually be applied only if all of the conditions in the productions that implement it are satisfied. For example, write-difference will only apply if the difference between the top and bottom numbers is known. If an operator is selected, but the conditions of the productions that implement it are not satisfied, an impasse arises. As described in Section 2, the default response to this type of impasse is to perform operator subgoaling.

Figure 5 shows a trace of Soar's problem solving as it performs a simple two-column subtraction problem, after the learning of control knowledge has been completed. Because Soar's performance prior to learning on this problem is considerably more complicated, it is described after this simpler case. The

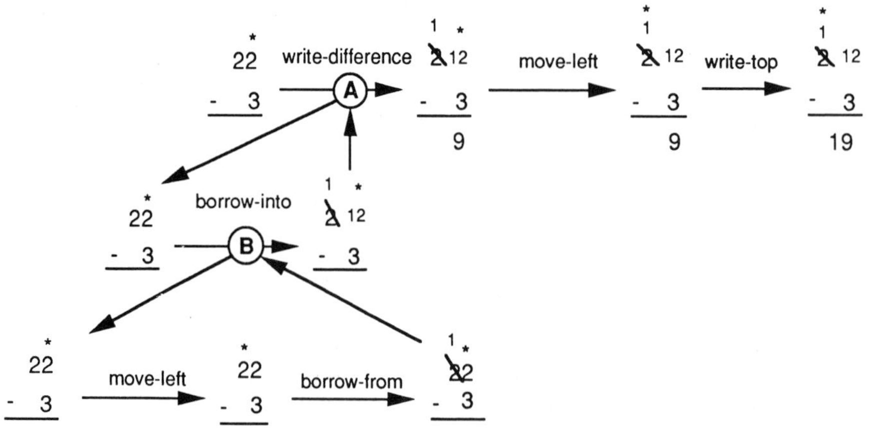

Fig. 5. Trace of problem solving after learning for 22 − 3.

top goal in this figure is to have the result of subtracting 3 from 22. Problem solving in the top goal proceeds from left to right, diving to a lower level whenever a subgoal is created in response to an impasse. Each state is a partially solved subtraction problem, consisting of the statement of the subtraction problem, a * designating the current column, and possibly column results and/or scratch marks for borrowing. Operator applications are represented by arrows going from left to right. The only impasses that occur in this trace are a result of the failure of operator preconditions—a form of operator no-change impasse. These impasses are designated by circles disrupting the operator-application arrows, and are labeled in the order they arise (A and B). For example, impasse A arises because write-difference cannot apply unless the lower digit in the current column (3) is less than the top digit (2).

For impasse A, operator subgoaling occurs when the subtraction problem space is selected in the subgoal. The preconditions of the write-difference operator are met when a state has been generated whose top digit has been changed from 2 to 12 (by borrowing). Once this occurs, the subgoal terminates and the operator applies, in this case writing the difference between 12 and 3. In this implementation of subtraction, operator subgoaling dynamically creates a goal hierarchy that is similar to the one programmed into the original implementation.

3.3. *Performance prior to learning*

Prior to learning, Soar's problem solving on this task is considerably more complicated. This added complexity arises because of an initial lack of knowledge about the results of simple arithmetic computations and a lack of knowledge about which operators should be selected for which states. Figure 6

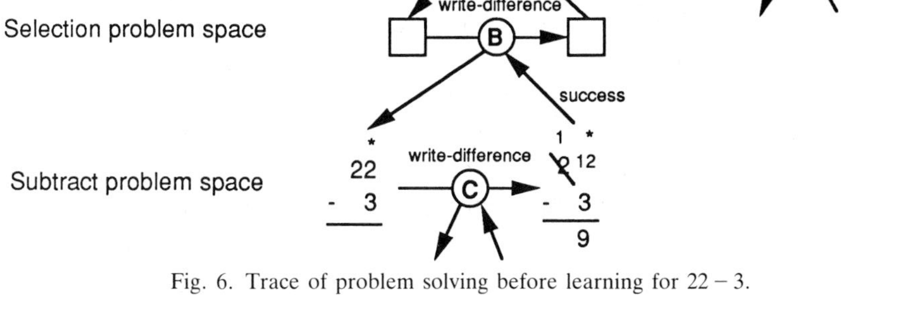

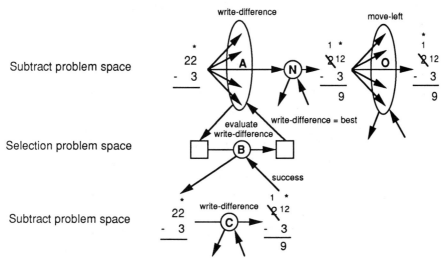

Fig. 6. Trace of problem solving before learning for 22 − 3.

shows a partial trace of Soar's pre-learning problem solving. Although many of the subgoals are missing, this small snapshot of the problem solving is characteristic of the impasses and subgoals that arise at all levels.

As before, the problem solving starts at the upper left with the initial state. As soon as the initial state is selected, a tie impasse (A) arises because all of the operators are acceptable and there are no additional preferences that distinguish between them. Default productions cause the selection space to be selected for this impasse. Within this space, operators are created to evaluate the tied operators. This example assumes that evaluate-object(write-difference) is selected, possibly based on advice from a teacher. Then, because there is no knowledge available about how to evaluate the subtraction operators, a no-change impasse (B) occurs for the evaluation operator. More default productions lead to a lookahead search by suggesting the original problem space (subtraction) and state and then selecting the operator that is being evaluated. The operator then applies, if it can, creating a new state. In this example, an operator subgoal impasse (C) arises when the attempt is made to apply the write-difference operator—its preconditions are not satisfied. Problem solving continues in this subgoal, requiring many additional impasses, until the write-difference operator can finally be applied. The lookahead search then continues until an evaluation is generated for the write-difference operator. Here, this happens shortly after impasse C is resolved. The system was given the knowledge that a state containing an answer for the current column is a (partial) success—such states are on the path to the goal. This state evaluation is then converted by default productions into an evaluation of "success" for the operator, and from there into a best preference for the operator. The creation of this preference breaks the operator tie, terminating the subgoals, and leading to the selection of the preferred operator (write-difference). The overall behavior of the system during this lookahead search is that of depth-first search—where backtracking occurs by subgoal termination—intertwined with operator subgoaling. Once this search is completed, further impasses (N) arise to actually apply the selected operator, but eventually, a solution is found.

One way in which multi-column subtraction differs from the classic AI search tasks is that the goal test is underspecified. As shown in Fig. 4, the goal test used here is that a result has been generated for each column of the problem. This determines whether some answer has been given for the problem, but is inadequate to determine whether the correct answer has been generated. The reason for this is that when solving a subtraction problem, the answer is in general not already available. It is theoretically (and practically) possible to use an addition procedure to test whether the subtraction procedure has generated the correct result. However, that corresponds to a deliberate strategy of "checking your work", rather than to the normal procedural goal test of determining whether the sequence of steps has been completed.

One consequence of having an underspecified goal test is that the combination of the problem space and goal test are not sufficient to ensure correct performance. Additional knowledge—the control knowledge which underlies the subtraction procedure—must also be provided in some form. VanLehn provided Sierra with worked-out examples which included the order in which the primitive external actions were to be performed [71]. The approach that we have taken is to provide advice to Soar [12] about which task operators it should evaluate first in the selection problem space. This ensures that the first answer generated during the lookahead search is the correct one.

3.4. Learning in subtraction

When chunking is used during subtraction problem solving, productions are created which reproduce the results of the subgoals in similar future situations. For the subgoals created because of tie impasses, the chunks create best preferences for the operators that led to the solution. These chunks essentially cache the results of the lookahead searches. A set of such chunks corresponds to a plan (or procedure)—they determine at every step what should be done—thus chunking converts Soar's behavior from search into plan (or procedure) following. When Soar is rerun on the same problem, the tie impasses do not arise and the solution is found directly, as in Fig. 5.

One important issue concerning the chunked productions is their generality. Does Soar only learn chunks that can apply to the exact same problem, or are the chunks general enough so that advice is no longer needed after a few subtraction problems have been completed? The answer is that the learned control chunks are quite general—so general that only one or two are required per operator. Once these chunks are acquired, Soar is able to solve perfectly all multi-column subtraction problems that have a positive answer. One sample control chunk for the borrow-into operator is shown in Fig. 7. Similar chunks are learned for each of the other major operators.

One reason for this generality is that operator subgoaling leads to a fine-grained goal hierarchy. There are a large number of relatively simple goals having to do with satisfying the preconditions of an operator. Because the problem solving for these goals is relatively minimal, the resulting chunks are quite general. A second reason for the generality of the learning is that

If the super-operator is write-difference,
  and the bottom digit is greater than the top digit,
then make a best preference for borrow-into.

Fig. 7. A control chunk for borrow-into.

inadequate; and allow flexible meta-level processing. Problem spaces separate control from action, allowing them (control and action) to be reasoned about independently; provide a constrained context within which the search for a desired state can occur; provide the ability to use weak problem solving methods; and provide for straightforward responses to uncertainty and error (search and backtracking). Chunking acquires long-term knowledge from experience; compiles interpreted procedures into non-interpreted ones; and provides generalization and transfer. The perceptual-motor system provides the ability to observe and affect the external world in parallel with the cognitive activity.

The fourth source of power is the interaction effects that result from the integration of all of the capabilities within a single system. The most compelling results generated so far come about from these interactions. One example comes from the mixture of weak methods, strong methods, and learning that is found in systems like R1-Soar. Strong methods are based on having knowledge about what to do at each step. Because strong methods tend to be efficient and to produce high-quality solutions, they should be used whenever possible. Weak methods are based on searching to make up for a lack of knowledge about what should be done. Such methods contribute robustness and scope by providing the system with a fall-back approach for situations in which the available strong methods do not work. Learning results in the addition of knowledge, turning weak methods into strong ones. For example, in R1-Soar it was demonstrated how computer configuration could be cast as a search problem, how strong methods (knowledge) could be used to reduce search, how weak methods (subgoals and search) could be used to make up for a lack of knowledge, and how learning could add knowledge as the result of search.

Another interesting interaction effect comes from work on abstraction planning, in which a difficult problem is solved by first learning a plan for an abstract version of the problem, and then using the abstract plan to aid in finding a plan for the full problem [41, 57, 70, 69]. Chunking helps the abstraction planning process by recording the abstract plan as a set of operator-selection productions, and by acquiring other productions that reduce the amount of search required in generating a plan. Abstraction helps the learning process by allowing chunks to be learned more quickly—abstract searches tend to be shorter than normal ones. Abstraction also helps learning by enabling chunks to be more general than they would otherwise be—the chunks ignore the details that were abstracted away—thus allowing more transfer and potentially decreasing the cost of matching the chunks (because there are now fewer conditions).

4.3. Scope and limits

The original work on Soar demonstrated its capabilities as a general problem solver that could use any of the weak methods when appropriate, across a wide range of tasks. Later, we came to understand how to use Soar as the basis for knowledge-based systems, and how to incorporate appropriate learning and perceptual-motor capabilities into the architecture. These developments increased Soar's scope considerably beyond its origins as a weak-method problem solver. Our ultimate goal has always been to develop the system to the point where its scope includes everything required of a general intelligence. In this section we examine how far Soar has come from its relatively limited initial demonstrations towards its relatively unlimited goal. This discussion is divided up according to the major components of the Soar architecture, as presented in Section 2: memory, decisions, goals, learning, and perception and motor control.

4.3.1. Level 1: Memory

The scope of Soar's memory level can be evaluated in terms of the amount of knowledge that can be stored, the types of knowledge that can be represented, and the organization of the knowledge.

Amount of knowledge. Using current technology, Soar's production memory can support the storage of thousands of independent chunks of knowledge. The size is primarily limited by the cost of processing larger numbers of productions. Faster machines, improved match algorithms and parallel implementations [13, 65, 66] may raise this effective limit by several orders of magnitude over the next few years.

Types of knowledge. The representation of procedural and propositional declarative knowledge is well developed in Soar. However, we don't have well worked-out approaches to many other knowledge representation problems, such as the representation of quantified, uncertain, temporal, and episodic knowledge. The critical question is whether architectural support is required to adequately represent these types of knowledge, or whether such knowledge can be adequately treated as additional objects and/or attributes. Preliminary work on quantified [43] and episodic [56] knowledge is looking promising.

Memory organization. An issue which often gets raised with respect to the organization of Soar's memory, and with respect to the organization of production memories in general, is the apparent lack of a higher-order memory organization. There are no scripts [59], frames [33], or schemas [1] to tie fragments of related memory together. Nor are there any obvious hierarchical structures which limit what sets of knowledge will be retrieved at any point in time. However, Soar's memory does have an organization, which is derived from the structure of productions, objects, and working memory (especially the context hierarchy).

What corresponds to a schema in Soar is an object, or a structured collection of objects. Such a structure can be stored entirely in the actions of a single production, or it can be stored in a piecemeal fashion across multiple productions. If multiple productions are used, the schema as a unit only comes into existence when the pieces are all retrieved contemporaneously into working memory. The advantage of this approach is that it allows novel schemas to be created from fragments of separately learned ones. The disadvantage is that it may not be possible to determine whether a set of fragments all originated from a single schema.

What corresponds to a hierarchy of retrieval contexts in Soar are the production conditions. Each combination of conditions implicitly defines a retrieval context, with a hierarchical structure induced by the subset relationship among the combinations. The contents of working memory determines which retrieval contexts are currently in force. For example, problem spaces are used extensively as retrieval contexts. Whenever there is a problem solving context that has a particular problem space selected within it, productions that test for other problem space names are not eligible to fire in that context. This approach has worked quite well for procedural knowledge, where it is clear when the knowledge is needed. We have just begun to work on appropriate organizational schemes for episodic and declarative knowledge, where it is much less clear when the knowledge should be retrieved. Our initial approach has been based on the incremental construction, via chunking, of multi-production discrimination networks [53, 56]. Though this work is too premature for a thorough evaluation in the context of Soar, the effectiveness of discrimination networks in systems like Epam [7] and Cyrus [19] bodes well.

4.3.2. Level 2: Decisions

The scope of Soar's decision level can be evaluated in terms of its speed, the knowledge brought to bear, and the language of control.

Speed. Soar currently runs at approximately 10 decisions/second on current workstations such as a Sun4/280. This is adequate for most of the types of tasks we currently implement, but is too slow for tasks requiring large amounts of search or very large knowledge bases (the number of decisions per second would get even smaller than it is now). The principal bottleneck is the speed of memory access, which is a function of two factors: the cost of processing individually expensive productions (the *expensive chunks* problem) [67], and the cost of processing a large number of productions (the *average growth effect* problem) [64]. We now have a solution to the problem of expensive chunks which can guarantee that all productions will be cheap—the match cost of a production is at worst linear in the number of conditions [68]—and are working on other potential solutions. Parallelism looks to be an effective solution to the average growth effect problem [64].

Bringing knowledge to bear. Iterated, parallel, indexed access to the contents of long-term memory has proven to be an effective means of bringing knowledge to bear on the decision process. The limited power provided by this process is offset by the ability to use subgoals when the accessible knowledge is inadequate. The issue of devising good access paths for episodic and declarative knowledge is also relevant here.

Control language. Preferences have proven to be a flexible means of specifying a partial order among contending objects. However, we cannot yet state with certainty that the set of preference types embodied in Soar is complete with respect to all the types of information which ultimately may need to be communicated to the decision procedure.

4.3.3. Level 3: Goals

The scope of Soar's goal level can be evaluated in terms of the types of goals that can be generated and the types of problem solving that can be performed in goals. Soar's subgoaling mechanism has been demonstrated to be able to create subgoals for all of the types of difficulties that can arise in problem solving in problem spaces [21]. This leaves three areas open. The first area is how top-level goals are generated; that is, how the top-level task is picked. Currently this is done by the programmer, but a general intelligence must clearly have grounds—that is, motivations—for selecting tasks on its own. The second area is how goal interactions are handled. Goal interactions show up in Soar as operator interactions, and are normally dealt with by adding explicit knowledge to avoid them, or by backtracking (with learning) when they happen. It is not yet clear the extent to which Soar could easily make use of more sophisticated approaches, such as non-linear planning [2]. The third area is the sufficiency of impasse-driven subgoaling as a means for determining when meta-level processing is needed. Two of the activities that might fall under this area are goal tests and monitoring. Both of these activities can be performed at the memory or decision level, but when they are complicated activities it may be necessary to perform them by problem solving at the goal level. Either activity can be called for explicitly by selecting a "monitor" or "goal-test" operator, which can then lead to the generation of a subgoal. However, goals for these tasks do not arise automatically, without deliberation. Should they? It is not completely clear.

The scope of the problem solving that can be performed in goals can itself be evaluated in terms of whether problem spaces cover all of the types of performance required, the limits on the ability of subgoal-based problem solving to access and modify aspects of the system, and whether parallelism is possible. These points are addressed in the next three paragraphs.

Problem space scope. Problem spaces are a very general performance model. They have been hypothesized to underlie all human, symbolic, goal-oriented behavior [37]. The breadth of tasks that have so far been represented in problem spaces over the whole field of AI attests to this generality. One way of pushing this evaluation further is to ask how well probem spaces account for the types of problem solving performed by two of the principal competing paradigms: planning [2] and case-based reasoning [20].[8] Both of these paradigms involve the creation (or retrieval) and use of a data structure that represents a sequence of actions. In planning, the data structure represents the sequence of actions that the system expects to use for the current problem. In case-based reasoning, the data structure represents the sequence of actions used on some previous, presumably related, problem. In both, the data structure is used to decide what sequence of actions to perform in the current problem. Soar straightforwardly performs procedural analogues of these two processes. When it performs a lookahead search to determine what operator to apply to a particular state, it acquires (by chunking) a set of search control productions which collectively tell it which operator should be applied to each subsequent state. This set of chunks forms a procedural plan for the current problem. When a search control chunk transfers between tasks, a form of procedural case-based reasoning is occurring.

Simple forms of declarative planning and case-based reasoning have also been demonstrated in Soar in the context of an expert system that designs floor systems [47]. When this system discovers, via lookahead search, a sequence of operators that achieves a goal, it creates a declarative structure representing the sequence and returns it as a subgoal result (plan creation). This plan can then be used interpretively to guide performance on the immediate problem (plan following). The plan can also be retrieved during later problems and used to guide the selection of operators (case-based reasoning). This research does not demonstrate the variety of operations one could conceivably use to modify a partial or complete plan, but it does demonstrate the basics.

Meta-level access. Subgoal-based problem solving has access to all of the information in working memory—including the goal stack, problem spaces, states, operators, preferences, and other facts that have been retrieved or generated—plus any of the other knowledge in long-term memory that it can access. It does not have direct access to the productions, or to any of the data structures internal to the architecture. Nonetheless, it should be able to indirectly examine the contents of any productions that were acquired by chunking, which in the long run should be just about all of them. The idea is to reconstruct the contents of the production by going down into a subgoal and retracing the problem solving that was done when the chunk was learned. In this way it should be possible to determine what knowledge the production cached. This idea has not yet been explicitly demonstrated in Soar, but research on the recovery from incorrect knowledge has used a closely related approach [23].

The effects of problem solving are limited to the addition of information to

[8] The work on Robo-Soar also reveals Soar's potential to exhibit reactive planning [11]. The current version of Soar still has problems with raw speed and with the unbounded nature of the production match (the expensive chunks problem), but it is expected that these problems will be solved in the near future.

working memory. Deletion of working memory elements is accomplished by a garbage collector provided by the architecture. Productions are added by chunking, rather than by problem solving, and are never deleted by the system. The limitation on production creation—that it only occurs via chunking—is dealt with by varying the nature of the problem solving over which chunking occurs [56]. The limitation on production deletion is dealt with by learning new productions which overcome the effects of old ones [23].

Parallelism. Two principal sources of parallelism in Soar are at the memory level: production match and execution. On each cycle of elaboration, all productions are matched in parallel to the working memory, and then all of the successful instantiations are executed in parallel. This lets tasks that can be performed at the memory level proceed in parallel, but not so for decision-level and goal-level tasks.

Another principal source of parallelism is provided by the motor systems. All motor systems behave in parallel with respect to each other, and with respect to the cognitive system. This enables one form of task-level parallelism in which non-interfering external tasks can be performed in parallel. To enable further research on task-level parallelism we have added the experimental ability to simultaneously select multiple problem space operators within a single problem solving context. Each of these operators can then proceed to execute in parallel, yielding parallel subgoals, and ultimately an entire tree of problem solving contexts in which all of the branches are being processed in parallel. We do not yet have enough experience with this capability to evaluate its scope and limits.

Despite all of these forms of parallelism embodied in Soar, most implementations of the architecture have been on serial machines, with the parallelism being simulated. However, there is an active research effort to implement Soar on parallel computers. A parallelized version of the production match has been successfully implemented on an Encore Multimax, which has a small number (2–20) of large-grained processors [66], and unsuccessfully implemented on a Connection Machine [15], which has a large number (16 K–64 K) of small-grained processors [9]. The Connection Machine implementation failed primarily because a complete parallelization of the current match algorithm can lead to exponential space requirements. Research on restricted match algorithms may fix this problem in the future. Work is also in progress towards implementing Soar on message-passing computers [65].

4.3.4. Learning

In [61] we broke down the problem of evaluating the scope of Soar's learning capabilities into four parts: when can the architecture learn; from what can the architecture learn; what can the architecture learn; and when can the architecture apply learned knowledge. These points are discussed in Section 4.1, and need not be elaborated further here.

One important additional issue is whether Soar acquires knowledge that is at the appropriate level of generalization or specialization. Chunking provides a level of generality that is determined by a combination of the representation used and the problem solving performed. Under varying circumstances, this can lead to both overgeneralization [29] and overspecialization. The acquisition of overgeneral knowledge implies that the system must be able to recover from any errors caused by its use. One solution to this problem that has been implemented in Soar involves detecting that a performance error has occurred, determining what should have been done instead, and acquiring a new chunk which leads to correct performance in the future [23]. This is accomplished without examining or modifying the overgeneral production; instead it goes back down into the subgoals for which the overgeneral productions were learned.

One way to deal with overspecialization is to patch the resulting knowledge gaps with additional knowledge. This is what Soar does constantly—if a production is overspecialized, it doesn't fire in circumstances when it should, causing an impasse to occur, and providing the opportunity to learn an additional chunk that covers the missing case (plus possibly other cases). Another way to deal with overspecialized knowledge is to work towards acquiring more general productions. A standard approach is to induce general rules from a sequence of positive and negative examples [35, 45]. This form of generalization must occur in Soar by search in problem spaces, and though there has been some initial work on doing this [48, 58], we have not yet provided Soar with a set of problem spaces that will allow it to generate appropriate generalizations from a variety of sets of examples. So, Soar cannot yet be described as a system of choice for doing induction from multiple examples. On the other hand, Soar does generalize quite naturally and effectively when abstraction occurs [69]. The learned rules reflect whatever abstraction was made during problem solving.

Learning behaviors that have not yet been attempted in Soar include the construction of a model of the environment from experimentation in it [46], scientific discovery and theory formation [31], and conceptual clustering [8].

4.3.5. Perception and motor control

The scope of Soar's perception and motor control can be evaluated in terms of both its low-level I/O mechanisms and its high-level language capabilities. Both of these capabilities are quite new, so the evaluation must be even more tentative than for the preceding components.

At the low-level, Soar can be hooked up to multiple perceptual modalities (and multiple fields within each modality) and can control multiple effectors. The critical low-level aspects of perception and motor control are currently done in a standard procedural language outside of the cognitive system. The resulting system appears to be an effective testbed for research on high-level aspects of perception and motor-control. It also appears to be an effective testbed for research on the interactions of perception and motor control with other cognitive capabilities, such as memory, problem solving, and learning. However, it does finesse many of the hard issues in perception and motor control, such as selective attention, shape determination, object identification, and temporal coordination. Work is actively in progress on selective attention [74].

At the high end of I/O capabilities is the processing of natural language. An early attempt to implement a semantic grammar parser in Soar was only a limited success [44]. It worked, but did not appear to be the right long-term solution to language understanding in Soar. More recent work on NL-Soar has focused on the incremental construction of a model of the situation by applying comprehension operators to each incoming word [32]. Comprehension operators iteratively augment and refine the situation model, setting up expectations for the part of the utterance still to be seen, and satisfying earlier expectations. As a side effect of constructing the situation model, an utterance model is constructed to represent the linguistic structure of the sentence. This approach to language understanding has been successfully applied to acquiring task-specific problem spaces for three immediate reasoning tasks: relational reasoning [18], categorical syllogisms, and sentence verification [3]. It has also been used to process the input for these tasks as they are performed. Though NL-Soar is still far from providing a general linguistic capability, the approach has proven promising.

5. Conclusion

In this article we have taken a step towards providing an analysis of the Soar architecture as a basis for general intelligence. In order to increase understanding of the structure of the architecture we have provided a theoretical framework within which the architecture can be described, a discussion of methodological assumptions underlying the project and the system, and an illustrative example of its performance on a multi-column subtraction task. In order to facilitate comparisons between the capabilities of the current version of Soar and the capabilities required to achieve its ultimate goal as an architecture for general intelligence, we have described the natural tasks for the architecture, the sources of its power, and its scope and limits. If this article has succeeded, it should be clear that progress has been made, but that more work is still required. This applies equally to the tasks of developing Soar and analyzing it.

Acknowledgement

This research was sponsored by the Defense Advanced Research Projects Agency (DOD) under contract N00039-86-C-0133 and by the Sloan Foundation. Computer facilities were partially provided by NIH grant RR-00785 to Sumex-Aim. The views and conclusions contained in this document are those of the authors and should not be interpreted as representing the official policies, either expressed or implied, of the Defense Advanced Research Projects Agency, the US Government, the Sloan Foundation, or the National Institutes of Health.

We would like to thank Beth Adelson, David Kirsh, and David McAllester for their helpful comments on an earlier draft of this article.

References

[1] F.C. Bartlett, *Remembering: A Study in Experimental and Social Psychology* (Cambridge University Press, Cambridge, England, 1932).

[2] D. Chapman, Planning for conjunctive goals, *Artif. Intell.* **32** (1987) 333–377.

[3] H.H. Clark and W.G. Chase, On the process of comparing sentences against pictures, *Cogn. Psychol.* **3** (1972) 472–517.

[4] G. DeJong and R.J. Mooney, Explanation-based learning: an alternative view, *Mach. Learn.* **1** (1986) 145–176.

[5] T.G. Dietterich, Learning at the knowledge level, *Mach. Learn.* **1** (1986) 287–315.

[6] O. Etzioni and T.M. Mitchell, A comparative analysis of chunking and decision analytic control, in: *Proceedings AAAI Spring Symposium on Limited Rationality and AI*, Stanford, CA (1989).

[7] E.A. Feigenbaum and H.A. Simon, Epam-like models of recognition and learning, *Cogn. Sci.* **8** (1984) 305–336.

[8] D.H. Fisher and P. Langley, Approaches to conceptual clustering, in: *Proceedings IJCAI-85*, Los Angeles, CA (1985) 691–697.

[9] R. Flynn, Placing Soar on the connection machine, Prepared for and distributed at the AAAI Mini-Symposium "How Can Slow Components Think So Fast" (1988).

[10] J.A. Fodor, *The Modularity of Mind* (Bradford Books/MIT Press, Cambridge, MA, 1983).

[11] M.P. Georgeff and A.L. Lansky, Reactive reasoning and planning, in: *Proceedings AAAI-87*, Seattle, WA (1987) 677–682.

[12] A. Golding, P.S. Rosenbloom and J.E. Laird. Learning general search control from outside guidance, in: *Proceedings IJCAI-87*, Milan, Italy (1987).

[13] A. Gupta and M. Tambe, Suitability of message passing computers for implementing production systems, in: *Proceedings AAAI-88*, St. Paul, MN (1988) 687–692.

[14] C. Hewitt and D. Kirsh, Personal communication (1987).

[15] W.D. Hillis, *The Connection Machine* (MIT Press, Cambridge, MA, 1985).

[16] W. Hsu, M. Prietula and D. Steier, Merl-Soar: applying Soar to scheduling, in: *Proceedings Workshop on Artificial Intelligence Simulation, AAAI-88*, St. Paul, MN (1988) 81–84.

[17] T.R. Johnson, J.W. Smith Jr and B. Chandrasekaran, Generic Tasks and Soar, in: *Working Notes AAAI Spring Symposium on Knowledge System Development Tools and Languages*, Stanford, CA (1989) 25–28.

[18] P.N. Johnson-Laird, Reasoning by rule or model? in: *Proceedings 10th Annual Conference of the Cognitive Science Society*, Montreal, Que. (1988) 765–771.

[19] J.L. Kolodner, Maintaining order in a dynamic long-term memory, *Cogn. Sci.* **7** (1983) 243–280.

[20] J.L. Kolodner, ed., *Proceedings DARPA Workshop on Case-Based Reasoning*, Clearwater Beach, FL (1988).
[21] J.E. Laird, Universal subgoaling, Ph.D. thesis, Carnegie-Mellon University, Pittsburgh, PA (1983); also in: J.E. Laird, P.S. Rosenbloom and A. Newell, *Universal Subgoaling and Chunking: The Automatic Generation and Learning of Goal Hierarchies* (Kluwer, Hingham, MA, 1986).
[22] J.E. Laird, Soar user's manual (version 4), Tech. Rept. ISL-15, Xerox Palo Alto Research Center, Palo Alto, CA (1986).
[23] J.E. Laird, Recovery from incorrect knowledge in Soar, in: *Proceedings AAAI-88*, St. Paul, MN (1988) 618–623.
[24] J.E. Laird and K.A. McMahon, Destructive state modification in Soar, Draft V, Department of EECS, University of Michigan, Ann Arbor, MI (1989).
[25] J.E. Laird and A. Newell, A universal weak method, Tech. Rept. 83-141, Department of Computer Science, Carnegie-Mellon University, Pittsburgh, PA (1983).
[26] J.E. Laird, A. Newell and P.S. Rosenbloom, SOAR: an architecture for general intelligence, *Artif. Intell.* **33** (1987) 1–64.
[27] J.E. Laird, P.S. Rosenbloom and A. Newell, Towards chunking as a general learning mechanism, in: *Proceedings AAAI-84*, Austin, TX (1984) 188–192.
[28] J.E. Laird, P.S. Rosenbloom and A. Newell, Chunking in Soar: the anatomy of a general learning mechanism, *Mach. Learn.* **1** (1986) 11–46.
[29] J.E. Laird, P.S. Rosenbloom and A. Newell, Overgeneralization during knowledge compilation in Soar, in: T.G. Dietterich, ed., *Proceedings Workshop on Knowledge Compilation*, Otter Crest, OR (1986).
[30] J.E. Laird, E.S. Yager, C.M. Tuck and M. Hucka, Learning in tele-autonomous systems using Soar, in: *Proceedings NASA Conference on Space Telerobotics*, Pasadena, CA (1989).
[31] P. Langley, H.A. Simon, G.L. Bradshaw and J.M. Zytkow, *Scientific Discovery: Computational Explorations of the Creative Processes* (MIT Press, Cambridge, MA, 1987).
[32] R.L. Lewis, A. Newell and T.A. Polk, Toward a Soar theory of taking instructions for immediate reasoning tasks, in: *Proceedings 11th Annual Conference of the Cognitive Science Society*, Ann Arbor, MI (1989).
[33] M. Minsky, A framework for the representation of knowledge, in: P. Winston, ed., *The Psychology of Computer Vision* (McGraw-Hill, New York, 1975).
[34] M. Minsky, *The Society of Mind* (Simon and Schuster, New York, 1986).
[35] T.M. Mitchell, Generalization as search, *Artif. Intell.* **18** (1982) 203–226.
[36] T.M. Mitchell, R.M. Keller and S.T. Kedar-Cabelli, Explanation-based generalization: a unifying view, *Mach. Learn.* **1** (1986) 47–80.
[37] A. Newell, Reasoning, problem solving and decision processes: the problem space as a fundamental category, in: R. Nickerson, ed., *Attention and performance* **8** (Erlbaum, Hillsdale, NJ, 1980).
[38] A. Newell, *Unified Theories of Cognition* (Harvard University Press, Cambridge, MA, 1990).
[39] A. Newell and P.S. Rosenbloom, Mechanisms of skill acquisition and the law of practice, in: J.R. Anderson, ed., *Cognitive Skills and Their Acquisition* (Erlbaum, Hillsdale, NJ, 1981) 1–55.
[40] A. Newell, P.S. Rosenbloom and J.E. Laird, Symbolic architectures for cognition, in: M.I. Posner, ed., *Foundations of Cognitive Science* (Bradford Books/MIT Press, Cambridge, MA, 1989).
[41] A. Newell and H.A. Simon, *Human Problem Solving* (Prentice-Hall, Englewood Cliffs, NJ, 1972).
[42] N.J. Nilsson, *Principles of Artificial Intelligence* (Tioga, Palo Alto, CA, 1980).
[43] T.A. Polk and A. Newell, Modeling human syllogistic reasoning in Soar, in: *Proceedings 10th Annual Conference of the Cognitive Science Society*, Montreal, Que. (1988) 181–187.
[44] L. Powell, Parsing the picnic problem with a Soar3 implementation of Dypar-1, Department of Computer Science, Carnegie-Mellon University, Pittsburgh, PA (1984).
[45] J.R. Quinlan, Induction of decision trees, *Mach. Learn.* **1** (1986) 81–106.
[46] S. Rajamoney, G.F. DeJong, and B. Faltings, Towards a model of conceptual knowledge

Artificial Intelligence 47 (1991) 327–346
Elsevier

Approaches to the study of intelligence

Donald A. Norman

Department of Cognitive Science A-015, University of California, San Diego, La Jolla, CA 92093, USA

Received April 1990

Abstract

Norman, D.A., Approaches to the study of intelligence, Artificial Intelligence 47 (1991) 327–346.

How can human and artificial intelligence be understood? This paper reviews Rosenbloom, Laird, Newell, and McCarl's overview of Soar, their powerful symbol-processing simulation of human intelligence. Along the way, the paper addresses some of the general issues to be faced by those who would model human intelligence and suggests that the methods most effective for creating an artificial intelligence might differ from those for modeling human intelligence. Soar is an impressive piece of work, unmatched in scope and power, but it is based in fundamental ways upon Newell's "physical symbol system hypothesis"—any weaknesses in the power or generality of this hypothesis as a fundamental, general characteristic of human intelligence will affect the interpretation of Soar. But our understanding of the mechanisms underlying human intelligence is now undergoing rapid change as new, neurally-inspired computational methods become available that are dramatically different from the symbol-processing approaches that form the basis for Soar. Before we can reach a final conclusion about Soar we need more evidence about the nature of human intelligence. Meanwhile, Soar provides an impressive standard for others to follow. Those who disagree with Soar's assumptions need to develop models based upon alternative hypotheses that match Soar's achievements. Whatever the outcome, Soar represents a major advance in our understanding of intelligent systems.

Introduction

> Human intelligence . . . stands before us like a holy Grail—Rosenbloom, Laird, Newell, and McCarl. [17]

How can human intelligence be understood? The question is an old one, but age does not necessarily lead to wisdom, at least not in the sense that long-standing interest has led to a large body of accumulated knowledge and understanding. The work under discussion here, Soar, attempts to provide an advance in our understanding by providing a tool for the simulation of thought, thereby providing a theoretical structure of how human intelligence might operate.

Soar has a lofty mission: providing a critical tool for the study of human cognition. The goal is most clearly stated by Allen Newell in his William James lectures "Unified theories of cognition". Newell thought the statement important enough to present it twice, both as the first paragraph of the first chapter and then as the final paragraph of the final chapter:

> Psychology has arrived at the possibility of unified theories of cognition—theories that gain their power by having a single system of mechanisms that operate together to produce the full range of cognition.
>
> I do not say they are here. But they are within reach and we should strive to attain them. (Newell [11])

Soar represents the striving. Among other things, Soar hopes to provide a coherent set of tools that can then be used by the research community in a variety of ways. Soar is built upon a number of fundamental assumptions about the nature of human cognition: within the broad range of theories subsumed under these assumptions, Soar can provide powerful and important benefits. Prime among the assumptions is that the fundamental basis for intelligent behavior is a physical symbol system.

In this paper I examine the power and promise of Soar from the point of view of a cognitive scientist interested in human cognition. The emphasis, therefore, is not on Soar's capabilities as a system of artificial intelligence as much as its ability to simulate the behavior of humans and to enhance our understanding of human cognition. The goal is to provide a friendly, constructive critique, for the goal of Soar is one all cognitive scientists must share, even if there is disagreement about the underlying assumptions. Because of the wide scope and generality of Soar, it can only be examined by asking about fundamental issues in the study of intelligence, issues that lie at the foundations of artificial intelligence, of psychology, and of cognitive science.

1. Psychology and the study of human cognition

Psychology tends to be a critical science. It has grown up in a rich and sophisticated tradition of carefully controlled experimentation, the power of the analysis of variance as the statistical tool, and counterbalanced conditions as the experimental tool. Occam's Razor is held in esteem—no theory is allowed to be more complex than it need be. This is a reasonable criterion if several competing theories all attempt to account for the same phenomena. However, because of psychology's emphasis on a theory for every experimental result, the interpretation has caused a proliferation of very simple theories for very simple phenomena. There is a strong bias against theories such as Soar—they are more complex than the community is willing to accept, even when the range is extremely broad and comprehensive.

There is another negative tendency within psychology. Students are taught to be critics of experimental design: give students any experiment and they will find flaws. Graduate seminars in universities are usually devoted to detailed analyses of papers, ripping them apart point-by-point. Each paper provides the stimulation for new experimental work, each responding to the perceived flaws in the previous work. As a result, the field is self-critical, self-sustaining. Experiments seem mainly to be responses to other experiments. It is rare for someone to look back over the whole body of previous work in order to find some overall synthesis, rare to look over the whole field and ask where it is going.

With so much careful experimentation in psychology, surely there ought to be a place for compiling and understanding the systematic body of knowledge. This goal is shared by many, but it is especially difficult in psychology for there has been no systematic effort to compile these data, and the data are often collected through experimental methods different enough from one another to confound any simple compilation.

Why do we have this state of affairs? In part because of the extreme difficulties faced by those who study human behavior. The phenomena are subtle, for people are sensitive to an amazing range of variables. Experimental scientists over the years have found themselves fooled by apparent phenomena that turned out to be laboratory artifacts. We are trained to beware of "Clever Hans", the nineteenth century counting horse, certified as legitimate by a committee of eminent scientists. Alas, Hans couldn't count at all: he responded to subtle, unconscious cues from his audience. Modern experimental rigor is designed to avoid these and countless other pitfalls.

The resulting caution may, however, be an over-reaction. Complete control can only be found in the laboratory, but of necessity, a laboratory experiment has to simplify the conditions that are to be studied, both in order to control all the factors that are not of immediate interest and so that one can make precise measurements of behavior. But the simplification of the environment may have eliminated critical environmental structure, thereby changing the task that the person is performing. And the simplifications of the response measure may mean that the real behavior of interest is missed. Perhaps the emphasis on experimental rigor and control has led to measurements of the wrong variables?

Soar wades into the psychological arena by proposing a coherent, systematic way to evaluate the experimental data that now exist. It takes those data seriously and suggests that the difficulty in providing cohesion in the past has more to do with the limited theoretical tools available than with the nature of the data. Soar proposes to provide a "unified theory of cognition".

2. Toward a unified theory of cognition[1]

The lack of systematic, rich data in psychology has led many in AI to rely on introspection and "common sense" as evidence. But common sense is "folk-psychology" and it does not have a good reputation among behavioral scientists as a source of legitimate measures of behaviour. In order to improve the quality of theory in cognitive science in general, there needs to be a systematic, cumulative set of reliable and relevant experimental data. Yet in psychology, there has been surprisingly little building upon previous work, little "cumulative science". Why this lack? The developers of Soar suggest that the difficulty results from the lack of good theoretical tools that would allow one generation of researchers to build upon the work of the previous generation. One important gap is a set of modeling tools, tools that permit one to evaluate theoretical assumptions against empirical research in a systematic, constructive fashion.

Soar is really an attempt to do psychology differently than the way it has usually been done. It provides a set of general mechanisms that are postulated to range over all the relevant phenomena of cognition. The idea is to provide concrete mechanisms that can be tested against the known phenomena and data of psychology. When Soar fails, this will point to a deficiency in the theory, leading to refinement of the mechanisms: truly a cumulative approach to theory building. In this method, not only the data, but also the inner structure of the theory has its say (see Newell's famous analysis "You can't play 20 questions with nature and win" [9]).

The problem for such theory-building in psychology is that any given theory never quite gets the phenomenon right. That would normally be alright if there was agreement that the attempt provides useful information. But in the culture of modern day psychology, the response to such theories is "See, it doesn't account for *Y*, so it's wrong." The developers of Soar advocate the more constructive approach of using the misfits to guide the future development: "Yes, it accounts for *X*, but not for *Y*—I wonder what we would need to change to make it handle *Y* better?" "Don't bite my finger", says Allen Newell, "but look at where it is pointing."

In this review I follow the spirit of Newell's admonition: I do not bite at Soar, but rather, I examine the direction in which it points. Of course, I was also trained as a psychologist, so at times, the review may seem more critical than supportive. But the critiques are meant to be constructive, to state where I feel the more fundamental problems lie.

I do not examine the details of the (very) large number of papers and demonstrations of Soar that have now appeared. Rather I focus on the

[1] This section has gained much from discussions with Paul Rosenbloom, Allen Newell, and Stu Card. Some of the material was inspired by an e-mail interaction with Stu Card.

overriding philosophy and method of approach. I conclude that for those who travel in this direction, Soar provides the most systematic, most thoughtful approach to the terrain. However, I will also question whether the direction of travel is appropriate, or perhaps, whether it might not be important to examine several different paths along the terrain of human cognition.

3. Soar

3.1. *An overview of Soar*

The study of human intelligence requires the expertise of many disciplines ranging in level from that of the individual cell to that of societies and cultures. Soar aims at an in-between level, one that it calls the *cognitive band*. Soar is built upon a foundation of cognitive theory, and even the choice of levels at which it operates has a theoretical basis, in this case an analysis of the time-frame of intelligent systems. Newell ([10]; also see [12]) has argued that different levels of scientific disciplines study phenomena that lie within different time frames. According to this argument, cognitive events take place in the time bands that lie between 10 msec and 10 sec., and it is in this region that Soar aims to provide an appropriate theoretical basis (see [17, Fig. 1]). Not all events relevant to human intelligence lie within this band, of course. Events that occur with a time scale less than 10 msec. are relevant to the computational or neural base. Thus, this is the region studied by those interested in architecture; it is where the connectionist systems work. Events that take place with a time scale greater than 10 sec. are most relevant to rational cognition, to the use of logic or rule-following, as in expert systems where the system operates by following rules stated within its knowledge base.

Soar stakes out the middle ground, that of the cognitive band. At the lower levels of its operation it overlaps within studies of the neural band: Soar makes no claims about this level and tries to be compatible with all approaches, including (especially?) connectionist approaches (e.g., [16]). At the higher levels, Soar attempts to match up with the rational band and the logicist and expert system communities.

3.2. *Soar's assumptions*

Soar builds upon a number of assumptions and like all theories, how you evaluate it depends to a large extent upon how well you accept these basic premises. The basic premises are these:

(1) That psychological evidence should be taken seriously.
(2) That intelligence must be realized through a representational system based upon a physical symbol system.

Is a problem space appropriate for all tasks? Again, it isn't clear, but I am not convinced that this poses any fundamental difficulty for Soar. Thus, many of us have argued that physical constraints and information in the environment plays a major role in human planning, decision making and problem solving. But if so, this information is readily accommodated by Soar. Thus, in the current version, the formulation of the problem space automatically encodes physical constraints [17, Section 2.3]. And when Soar gets the appropriate I/O sensors, it should be just as capable of using environmental information as any other model of behavior. Here the only restriction is the state of today's technology, but in principle, these factors are readily accounted for.

5. Soar as artificial intelligence

How well does Soar do as a mechanism for AI? Here, Soar falls between the cracks. It is neither logic, nor frames, nor semantic nets. Soar classifies itself as a production system, but it is not like the traditional forms that we have become used to and that fill the basic texts on AI. As theoretical AI, Soar has several weaknesses, many shared by other approaches as well. In particular, Soar suffers from:

- weak knowledge representation;
- unstructured memory;
- the characterization of everything as search through a problem space.

Weak knowledge representation certainly stands out as one of the major deficits. In this era of highly sophisticated representational schemes and knowledge representation languages, it is somewhat of a shock to see an AI system that has no inheritance, no logic, no quantification: Soar provides only triples and a general purpose processing structure. How does Soar handle reasoning that requires counterfactuals and hypotheticals and quantifiers? How will it fare with language, real language? What about other forms of learning, for example, learning by being told, learning by reflection, learning by restructuring, or learning by analogy? How will Soar recover from errors? All unanswered questions, but never underestimate the sophistication of a dedicated team of computer professionals. Soar will master many or even all of these areas. In fact, in the time that elapsed between the oral presentation of the Soar paper under review and now, the final writing of the review, Soar has made considerable progress in just these areas.

What about other methods of deduction and inference? We have already noted Soar's weaknesses in doing inference.

Technically, Soar has all the power it needs. It is, after all, Turing-equivalent, and with the basic structure of triples it can represent anything that it needs. In fact, one of the assumptions of Soar is that it should start with only the minimum of representation and process: everything else that might be needed is learned. It gains considerable speed with experience—through chunking—and in any event, speed was never a prerequisite of a theoretical structure.

Soar gets its main strength by virtue of its uniformity of architecture, representation, and learning. It can solve anything because it is so general, so unspecialized. It then gets its power through the learning mechanism: the assumption is:

- weak methods + chunking → strong methods;
- the tuning of preferences → strength.

Soar has many positive features. It is a production system, but with a major difference. Conflict resolution, a critical feature of traditional production systems, has disappeared. All relevant Soar productions are executed in parallel. The execution puts all their memory data into working memory, where the decision procedure selects a relevant action to be performed from the information in working memory. Soar can be both goal-driven and data-driven. And the strategy of action is flexibly determined by the kind of information available within working memory.

5.1. Soar and its competition

How does Soar compare to other AI systems? Restricting the consideration to those that aspire to a unified theory of intelligence, and then further restricting it to evaluate the systems in terms of their relevance to human cognition, the answer is that there really isn't much competition. Of the more traditional AI systems, only Soar is viable. Soar's principles and structure seem much more in harmony with what we know of human processing than systems such as the traditional expert system approach to reasoning, or the decision processes of knowledge representation languages, various database systems and truth-maintenance systems, and logic programming. Work on explanation-based learning [4] could potentially be compared, but for the moment, there are no unified, grand systems to come out of this tradition (with the exception of Soar itself, which is a variant of explanation-based learning).

Psychologists have a history of system building as well that should be considered. Thus, Soar could be compared to the approach followed by Anderson in his continual refinements of his computer models (e.g., ACT*, [1]), or by the earlier work of Norman, Rumelhart, and the LNR Research Group [15]. But of these, only ACT* is active today. Here, I would probably conclude that ACT* is superior in the way it models the finer details of the psychological processes that it covers, but that its scope is quite restricted: ACT* is an important influential theory, but it has never been intended as a general, unified theory of all cognitive behavior.

There are numerous small systems, each devoted to the detailed modeling of restricted phenomena. Connectionist modeling fits this description, with perhaps the largest and most detailed simulation studies being those of Rumelhart and McClelland in their simulation of a wide variety of data on word recognition and perception [6, 18, 20]. In all these cases, although the work provides major contributions to our understanding of the phenomena being modeled, they are restricted in scope, hand-crafted for the task (even if the underlying representational structures are learned) and no single system is intended to be taken as a unified theory, applicable to a wide range of phenomena.

There is one major system, however, which does attempt the same range of generality—the genetic algorithm approach of Holland, Holyoak, Nisbett, and Thagard [5]. This work comes from a strong interdisciplinary group examining the nature of cognition and its experimental and philosophical basis. Its computer modeling tools do provide an alternative, a kind of cross between connectionist modeling and symbolic representation, with an emphasis on learning. How do these two systems compare? So far, Soar has the edge, in part because of the immense amount of effort to the development of a wide-ranging, coherent model. But the approach of Holland et al. [5] has the capability to become a second unified theory of cognition, one that would allow more precise comparison with the assumptions of Soar. It will be a good day for science when two similar systems are available, for comparisons of the performance on the same tasks by these two systems with very different underlying assumptions can only be beneficial. Indeed, this is one of the hopes of the Soar enterprise: the development of competing models that can inform one another.

6. Reflections and summary

6.1. *Soar's stengths and weaknesses*

The strength of Soar is that it starts with fundamental ideas and principles and pushes them hard. It derives strength and generality from a uniform architecture, uniform methods, and uniform learning. Weak methods are general methods, and although they may be slow, they apply to a wide range of problems: the combination of weak methods plus a general learning mechanism gives Soar great power. The learning method allows for specialization, for the chunking of procedures into efficient steps, tuned for the problem upon which it is working.

Learning within Soar is impressive. I was prepared to see Soar gradually improve with practice, but I was surprised to discover that it could take advantage of learning even within its first experience with a problem: routines learned (chunked) in the early phases of a problem aided it in the solution of the later phases, even within its first exposure. Soar may indeed have taken advantage of both worlds of generality and specialization: an initial generality that gives it scope and breadth, at the tradeoff of being slow and inefficient, plus chunking that provides a learned specialization for speed and efficiency.

The weaknesses of Soar derive from its strengths. It has a weak knowledge representation language and a weak memory structure. It has no formalism for higher-order reasoning, for productions, for rules, or for preferences. It is not clear how well Soar will do with natural language (where reasoning and quantification seem essential), or with argumentation, or for that matter, with simple input and output control. Everything in Soar is search: how far can that be carried?

6.2. Soar as a theoretical tool for psychology

Soar claims to be grounded upon psychological principles, but the psychology is weak. As I have pointed out, this is no fault of Soar, but it reflects the general status of psychological theory, which in turn reflects the difficulty of that scientific endeavor. Still, unsettled science provides shaky grounds for construction. How can I, as a psychologist, complain when someone takes psychological data seriously?

The problem is the sort of psychological evidence that is considered. As I indicated at the start of this review, there are different ideas about the nature of the appropriate evidence from psychology. The Soar team takes the evidence much more seriously than do I.

One basic piece of psychological evidence offered as support for the chunking hypothesis is the power law of learning, that the relationship between speed of performance and number of trials of experience follows a power law of the form $Time = k(trials)^p$ over very many studies, and with the number of trials as large as 50,000 (or more: see [13]). Yes, the ability of Soar to produce the power law of learning is impressive. At the time, it was the only model that could do so (now however, Miyata [8] has shown how a connectionist model can also yield the power law of learning).

Soar handles well the data from the standard sets of problem-solving tasks, for inference, and for other tasks of think-aloud problem solving. But how much of real cognition do these tasks reflect? There is a growing body of evidence to suggest that these are the sorts of tasks done primarily within the psychological laboratory or the classroom, and that they may have surprisingly little transfer to everyday cognition. For example, consider the set of problems against which Soar tests its ability to mimic human problem solving: the Eight Puzzle, tic-tac-toe, Towers of Hanoi, missionaries and cannibals, algebraic equations, satisfying local constraint networks, logical syllogisms, balance beam problems, blocks world problems, monkey-and-bananas, and the water-jug problems. These are indeed the traditional problems studied in both the human and artificial intelligence literature. But, I contend, these are not the typical problems of everyday life. They are not problems people are particularly good at. One reason psychologists study them is that they do offer so many difficulties: they thereby provide us something to study.

But if this is not how people perform in everyday life, then perhaps these should not be the baseline studies on which to judge intelligent behavior. If I am right, this stands as an indictment of human psychology, not of Soar, except that Soar has based its case on data from the human experimental literature.

6.3. The choice of phenomena to be modeled

How has Soar chosen the set of phenomena that it wishes to consider? Not clear. Thus, there is a well-established and rich core of knowledge about human short-term memory, and although the current theoretical status of the concept is unclear, the phenomena and data are still valid. The literature is well known to the developers of Soar, and key items are summarized in Newell's William James lectures. One of the major developments over the years is the finding that items in STM decay: not that less and less items are available, but that only partial information is available from any given item. Two major methods have been developed for representing this decay, one to allow each item to have some "activation value" that decreases with time or interference from other items (thus decreasing its signal-to-noise ratio), the other that each item is composed of numerous "micro-features", and each of the features drops out probabilistically as a function of time or interference from other items, so the main item gets noisier and noisier with time.

Soar decides to use neither of these mechanisms of memory loss. Why? Loss of activation is rejected, probably because activation values are simply not within the spirit of representation chosen for Soar ("The simplest decay law for a discrete system such as Soar is not gradual extinction, but probabilistic decay", Chapter 6 of the William James lectures [11]). And loss of microfeatures is not possible because the Soar representation is wholistic: internal components cannot be lost.

Does this difference matter? It is always difficult to assess the impact of low-level decisions upon the resulting global behavior. Clearly, the choice rules out the simulation of recognition-memory operating characteristics (e.g., [29]). This kind of decision permeates the model-building activity, and it isn't always easy to detect where a basic assumption is absolutely forced by the phenomena or universal processing constraints, where selected for more arbitrary reasons.

In general Soar seems on strongest ground when it discusses the highest-order of the cognitive band: tasks that clearly make use of symbol processing, especially problem-solving tasks. At the lowest level, it is weak on time-ordered tasks, both on the effects of time and activity rate on performance and cognition, and also on the simulation of tasks that require controlled rates of production. At the middle level, it is weakest on issues related to knowledge representation: the existing representation has little overall structure and none of the common organizational structures or inference rules of knowledge representation languages.

Soar also espouses the software-independence approach to modeling. That is, psychological functions are assumed to be independent of hardware implementation, so it is safe to study the cognitive band without examination of the implementation methods of the neural band, without consideration of the physical body in which the organism is imbedded, and without consideration of non-cognitive aspects of behavior. How big a role does the biological implementation of cognition play? What constraints, powers, and weaknesses result? What of the body, does it affect cognition? How about motivation, culture, social interaction. What about emotions? The separation of these aspects into separate compartments is the common approach to cognition of the information processing psychologist of an earlier era, but the psychologist of the 1990s is very apt to think the separation cannot be maintained. Certainly the connectionist takes as given that:

(1) There is continuous activation.
(2) The implementation makes a major difference.
(3) Time is important.
(4) Major biases and processing differences can result from extra-cognitive influences.

How do we weigh these various considerations? The field is young, the amount of knowledge low. Soar may be right. But it does not implement the only possible set of alternatives.

And how does Soar react to criticisms of this sort? Properly: Soar aspires to set the framework for general models of cognition. It tests one set of operating assumptions. The goal, in part, is to inspire others to do similar tasks, perhaps with different sets of assumptions and mechanisms. But then they are all to be assessed with the same data. The goal is not to show Soar right or wrong, the goal is to advance the general state of knowledge. With this attitude, Soar—and the science of cognition—can only win.

6.4. Soar as a modeling tool for AI

Maybe Soar should be evaluated separately for its role as a tool for artificial intelligence and for psychological modeling. Personally, that is my view, but the Soar community has soundly rejected this idea. One of the basic methodological assumptions, (M2), is that general intelligence can be studied most usefully by not distinguishing between human and artificial intelligence. But I am not convinced. Human intelligence has evolved to meet the demands of the situations encountered through evolutionary history, where survival and reproduction were critical aims. The brain has a biological basis and the sensory, motor, and regulatory structures reflect the evolutionary history and the demands made upon them over a time course measured in millions of years. Human intelligence is powerful, but restricted, specialized for creativity, adaptivity, and robustness, with powerful perceptual apparatus that probably dominates the mechanisms of thought. Human language is also the product of an evolutionary struggle, and its properties are still not understood by the scientific community, even though virtually all humans master their native, spoken language. The properties of biological and artificial systems are so dramatically different at the hardware level (the neural band), that this must certainly also be reflected at the cognitive level (see [7]).

Good artificial intelligence may not be good psychology. Soar attempts to be both, but by so doing, I fear it weakens its abilities on all counts. By attempting to account for the known experimental results on cognition, it is forced to adopt certain computational strategies that may hamper its performance on traditional tasks of artificial intelligence. And by being developed from the traditional framework of information processing artificial intelligence, it may limit the scope of human mechanisms that it tries to duplicate.

6.5. *How should Soar be judged?*

How should Soar—or any other model of intelligence—be judged? On the criteria of practical and theoretical AI I think the answer is clear. One uses a standard set of benchmarks, probably similar to what Soar has done. Here the answer is given by how well the system performs. On the issue of the simulation of human cognition, the answer is far from clear. We don't have a set of benchmark problems. If I am to be a constructive critic (look where Soar is pointing), I have to conclude that what it does, it does well: in this domain it has no competiton.

Soar does not aspire to be *the* tool for human simulation. Rather, it hopes to set an example of what can be done. Others are urged to follow, either by building upon Soar or by providing their own, unified theory of cognition, to be tested and compared by attempting to account for exactly the same set of data.

One practical barrier stands in the way of the systematic use and evaluation of Soar by the research community: the difficulty of learning this system. Today, this is not an easy task. There is no standard system, no easy introduction. Programming manuals do not exist. Until Soar is as easy to master as, say, LISP or PROLOG, there will never be sufficient people with enough expertise to put it to the test. If Soar usage is to go beyond the dedicated few there needs to be a standard system, some tutorial methods, and a standard text.

6.6. *Conclusion: Powerful and impressive*

In conclusion, Soar is a powerful, impressive system. It is still too early to assess Soar on either theoretical or practical grounds, for either AI or psychology, but already it has shown that it must be taken seriously on both counts. The chunking mechanism is a major contribution to our understanding of learning. The exploitation of weak methods provides a valuable lesson for system builders. And the use of uniform structures may very well provide more benefits than deficits. I am not so certain that we are yet ready for unified theory, for there are many uncertainties in our knowledge of human behavior and of the underlying mechanisms—our understanding of the biological structure of processing is just beginning to be developed, but already it has added to and changed some of our ideas about the memory systems. But for those who disagree or who wish to explore the terrain anyway, Soar has set a standard for all others to follow.

Acknowledgement

This article has benefited from the aid of several reviewers as well as through discussions and correspondence with Stu Card, David Kirsh, Allen Newell, Paul Rosenbloom, and Richard Young. My research was supported by grant NCC 2-591 to Donald Norman and Edwin Hutchins from the Ames Research Center of the National Aeronautics and Space Agency in the Aviation Safety/Automation Program. Everett Palmer served as technical monitor. Additional support was provided by funds from the Apple Computer Company and Digital Equipment Corporation to the Affiliates of Cognitive Science at UCSD.

References

[1] J.R. Anderson, *The Architecture of Cognition* (Harvard University Press, Cambridge, MA, 1983).

[2] J.R. Anderson, *Cognitive Psychology and Its Implications* (Freeman, New York, 1985).

[3] R.A. Brooks, Intelligence without representation, *Artif. Intell.* **47** (1991) 139–159, this volume.

[4] T. Ellman, Explanation-based learning: a survey of programs and perspectives, *ACM Comput. Surv.* **21** (1989) 163–221.

[5] J.H. Holland, K.J. Holyoak, R.E. Nisbett and P.R. Thagard, *Induction: Processes of Inference, Learning, and Discovery* (MIT Press, Cambridge, MA, 1987).

[6] J.L. McClelland and D.E. Rumelhart, An interactive activation model of context effects in letter perception, Part I: An account of basic findings, *Psychol. Rev.* **88** (1981) 375–407.

[7] C. Mead, *Analog VLSI and Neural Systems* (Addison-Wesley, Reading, MA, 1989).

[8] Y. Miyata, A PDP model of sequence learning that exhibits the power law, in: *Proceedings 11th Annual Conference of the Cognitive Science Society*, Ann Arbor, MI (1989) 9–16.

[9] A. Newell, You can't play 20 questions with nature and win, in: W.G. Case, ed., *Visual Information Processing* (Academic Press, San Diego, CA, 1973).
[10] A. Newell, Scale counts in cognition, 1986 American Psychological Association Distinguished Scientific Award Lecture.
[11] A. Newell, *Unified Theories of Cognition* (Harvard University Press, Cambridge, MA, 1990); 1987 William James lectures at Harvard University.
[12] A. Newell and S.K. Card, The prospects for psychological science in human-computer interaction, *Hum.-Comput. Interaction* **1** (1985) 209–242.
[13] A. Newell and P.S. Rosenbloom, Mechanisms of skill acquisition and the law of practice, in: J.R. Anderson, ed., *Cognitive Skills and Their Acquisition* (Erlbaum, Hillsdale, NJ, 1981).
[14] D.A. Norman, Reflections on cognition and parallel distributed processing, in: J.L. McClelland, D.E. Rumelhart and the PDP Research Group, eds., *Parallel Distributed Processing: Explorations in the Microstructure of Cognition* **2**: *Psychological and Biological Models* (MIT Press/Bradford, Cambridge, MA, 1986).
[15] D.A. Norman, and D.E. Rumelhart, The LNR Research Group, *Explorations in Cognition* (Freeman, New York, 1975).
[16] P.S. Rosenbloom, A symbolic goal-oriented perspective on connectionism and Soar, in: R. Pfeifer, Z. Schreter, F. Fogelman-Soulie and L. Steels, eds., *Connectionism in Perspective* (Elsevier, Amsterdam, 1989).
[17] P.S. Rosenbloom, J.E. Laird, A. Newell and R. McCarl, A preliminary analysis of the Soar architecture as a basis for general intelligence, *Artif. Intell.* **47** (1991) 289–325, this volume.
[18] D.E. Rumelhart and J.L. McClelland, An interactive activation model of context effects in letter perception, Part II: The contextual enhancement effect and some tests and extensions of the model, *Psychol. Rev.* **89** (1982) 60–94.
[19] D.E. Rumelhart and D.A. Norman, Accretion, tuning and restructuring: three modes of learning, in: J.W. Cotton and R. Klatzky, eds., *Semantic Factors in Cognition* (Erlbaum, Hillsdale, NJ, 1978).
[20] M.S. Siedenberg and J.L. McClelland, A distributed, developmental model of word recognition and naming, *Psychol. Rev.* **96** (1989) 523–568.
[21] P. Smolensky, On the proper treatment of connectionism, *Brain Behav. Sci.* **11** (1988) 1–74.
[22] L.R. Squire, *Memory and Brain* (Oxford University Press, New York, 1987).
[23] L.R. Squire, and S. Zola-Morgan, Memory: Brain systems and behavior, *Trends Neurosci.* **11** (4) (1988) 170–175.
[24] M. Tambe and P.S. Rosenbloom, Eliminating expensive chunks by restricting expressiveness, in: *Proceedings IJCAI-89*, Detroit, MI (1989).
[25] E. Tulving, Episodic and semantic memory, in: E. Tulving and W. Donaldson, eds., *Organization of Memory* (Academic Press, San Diego, 1969).
[26] E. Tulving, *Elements of Episodic Memory* (Oxford University Press, New York, 1983).
[27] E. Tulving, Remembering and knowing the past, *Am. Sci.* **77** (1989) 361–367.
[28] K. VanLehn, W. Ball and B. Kowalski, Non-LIFO execution of cognitive procedures, *Cogn. Sci.* **13** (1989) 415–465.
[29] W.A. Wickelgren and D.A. Norman, Stength models and serial position in short-term recognition memory, *J. Math. Psychol.* **3** (1966) 316–347.

Index